Blackmaition

Manchester University Press

Blackmail, scandal, and revolution

London's French *libellistes*, 1758–92

SIMON BURROWS

Manchester University Press

Manchester and New York

distributed exclusively in the USA by Palgrave

Published by Manchester University Press
Oxford Road, Manchester M13 9NR, UK
and Room 400, 175 Fifth Avenue, New York, NY 10010, USA
www.manchesteruniversitypress.co.uk

Distributed in the United States exclusively by
Palgrave Macmillan, 175 Fifth Avenue,
New York, NY 10010, USA

Distributed in Canada exclusively by
UBC Press, University of British Columbia, 2029 West Mall,
Vancouver, BC, Canada V6T 1Z2

British Library Cataloguing-in-Publication Data
A catalogue record for this book is available from the British Library

Library of Congress Cataloging-in-Publication Data applied for

ISBN 978 0 7190 6527 9 paperback

First published by Manchester University Press in hardback 2006

This paperback edition first published 2009

Printed by Lightning Source

For Andrea

Hanım canım

Contents

Illustrations

Tables

Acknowledgements

This work evolved out of a project on the *libelliste* Charles Théveneau de Morande. I have been researching Morande sporadically since 1989, when I first encountered his journalism and read Robert Darnton's account of his influence. Professor Darnton encouraged my study of Morande and, although we have reached very different conclusions, his work has provided inspiration and a point of reference ever since.

I would also like to thank the following for academic advice and support, useful references, or comments on papers or extracts: David Adams, Hannah Barker, Laurence Brockliss, Kimberly Chrisman, Jonathan Conlin, Simon Dixon, Alan Forrest, Dena Goodman, Russell Goulbourne, Vivian Gruder, William Jennings, Tom Kaiser, Iain McCalman, Roger Mettam, David Parker, Jeremy Popkin, Munro Price, Barry Shapiro, Alexandre Stroev, and Christopher Todd. Above all, Colin Jones, Jenny Skipp, and an anonymous reviewer for Manchester University Press made numerous valuable comments on the original manuscript, and my father, Peter Burrows, has been invaluable as a proof-reader and indexer. I am also grateful to Martin Sumpter in Paris and Danalee Burrows in London for their hospitality.

I owe particular thanks to Bernard Leblanc, *savant* and historian of Arnay-le-Duc, for sharing his impressive knowledge and personal library, and to Paul Agnani for checking sources and exchanging ideas as he prepared a master's thesis on 'Libelles et diplomatie à la fin du dix-huitième siècle'. Paul has been a generous comrade in arms, and kindly sent me a copy of his thesis as I made final amendments to my manuscript. I am also grateful to the custodian of the Morande–Beaumarchais correspondence, who wishes to remain anonymous.

Among many helpful librarians and archivists, I am especially grateful to the staff of the Archives du Ministère des affaires étrangères in Paris, the Bibliothèque municipale de Tonnerre, the Médiathèque d'Orlèans, the Bibliothèque publique et universitaire de Neuchâtel, and Special Collections in the Brotherton Library at Leeds University, and particularly to Philippe Henrat at the Archives nationales, Bob Thomson at Harrow Library, and I. A. Mayr at the Bayerisches Hauptstaatsarchiv.

At Manchester University Press, Alison Welsby and Jonathan Bevan have been helpful, encouraging, and supportive. The Brotherton Library at Leeds

University, the British Library, the British Museum Department of Prints, and Routledge have kindly granted permission to reproduce illustrations.

I have received financial support from several sources. A Sabbatical Fellowship at the Humanities Research Centre at the Australian National University in Canberra facilitated my early research; while a British Academy Small Research Grant allowed me to complete work in Paris; and the universities of Waikato and Leeds allowed me generous sabbaticals. Additional funding came from a Humanities Research Scheme Award at Waikato and the School of History and Humanities Research Leave Scheme at Leeds. Finally, a Research Leave Award from the Arts and Humanities Research Board Research Leave Scheme provided sabbatical leave to complete the book. I am deeply grateful for the help I have received from all these sources.

I am also grateful to my infant daughter Hannah Kura for sleeping through the night almost since birth and being a source of unending joy. Finally, my wife, Andrea, has accepted long absences, critiqued drafts, spent holidays as an unpaid research assistant, indulged my taste for antiquarian books, and tolerated my passion for long-dead rogues. This book is dedicated to her, in recognition of her devotion, with gratitude and adoration.

Simon Burrows
Leeds

Abbreviations

AAE	Archives du Ministère des affaires étrangères, Paris
ADCO	Archives départementales de la Côte d'Or, Dijon
Add. MS	Additional Manuscript (in BL)
AN	Archives nationales, Paris
Arsenal	Bibliothèque de l'Arsenal, Paris
BBTI	*British Book Trade Index*
BCE	Gunnar and Mavis von Proschwitz, *Beaumarchais et le Courier de l'Europe: documents inédits ou peu connus*, 2 vols, *SVEC* 273-4 (Oxford: Voltaire Foundation, 1990)
BHVP	Bibliothèque historique de la ville de Paris
BL	British Library, London
BMT	Bibliothèque municipale de Tonnerre
BN	Bibliothèque nationale, Paris
BPUN	Bibliothèque publique et universitaire de Neuchâtel, archives of the STN
CBW	Jacques-Pierre Brissot de Warville, *Correspondance de Brissot de Warville* [with the STN], edited by Robert Darnton, at http://163.1.91.50/x_vfetc/textual/corres/brissot/bris_intro/bris_intro_003.html (consulted on 8 May 2001)
CPA	Correspondance politique, Angleterre (in AAE)
CSB	Charles-François de Broglie, *Correspondance secrète du comte de Broglie avec Louis XV*, edited by Didier Ozanam and Michel Antoine, 2 vols (Paris: Klincksieck, 1956–61)
CSCV	*Correspondance secrète inédite sur Louis XVI, Marie-Antoinette, la cour et la ville de 1777–1792*, edited by M. de Lescure, 2 vols (Paris: Plon, 1866)
CSI	Louis XV, *Correspondance secrète inédite de Louis XV*, M. E. Boutaric, 2 vols (Paris: Plon, 1866)
CSMT	*Correspondance secrète entre Marie-Thérèse et le comte de Mercy-Argenteau*, edited by A. von Arneth and M. Geoffroy, 2nd edition, 3 vols (Paris: Firmin-Didot: 1874–75)
CSP	*Correspondance secrète, politique et littéraire, ou mémoires pour servir à l'histoire des cours, des sociétés et*

	de la littérature en France, depuis la mort de Louis XV, 18 vols (London: John Adamson, 1787–90)
ESTC	*English Short Title Catalogue*
LMA	London Metropolitan Archives, London EC1
MD	Mémoires et documents (series, in AAE)
MO	Médiathèque d'Orléans, Lenoir papers
MSB	Louis Petit de Bachaumont (attrib.), *Mémoires secrets pour servir à l'histoire de la république de lettres en France, depuis 1762 jusqu'à nos jours*, 36 vols (London: John Adamson, 1777–87)
PRO	Public Record Office, Kew (now also known as National Archives)
STN	Société typographique de Neuchâtel
SVEC	*Studies on Voltaire and the Eighteenth Century*
ULBC	University of Leeds, Brotherton Library, Brotherton Collection, papers of the chevalier d'Eon

Notes on conventions, translations, and terminology

My choice between editions of rare works has often been based on cost and accessibility. In general, I used the nearest available edition, regardless of language. Where I had a choice between English and French editions, I used the former. Where there are significant textual differences between editions and/or translations and original language versions, I have consulted two or more editions of the same work. These are all noted in the bibliography, and footnotes make clear which edition is referenced. Occasionally, this means that I have quoted from a French edition where an English edition exists. In such cases, and any other where an English source is not indicated, translations are my own. In the case of short French quotations and pamphlet titles where the English equivalent is nearly identical, I have given just the original French on the grounds of readability. In all translations I have, as far as possible, attempted to render the flavour of the original. Quotations maintain the original spelling and punctuation as far as this is discernible.

Owing to the length of many eighteenth-century titles, I have sometimes used shortened forms in the text and first note references. Subsequent notes use truncated forms of the first reference. Full versions can be found in the bibliography. For reasons of brevity, the secondary source bibliography lists only works that appear at least twice in the notes. Editions of correspondence appear in the bibliography under the name of the author if there is a single or dominant author's name in the title; where several authors are given equal prominence, the edition appears under its title.

Where there is no agreed spelling of personal names, I have adopted the spelling preferred by the individual, if known. Where, as in the case of La Fite de Pelleport, multiple spellings exist, I have adopted arbitrary but common variants. Place names appear in standard English spelling where possible. Noble titles are given according to the nationality of the person concerned, except in cases where quotations or footnotes require otherwise. The particle 'de' has been dropped from shortened versions of French names; 'd'' and 'du' are maintained.

In the bibliography, compound names appear under the abbreviated form of the name commonly used in the main body of the text and footnotes, e.g. Charles-Claude Théveneau de Morande's works appear under 'Morande', while Jacques-Pierre Brissot de Warville appears under 'Brissot'. Printed sources are listed only if cited.

Prologue

In early 1778, as war-clouds darkened the horizon, Nathaniel Parker Forth, principal agent of the British embassy in Paris, crossed the English Channel with a locked trunk containing a sensitive cargo destined for the French government.[1] It bore the seal of the British prime minister, Lord North, was exempted from examination by customs, never left Forth's sight, and was delivered to the private study of his Paris residence. On 6 February, the very day when France and Britain's rebel American colonies signed a treaty of friendship, Forth wrote to Louis XVI's closest minister, the comte de Maurepas, to announce his arrival. 'Je suis heureux quand je pense', he wrote, 'que je suis actuellement assis dessus un coffre contenant des horreurs capable de detruire la tranquillité de tant de grandes et respectables personnages.' ['I am happy to reflect that I am currently sitting on top of a chest containing horrors capable of destroying the peace of mind of so many great and respectable persons.'][2] Maurepas at once informed the lieutenant of police, Jean-Charles-Pierre Lenoir, who instructed his most trusted secretary to collect the chest and escort it to the Bastille.[3] Louis XVI was delighted with Forth and granted him generous compensation for expenses and special permission to remain in France should war break out.[4]

The 'horreurs' inside this mysterious chest comprised the entire print-run of what Maurepas, Forth, and Lenoir termed a 'libelle'. This gives us little idea of its precise content, as a 'libelle' could be a libellous work, a pamphlet, or a lampoon. However, Lenoir's unpublished memoirs reveal that this particular *libelle* was an obscene attack on the French court.[5] A more helpful and evocative description of the pamphlet survives in a bilingual handbill in a French archive. It announces:

> In the press and in a few days will be published, Price 10s. 6d. A PAMPHLETT entitled LE GUERLICHON FEMELLE OU LA REINE CHAUDE ET SA SUR-INTENDANTE [*The Fancywoman*[6] *or the Hot Queen and her* [*Female*] *Super-intendent*] Being a minute, exact, authentic and genuine Account of the most private Memoires, of a certain neighbouring hostile Court, giving an ample Detail of the secret Reasons which have occasioned the different Deaths, Marriages, Preferments at that Court for these last Ten Years. COMPRISING A faithful Narrative of the hidden Causes which reciprocally instigated the late DAUPHIN and his ROYAL FATHER against each other, and of the events which followed.

The handbill went on to imply that the work contained secret anecdotes about the ladies of the court, Louis XVI's impotence, and plots and murders in the heart of the ministry and royal family. In particular, it suggested that Louis XVI's father (the dauphin) had been involved in parricidal attempts to assassinate Louis XV, and that in revenge Louis XV and his first minister Choiseul had murdered him and his wife. Then, in a final twist, the poetic, ghostly voice of the dauphin implies that Louis XV, in turn, was killed by his daughter Adelaïde and Maurepas:

> But Revenge does not Sleep even in a Father's Breast,
> *Le Poison de* CHOISEUL *me soulage de mes Maux*
> *Et mon Père quoique Roi devient mon Bourreau:*
> '*Ton Fils, et sa Femme, sont Morts de tes Coups –*
> ADELAIDE, *et* MAUREPAS *feront autant pour vous – !*'
>
> [Choiseul's poison soothes my sufferings
> And my father, although king, becomes my executioner:
> 'Your son and his wife, are dead from your blows –
> Adelaïde and Maurepas will do the same for you.']⁷

The chest containing the *Guerlichon* remained untouched under seal until 1785, when Lenoir ordered the destruction of the hoard of illegal books held in the Bastille. However, he also ordered a small sample of each title held back, and they remained in the Bastille until the fortress was stormed in 1789.⁸

The *Guerlichon* incident reveals the desperation of the Bourbon monarchy to control its image in the decades before the revolution, and was not an isolated event. Between the late 1750s and early 1790s the French government attempted to silence a series of blackmailer-pamphleteers (*libellistes*) operating out of London, using a variety of methods, with varying degrees of success. The activities of the *libellistes*, the texts they produced, their influence on public opinion in Britain as well as France, and the attempts of the French government to control them are the subject-matter of this book.

Notes

1 On Forth, see Marion Ward, *Forth* (London: Phillimore, 1982).
2 CPA 528 fo. 275, Forth to Maurepas, 6 February 1778.
3 Ibid., and fo. 279, Lenoir to Maurepas, Paris, 7 February 1778.
4 CPA 528 fo. 277, Maurepas to Forth, 6 February 1778; fos 387–8, Forth to Maurepas, 20 February 1778; CPA 529 fo. 147, Vergennes to Forth, 17 March 1778. For Forth's expenses see CPA 528 fo. 389.
5 MO, MS 1422 p. 104.
6 I have borrowed Ward's translation of 'Guerlichon femelle'.
7 CPA 528 fo. 95.
8 MO, MS 1422 p. 104; Pierre-Louis Manuel, *La Police de Paris dévoilée*, 2 vols (Paris: Garnery, l'an II de la liberté [1791]), I, 36–9. See also appendix. It is possible that the entire edition was destroyed in 1785, for in contrast with other works stored in the Bastille, no copies of this title survive.

Introduction

The French blackmailer-*libellistes* operating out of London between 1758 and 1792 were involved in one of the most shadowy and, in the eyes of the Bourbon government, most criminal and dangerous aspects of a vast and influential international clandestine publishing industry.[1] Their publications were among the most scandalous political texts of the eighteenth century.[2] Such works have attracted considerable attention from historians, many of whom stress the central role of scurrilous pamphlets in undermining the monarchy and covering leading political figures in contempt, above all Louis XV and Louis XVI's queen, Marie-Antoinette.[3] It has even been suggested that such pamphlets had a greater role in revolutionary causation than leading enlightenment thinkers such as Montesquieu, whose writings empowered opposition under the monarchy, or Rousseau, who so inspired egalitarian Jacobin politicians such as Robespierre and the militant, artisanal *sans culottes*. Thus scandalous pamphleteering has been heavily implicated in the origins of the French revolution of 1789.

Nevertheless, this monograph offers the first collective study of the *libellistes*, their works, and their significance.[4] In the process, it radically revises existing perceptions of the role of gutter pamphlets, pamphleteers, 'political pornography', and clandestine pamphleteering under the late *ancien régime* (i.e. prerevolutionary period).[5] It contends that the social origins, career paths, and motives of the *libellistes* have been misunderstood; their political role and influence misread; the nature of their pamphlets misconstrued; and their wider political significance largely overlooked. To appreciate the *libellistes'* significance, however, it is first necessary to consider how *ancien régime* French politics functioned and the current state of historical thinking about scandalous pamphleteering and the origins of the French revolution. This is the main purpose of this introductory chapter.

Before 1789, France was ruled by the Bourbon dynasty as a hereditary absolute monarchy. Succession to the Crown was determined by the principles of Salic law and primogeniture: females could not inherit the throne. The king was at the head of the executive, legislative, and judicial branches of government. Since the last meeting of the Estates-General, the old representative body of the kingdom, in 1614, there had been in effect no elective checks on the king's exercise of any of these functions.[6] Power was strongly centralised: the heart of government was the Royal Council, composed of the king and hand-picked ministers, who owed their position to royal favour and were often fierce rivals. Hence the royal court at Versailles served as a magnet for those who wished to exercise social, cultural, or political influence. Contemporaries therefore used the term 'court' ambiguously, to denote the royal government, 'court aristocracy', or 'the court' in its modern, institutional sense. These ambiguities are replicated in the work of the *libellistes*, many of whom castigated the court, and throughout this book.

The *libellistes*' antipathy to the court was a manifestation of a growing gulf between France's political centre of gravity at Versailles and the capital, Paris, which increasingly assumed the mantle of commercial and cultural leadership. Louis XIV (ruled 1643–1715) established his court at Versailles partly as a means of control and surveillance over the aristocracy. However, under his successors, Louis XV (1715–74) and Louis XVI (1774–92), the tight control exercised by Louis XIV gradually broke down.[7] Increasingly, leading nobles maintained residences in Paris as well as Versailles. Thus the importance of Versailles as a centre for artistic and literary patronage, and hence the arbiter of fashion and taste, declined. This process accelerated under Louis XVI. He and Marie-Antoinette surrounded themselves with a select circle of friends, thereby alienating many of France's traditional leading families, who began to stay away from court. Scions of several such families would play a leading role in the early stages of the revolution.[8] However, more serious political problems were looming in the *ancien régime*'s final years.

From 1756 to 1789 the Bourbon monarchy faced a continuing fiscal-military-political crisis. At heart the problem was a simple one: how could France continue as a leading power both in Europe and overseas? This was not a challenge facing her main rivals. Prussia, Russia, and Austria limited their ambitions to landward expansion. France's greatest colonial rival, Britain, relied on maritime power. France's attempts to maintain a massive army and a large fleet placed her finances under great strain, especially as, unlike Britain, she lacked well-developed fiscal and financial systems for raising cheap loans. Instead, her tax-collection was farmed out and borrowing was arranged by profiteering middlemen. The Bourbons paid dearly for their loans, but the only alternative was root-and-branch reform of France's inequitable tax system, especially the fiscal privileges of the nobility and clergy.

The need for reform was made more pressing by defeat in the defining conflict of the period, the Seven Years' War (1756–63), in which the combined might and population resources of France, Russia, and Austria proved unable to triumph over Frederick the Great's Prussia and Britain. The Peace of Paris in February 1763 proved particularly humiliating for France, since Britain stripped her of colonial possessions in Canada and India. Defeat was all the more bitter for many French subjects because the war was effectively waged on behalf of the old enemy, Austria, with whom France signed a defensively orientated alliance in 1756. Although the alliance raised eye-brows, the foreign minister, the duc de Choiseul, had sound geo-strategic motives. By neutralising the threat of Austro-French conflict in the Low Countries and north Italy, the treaty of Versailles freed France to pursue her colonial rivalry with the British. Two further aspects of the alliance are also worthy of note. First, Madame de Pompadour, who involved herself in pol-itics to a much greater degree than Louis XV's previous lovers, played a sig-nificant role in promoting and brokering the alliance. This made her an obvious scapegoat for malcontents and opponents of the war. Second, the alliance included provisions for the marriage of the future Louis XVI, to an Austrian princess, Marie-Antoinette, the daughter of Empress Maria-Theresia. Thus, when Marie-Antoinette arrived in France in 1770, she was already associated with an unpopular alliance and humiliating defeat.

The war exposed the weaknesses of the French state and all but destroyed the prestige of the Bourbon monarchy. Choiseul dedicated the remainder of his ministry to repairing the damage by reforming the state, and subsequent ministries followed suit. In the process, they ran into determined opposition. The focus for institutional opposition to the policies of Bourbon govern-ments was the thirteen (subsequently fifteen) sovereign law-courts or *par-lements*, above all the *Parlement* of Paris, whose jurisdiction covered half of France. Despite having limited fiscal and legislative powers, the *parlements'* political role and authority was very different from those of their British namesake. Their member magistrates were not elected but purchased their offices, which were hereditary and conferred nobility. The *parlements'* primary role was to serve as high courts of appeal over their (very unequal) jurisdictions. Their fiscal and legislative functions were limited to consent-ing to new taxes and 'enregistering' royal edicts. The *parlements* had no say in the choice of ministers and possessed no power to scrutinise budgets or propose legislation. They could, however, exert pressure through formal 'remonstrances' to the Crown, which often contained propagandist rehearsals of their own political claims, or through judicial strikes that para-lysed the administration of justice. However, the king had considerable coer-cive weapons against the *parlementaires*. They included the notorious *lit de justice* – a royal session of a *parlement* at which he or his representative commanded registration – and, if all else failed, his dreaded *lettres de cachet*, by which he could send the *parlements* or their ringleaders to prison or inter-nal exile.[9]

Although the *parlementaires* belonged to a privileged elite, they increas-ingly claimed to represent the French people and champion their interests. As the only institutional bodies with the legal authority to challenge the acts of the absolute monarchy, the *parlements* were in a unique position to do so. Consequently they played a leading role in political controversy, above all taking the side of the Jansenists in their struggle with the Jesuits and their allies at court, the so-called *dévot* party. In essence, Jansenism was an austere early seventeenth-century brand of Augustinian Roman Catholicism, and its adherents' argument with the Jesuits was doctrinal. By stressing the necessity of divine grace for salvation, admiring the 'purity' of the early Church, and opposing Papal and episcopal pretensions, Jansenists inevitably came into conflict with the Jesuits. The Jesuit order, established to spearhead the Catholic counter-reformation, was wealthy and very influential. Jesuits helped persuade Louis XIV to abandon the toleration granted to Protestant *huguenots* by the edict of Nantes and encouraged his attempts to stamp out Jansenism, which he considered a threat to episcopal control and a mask for republican tendencies. Louis XV continued the persecution of Jansenism, which from the 1720s gained a dangerous populist dimension following alleged miracles at the grave of a Jansenist divine in Paris.

In the early 1760s, the political balance tilted decisively in favour of the Jansenists, as Choiseul sought the *parlements*' acquiescence to his policy of post-war reconstruction. The Jesuits' fate was sealed in 1762, when they maladroitly appealed to the Paris *Parlement* to overturn a legal judgement prejudicial to their order. The *parlement* found against the Jesuits and opened proceedings for abuse of appeal. It duly condemned Jesuit doctrines, banned them from recruiting, and dissolved their organisational structure. Choiseul did nothing to intervene, and in November 1764 Louis XV reluctantly suppressed the order. The suppression took the political heat out of religious debates in France. However, by the same token, religion ceased to be a cloak for politics: henceforth political discourses – and underground pamphleteering – focused primarily on questions of secular government and became more directly critical of the Bourbon regime.[10]

The triumph of the *parlements* was short-lived. By 1770, hostile forces were lining up against them and Choiseul. Their isolation was intensified by the emergence of a new royal mistress, Madame du Barry, a plebian courtesan with a seedy past and close ties to Choiseul's enemies and the *dévots*. Finally, in December 1770, after he appeared to encourage Spanish resistance to British attempts to settle the Falkland Islands, the normally pacific Choiseul was dismissed by Louis XV. The leading voice in government now passed to a triumvirate composed of Chancellor René-Charles-Augustin de Maupeou; the abbé Joseph-Marie Terray, controller-general of Finances; and the duc d'Aiguillon, who served as foreign minister from June 1771 to 1774. All three had good motives for reshaping and chastening the *parlements*. Maupeou hoped to strengthen his voice in government; Terray to ensure the passage of a radical financial reform package; d'Aiguillon to secure his political future after the so-called Brittany affair, a crisis which culminated in the Breton *Parlement*'s attempting to impeach him over his actions as provincial Commander in Brittany during the 1760s. In 1770, the Paris *Parlement* found against d'Aiguillon, but the decision was quashed by Louis XV. United more by self-interest and opportunism than by ideology, this triumvirate embarked on a radical reform of the *parlements*.

The Maupeou reforms involved a massive overhaul of the upper strata of the French judicial system and a large-scale purge of the *parlementaires*.

In February 1771, the Paris *Parlement*'s jurisdiction was divided between six *Cours supérieures* and a rump *parlement* was stripped of much of its power. Magistrates who refused to serve were sacked, venal offices in the *parlements* abolished, and a system of salaries introduced in their place. As other *parlements* protested, they, too, were remodelled, and four abolished outright. These measures were met with the biggest explosion of political pamphleteering since the Fronde rebellions of the mid-seventeenth century. Nevertheless, with the resolute support of the king, Maupeou and his colleagues were able to face down the so-called *patriote* opposition. Their reforms proved abortive only because Louis XV suddenly succumbed to smallpox in May 1774, and his grandson and successor, Louis XVI, recalled the old *parlements*.[11]

Historical opinion is divided on the Maupeou crisis. Some historians have praised Maupeou's perspicacity and seen his policies as a final chance for the monarchy to reform itself.[12] Such an interpretation overlooks persistent reform efforts by other ministries and seems tenuous and over-deterministic. In 1771 no-one could foresee the revolution and, far from following a predetermined plan, Maupeou and his associates blundered into draconian measures. Nevertheless, the crisis had far-reaching implications because it exposed the lack of effective institutional safeguards against the abuse of state power by the monarch or his ministers.[13]

The accession of Louis XVI, and France's victorious participation in the American revolutionary war (1778–83), did little to change the monarchy's fundamental political problem. Finances still urgently needed reform, and the *parlements*, though chastened, continued to obstruct fiscal reforms. Indeed, victory exacerbated the problems, not least because the Swiss-born banker and controller-general Jacques Necker, having financed the war entirely through loans, declared royal finances to be in healthy surplus in his celebrated *Compte-rendu des finances* [*Financial Accounts*], which was published in 1781. Necker's figures were misleading, since they omitted many items of extraordinary expenditure, but most contemporaries, dazzled by his unprecedented disclosure of royal accounts and the power of wishful thinking, took him at his word. The monarchy's debt escalated under his successor, Charles-Alexandre de Calonne, who ostentatiously embarked upon a programme of public expenditure to shore up public confidence. Eventually, the house of cards collapsed. In 1786 Calonne was forced to inform the king of impending bankruptcy and proposed a radical fiscal reform package that would have hit the privileged orders hard. In an attempt to outflank opposition, Calonne also proposed that the king summon a long-forgotten and hand-picked body, the Assembly of Notables, to ratify the reforms, thereby trumping the *parlements*' claims to represent the nation. However, the Notables gave the reforms a frosty reception, and their resistance to the Crown's financial package precipitated a political crisis that culminated in the convening of an Estates-General in May 1789. This was the event that precipitated the revolution.

When the Estates-General met, an impasse over the method of voting led the representatives of the Third Estate (commoners) to declare themselves a National Assembly. They invited the privileged orders to join them and promised to make France a constitutional monarchy. Although Louis XVI appeared to acquiesce, fears of a royal counter-coup caused by suspicious troop movements and the appointment of a reactionary ministry under the baron de Breteuil led to a popular rising in Paris in July and the storming of the Bastille. In the provinces, agitation and fear of noble-backed counter-revolutionary conspiracies continued throughout the summer, and in October, in a re-run of the July, further troop movements provoked demonstrations in Paris, a march on Versailles, and the forced return of the royal family to Paris, where they could be observed closely. By this time, too, the National Assembly had produced its blueprint for a liberal constitution, the Declaration of the Rights of Man and Citizen, which proclaimed civic and fiscal equality, freedom of expression and conscience, and guarantees against ministerial despotism and arbitrary arrest. This measure also consolidated the Assembly's decisions of 4 August, when it attempted to assuage peasant unrest in the provinces by abolishing feudal privilege and obligations. However, the revolutionary djinn could not so easily be put back in the bottle. Although the new constitution was promulgated in September 1791, it was loudly criticised from both ends of the political spectrum and proved unworkable, not least because Louis XVI had proved his unwillingness to accept a reduced political role by his abortive flight to Varennes the previous June. Economic crisis and the outbreak of war with Prussia and Austria in April 1792 unleashed further political pressures, and in August 1792 a popular rising in Paris overthrew both the king and the constitution. A republic was declared, and the following January Louis XVI went to the scaffold. Marie-Antoinette followed him in October.

Historical interest in the role of scandalous pamphleteering in the political life of the *ancien régime* and revolution has fluctuated according to developments in the wider contours of revolutionary historiography. A first wave of interest occurred between about 1870 and 1914, and coincided with the heyday of empirical political history. This period saw the republication of several eighteenth-century scandalous texts which, despite the frequent inclusion of academic introductions, probably aimed primarily at *fin de siècle* libertines.[14] By 1900 this prurient interest had given rise to genuine historical curiosity and serious bibliographic research, culminating in a series of monumental studies of anti-Marie-Antoinette literature by Henri d'Almeras and Hector Fleischmann. They identified and examined all the major texts and often gave valuable insights into their production and authorship. Their work revealed the existence of a significant corpus of scandalous and pornographic texts attacking the monarchy, and served as a valuable bibliographic guide for later historians.[15]

After World War One, following the rise of Marxist history and resultant disdain for 'petite histoire', interest in scandalous texts waned. According to the Marxist Vulgate, the revolution was primarily the outcome of vast impersonal forces, notably the rise of commercial capitalism and the decline of the old feudal nobility. Prior to the revolution, a new capitalist class, the bourgeoisie, had accumulated great economic wealth, but had been denied the social prestige and political power that should have accompanied it by the nobility, who monopolised state positions and institutions and enjoyed considerable fiscal and social privileges. The revolution of 1789 marked the triumph of the bourgeoisie, who seized control of the levers of political power, established an elective National Assembly, and forged a state conducive to their needs. They suppressed noble titles; abolished privilege; established equality of opportunity and equality before the law; replaced venal office-holders with elected officials; and abolished restraints on trade. Marxist historians generally had little interest in the texts of the French enlightenment, which they believed merely articulated bourgeois ideology and class interest. The ideas they contained were merely the froth on the waves of great underlying social forces. If they noticed them at all, Marxist scholars doubtless viewed scandalous pamphlets as the scum on the froth.

Interest in both the enlightenment and scandalous pamphleteering has revived following the undermining of the Marxist orthodoxy by revisionist historians. At the heart of the revisionist challenge lies a reconsideration of class divisions and the economic condition of *ancien régime* France. Research published between the late 1950s and early 1970s increasingly suggested that the French social elite was not as fractured as the Marxist interpretation supposed. Rich bourgeois and aristocratic nobles mixed socially and led similar lifestyles; successful bourgeois families aspired to purchase landed estates and noble titles; and the greatest industrial ventures tended to be owned and run by noble landowners. Nor, it transpired, could most of the French bourgeoisie be characterised as capitalists: most were professionals, landowners, or state office-holders. Many of them also owned considerable 'privileges'.[16] Equally, the French economy was not as 'backward' in comparison to commercialised Britain as had long been supposed. It thus became hard to argue that it was unduly hampered by 'feudalism', or that a great gulf existed between a privileged, feudal, landed, reactionary, noble class and a dynamic, urban, capitalist bourgeoisie. The cataclysm of 1789 thus appeared to be, in George V. Taylor's oft-quoted phrase, 'essentially a political revolution with social consequences and not a social revolution with political consequences'.[17] This cleared the way for new post-revisionist interpretations of the revolution based on political-cultural rather than socio-economic approaches.

Post-revisionist historians – as advocates of political-cultural interpretations of the revolution are known – are generally more united in their approach to the problem of the revolution's origins than in their explanations. Most are committed to two related propositions. First, the revolution was a defining moment in the emergence of modern western democratic political culture. Second, the political culture that emerged from the revolution drew heavily on the ideology, norms, and discursive practices of the 'public sphere'. According to the German philosopher Jürgen Habermas, whose ideas provide a touchstone for post-revisionists, the 'public sphere', a newly emerged 'space' for public discussion, was formed by the burgeoning print media and new forms of sociability which developed across the eighteenth century.[18] Post-revisionists therefore believe that a key to understanding the revolution and its origins lies in the rise of the public sphere, whether as an ideological construct, a forum for debate, or in the discourses that prevailed there. However, they have very different understandings of the relative significance of 'discourses', 'public opinion', and the institutional basis of the public sphere. Some leading post-revisionists, including François Furet, Keith Michael Baker, Mona Ozouf, and Lynn Hunt, draw heavily on French semiotic theorists such as Pierre Bourdieu, who believe that verbal expression shapes the parameters of material reality. Hence they focus excessively on abstract 'discourses' and 'political vocabulary' at the expense of political events.[19] Others, such as Thomas Kaiser and Jeremy Popkin, pay much more attention to how everyday decisions by politicians and publishers played a large part in shaping prerevolutionary and revolutionary political culture. Their approach complements the work of the new British school of French revolutionary historians, led by Julian Swann, John Hardman, and Munro Price, which emphasises political contingency. The role of clandestine scandalous literature has attracted the attention of members of all these groups, not least because scurrilous works provide a bridge between abstract discourses and everyday court politics.

Since the late 1960s, the central figure in historiographical debates about the role of clandestine publishing and subversive literature has been Robert Darnton. In two seminal articles, published in 1968 and 1971, Darnton argued that pornographic political *libelles* played a central role in a process of 'desacralising' the French monarchy, by stripping its personnel and key institutions of the respect and sacred aura which conferred their legitimacy and hence ensured their survival. Thus scandalous *libelles* were highly implicated in the collapse of the Bourbon monarchy and the origins of the revolution. Moreover, Darnton singled out two London-based figures, Charles-Claude Théveneau de Morande and the future revolutionary Jacques-Pierre Brissot de Warville, as classic examples of the pamphleteers who produced such *libelles* and dragged the monarchy's reputation through the gutter, thereby wrecking its reform attempts.[20] Darnton labelled the *milieu* in which such pamphleteers operated 'Grub Street'.

In essence, Darnton's 'Grub Street' theory suggests that the key links between enlightenment and revolution lie in the output of lesser writers excluded from a gravy-train of patronage, state pensions, academy places, and awards, rather than in the works of great *philosophes* like Voltaire, Montesquieu, Diderot, and Rousseau. It contends that by the late 1770s, in an overstocked literary market-place, the most lucrative places were monopolised by careerist time-servers like Jean-Baptiste-Antoine Suard, who followed an entrenched enlightenment party line.[21] According to Darnton, Suard's urbanity and carefully cultivated connections won him literary fame and fortune without his publishing a major work. Such nonentities blocked the progress of budding Voltaires and future revolutionaries such as Brissot, who seethed with frustration and rebelled against the *ancien régime* establishment and its system of patronage, censorship, and licensing.

Nevertheless, embittered 'Grub Street hacks' needed to eat, and thus many were reduced to writing pornographic *libelles*, blackmail, or spying for the police. Darnton insinuated that Brissot, the pivotal figure in his theory, had probably done all these things: 'he was probably a spy, and his spying probably concerned the *libelle* style of pamphleteering that contributed to his support before the revolution and his downfall during it.'[22] However, Brissot and his fellow 'hacks' never forgave the regime that forced them to adopt such 'degrading' expedients. Their anger, Darnton asserted, was released in their works, where 'they expressed the passion of men who hated the old regime in their guts' and began the 'political education' of the people, who, unable to comprehend Rousseau, 'would soon be reading *Le Père Duchesne* [Jacques-René Hébert's outspoken and obscene revolutionary newspaper]'.[23]

However, Darnton's classic example of a Grub Street pamphlet was written not by Brissot but by his arch-enemy, Morande. Morande's *Le Gazetier cuirassé, ou anecdotes scandaleuses de la cour de France* [*The Armour-Plated Gazetteer, or Scandalous Anecdotes of the French Court*] (1771), the most notorious *libelle* of the Maupeou crisis, was, according to Darnton, a characteristically nihilistic tract and 'virtually a prototype of the genre'.[24] A systematic attack on a corrupt and vice-ridden establishment, it denounced the sexual depravity of aristocrats and the royal mistress, linked them to corruption in army, Church and state, and castigated Maupeou's reform programme. According to Darnton:

> Morande . . . and his fellow hacks had no interest in reform. They hated the system in itself: and they expressed that hatred by desanctifying its symbols, destroying the myths that gave it legitimacy in the eyes of the public, and perpetrating the countermyth of degenerate despotism.[25]

When the revolution broke out, many of Darnton's 'hacks' – including Brissot, Jean-Paul Marat, Pierre-Louis Manuel, Antoine-Joseph Gorsas, and Jean-Louis Carra – became Jacobin activists, pursued distinguished political and journalistic careers, and helped dismantle the hated monarchy and its institutions. Darnton's image of Brissot and, by extension, other revolutionaries involved in prerevolutionary pamphleteering is now widespread in historical literature.[26]

Combining explanatory simplicity with masterful exposition, Darnton's 'Grub Street' thesis proved compelling and influential. It appeals to the human urge for a narrative in which the repressed underdog turns the tables and the common-sense assumption that causal links must exist between enlightenment and revolution. It also offered something to all camps in the revolution debate. Revisionists and post-revisionists were attracted to his concept of 'desacralisation' and 'Grub Street theory' because they offered rich explanatory possibilities while providing a credible non-Marxist explanation for revolutionary anti-aristocratic rhetoric. Meanwhile, die-hard Marxists could embrace the idea of a literary proletariat rebelling against a privileged academic elite. Darnton's ideas also inspired gender historians seeking to explain the marginalisation of women in revolutionary political culture, particularly Sarah Maza and Lynn Hunt. They have focused particular attention on pornographic pamphlets against Marie-Antoinette – a figure about whom Darnton says little – arguing that by vilifying the queen, they damaged the political cause of all women. By treating her as a representative figure, the discourses they promoted led to the exclusion of women from republican political life and their confinement within a private sphere of family and domesticity.[27]

Such ideas have become common-place in general historical literature. For example, Munro Price's recent treatment of high politics has a section on rumours and pamphlets concerning Marie-Antoinette, which concludes: 'There is no evidence whatever that the queen or any of her friends had lesbian or any other unorthodox tastes. Yet none of this affected the spread of underground literature against Marie-Antoinette, nor the remarkable extent to which it was believed by the public. By 1789, the queen's unpopularity had begun to threaten the Crown itself.'[28] An essay by Tim Blanning entitled 'Louis XVI and the public sphere' published in 2004 goes even further, devoting over half of its space to attacks on Marie-Antoinette. He asserts that 'it was when it became known that the queen was pregnant for the first time [in 1781] that the real flood of pornographic *libelles* began', and that from 1785, following the diamond necklace scandal, they became a torrent.[29] Likewise, Jacques Revel's article 'Marie-Antoinette' in the *Dictionnaire critique de la révolution française*, the crowning achievement of French post-revisionism, states:

> In any case the queen's fate had long since been decided by public opinion. In the very first years of the revolution an abundant pamphlet literature had made her its target. It began not in 1789 but . . . in the 1770s, with several periods of particularly high intensity, such as . . . the aftermath of the 'affair of the necklace'. Much of this material was prepared, usually in London, by professional satirists [*libellistes*].[30]

Such accounts have even entered popular culture,[31] and amount, according to Vivian Gruder, to a veritable 'pornographic interpretation' of the revolution and its origins.[32]

This Darntonesque, 'pornographic school' account of subversive pamphleteering has been questioned on several grounds. First, critics have charged that Darnton's interpretation exaggerates the significance of illegal works, since pornographic *libelles* and scandalous memoirs formed only part of France's rich print culture. Many historians highlight the significance of other forms of potentially subversive printed product, not all of them illegal. These include newspapers and periodicals, and even legal trial briefs, which were uncensored and, if related to *causes célèbres*, sold in their thousands.[33] Others feel that Darnton trivialises the enlightenment, by ignoring the role of ideas, and hence the cultural influence of major enlightenment thinkers.[34] Harvey Chisick goes so far as to contend that 'what is significant about the Grub Street mode of radical devalidation, apart from its existence, is its marginality'.[35]

Second, the desacralisation model of 'ideological erosion' (the phrase is Darnton's own)[36] is crude, particularly Darnton's image of public opinion as a unitary, invincible, concrete force, opposed to monarchy, and working inevitably to bring about the revolution. Thomas Kaiser feels it lacks sufficient traction to explain the revolution, while Daniel Gordon considers it 'theoretically weak'.[37] Gordon argues that the state was 'the most dynamic force' in eighteenth-century France and had multiple claims to legitimacy. Hence its collapse in 1789 cannot be attributed primarily to the stripping of the monarchy's religious foundations.[38] Likewise, Roger Chartier believes that desacralisation theory over-simplifies the complex, little-understood ways by which readers appropriate texts, treating readers' minds as 'soft wax' on which writers stamp their opinions.[39]

Third, commentators have detected several problems with the dynamics of Darnton's model, not least because many authors who fit the Grub Street profile never became revolutionaries, and some were drawn to counter-revolution.[40] In addition, Jeremy Popkin argues that Darnton overlooks the crucial importance of patronage under the *ancien régime*.[41] Other scholars have denied that a literary underclass was developing in the 1780s and commented on the openness of the French cultural elite.[42] Elizabeth Eisenstein has also observed that beyond French borders, most literary exiles and 'other cultural intermediaries . . . propagated the enlightenment without turning to crime'.[43] Finally, the case studies which underpin the 'Grub Street' theory remain contentious. Recent studies rehabilitate Suard and challenge Darnton's portrayal of Morande.[44] Brissot, meanwhile, has emerged as a well-connected and well-respected *philosophe*,[45] and new evidence published by the present author casts doubt on Darnton's insinuations that he published pornographic *libelles* or spied for the police.[46] But if he did, as Eisenstein notes, it seems unlikely that he felt 'degraded' by serving as an agent of a royal official.[47] Even Darnton now accepts that Brissot was probably not one of the London *libellistes*, although he still insists that he was 'probably' a spy.[48]

Moreover, the term 'Grub Street' is problematic. Franco Venturi notes that it originally referred to a road in London where the back-street printing trade was concentrated in the early eighteenth century and hence ill describes the 'Parisian literary proletariat in the [seventeen-]eighties'.[49] Darnton has responded that 'Grub Street' is a 'metaphorical landscape and social *milieu*' rather than a real place, but this is not particularly helpful.[50] It fails to clarify whether writers entered 'Grub Street' because of their poverty or their behaviour, and, if the latter, whether they had to resort to subversive, illegal, pornographic, or other morally suspect expedients before setting their virtual feet on its metaphorical cobbles. The term 'Grub Street' is thus pejorative, misleading, and ultimately meaningless, particularly for figures like Brissot, whom it strips of intellectual credibility and moral integrity. Thus, the chapters that follow avoid using it and refer to *libellistes* rather than 'Grub Street hacks'. Nevertheless, as deployed hereafter, *libelliste* serves as a short-hand for 'blackmailer-*libelliste*' and thus has connotations of its own. It will not be applied to pamphleteers who were not involved in extortion except when quoting from contemporary sources.

Finally, there are problems of chronology in the 'pornographic' interpretation. The best-selling 'libels and court satires' in Darnton's recently published statistics of the French illegal book trade of the Société typographique de Neuchâtel between 1769 and 1789 attack Louis XV and his mistresses rather than Louis XVI or Marie-Antoinette.[51] Moreover, Vivian Gruder has recently argued that while rumours, epigrams, and gossip against the queen circulated among courtiers from an early stage, pornographic *libelles*, prints, caricatures, and songs attacking Louis XVI and Marie-Antoinette were comparatively rare before the revolution. They were, she suggests, more a consequence than a cause of the political crisis that destroyed the *ancien régime*.[52] The current study builds upon, extends, and revises her arguments.

Despite the heat and scholarship generated by these debates, no critic of Darnton or the 'pornographic school' has hitherto offered a rounded alternative account of the cultural and political role of prerevolutionary scandalous pamphleteering. Likewise, although Darnton's position has evolved, the most cogent objections to his work remain valid. Darnton acknowledges that his early published work took insufficient account of patronage and over-states links between 'Grub Street' writers and the revolution.[53] As Thomas Kaiser has pointed out, the 'alienated hacks' line does not feature in Darnton's study of *Forbidden Best-Sellers of Pre-Revolutionary France* (1996), which instead makes maximum use of desacralisation theory.[54] However, it still pays little attention to patronage and reiterates an account of 'ideological erosion' and public opinion based on metaphor rather than a detailed model of process: 'Like the drip, drip, drip of water on stone', Darnton writes, 'the denunciations of dissolute kings and wicked ministers wore away the layer of sacredness that made the monarchy legitimate in the eyes of its subjects' until, by 1788, 'the regime stood condemned. It had lost its final round in the long struggle to contain public opinion.'[55] Moreover, Darnton has reiterated his belief that tensions between enlightenment establishment and budding writers can help to explain the revolution.[56]

Nevertheless, critics of Darnton and the 'pornographic interpretation' dismiss the illegal sector at their peril. Francophone publishing networks beyond French frontiers were extensive and supplied a clandestine trade that, according to one estimate, accounted for perhaps half of all books sold in France.[57] Scandalous works formed a significant part of this total, and hence there is an urgent need to explore their role within *ancien régime* politics and print culture. Before this can be achieved, many questions remain to be resolved. The mechanisms and full extent of patronage are still uncertain, and thus it remains unclear how much autonomy was available to writers, especially those beyond French borders. Much more needs to be known about the motives and aspirations of authors. Should their activities and products be seen primarily as the manifestations of political manoeuvring among social elites, or did they often act on their own initiative or for ideological reasons? There is still room for debate about the importance and role of both political pamphleteering and scandalous texts. What role, too, did government, ministers, courtiers, the *parlements*, and private individuals play in pamphleteering? How widely were seditious texts available? How did readers understand and respond to them? And what were the links between pamphleteers, pamphleteering, and the revolution?

In particular, surprisingly little is known about the group from which Darnton drew his examples of 'Grub Street hacks': French exile *libellistes* who wrote in the hope of suppression fees. Who were they and what motivated them? How were their works produced or disseminated, and by whom? What were their backgrounds? How many of them were there? Did they have links with the elite, or were they freelancers? How far would the French or British ministries go to control them, and what do their policies reveal? How were attempts to control the *libellistes* received and reported? And did they become radical revolutionaries, as Darnton's analysis suggests?

These questions suggest that the *libellistes* and their writings – not all of which were pornographic – are worthy of study from at least three points of view. First, blackmailer-*libellistes* are a phenomenon that has not been subjected to systematic study.[58] Moreover, in the late eighteenth and early nineteenth centuries, the London *libellistes* were not a unique phenomenon: Britain, too, had writers who relied on suppression fees.[59] They, together with their French-born *confrères*, contributed to the enduring image of the London press of the period as intrinsically corrupt.[60]

Secondly, the topic has a significant historiographical interest, because the *libellistes* represent an extreme case. Operating in a constitutional monarchy under the most liberal press regime in Europe, they enjoyed more freedom, both legal and *de facto*, than any other French enlightenment writers. What they did, what they wrote, and how they interacted with the authorities tested the limits of the law, their imagination, and the possible. The *libellistes* therefore offer a case study of the limits of expression, thought, action, patronage, authority, loyalty, and identity among *ancien régime* French subjects. By revealing the contexts, networks, and ideological frameworks within which they operated, it is possible to re-examine many of the issues in dispute between the advocates of the 'pornographic school' and their critics. Because they occupied an unstable position between 'liberal' Britain and 'despotic' France, they also offer a unique vantage point from which to appraise French perceptions of Britain and vice versa.

Thirdly, the *libellistes* undoubtedly had an influence both in France and in Britain that transcended the texts they produced, not least because several of them enjoyed a high public profile and, together with some of their associates, ranked among the most colourful characters of their day. Among them were the cross-dressing ex-diplomat Charles-Geneviève-Louise-Auguste-André-Timothée d'Eon de Beaumont; Simon-Nicolas-Henri Linguet, author of the most sensational journalism of the prerevolutionary era; the charismatic and audacious comtesse de La Motte, who pulled off the most spectacular fraud of the century; and Morande, the most notorious black-mailer-*libelliste* of all. The *libellistes*' associate Pierre-Augustin Caron de Beaumarchais, creator of Figaro, also had a high public profile. Moreover, *libelles* and blackmail were only part of the scandal associated with the *libellistes*. Many contemporaries were horrified that their behaviour went unpunished; others were alarmed by rumours of the French authorities' attempts to silence them, since plans to suborn English press freedom or encourage the reform of London's policing smacked of despotism and unreasonable interference in the domestic policy of a sovereign power. Allegations of kidnap and assassination plots were yet more chilling. As a result, the activities of the *libellistes* and their adversaries nourished debates on both sides of the Channel about state power and the individual, liberty and licence, freedom and despotism.

The history of the circumstances in which scandalous *libelles* were produced, disseminated or suppressed, as well as the reports and stories to which they gave rise, thus holds as much interest as, and probably more importance than, the *libelles* themselves. It is a tale which deserves to be told. Fortunately, despite the necessarily secretive nature of blackmail, primary source material is extensive and rich, if uneven. The *libellistes* and their associates published and wrote a great deal, and in the cases of d'Eon, Morande, Brissot, the comte and comtesse de La Motte, and Beaumarchais, a large volume of relevant documentation survives.[61] The first five all produced autobiographical texts.[62] In addition, the archives of the French foreign ministry and the Bastille papers in the Bibliothèque de l'Arsenal contain hundreds of documents relating to the *libellistes*' activities. Further scattered references appear in published memoir sources; contemporary pamphlets; clandestine newsletters; contemporary correspondence; the papers of prominent individuals; and police sources, including the extensive, if somewhat unreliable, memoirs of Lenoir.[63] Unfortunately, British sources on the *libellistes* are somewhat thinner, although much valuable newspaper material survives, including large collections of cuttings made by d'Eon and preserved in the British Library and the Brotherton Collection at Leeds University.[64] Official British reactions often have to be deduced from French diplomats' reports, as the references in British diplomatic and political correspondence are sparse.

Perhaps the most interesting aspect of these sources is the ambiguities and paradoxes they reveal in contemporary attitudes. Inside France, scandalous publications were illegal, but many were highly sought-after. Members of the courtly elite both decried *libelles* and indulged in reading and, in all probability, composing them. Among the British elite, *libelles* commanded high prices, and several were translated. Yet to many contemporaries the *libellistes* were literary buccaneers, no better than highwaymen.[65] Nevertheless, the *libellistes* also had significant defenders in print and person: for they could be viewed as heroic victims of French despotism, champions of press freedom, and pioneers of the public's right to know about affairs thitherto regarded as 'the King's secret'.

Furthermore, in England the *libellistes*' activities were sheltered by libel and blackmail laws that offered no effective protection to non-residents.[66] Hence, they plied their trade with impunity, at least from a legal point of view, and in consequence French ministers, police agents, and private individuals often resorted to violent, clandestine, illegal, or 'despotic' means to control them.[67] The London populace regarded such actions as serious infringements of British liberties, and on several occasions mobs were mobilised to defend individual *libellistes*. The story of the clandestine publishing activities of the London *libellistes* thus transcends the history of the production, dissemination, and occasional suppression of scandalous pamphlets. It is also a study in how the political cultures, public spheres, and government agencies of eighteenth-century France and Britain actually operated.

In consequence, this study of the London *libellistes* offers a major reassessment of the Darntonian and pornographic school views of political pamphleteers and pamphleteering. Its opening chapter examines the *libellistes*' backgrounds, career paths, political connections, and attitudes and shows a marked divergence from the expectations established by the 'Grub Street' model. The second chapter explores how the London *libelle* industry was organised, how widely its products were disseminated, the patronage links of the *libellistes*, and how readers appear to have responded to their works. It uncovers an extensive French publishing and bookselling industry in London, and offers a radical re-evaluation of the *libelles*' political significance. Chapters three and four show what the French government and officials thought about *libellistes*, how they attempted to control them, and with what results. They indicate that when it chose to do so, the monarchy generally succeeded in preventing publication and circulation of the types of *libelle* which it considered most noxious. These included *libelles* against Marie-Antoinette: owing to their centrality in the 'pornographic interpretation', the fifth chapter is devoted to them. It reinforces and extends Gruder's contention that *libelles* against the queen were extremely rare prior to 1789, before establishing when key texts became available and what messages they contained. The sixth chapter considers the messages contained in other London-produced *libelles* which were available up to 1789, and the constructions they placed on the French regime. The final chapter uncovers the ways in which the *libellistes*, their activities, and those of French government agents sent to deal with them were reported to the public, and how these stories interacted with prevailing discourses concerning despotism and freedom. The findings of these chapters are spelt out in the conclusion, and have broad implications for our understanding of both prerevolutionary pamphleteering and late eighteenth-century British and French political culture.

Notes

1 On French clandestine publishing, see Robert Darnton's *Forbidden Best-Sellers of Pre-Revolutionary France* (London: Harper Collins, 1996) and *The Corpus of Clandestine Literature in France 1769–1789* (New York: Norton, 1995); Elizabeth L. Eisenstein, *Grub Street Abroad: Aspects of the French Cosmopolitan Press from the Age of Louis XIV to the Enlightenment* (Oxford: Clarendon Press, 1992). See also Raymond Birn, *Pierre Rousseau et les philosophes de Bouillon*, SVEC 29 (Oxford: Voltaire Foundation, 1964); J.-P. Belin, *Le Commerce des livres prohibés à Paris de 1750–1789* (New York: B. Franklin, 1967 [original edition, Paris: 1913]).

2 These texts are discussed in chapters five and six below.

3 This literature is discussed later in this introduction.

4 For previous treatments see Peter Wagner, *Eros Revived: Erotica of the Enlightenment in England and America* (London: Paladin, 1988), pp. 91–100; Henri d'Almeras, *Marie-Antoinette et les pamphlets royalistes et révolutionnaires* (Paris: Librarie mondiale, 1907); Hector Fleischmann, *Les Pamphlets libertins contre Marie-Antoinette* (Paris, 1908; republished Geneva: Slatkine reprints, 1976), pp. 102–29, 186–204, and *Marie-Antoinette libertine* (Paris: Bibliothèque des curieux, 1908), pp. 33–78; Paul Agnani, 'Libelles et diplomatie à la fin du dix-huitième siècle d'après la Correspondance Politique, Angleterre conservée aux Archives du Ministère des affaires étrangères, 1771–1783' (unpublished *mémoire de maîtrise*, University of Besançon, 2004).

5 The term 'political pornography' is problematic. While other scholars use it frequently, Darnton appears careful to avoid the term, and with justification. Although this book uses the term, it does so sparingly, since most prerevolutionary works by the London *libellistes* are not pornographic in the accepted sense: see below, chapter six.

6 However, provincial representative Estates survived in Brittany and Burgundy. Some municipal authorities were also elected.

7 See esp. Norbert Elias, *The Court Society*, transl. Edmund Jephcott (Oxford: Blackwell, 1983).

8 See Thomas E. Kaiser, 'Ambiguous identities: Marie-Antoinette and the House of Lorraine from the affair of the minuet to Lambesc's charge' in Dena Goodman (ed.), *Marie-Antoinette: Writings on the Body of a Queen* (New York and London: Routledge, 2003); Daniel Wick, *A Conspiracy of Well-Intentioned Men: The Society of Thirty and the French Revolution* (New York and London: Garland, 1987).

9 For recent studies see Bailey Stone, *The Parlement of Paris, 1774–1789* (Chapel Hill, NC: University of North Carolina Press, 1981); John Rogister, *Louis XV*

and the Parlement of Paris, 1737–55 (Cambridge: Cambridge University Press, 1995); Julian Swann, *Politics and the Parlement of Paris under Louis XV, 1754–74* (Cambridge: Cambridge University Press, 1995).

10 On Jansenism see C. Maire, *De La Cause de Dieu à la cause de la nation. Les jansénistes au XVIIIe siècle* (Paris: Gallimard, 1998); Dale Van Kley, *The Jansenists and the Expulsion of the Jesuits from France, 1757–1765* (New Haven, CT: Yale University Press, 1975).

11 On the Maupeou coup see: Durand Echeverria, *The Maupeou Revolution: A Study in the History of Libertarianism: France, 1770–1774* (Baton Rouge, LA: Louisiana State University Press, 1985). On the *parlements*' pamphleteering and propaganda see Shanti Marie Singham, ' "A conspiracy of twenty million Frenchmen": public opinion, patriotism, and the assault on absolutism during the Maupeou years, 1770–1775' (unpublished Ph.D. thesis, Princeton University, 1991).

12 See for example Alfred Cobban, *A History of Modern France*, vol. I, *1715–1799* (Harmondsworth: Penguin, 1957), pp. 95–6; Robert Darnton, 'The high enlightenment and the low-life of literature in prerevolutionary France', *Past and Present* no. 51 (1971).

13 This interpretation dates back to Jean Egret, *Louis XV et l'opposition parlementaire, 1715–1775* (Paris: A. Collin, 1970) and William Doyle, 'The parlements of France and the breakdown of the old regime, 1770–1788', *French Historical Studies* 6:4 (1970).

14 Common imprints include Le Coffret des Bibliophiles in Paris and Société des Bibliophiles cosmopolites in Neuchâtel.

15 D'Almeras, *Marie-Antoinette et les pamphlets*; Fleischmann, *Pamphlets libertins*; Fleischmann, *Marie-Antoinette libertine*.

16 See especially two seminal essays by George V. Taylor, 'Noncapitalist wealth and the origins of the French revolution', *American Historical Review* 72:2 (1967) and 'Types of Capitalism in Eighteenth-Century France', *English Historical Review* 79:3 (1964); Guy Chaussinand-Nogaret, *The French Nobility in the Eighteenth Century: From Feudalism to Enlightenment*, transl. William Doyle (Cambridge: Cambridge University Press, 1985).

17 Taylor, 'Noncapitalist wealth', p. 491.

18 Jürgen Habermas, *The Structural Transformation of the Public Sphere: An Inquiry into a Category of Bourgeois Society*, transl. Thomas Burger (Cambridge, MA: MIT Press, 1989 [original German edition, 1962]). Recent assessments of Habermas include Hannah Barker and Simon Burrows (eds), *Press, Politics and the Public Sphere in Europe and North America 1760–1820* (Cambridge: Cambridge University Press, 2002); James van Horn Melton, *The Rise of the Public in Enlightenment Europe* (Cambridge: Cambridge University Press, 2001).

19 See, for example, Keith Michael Baker, *Inventing the French Revolution: Essays on French Political Culture in the Eighteenth Century* (Cambridge: Cambridge University Press, 1990); Mona Ozouf, 'Public opinion at the end of the ancien regime', *Journal of Modern History* 60 supplement (1988).

20 Robert Darnton, 'The Grub Street style of revolution: J.-P. Brissot, police spy', *Journal of Modern History*, 40:4 (1968) and Darnton, 'High enlightenment'.

21 Darnton elaborates this case in 'A police inspector sorts his files: the anatomy of the Republic of Letters' in Robert Darnton, *The Great Cat Massacre and Other*

Episodes in French Cultural History, first Vintage Books edition (New York: Vintage, 1985 [first edition, 1984]) and 'The facts of literary life in eighteenth-century France' in Keith Michael Baker (ed.), *The French Revolution and the Creation of Modern Political Culture*, vol. I, *The Political Culture of the Old Regime* (Oxford: Pergamon, 1987).

22 Darnton, 'Grub Street', p. 325.

23 Darnton, 'High enlightenment', pp. 115, 110.

24 Quote ibid., pp. 105–6; p. 110 asserts that a 'spirit of nihilism' characterised the *libelles*.

25 Ibid., p. 109.

26 See Simon Schama, *Citizens: A Chronicle of the French Revolution* (London: Viking, 1989), p. 227; Colin Jones, *The Great Nation: France from Louis XV to Napoleon* (London: Allen Lane, 2002), p. 455; Leigh Whalley, *Radicals: Politics and Republicanism in the French Revolution* (Stroud: Sutton, 2000), p. 14; D. M. G. Sutherland, *France 1789–1814: Revolution and Counter-Revolution* (London: Fontana, 1985), p. 120. However, in *The French Revolution and Empire: The Quest for a Civic Order* (Oxford: Blackwell, 2003), p. 112, Sutherland reverses his previous view.

27 See esp. Sarah Maza, 'The diamond necklace affair revisited (1785–1786): the case of the missing queen' and Lynn Hunt, 'The many bodies of Marie-Antoinette: political pornography and the problem of the feminine in the French Revolution', both published in Lynn Hunt (ed.), *Eroticism and the Body Politic* (Baltimore, MD, and London: Johns Hopkins University Press, 1991). These and other treatments of anti-Marie-Antoinette pamphlets appear in Goodman (ed.), *Marie-Antoinette*. See also Antoine de Baecque, 'Pamphlets: libel and political mythology' in Robert Darnton and Daniel Roche (eds), *Revolution in Print: The Press in France, 1775–1800* (Berkeley and Los Angeles: University of California Press, 1989); Chantal Thomas, *The Wicked Queen: The Origins of the Myth of Marie-Antoinette*, transl. Julie Rose (New York: Zone Books, 1999). The classic study of women's exclusion from revolutionary political life remains Joan Landes, *Women and the Public Sphere in the Age of the French Revolution* (Ithaca, NY: Cornell University Press, 1988).

28 Munro Price, *The Fall of the French Monarchy: Louis XVI, Marie-Antoinette and the Baron de Breteuil* (London: Macmillan, 2002), 16. On Marie-Antoinette's lesbian image see Elizabeth Colwill, 'Pass as a woman, act like a man: Marie-Antoinette as tribade in the pornography of the French revolution' in Goodman (ed.), *Marie-Antoinette*.

29 T. C. W. Blanning, 'Louis XVI and the public sphere' in Malcolm Crook, William Doyle, and Alan Forrest (eds), *Enlightenment and Revolution: Essays in Honour of Norman Hampson* (Aldershot: Ashgate, 2004), quote at p. 65. See also T. C. W. Blanning, *The Culture of Power and the Power of Culture: Old Regime Europe 1660–1789* (Oxford: Oxford University Press, 2002), pp. 406–17.

30 Jacques Revel, 'Marie-Antoinette' in François Furet and Mona Ozouf (eds), *A Critical Dictionary of the French Revolution*, transl. Arthur Goldhammer (Cambridge, MA: Belknap Press, 1989), p. 262.

31 See, for example, Mark Steel, *Vive la Révolution: A Stand-Up History of the French Revolution* (London: Scribner, 2003), pp. 38–43. Steel, a left-wing British comedian, offers a passionate response to conservative revisionists, above all Schama.

32 Vivian R. Gruder, 'The question of Marie-Antoinette: the queen and public opinion before the revolution', *French History* 16:3 (2002), p. 272. In addition to Darnton's *oeuvre* and works cited in n. 27 above, important contributions to this interpretation include Lynn Hunt's *The Family Romance of the French Revolution* (Berkeley, CA: University of California Press, 1992) and 'Pornography and the French Revolution' in Lynn Hunt (ed.), *The Invention of Pornography: Obscenity and the Invention of Modernity* (New York: Zone Books, 1993); Jacques Revel's 'Marie-Antoinette' and 'Marie-Antoinette in her fictions: the staging of hatred' in Bernadette Fort (ed.), *Fictions of the French Revolution* (Evanston, IL: Northwestern University Press, 1991); Sarah Maza's *Private Lives and Public Affairs: The Causes Célèbres of Prerevolutionary France* (Berkeley, CA: University of California Press, 1993) and 'L'Image de la souveraine: féminité et politique dans les pamphlets de l'affaire du collier' in Harvey Chisick (ed.), *The Press in the French Revolution*, *SVEC* 287 (Oxford: Voltaire Foundation, 1991); Jean-Marie Goulemot, *Forbidden Texts: Erotic Literature and its Readers in Eighteenth-Century France*, transl. James Simpson (Cambridge: Polity, 1994 [original French edition, 1991]), esp. pp. 24–5; Wagner, *Eros Revived*, pp. 91–100. For a more extensive bibliography see Colwill, 'Pass as a woman', pp. 162–3, n. 7. For critical essays on Darnton's work, see Haydn T. Mason (ed.), *The Darnton Debate: Books and Revolution in the Eighteenth Century* (Oxford: Voltaire Foundation, 1998).

33 On trial briefs see Maza, *Private Lives*.

34 See esp. Daniel Gordon, 'The great enlightenment massacre', Jeremy D. Popkin, 'Darnton's alternative (to the) enlightenment', and Elizabeth L. Eisenstein, 'Bypassing the enlightenment: taking an underground route to revolution' all in Mason (ed.), *Darnton Debate*; John Lough, 'The French literary underground reconsidered', *SVEC* 329 (Oxford: Voltaire Foundation, 1995). Popkin contends that Darnton has studied the enlightenment's 'other'.

35 Harvey Chisick, 'Introduction' in Chisick (ed.), *Press in Revolution*, p. 8.

36 See Darnton, *Forbidden Best-Sellers*, p. 20.

37 Thomas E. Kaiser, 'Enlightenment, public opinion and politics in the work of Robert Darnton' in Mason (ed.), *Darnton Debate*, esp. pp. 191–2; Gordon, 'Enlightenment massacre', p. 132.

38 Gordon, 'Enlightenment massacre', p. 151.

39 Roger Chartier, *The Cultural Origins of the French Revolution* (Durham, NC, 1991), esp. ch. 4.

40 See esp. Darrin M. McMahon, 'The counter-enlightenment and the low-life of literature in pre-revolutionary France', *Past and Present* no. 159 (1998).

41 Jeremy D. Popkin, 'Pamphlet journalism at the end of the old regime', *Eighteenth-Century Studies* 22:3 (1989).

42 Lough, 'French literary underground'; Eisenstein, 'Bypassing enlightenment', p. 163.

43 Eisenstein, *Grub Street Abroad*, p. 138.

44 Daniel Gordon, *Citizens Without Sovereignty: Equality and Sociability in French Thought, 1670–1789* (Princeton, NJ: Princeton University Press, 1994); *BCE*; Simon Burrows, 'A literary low-life reassessed: Charles Théveneau de Morande in London, 1769–1791', *Eighteenth-Century Life* 22:1 (1998).

45 Dena Goodman, *The Republic of Letters: A Cultural History of the French Enlightenment* (Ithaca, NY: Cornell University Press, 1994), pp. 281–8; Leonore

Loft, *Passion, Politics and Philosophie: Rediscovering J. -P. Brissot* (Westport, CT: Greenwood, 2002). See also Frederick A. De Luna, 'The Dean Street style of revolution: J. -P. Brissot, *jeune philosophe*', *French Historical Studies* 17:1 (1991).

46 Simon Burrows, 'The innocence of Jacques-Pierre Brissot', *Historical Journal* 46:4 (2003); Robert Darnton, 'The Brissot dossier', *French Historical Studies* 17:1 (1991). A further allegation, that Brissot published pamphlets designed to manipulate stock prices, in Robert Darnton, 'Ideology on the Bourse' in Michel Vovelle (ed.), *L'Image de la révolution française*, 4 vols (Paris and New York: Pergamon, 1990), subsequently republished in Robert Darnton, *George Washington's False Teeth: An Unconventional Guide to the Eighteenth Century* (New York, 2003), has provoked a fascinating refutation by Richard Livesey and James Whatmore, 'Étienne Clavière, Jacques-Pierre Brissot et les fondations intellectuelles de la politique des Girondins', *Annales historiques de la révolution française* 72:3 (2000).

47 Eisenstein, 'Bypassing enlightenment', p. 162.

48 The reasons for this apparent *volte face* are not clear. Robert Darnton, 'The skeletons in the closet: how historians play god' in Darnton, *George Washington's False Teeth*, first published in 2002, only states (pp. 169–70), 'Did Brissot collaborate on smutty pamphlets? Having read through the elaborate reports by French agents in London . . . at the Quai d'Orsay, I think it unlikely.' However, Darnton, 'Grub Street' reveals (n. 54) that by 1968 he had already determined that these records portrayed Brissot as the *libellistes*' associate, not their collaborator, yet still made the previously quoted insinuations about Brissot's involvement in 'the *libelle* style of pamphleteering'.

49 Franco Venturi, *The End of the Old Regime in Europe, 1776–1789*, transl. B. Litchfield, 2 vols (Princeton, NJ: Princeton University Press, 1991), I, 427, n. 7. See also De Luna, 'Dean Street', p. 185; Eisenstein, 'Bypassing enlightenment', p. 159; Gordon, 'Enlightenment massacre', p. 136. Eisenstein notes that when Darnton attempted to translate 'Grub Street', he settled for the equally inappropriate and anachronistic 'Bohème littéraire'.

50 Robert Darnton, 'Two paths through the social history of ideas' in Mason (ed.), *Darnton Debate*, p. 264.

51 Darnton, *Corpus*, p. 207.

52 Gruder, 'Question of Marie-Antoinette'.

53 Darnton, 'Two paths', pp. 254, 279. Ironically, patronage features prominently in Darnton's treatment of the Kornmann group of pamphleteers and Clavière's stable of writers in his unpublished thesis, 'Trends in radical propaganda on the eve of the French revolution (1782–1788)' (D.Phil. thesis, University of Oxford, 1964). Part of this analysis appears in Darnton, 'Ideology on the Bourse'.

54 Kaiser, 'Enlightenment, public opinion and politics', pp. 194–5.

55 Darnton, *Forbidden Best-Sellers*, quotes at pp. 216, 246.

56 Darnton, 'Two paths', esp. p. 266.

57 Roger Chartier, 'Book markets and reading in France at the end of the old regime' in Carol Armbruster (ed.), *Publishing and Readership in Revolutionary France and America* (Westport, CT: Greenwood, 1993), p. 125, notes that only 40 per cent of 1,548 known French titles published in 1764 had received formal legal permission, though others may have received oral consent.

58 See, however, Angus McLaren, *Sexual Blackmail: A Modern History*, (Cambridge, MA: Harvard University Press, 2002), and Frances Wilson's

biography of Harriet Wilson, *The Courtesan's Revenge* (London: Faber, 2003). See also Lynda M. Thompson, *The 'Scandalous Memorialists': Constantia Phillips, Laetitia Pilkington and the Shame of 'Public Fame'* (Manchester: Manchester University Press, 2000).

59 See the works mentioned in n. 58 above. Anna Clark, *Scandal: the Sexual Politics of the British Constitution* (Princeton and Oxford: Princeton University Press, 2004) notes that scandals often began when blackmail attempts failed.

60 For miscellaneous reports of newspaper suppression fees, see Arthur Aspinall, *Politics and the Press, c. 1750–1850* (Brighton: Harvester, 1973); Robert Harris, *A Patriot Press: National Politics and the London Press in the 1740s* (Oxford: Clarendon, 1993); Roger Wilkes, *Scandal: A Scurrilous History of Gossip* (London: Atlantic Books, 2002). Hannah Barker, *Newspapers, Politics, and Public Opinion in Late Eighteenth-Century England* (Oxford: Oxford University Press, 1998), compellingly refutes arguments that the British press was intrinsically corrupt. For links between foreign journalists and the London press see Simon Burrows, *French Exile Journalism and European Politics, 1792–1814* (Woodbridge: Royal Historical Society, 2000).

61 For d'Eon's papers see BMT; ULBC; AN, 277AP; CPA 445–576 *passim* and CPA suppléments 13, 16, and 17; and Add. MSS 11,339–41. Some have been published in Frédéric Gaillardet, *Mémoires du chevalier d'Eon*, réédités à Paris (Paris: Bernard Grasset, 1935 [original edition, Paris, 1836]); Charles-Geneviève-Louise-Auguste-André-Timothée d'Eon de Beaumont, *The Maiden of Tonnerre: The Vicissitudes of the Chevalier and the Chevalière d'Eon*, transl. and edited by Roland A. Champagne, Nina Ekstein, and Gary Kates (Baltimore and London: Johns Hopkins University Press, 2001); and d'Eon's own publications, especially his *Lettres, mémoires et négociations particulières du chevalier d'Eon* (London: Dixwell, 1764). Records concerning Morande exist in CPA 502–77 *passim*, CPA suppléments 17, 28, and MD Angleterre, 73; AN, 277AP/1; Arsenal, MS 12,247 and MS 12,345. His correspondence with Beaumarchais is in private hands, but extensive selections appear in *BCE*. Other items appear in Pierre Augustin Caron de Beaumarchais, *Correspondance*, edited by Brian Morton and D. Spinelli, 4 vols (Paris: Nizet, 1969–78) and Louis de Loménie, *Beaumarchais et son temps*, 2 vols (Paris: Michel Levy frères, 1856). For the La Mottes, see esp. AN, F⁷4445² and PRO, FO95/631. Major collections of Brissot's papers survive in BN, nouvelles acquisitions françaises MSS 9533–4 and AN, 446AP. His correspondence with the STN (BPUN, MS 1128) has been published by Darnton on-line: see *CBW*.

62 See Charles-Claude Théveneau de Morande, *Réplique de Charles Théveneau Morande à Jacques-Pierre Brissot* (Paris: Froullé, 1791); Jacques-Pierre Brissot de Warville, *Mémoires de Brissot sur ses contemporains et la révolution française*, edited by F. de Montrol, 4 vols (Paris: Lavocat, 1830–32). There are several editions of the comtesse de La Motte's *Mémoires justificatifs*, first published in English and French in 1789, and her revised life-story, published in 1791. References are from the following editions unless specified: Jeanne de Saint-Rémy de La Motte, *Memoirs of the Countess de Valois de La Motte* (Dublin: John Archer and William Jones, 1790); Jeanne de Saint-Remy de Valois de La Motte, *The Life of Jane de St Remy de Valois*, 2 vols (Dublin: P. Wogan, P. Bryce, J. Moore, and J. Rice, 1792 [original edition London, 1791]). See also the probably spurious *Second Mémoire justificatif de la comtesse de La Motte-Valois*

(London, 1789); Marc-Antoine-Nicolas de La Motte, *Mémoires inédits du comte de Lamotte-Valois sur sa vie et son époque (1754–1830)*, edited by Louis Lacour (Paris: Poulet-Malassis et de Broise, 1858); and Jeanne de Saint-Rémy de La Motte, *Mémoire pour dame Jeanne de Saint-Rémy de Valois, épouse du comte de la Motte* (Paris: Cellot, 1785), a trial brief prepared by her lawyer Doillot. Draft portions of d'Eon's heavily fictionalised unpublished autobiography in ULBC are reproduced in d'Eon, *The Maiden of Tonnerre*, edited by Champagne, Ekstein, and Kates.

63 These sources are listed in the text and bibliography. Lenoir's manuscripts are in MO, MSS 1421–3.

64 Add MS 11,340; ULBC, files 58, 60.

65 See CPA 518 fos 78–90, 'Le Mandrin littéraire ou Anecdotes du *Gazetier cuirassé*', fo. 78. Annotations on this manuscript indicate that d'Eon was the author.

66 Britain had been free of pre-publication controls since the 1690s. English law was draconian in the case of seditious libels, but offered less protection to individuals: to be awarded damages, plaintiffs had to prove damage to their reputation, whereas in France insult was sufficient. The English law of blackmail protected only residents. In many cases, libel and blackmail victims preferred not to chance their reputations before a court. On the problems these laws presented, see chapters three and four below and McLaren, *Sexual Blackmail*, ch. 1.

67 See chapters three and four below and Simon Burrows, 'Despotism without bounds: the French secret police and the silencing of dissent in London', *History* 89:4 (2004).

1

London's French *libellistes*

The London *libellistes* produced some of the most scandalous texts of the *ancien régime*, but remain shadowy and enigmatic figures. Although Robert Darnton has propelled them to the centre of the historical stage, no historian has attempted a systematic survey of their careers. This is regrettable because, as the most criminal and scandalous of *ancien régime* authors, they appear more likely than any other group to fit the 'Grub Street' paradigm, which, although contentious, offers the only coherent model for 'criminal' writers. This chapter therefore profiles the *libellistes* individually and collectively in order to assess the validity of this model and postulate an alternative one.

There are good reasons to expect Darnton's model to fit the *libellistes*. His account of desperate and frustrated literary failures, who made nihilistic attacks on the monarchy through bitter hatred rather than deep-seated ideology and in due course embraced revolutionary extremism, presupposes that Grub Street pamphleteers were masterless men and women. It also implies that they were impoverished and saw themselves as outsiders to the establishment. This profile apparently resembles the *libellistes* in several ways. The *libellistes*' pamphlets were often highly antagonistic to the government, suggesting that they considered themselves remote from it. Their resort to blackmail implies that they were free from patronage bonds and believed scandalmongering would be more profitable than legitimate literary activities. However, the life-histories of the sixteen *libellistes* known to have operated in London in the period 1758–92 reveal that their social background, political trajectories, motives, and ideologies bear little resemblance to the Grub Street model. This would remain true if the sample were extended to include their known and suspected close collaborators.[1]

Pillement de Fauques[2]

Marianne-Agnès Pillement de Fauques, who was born in Avignon or the Comtat Venaissin around 1720 and died, probably in London, some time after 1785, exemplifies many of the problems with Darnton's model.[3] Destined for the Church from childhood, she bowed to family pressure to become a nun, but absconded ten years later. She was absolved from her vows, whereupon her family disowned her. She went to Paris, took a string of lovers, and, in the early 1750s, began publishing novels.[4] She thus embraced a literary career through necessity. Eventually, she was seduced by an English aristocrat but, when he abandoned her, continued the parallel lives of writer and courtesan in London until she married a Prussian officer.[5] In England, Fauques gained a certain notoriety, when a suppression fee was paid for a French edition of her *L'Histoire de Madame la marquise de Pompadour*, a work first published as *The History of the Marchioness de Pompadour* in 1758.[6] However, in a letter written in 1760, Fauques boasts of the obstacles she has overcome to become a female author and of attracting praise from Frederick the Great.[7]

A letter from Madame Hervé to her friend Madame Geoffrin, the celebrated *salonnière*, paints a much less flattering portrait of Fauques. It describes her as an 'aventurière' and 'pauvre . . . n'ayant je crois aucun moyen de subsister que par son esprit et son corps, dont le dernier . . . ne luy rapporte pas beaucoup à présent.' ['poor . . . having, I believe, no means of support but her wit and her body, the latter of which does not . . . bring her much at present.'] Madame Hervé reports that Fauques produced her *History of Pompadour* in collaboration with an unnamed Frenchman, who translated her drafts into English. This collaborator wrote other 'infamous works' and was a gentleman but scraped a living by his pen because his family had disowned him. Fauques, too, claimed to come from a 'très bonne maison' ['very good family'], but Madame Hervé believed her an impostor who lacked sources at court and compiled her biography from Parisian street gossip and her own imagination.[8] The *Dictionnaire de biographie française* concurs, dismissing the work as an 'absurd pamphlet'.[9] Thus, if Madame Hervé's testimony is trustworthy, Fauques was a freelancer, as the Grub Street model would suggest, but she was also an adventuress who lived in a *demi-monde* of rogues, criminals, and prostitutes. She became a *libelliste* primarily to earn a dishonest crust, not from ideological motives or frustrated ambition.

Théveneau de Morande

Darnton's archetypical *libelliste*, Morande also had a background in petty crime, prostitution, and living by his wits. His criminality pre-dated his literary career and contributed to its success. Nor were his works, on close examination, politically nihilistic or revolutionary. Instead there is good reason to link him ideologically to *patriote* reformist opposition to the monarchy. He certainly never embraced republicanism and courageously opposed revolutionary Jacobinism.

Morande was born in 1741 at Arnay-le-Duc, Burgundy,[10] the son of a *procureur du roi* (attorney) named Louis Théveneau. His paternal grandfather was a doctor, while his mother came from prosperous merchant stock.[11] None of his relatives were nobles: the title 'chevalier de Morande' originated as a fraudulent ruse to gain entry to society. Morande was educated in Dijon, where he acquired a taste for debauchery and gambling, exasperating his father, who in 1759 enrolled him in the dragoons.[12] Morande campaigned briefly in Germany, but his military career ended in injury, and possibly desertion.[13] He returned to Burgundy and a life of gambling, duelling, and womanising. Several times his father had him arrested by *lettres de cachet*, but he always escaped.[14] Finally, he fled to Paris, where, on 15 February 1765, he was arrested as a gambler, conman, and libertine, while undergoing mercury treatment for syphilis. His condition deteriorated rapidly in prison, and he was soon released.[15] In 1768 he was arrested again, following petitions from his family and Mademoiselle Danezy, an opera-girl who demanded protection.[16]

The archives of the Bastille concerning Morande's imprisonment indicate that he was involved in a range of petty crime, possibly including pederasty. However, he also mixed in exalted company and was probably a client of the prince de Limbourg.[17] He had contacts at Versailles; had access to several foreign embassies and the homes of the duc de Bethune and the duchesse de Châtillon; and had been unofficially adopted by a wealthy, childless, Burgundian *parlementaire*, La Saule.[18] However, his most important contacts were high-class courtesans and the mistresses of aristocrats. Morande insinuated himself into the affections of several such women, acting as a pimp and exploiting their fortunes.[19] Their *milieu* supplied anecdotes that he later incorporated into his accounts of opera-girls, brothels, and the peccadilloes of high society.[20] Naturally, he also made powerful enemies, including, apparently, Jacques de Flesselles, who was at that time intendant of Lyon, and the duc de La Vrillière, the minister who issued *lettres de cachet*.[21]

In 1769, Morande was released from prison once more on the grounds of ill-health, repentance, and good behaviour, after family solicitations.[22] However, he was soon up to his old tricks, extorting 'loans' with physical menaces.[23] On 14 May 1770, his arrest was ordered again, but he was alerted and fled to London.[24] There, Morande married his landlady's daughter, Elizabeth Sinclair,[25] and mixed with his fellow exiles, regaling them with witty and salacious anecdotes. These were the origin of the *Gazetier cuirassé* (Darnton's archetypical *libelle*), which he published in July 1771.[26]

Thereafter, Morande turned to blackmail, targeting, among others, the duc de Bethune; Voltaire; Pompadour's brother, the marquis de Marigny; the pamphleteer and courtier, the comte de Lauraguais; and the marquis de la Vilette.[27] Finally, and most successfully, he threatened to publish a scandalous biography of Madame du Barry entitled *Mémoires secrets d'une femme publique depuis son berceau jusqu'au lit d'honneur* [*Secret Memoirs of a Public Woman from her Cradle to the Bed of Honour*]. The machinations leading to the suppression of this work are discussed in chapter three. Here we need note only that the successful negotiator was an agent more versatile, colourful, and cunning than Morande himself: the playwright Beaumarchais. Beaumarchais had provoked royal displeasure by publishing scathing satirical trial briefs attacking Louis Valentin Goëzman, a corrupt magistrate in the Maupeou *Parlement*, who had found him guilty of forgery. The verdict was overturned on appeal and Goëzman was struck off. Nevertheless, Beaumarchais's trial briefs, which brought the whole Maupeou system into disrepute and bore the hallmarks of the *patriote* opposition, were condemned and burned.[28] He therefore undertook his mission to recover royal favour.

The choice of the witty, urbane, libertine Beaumarchais was shrewd, particularly given his sympathies with the *patriote* opposition. Royal agent and *libelliste* enjoyed a natural *rapport*. Within months, Morande was serving as Beaumarchais's auxiliary in a feud with another *libelliste*, the chevalier d'Eon, and seconding his efforts to channel French aid to the American insurgents. However, the British were suspicious of their liaison and ordered Morande from London when war broke out.[29] He moved to Great Stanmore in Middlesex, then a village outside the capital, and withdrew from espionage. However, in 1781, following the destruction of a French spy-ring headed by Henri de La Motte (no relation of the aforementioned comte and comtesse), Morande offered his services again. From 1781 to 1791 he worked successively for the French naval and foreign ministries on a stipend of 1,000 *Louis*.[30] He also liaised with Beaumarchais and subsequently the Paris police to help identify and apprehend several *libellistes* and French expatriates, including Brissot, whom he framed.[31]

Morande's enemies accused him of betraying de La Motte, who was hanged, drawn, and quartered at Tyburn in July 1781. They alleged that he received a 200-guinea bounty which he spent establishing fabulous gardens at Stanmore, and that he and Beaumarchais betrayed any French convoy in which the latter had no financial stake.[32] Both allegations are probably untrue. Morande was established at Stanmore three years before La Motte's arrest and lived in a modest rented property.[33] Newspaper accounts reveal that La Motte was betrayed by a smuggler named Stephen Ratcliffe. Morande's name and handwriting are not found in official files or newspaper reports concerning the case.[34] Testimony concerning the betrayal of French shipping is also suspect, especially as it apparently originates with d'Eon.[35]

Between 1784 and 1791, Morande also served Beaumarchais and the French government as editor of the newspaper the *Courier de l'Europe*.[36] Nevertheless, from 1787, he found an independent editorial voice and castigated the abuses of the *ancien régime*, especially money-grubbing courtiers, avaricious clergymen, commercial corruption, and the partisan *esprit de corps* of France's corporate bodies. He welcomed the revolution, believing that it would regenerate France morally, politically, economically, and militarily. However, he also saw the revolution as part of a pan-European rejection of ministerial despotism and movement towards liberty, acclaiming popular disturbances across the continent as manifestations of this process.[37] The same themes appear in his newspaper the *Argus patriote*, published in revolutionary Paris in 1791 and 1792, and the *Gazetier cuirassé*. It appears that far from producing nihilistic *libelles* to tear down the monarchy, as Darnton argued, Morande remained a reformist patriot throughout his writing career.[38] Nor was he ever a republican. He described himself as a *patriote royaliste* struggling to reconcile extremes of left and right. This defence of constitutional monarchy was apparently sincere, for he consistently adopted positions well to the left of his former royalist paymasters, aligning himself with the *feuillant* faction. Both d'Eon, with whom he was reconciled, and Manuel, an arch-enemy, believed his patriotism was genuine.[39]

Morande's decision to return to Paris in May 1791 to defend the constitutional monarchy against radicals such as Brissot was courageous and nearly cost him his life. Brissot almost certainly orchestrated Morande's arrest in the wake of the September 1792 prison massacres, when Parisian mobs murdered royalist sympathisers.[40] Released for wrongful imprisonment, Morande fled to Arnay-le-Duc, where he lived under surveillance but otherwise unmolested throughout the Terror.[41] In 1793, he apparently offered, via an intermediary, to testify against Brissot at the trial of the Girondins.[42] He died in Arnay in 1805.[43]

Contemporaries depict Morande as a demonic figure, a dishonoured, scurrilous libeler, base coward, and ungrateful monster. Historians have followed such judgements: Paul Robiquet describes him as 'Figaro vivant et réel, si retors qu'il a exploité Beaumarchais lui-même' ['a flesh and blood Figaro, so devious that he exploited Beaumarchais himself']; Peter Wagner sees him as 'tsar of the London pamphleteers'; and Gary Kates finds him 'the incarnation of an eighteenth-century rogue'.[44] These descriptions are largely justified. Morande never ceased to resort to calumny against opponents or victims. Nor was his friendship a particular boon, for Beaumarchais suffered a constant barrage of requests for money and extortion threats.[45] However, Morande does not fit the Darntonian model of 'Grub Street hack'. He was certainly no nihilist, and was happy to reconcile himself with a reforming monarchy. This was not mere cynicism: despite his moral terpitude, he had a sincere reformist ideology so deep-rooted that he never moved beyond it. As the revolution lurched leftwards in 1791–93, it left him behind. Nor did he become a *libelliste* because of literary failure. Instead, his criminality preceded his early writings, which grew out of the material and contacts it had provided. His decision to serve as a spy was part of his reconciliation with the French government, and apparently stemmed from genuine repentence. But it was also motivated by a desperate need for money to support an extravagant lifestyle and pressing debts.

La Fite de Pelleport

The marquis Anne-Gédeon de La Fite de Pelleport, who was linked to more blackmail pamphlets than any other *libelliste*, had much in common with

Morande. Both had a military background. Both were imprisoned at the request of their families, and it seems likely that Pelleport, like Morande, indulged in gambling, vice, and petty crime before resorting to *libelles*.[46] Both had contacts at Versailles and in diplomatic circles. Both turned to journalism and espionage, and both, like Fauques, married foreigners. Although Pelleport's political affiliations and espionage activities are murky and ambiguous, he probably turned against the revolution earlier than Morande, and perhaps became a counter-revolutionary activist.

Pelleport was a nobleman of modest means. The son of an equerry in the household of Louis XVI's oldest brother, the comte de Provence (the future Louis XVIII), he was born in Stenay-sur-Meuse on 11 May 1754 and educated at the prestigious *école militaire*.[47] He served briefly in India, but was expelled from two regiments for conduct unbecoming to an officer, whereafter his father had him imprisoned repeatedly by *lettres de cachet*. His prospects were further blighted when his father remarried.[48] Intriguingly, Pelleport's new stepmother's brother was the celebrated police officer Joseph d'Hémery, an inspector of the book trade, who prepared files on Paris's literary population between 1748 and 1753.[49] Thus Pelleport was probably well acquainted with tales of literary buccaneers and police methods before his involvement in the *libelle* trade. He also had family contacts at court and connections with publishers, journalists, and pamphleteers such as Brissot.

Pelleport met Brissot through a mutual friend, Edmé Mentelle, a professor at the *école militaire*. They became friends, and in 1779 Pelleport introduced Brissot to his Swiss publisher, the Société typographique de Neuchâtel.[50] By then, Pelleport was living in Neuchâtel, scraping a living as a schoolteacher and writing articles for the *Journal hélvetique*. There, he married Anne Leinhard, a chambermaid of Rousseau's friend Pierre-Alexandre du Peyrou.[51] His bride brought him a small dowry, which Pelleport lost in ill-judged maritime speculations, and rapidly bore four healthy children. In consequence, Pelleport left his family to seek his fortune.[52] His first stop was The Hague, where he worked for the French ambassador, the duc de La Vauguyon.[53] Thereafter, he travelled to London, probably in July 1782.[54]

In London, Pelleport encountered David Boissière, a bookseller-publisher specialising in *libelles*. With Boissière's assistance, Pelleport published the *Petits Soupers de l'hôtel de Bouillon* [*Intimate Suppers at the Bouillons' Town-House*], for which he attempted to extort a suppression fee from the princesse de Bouillon, before graduating to *libelles* against the queen. Thereafter, he also published *Le Diable dans un bénitier et le gazetier cuirassé transformé en mouche* [*The Devil in a Font and the Gazetier Cuirassé Transformed into a Spy*], a satirical *exposé* of French espionage and secret police activities.

Brissot, in London to establish his ill-fated *Lycée* [Lyceum], claims to have discouraged Pelleport's *libelles* against Marie-Antoinette, offering to pay his costs if he would suppress them.[55] He found Pelleport alternative work as a translator for the British political philosopher and radical deist David Williams and on the staff of the *Courier de l'Europe*, which was at that time edited by Alphonse-Joseph de Serres de La Tour .[56] However, in late 1783, La Tour's business partner, the Scottish *entrepreneur* and soldier of fortune Samuel Swinton, wrested control of the paper from him and installed Morande as editor. Seeking new projects and new capital, La Tour and Pelleport began to cultivate Brissot's business partner, Desforges d'Hurecourt, turning him against Brissot.[57] By May 1784, Desforges was shirking his financial obligations and demanding the liquidation of their partnership.[58] Pelleport's and La Tour's seduction of Desforges was encouraged by Swinton and Morande, who blamed a decline in the *Courier de l'Europe*'s readership on Brissot's *Journal du Lycée*.[59] Pelleport, who intended to launch his own paper, the *Mercure d'Angleterre*, probably also hoped to destroy a rival publication. Brissot never forgave any of them.

The *Mercure d'Angleterre* proved Pelleport's undoing. On learning his plans, Swinton offered to reprint the paper at Boulogne, where it would evade British stamp duties. Pelleport took the bait, went to inspect Swinton's premises, and was delivered to the authorities by his travelling companion, a certain Buard.[60] He was sent to the Bastille, where he remained for four years. While there, he encountered the comtesse de La Motte, who later sought his advice about selling her own *libelles*.[61] He finally emerged from prison in 1788, after a campaign by the chevalier de Paulet, head of the school for military orphans, who had been touched by the plight of Pelleport's wife and children.[62] On his release, Pelleport retired to Stenay. By mid-1789 he was back in Paris. There, on 14 July, he encountered the crowd that had just stormed the Bastille and tried to save its deputy-governor, de Losme, who had treated him kindly. He failed to save his benefactor, and was savaged by the mob and left for dead.[63] The experience probably turned him against the revolution.

Pelleport was soon associating with committed counter-revolutionaries, but his true loyalties are opaque. In late 1789, he left France. He probably went to Ireland, but by January 1790 he was back in Paris, wishing to renew his acquaintance with the comtesse de La Motte.[64] Shortly afterwards, he was recruited as a secret agent by the royalist-leaning foreign minister, Claude-Antoine de Valdec Delessart, and served on missions to London, Germany, Spain, and north Italy.[65] In February 1792, Pelleport's brother and Pierre-Jean Lambelet, who served as messengers between Pelleport and Delessart, were arrested. When Pelleport returned to France to protest, he, too, was arrested and accused of conspiring against the state. His case was debated in the Legislative Assembly and Diplomatic Committee, where radicals hoped to implicate Delessart in treason. These moves were led by Brissot, who asserted that Pelleport was a 'parfait arisocrate' and had visited the headquarters of the émigré army at Coblenz. Nevertheless, the Assembly rejected calls for Delessart to state Pelleport's business and accepted his explanations.[66] Pelleport was released, and in late 1792 he was re-employed by the Dantonist foreign minister, François Deforgues, who sent him to Belgium masquerading as an émigré. He was denounced and arrested by the Austrians, who allowed him to turncoat and work for them. Declared an émigré, he had difficulty returning to France following Bonaparte's accession, not least because his eldest son was a counter-revolutionary activist.[67] Pelleport died in Liège on 26 March 1807. Although his papers were reported to survive at the family château at Champlévrier as late as 1910, it has since passed into other hands, and their whereabouts are unknown.[68]

The comte and comtesse de La Motte

Captivatingly beautiful, sparklingly vivacious, breathtakingly mendacious, sexually promiscuous, and supremely self-confident, the comtesse de La Motte was the most audacious, imaginative, and venomous of the *libellistes*. Volatile and prone to violent passions, she was also the most excessive in her demands and increasingly unstable. Nevertheless, she and her husband fit a now-familiar profile, not least because they were the masterminds behind the diamond necklace affair, an intrigue of such labyrinthine complexity and ambition that those of Morande, Pelleport, or even Beaumarchais pale by comparison.

   The diamond necklace affair began as the biggest con-trick of the eighteenth century. The full details of the La Mottes' conspiracy have still not been unravelled by historians and probably never will be, since the surviving documents were carefully weeded, possibly to protect cardinal Rohan, the grand almoner of France and a distant cousin of the queen, who was implicated in the affair. Although Louis XVI interviewed the cardinal in person and became convinced of his guilt,[69] historians have usually followed the Paris *Parlement*'s judgement of 31 May 1786 and seen him as the La Mottes' dupe. In this version, the comtesse de La Motte persuaded the cardinal, who had incurred Marie-Antoinette's disfavour, that the queen wished him to purchase a fabulous diamond necklace for her secretly from the court jewellers, Böhmer and Bassenge. To convince Rohan of their connection with Marie-Antoinette, the La Mottes hired a young prostitute, Nicole Guay d'Oliva, to impersonate the queen in a fleeting moonlit meeting with the cardinal in the gardens at Versailles. Rohan was duped and a contract of sale was drawn up, on which the queen's signature was forged by the comtesse's lover, Marc-Antoine Rétaux de Villette. The cardinal duly entrusted delivery of the necklace to the comtesse, whose husband peddled the jewels around Europe. The fraud was discovered only when the first payment became overdue and the jewellers demanded restitution from the queen, who referred the matter to her husband. The comtesse, who had stayed in France, presumably gambling on a cover-up, was arrested.[70] So were a crowd of other suspects, including Rohan and his associate, the magician and self-styled Grand Copt, the comte de Cagliostro.

   Rohan's arrest could not pass unnoticed, and as rumours began to fly,

REPRÉSENTATION EXACTE

DU GRAND COLLIER EN BRILLANTS DES Srs BOEHMER ET BASSANGE

Gravé d'après la grandeur des Diamans

1 The diamond necklace

Louis XVI naïvely ordered a public trial to clear his wife's name of all suspicion.[71] Predictably, the accused parties printed their trial briefs and whipped up a fever of speculation, for the case involved more than the fate of the cardinal and honour of the House of Rohan: the queen's reputation was also at stake.[72] Although he made no suggestion that she was involved, the cardinal's defence was premised upon the claim that he might reasonably have believed that Marie-Antoinette would initiate a secret midnight assignation and seek to acquire jewellery by clandestine means. Thus to acquit the cardinal was to condemn the queen's morals, and suggest that the magistrates in the *parlement* credited rumours spread by her enemies at court. The case provided the *parlementaires* with the opportunity to settle political scores and pitted the powerful Rohan clan and their allies, including the comte de Vergennes, France's foreign minister from 1774 to 1787, against the queen's adherents, led by the baron de Breteuil, minister of the king's household. In the final verdict, the cardinal, Cagliostro, and d'Oliva were found innocent. Rétaux de Villette was banished for life and the comte de La Motte condemned in his absence. The comtesse was found guilty, whipped, branded, and imprisoned for life, but subsequently escaped to London, apparently with inside assistance.

Many aspects of the affair remain mysterious. For example, it beggars belief that a courtier of Rohan's standing could mistake a common prostitute for the queen or a crude and inaccurate forgery for Marie-Antoinette's signature. Did he really believe that she would resort to such clandestine intrigues, and by these means restore him to public favour? But if he was involved in the scam, what did he hope to gain? It is true that his family faced enormous financial problems following the bankruptcy of his cousin, the prince de Guémenée, who in 1781 owed his creditors 32 million *livres*. Moreover, even if the fraudulent contract of sale is overlooked, he cannot have expected to avoid paying for goods he received on credit. Indeed, the Rohan clan did eventually repay the jewellers, although it took almost a century.[73] Perhaps the cardinal was so bewitched by the comtesse that he lent himself to her schemes to secure her favours? If so, his gullibility and lechery exceeded all reason. There must be questions, too, about the jewellers, who were so desperate to sell the necklace that they accepted a crudely forged contract.

Historians have also speculated about who assisted the comtesse to escape and whether she might really have had contacts at court, as she claimed. In particular, d'Oliva's needless – and dangerous – insistence under interrogation that, after her assignation in the Versailles gardens, she was driven back to Paris in a coach bearing the royal livery has raised questions. Evelyne Lever has recently revived speculations that the comtesse really had befriended the queen, and that Marie-Antoinette was lying when she denied they had ever met. Possibly, the queen even orchestrated the scene in the gardens, just as La Motte's *Mémoires* claimed, presumably as a joke at the cardinal's expense.[74] Although it is conceivable that the queen might have lied to avoid giving the impression that she associated with adventuresses and distance herself from hostile rumours, it seems improbable. The comtesse was a perjuror and fraudster. In contrast, the queen conducted herself with quiet dignity when on trial for her life in 1793, meeting the most revolting and malicious accusations head-on.[75] To lie about her relations with the comtesse would, moreover, have been extremely dangerous if contrary evidence were ever uncovered.

Although no detailed examination of the impact of the diamond necklace affair on public opinion exists, the incident has been widely credited with fatally undermining both Marie-Antoinette and the French monarchy. This study suggests, however, that any such conclusion is exaggerated and based on suspect chronology. None of the dozens of pamphlets to which the affair gave rise in 1785–86 implicated the queen,[76] and the most serious allegations made against her emanated from Madame de La Motte during her London exile. They first appeared in her *Mémoires*, which were not published until 1789.

Madame de La Motte was born Jeanne de Saint-Rémy on 27 July 1756. Her father, an impoverished nobleman, owned a tiny estate at Fontette outside Bar-sur-Aube. A crapulous debauchee who seduced and married his gatekeeper's daughter, he sold his lands and rooms in his château piecemeal until the night in 1760 when he fled with his family. He died on 16 February 1762, in abject poverty, in the Hôtel Dieu [pauper hospital] in Paris. Shortly thereafter, Jeanne's mother and her brutal new lover began sending her to beg on the streets, with instructions to claim descent from the Valois king Henri II. Remarkably, this claim was later authenticated by royal heralds. The marquise de Boulainvilliers heard the little beggar's claims, asked her story, and decided to adopt her. She had Jeanne educated, found her a position with a dressmaker, and in 1776, having had Jeanne's genealogy authenticated, obtained her and her siblings royal pensions of 800 *livres*. She then placed Jeanne and her younger sister, Marie-Anne, in a finishing establishment for young ladies, and thereafter the Abbey de Longchamp, an institution reserved for noblewomen.[77]

In 1779, the Saint-Rémy sisters returned to Bar-sur-Aube to attempt to reclaim lost ancestral possessions. There, Jeanne began a passionate love-affair with an impoverished gendarme officer, comte Marc-Antoine-Nicolas de La Motte.[78] Jeanne fell pregnant and, on 6 June 1780, married her lover. One month later she gave birth to twin sons, who died within weeks.[79] This tragedy was followed by a series of miscarriages.[80] Jeanne's husband's pretensions to nobility were tenuous. His marriage certificate describes him as 'écuyer' [squire]. His father was an officer in the gendarmerie and the title comte was usurped.[81] His position in the gendarmerie was ill calculated to meet the aspirations of a proud and beautiful wife who claimed descent from royalty, so he resigned his post.[82] In late 1781 the young couple moved to Paris, where they contracted debts and lived one step ahead of landlords, creditors, bailiffs, and the police.[83]

Jeanne was now assembling the networks, facilities and knowledge that she would use to acquire the diamond necklace. She had already met the cardinal de Rohan, who promised to be her protector. Now she rented rooms at Versailles, employed a growing retinue of servants, and befriended Rétaux de Villette. She began to claim she had influence at Versailles, gathering around her people who wished to profit from her reputed credit with the queen.[84] There was little unusual about this. The police would recognise

2 The comtesse de La Motte

Jeanne as a *faiseuse d'affaires*, someone who offered to procure favours at court, using real or imaginary influence. Lenoir reports that she was also a prostitute and once entertained the libertine prince and future revolutionary, the duc d'Orléans, at an intimate supper.[85] Thus she was ideally placed to implement her scheme. She had beauty and seductiveness, the refinement and education of a lady, experience of intrigue, contacts in the Parisian *demi-monde* of adventurers and prostitutes, a reputation for having influence at court, and a willing dupe. Her activities and associates resembled those of Fauques, Morande, and Pelleport: the comtesse differed only in the scale of her ambitions.

The comtesse turned *libelliste* only after her sensational escape from prison and arrival in London in 1787. There she rejoined her husband and sought assistance from a sucession of British speculators, refugee ghost-writers, and the British journalist Peter Stuart. However, the comtesse's blackmail activities came to an abrupt end with her untimely and tragic death on 23 August 1791. Her husband returned to France in early 1789 and survived the revolution.

Although the comtesse hoped to profit from the revolution, it is likely that, when put to the test, her sympathies, like those of Morande and Pelleport, ultimately lay with the monarchy. In an insightful treatment of textual differences between her original *Mémoires* of 1789 and her *Vie de Jeanne de Saint-Rémy de Valois* [*The Life of Jane de Saint-Remy de Valois*], published in 1791, Iain McCalman suggests that the comtesse's attitude to the queen softened with time. As revolutionary attacks on the queen were reaching fever pitch by 1791, this may indicate that she repented her repellent portrayal of Marie-Antoinette in the *Mémoires*. However, it is not certain that such changes should be viewed in this light, especially as the comtesse may have been reorientating her material to suit British tastes.[86]

The comte de La Motte may also eventually have recanted. In his case, moderate revolutionary sympathies appear to have evolved into committed royalism by the restoration of the monarchy in 1814. In January 1792, he presented himself at the Conciergerie prison, seeking to overturn his sentence in the diamond necklace trial and to sue the judges and ministers responsible.[87] The sentence was quashed in July 1792, but he was still in the Conciergerie at the time of the September massacres, which he was lucky to survive.[88] Thereafter he was released and joined relatives in Tonnerre. He claims he was approached to testify against the queen, but refused, not wishing to be involved. In December 1793 he was arrested and accused of being an enemy agent. Released the following October, he remarried and bought a country estate with compensation granted by the revolutionary government for property confiscated following the diamond necklace trial.[89] He refused service under Bonaparte and welcomed the restoration. If his word can be trusted, he was denounced for distributing royalist propaganda as the Napoleonic regime fell.[90] Thereafter, he worked for Louis XVIII's police, frequented royalist *salons*, and was given a variety of sinecures by an old friend, the comte de Beugnot, who was successively *directeur-général de la police*, naval minister, postmaster-general, and minister of state.[91] Nevertheless, La Motte did not abandon intrigue. He frittered away his fortune, and even attempted to sell a fabricated correspondence between the royal family, Robespierre, and Marat.[92] Despite being hit by a stray bullet during the 1830 revolution and making several suicide attempts, he died naturally in a charitable institution in 1831.[93]

Thus far, the *libellistes* fit a discernible pattern. All were impoverished fallen nobles or commoners falsely claiming nobility; all had been involved in petty crime or intrigue before turning to *libelles*; and available evidence suggests that those who survived into the 1790s favoured a reformed monarchy over Jacobin republicanism. The next two *libellistes* deviate from this pattern. Neither had a history of criminality, and both had distinguished careers before resorting to blackmail. The chevalier d'Eon was a successful diplomat and writer; Linguet was a controversial pamphleteer, *anti-philosophe*, and radical lawyer who later became the most celebrated journalist of his era.[94] Nevertheless, there are also striking parallels between both men and previous *libellistes* in terms of social background and politics.

Linguet

Simon-Nicolas-Henri Linguet was born on 14 July 1736. His father was a Jansenist, and had been dismissed as sub-principal at the College of Navarre in Paris in 1731.[95] An academic prodigy, Linguet studied at the University of Paris. He mingled in anti-*philosophe* circles, wrote miscellaneous literary works, entered the legal profession, and, aged thirty, published his *Théorie des lois civiles*. At the Bar he won a string of celebrated cases, and served as d'Aiguillon's representative during the Brittany affair. Arrogant and outspoken, he made impassioned pleadings which attacked the legal establishment and made him powerful enemies. In due course he was banned from appearing before the *parlement*. Thereafter, he made an ill-starred foray into journalism as editor of Charles-Joseph Panckoucke's *Journal de politique et de littérature*. Within months he was sacked, following complaints about a scathing attack on the Académie française and ministerial pressure from Vergennes and Miromesnil.[96] Having alienated the literary establishment, powerful ministers, and the *parlements*, Linguet went into self-imposed exile in England, intent on protesting his case to the public. In his new journal, the *Annales civiles, politiques, et littéraires*, launched in April 1777, he presented himself as a victim of persecution. He announced his position in an 'openly libelous' *Lettre de M. Linguet à M. le comte de Vergennes* [*Letter from Mr Linguet to the comte de Vergennes*], a pamphlet that Darline Gay Levy describes as 'an unambiguous declaration of independence from professional enslavement and political servitude under a despotic regime'.[97] Such statements did not ingratiate him with the French government, whose permission he needed if his journal were to circulate inside France. Linguet's solution was to resort to blackmail.

Linguet did not produce his *Annales* in London for long. As war loomed, he relocated to the Austrian Netherlands (Belgium), but in September 1780, he was lured to Paris and arrested, ostensibly for denigrating the duc de Duras, who had petitioned for a *lettre de cachet*. There were other motives, however. The police suspected that Linguet was the author of an anti-ministerial manuscript discovered in a raid on Provence's château at Brunoy. Equally, by April 1780, when the *lettre de cachet* was issued, Vergennes had grown weary of his constant opposition to French foreign policy.

Linguet was released in May 1782. Almost immediately he broke the conditions of his internal exile, left France, and returned to England. In 1783, he relaunched the *Annales* with his mendacious and sensational *Mémoires sur la Bastille*. The following year he began campaigning for the reopening of the river Scheldt, a move long blocked by the Dutch, who feared Belgian competition. The Austrian government was delighted. It allowed him to be naturalised, ennobled him, and backed his demands for permission to return to France to seek compensation from d'Aiguillon, Panckoucke, the Parisian order of lawyers, and various other enemies. Secure in the support of the Austrians and Louis XVI, who enjoyed his journalism, Linguet returned to Paris, where in March 1787 he won damages from d'Aiguillon and became a popular hero.

The response of Linguet to the revolutionary crisis was complex, and largely determined by his pre-existing ideas concerning the social question. Linguet believed that wealth was concentrated too much at the top of the social pyramid. He had long been convinced that significant redistributive justice was necessary if Europe was to evade violent social revolution and that the entrenched power of wealthy elites prevented reform. Nevertheless, he construed the issue largely in administrative terms: the basic political problem concerned the means to assuage the suffering, and negate the threat, of growing numbers of impoverished and desperate people. He therefore advocated an alliance of monarchy and the mass of the Third Estate against privileged elites. Although supportive of the Third Estate in early 1789, he was disappointed by their bourgeois leadership's failure to address social questions. However, after the fall of the Bastille he decided that he had too much to lose by educating the lower orders for a social revolution. When rumours that he had betrayed 'le peuple' began to circulate, he fled to Belgium, where a rebellion against the centralising reforms of Joseph II was in full swing. There, Linguet's ambiguous position as an advocate for both 'le peuple' and absolutism proved as problematic as ever. Neither side trusted him, and he was arrested by the Austrian authorities. Released in December 1789, he embraced the cause of Belgian independence.

Linguet returned to France after overtures from the radical journalist Camille Desmoulins, and aligned himself briefly with the radical Cordeliers club. However, in mid-1792 he abandoned journalism and retired to his newly acquired château at Marne-les-Saint-Cloud. There, he turned his attention to social reforms and tried to create a model commune. He was elected mayor and sank his money into providing welfare, volunteers, and crops for the poor. Nevertheless, the former spokesman for absolute monarchy was considered suspect and arrested. He was executed on 27 June 1794, less than a month before the fall of Robespierre ended the Terror. The key evidence against him was a letter from the *Armoire de fer*, Louis XVI's secret strong-box. Nevertheless, Linguet made a strange counter-revolutionary, for his social schemes would later be championed by spokesmen for *sans culotte* egalitarianism such as Jacques Roux and the proto-socialist Gracchus Babeuf.

Linguet differs from other *libellistes* in several ways. His political positions are better documented, yet were so complex and idiosyncratic that they confused contemporaries and defy categorisation by historians. As an advocate of absolutism with revolutionary social ideas, a commoner who achieved nobility, and an egotistical political crusader, Linguet's career contains paradoxes. Nevertheless, like other *libellistes*, he was a monarchist reformer for most of his life. In one respect, he resembles the 'Grub Street' model more than Morande, Fauques, Pelleport, and the La Mottes, for he resorted to *libelles* following a check to his literary ambitions.[98] However, his grievance was clearly defined and very specific, though aggravated by a strong sense of personal entitlement and merit. These were characteristics he shared with d'Eon.

D'Eon

The chevalier d'Eon (1728–1810) is not usually thought of as a *libelliste*, perhaps because Darnton's portrayal of Grub Street is indelibly linked to smut-mongering.[99] However, in the minds of contemporaries his actions were similar: he threatened to print damaging revelations and sought to sell his silence. He also enjoyed complex relationships with other *libellistes*, particularly Morande, and frequently played an ambiguous role towards the monarchy he served.

The chevalier d'Eon came from Tonnerre in Burgundy and belonged to the lowest ranks of the provincial nobility. His father was a functionary who rose to become sub-delegate of the intendant of Paris, and hence a significant figure in Burgundy.[100] An uncle was prominent in the Paris police, and Christophe de Beaumont, the conservative archbishop of Paris and scourge of the Jansenists, was a relative. D'Eon studied law at the Collège Mazarin and then took a post in the office of Louis-Jean Bertier de Sauvigny, intendant of Paris, who encouraged him to publish works on finance and administration. By his mid-twenties, his talents were attracting powerful patrons, and in 1756 he was inducted into France's clandestine espionage network, the *Secret du roi*. Orchestrated by the comte de Broglie, the *Secret*, unbeknown to Louis XV's foreign ministers, followed a policy line different from that of the official foreign ministry. Louis XV was not the only monarch to follow such a dangerous policy – Alexander I did something similar in the Napoleonic wars – but eventually the inherent contradictions of his conflicting policies became apparent.[101]

D'Eon's first appointment in the *Secret* was as secretary to Alexander Douglas, French *chargé d'affaires* at St Petersburg, assisting him to secure a rapprochement between France and Russia on the eve of the Seven Years' War. Thereafter, d'Eon joined French forces campaigning in Germany, where he apparently first encountered his arch-enemy, the comte de Guerchy. D'Eon later claimed that on 19 August 1761 at Hoxter, Guerchy refused orders to assist him in evacuating munitions while under enemy fire. He also blamed him for several *débâcles*, including the loss of the French baggage train at Minden.[102]

A year later, d'Eon accompanied the duc de Nivernais to the peace negotiations in London, armed with a secret order signed by Louis XV instructing him to explore routes for invading England. When Nivernais left England after the peace, d'Eon harboured unrealistic hopes of replacing him as ambassador. Instead, his career began to unravel rapidly after he was overlooked in favour of the inexperienced, aristocratic Guerchy. D'Eon deeply resented the slight, which he attributed to Guerchy's life-long friendship with the duc de Praslin, France's foreign minister from 1761 to 1766. Relations between the two men deteriorated quickly, and before Guerchy even reached London he was accusing d'Eon of recklessly overspending on his ambassadorial residence.[103] Worse still, by the autumn of 1763, Broglie was out of favour and Louis XV was closing down the *Secret*. To cap it all, Praslin informed d'Eon that he would be demoted to ambassador's secretary owing to budgetary constraints. D'Eon protested vociferously, and so, on 4 October 1763, Praslin sent him a letter of recall.

Fearing disgrace, d'Eon refused to take leave of the British court, and defied orders to hand his diplomatic papers to Guerchy, insisting he could accept only orders direct from the king. Gary Kates suggests that d'Eon's refusal to return to France stemmed from his ambiguous position as spy for the *Secret* and official of the foreign minister. However, as d'Eon refused recall after recall, even from Broglie, clearly his main motive was money. If he returned to France or surrendered his papers, especially Louis XV's secret order, he would have no leverage when he sought reimbursement for his extravagant spending, which included vast purchases of wine used to ingratiate himself with the British elite. Instead, d'Eon decided to use the threat of publishing or selling his the most compromising papers to blackmail the French government, and in 1764 he published a selection of his diplomatic correspondence, entitled *Lettres, mémoires et négociations particulières du chevalier d'Eon*, to prove he was serious. This work covered Guerchy with ridicule and contained allegations that he and Praslin had plotted to assassinate d'Eon with the aid of embassy staff and a soldier of fortune named Pierre-Henri Treyssac de Vergy.[104]

Ultimately, d'Eon's attempt to win reimbursement and rehabilitation was partially successful. In 1766, Louis XV agreed a financial settlement and offered to restore d'Eon to favour when a suitable post became available.[105] Louis probably never intended to honour his promise, for it remained unfulfilled in 1770, when rumours began to circulate which, if confirmed, would permanently disqualify d'Eon from royal service. It was whispered that d'Eon was a woman.[106] These rumours, which may have originated with d'Eon himself,[107] unleashed a fever of speculative betting on his sex, conducted via insurance policies, since taking wagers was illegal. In 1777, the verdict in a case between gamblers in the Court of King's Bench determined that d'Eon was legally female.[108] Although this had serious implications for

3 The chevalier d'Eon

d'Eon – as a woman he would enjoy far fewer rights – he made no representation to prevent the case being brought, although innocent third parties were entitled to do so.[109] Instead, he accepted the judgement and shortly afterwards agreed to dress as a woman in order to return to France. This gender transformation served several purposes. Convincingly refuting Freudian interpretations, Gary Kates argues that it was inspired by politics rather than sexuality, and was a means of escaping a dead-end career.[110] However, by becoming a woman, d'Eon also remained a celebrity while marginalising himself permanently from political life, and greatly reduced his chances of being kidnapped or assassinated by his enemies.

D'Eon maintained connections with the *libelle* industry for most of the 1770s. In 1774 he helped broker a settlement with Morande, and, shortly afterwards he negotiated a final settlement of his own claim with Beaumarchais.[111] Unfortunately, instead of remunerating d'Eon directly, Beaumarchais paid large sums to d'Eon's friend and creditor, George Washington Shirley, Earl Ferrers, who invested them in developing his estates. Worse still, Beaumarchais and Morande attempted to persuade d'Eon to reveal his true nature to them so that they could corner the market in insurance policies on his sex. Furiously indignant, d'Eon rejected their offers and the quarrel spilled over into the press.[112] After public and mutual recriminations, d'Eon challenged Morande to a duel and, when Morande refused to fight a woman and evaded challenges from d'Eon's allies,[113] prosecuted him for libel. The case was rejected on the grounds that the offence was mutual.[114] Because of the dispute, d'Eon secretly withheld many papers from Beaumarchais and left them in England when he returned to France.

In 1785, d'Eon returned to London to sue Ferrers's sibling and heir, Robert, for the principal and interest owed on monies paid to Ferrers by Beaumarchais.[115] D'Eon was desperate for cash to pay rent on rooms he had retained in London, because his landlord, Joseph Lautens, was threatening to sell his possessions and papers.[116] D'Eon successfully petitioned Vergennes for 6,000 *livres* (£250) to pay Lautens's bill,[117] but the death of Robert Ferrers, deeply endebted, ended his hopes of achieving financial security.[118] D'Eon remained in London, where his litigation dragged on at least until 1792.[119] He spent his last years in poverty. Although the dying monarchy redeemed his last remaining papers in early 1792, he struggled financially.[120] He kept afloat with a £500 advance for his never-completed memoirs.[121] When he died, still in London, in 1810, his elderly landlady discovered the truth about his sex. He was male.[122]

Like many other *libellistes*, d'Eon initially welcomed the French revolution, believing it would regenerate and purify the political system to which he had fallen victim. In May 1792, he even offered to lead a unit of Amazons against France's enemies.[123] His request amused the National Assembly, but in January 1793 the recently installed republican government sent him a passport.[124] D'Eon claimed he was prevented from returning to France by the outbreak of war on 1 February 1793, blockade, and his debts.[125] The Terror was also a motivating factor, as d'Eon risked being treated as an émigré and feared arrest and execution. However, though he never admitted it, the execution of Louis XVI on 21 January 1793 was probably a decisive factor in his decision and turned him against the new republic.[126] Olivier Blanc claims d'Eon was involved in counter-revolutionary activities including circulating false *assignats*,[127] but he never renounced his admiration for the early stages of the revolution. A note written for his memoirs in 1805 or 1806 apparently reveals d'Eon's true feelings. It asserts that 'la France gangrenée par le luxe depradateur de la cour auguste de Louis XIV et de Louis XV a grand besoin d'une crise violente pour se regenerer sous le regne vertueux de Louis XVI' ['France, rendered gangrenous by the depredatory indulgence of the court of Louis XIV and Louis XV has great need of a violent revolution to regenerate itself under the reign of Louis XVI']. Later he decided this statement was imprudent, and redrafted the passage as an anodyne statement praising Louis XV's virtues and condemning the 'perverse' ministers who had usurped his power.[128] Nevertheless, d'Eon's approbation of the early revolution was ambiguous and, in the final two decades of his life, he embraced the millenarianism popular in émigré circles.[129]

D'Eon's life is full of paradoxes. Despite a deep sense of personal honour and insistence on his loyalty to the monarchy, he resorted to blackmail in support of extravagant compensation claims. He was a committed Christian who based his life on a lie. And while insisting on a female identity, he also relished violent displays of virility and meted out savage canings to enemies, including Morande, Vergy, and the veteran pamphleteer Ange Goudar, who wrote several pamphlets for Guerchy.[130] He differs from other *libellistes* in several ways, above all because he had been a middle-ranking state servant with connections close to the heart of government. However, he also had much in common with them. Like many *libellistes*, he came from minor noble stock and lacked the financial resources and generations-old networks of the aristocratic elite. His career was unlikely to survive a serious setback, so he had little to lose by rebelliousness. He also had an exaggerated sense of personal merit, entitlement, and his own importance. He seems to have been utterly convinced of the rectitude of his demands, and probably believed that his enemies were as repugnant as he depicted them. Like his most successful *libelliste confrères*, he also had extensive connections in the British elite, French exile community, and London publishing scene. This made him an ideal spy, a role he shared with other *libellistes*. Indeed, the lessons of d'Eon's situation were not lost on his fellow Burgundian and keenest imitator, Morande, who on arrival in London assiduously cultivated him.[131] The two men had much in common, and their families were even distantly related by marriage.[132] Besides a common *pays*, both had been educated for the law, both saw action in the Seven Years' War, and their fathers were acquainted. They also had similar political outlooks, for d'Eon, like Morande, appears to have been a reformist *patriote*: though a state servant, he considered himself an outsider to the established elite and an enemy and victim of ministerial despotism. Thus he could support the revolution in its early stages, and possibly even accept a republic; but he could never accept the king's execution, Terror, revolutionary dechristianisation, and other extreme manifestations of Jacobinism.

Vergy

Unlike most other *libellistes*, Vergy did not target the monarchy. Instead, driven by a desperate need for money, he sought revenge on Guerchy, his former employer, by threatening to publish his *Guerchiade* in 1767.[133] A *soi-disant* lawyer at the Bordeaux *Parlement* and former secretary to d'Aiguillon, Vergy travelled to London hoping to serve Guerchy in a similar capacity. Instead, Guerchy prevaricated before employing him as a spy, pamphleteer, and, possibly, hired sword, in his feud with d'Eon. By December 1763, growing impatient, Vergy turned coat and began preparing a pamphlet defence of d'Eon. This *Lettre aux françois* never appeared, because Vergy agreed to suppress it to avoid prosecution when, following complaints from Guerchy, the British attorney-general ruled it defamatory.[134] Vergy's reconciliation with the ambassador was shortlived. Within weeks he was arrested for debt, whereupon Guerchy ignored his pleas for a few guineas to secure his release.[135] This proved a fatal mistake. Vergy was released in October 1764, probably with d'Eon's assistance, and the following month testified to a British court that, just as the chevalier alleged, he had been involved in a conspiracy against him orchestrated by Praslin and Guerchy.[136] As Vergy promised to recount the tale of the conspiracy in his *Guerchiade*, his initial suppression fee of 100 *Louis* (approximately £105) was modest.[137]

Most surviving information about Vergy's background emanates from d'Eon, so must be treated cautiously. D'Eon, who was assiduous in gathering and publishing information on his enemies, quickly discovered that Vergy's name was usurped and that the Paris police considered him a gambler, libertine, and thief. He was being pursued by creditors and had been chased from the home of the comte d'Argental, French ambassador to Parma.[138] British newspaper obituaries add that Vergy quickly dissipated 100,000 crowns (almost £13,000) inherited from his father in high living. He arrived in London with next to nothing, spent eight out of ten years there in the Fleet and Marshalsea debtors' prisons, and died owning just three-and-a-half pence, the clothes he wore, and a trunk full of papers.[139] His will bequeathed land worth 30,000 *livres* revenue to his wife, but when the police traced her, she revealed that Vergy owned nothing. His relatives refused to transport his body to France, so he was buried in St Pancras several months after his death.[140] His wife was probably a *femme galante* or courtesan, for Lenoir reported that she used several different names and was living 'in great splendour and high estate' in Paris.[141] It seems, therefore, that Vergy came from a similar world to Morande. Originally from a well-to-do legal family, he fell into petty crime among gamblers and prostitutes before fleeing to

London, where he planted newspaper articles announcing that he was a famous literary figure.[142] D'Eon saw through him immediately. Vergy may have failed at blackmail, too, for d'Eon claims that the *Guerchiade* was eventually published. However, besides the manuscript samples from the first *canto* which Vergy sent to Guerchy, no trace of it has been found.[143]

Lenoir de La Bussière, Campagnol, and Dom Louis

The obscurity which surrounds Vergy's biography is also typical of the remaining eight *libellistes*. Very little indeed is known about three of them, yet even they clearly shared many characteristics with other *libellistes*. Lenoir de La Bussière's brief appearance in diplomatic correspondence sheds little light on his background. A destitute shipwreck victim, he threatened to make a public appeal for funds in the British press in order to shame the French *chargé d'affaires*, Garnier, who had ignored his requests for financial aid to travel to France.[144] There is no mention of a title, but since he intended to return to Versailles, he probably had connections at court. His subsequent decision to renounce blackmail or a public appeal because they would be dishonourable also suggests an aristocratic outlook. His use of the particle 'de' indicates at least aspirations to nobility.

Madame Campagnol, author of a *libelle* entitled *Considérations sur les moeurs de mon siècle, par un homme d'Etat sans perruque* [*Considerations on the Morals of my Century, by a Statesman without a Wig*], had similar pretensions, using the alias de Vernancourt. Beaumarchais's secretary and first biographer, Paul-Philippe Gudin de La Brenellerie, reports that she claimed to be a lady of quality, though he clearly doubted it.[145] She is known to have socialised with other *libellistes*, notably d'Eon, Jean-Joseph Janiau de Vignoles, and Morande, but beyond that she is an enigma.[146]

Dom Louis, a monk in the abbey of Saint-Denis, is equally mysterious. He absconded around the end of 1781 and fled to London, where he became a protégé of Lady Spencer, who also liaised between the French authorities and the La Mottes.[147] In 1783, Dom Louis was reported to be writing a *libelle* entitled *Les Rois de France jugés au tribunal de la raison* [*The Kings of France Judged at the Court of Reason*] by the police agent Receveur de Livermont.[148] Besides preparing this pamphlet, which never appeared, Dom Louis reputedly published *L'Enfer enfermé, et le paradis ouvert à tous les hommes* [*Hell Closed Down, and Heaven Opened to Every Man*].[149] Nothing more is known of him.[150] This leaves five *libellistes* whose lives and identities are a little better documented.

Linsing

The baron de Linsing (or Linsingen) had an unremarkable military career, until a series of bouts of violent insanity brought him notoriety. Consequently, he had trouble hiring servants, especially after he thrust a rapier through the heart of his favourite dog. In 1773, Linsing was sent to the Bastille for falsely accusing his benefactress, the princesse de Beauvau, of poisoning him, and threatening her brothers, the Rohan-Chabot. However, he escaped while being transferred between prisons and fled to London.[151] There he turned his hand to *libelles*, claiming that his long and costly military service and an ancient German lineage entitled him to special consideration. Eventually, Linsing was paid off, but he continued to scandalise London by quarreling publicly with other Frenchmen, including relatives and friends of the naval minister, Antoine-Gabriel de Sartine.[152] These quarrels culminated in a duel in which he injured a French officer called Rauçonnet. As a result he was imprisoned again, briefly, until d'Eon secured a reconciliation and his release.[153] Thereafter, he disappears from the diplomatic record, having reputedly left for Portugal in September 1776.[154]

Vignoles

The life of the defrocked monk Vignoles, author of a journal suppressed by Beaumarchais, is similarly opaque. Having taken the habit at the abbey of Joyenval in 1739, he later fled to Holland with his pregnant mistress. He set himself up in business, went bankrupt, and fled to London. There, in the 1760s and 1770s, he was a close associate of d'Eon, serving as his secretary, legal advisor, and hired pen. The British considered him an Austrian spy and intriguer.[155] Barthélemy Tort de La Sonde, the disgraced one-time secretary to the French ambassador Adrien-Louis de Bonnières de Souastres, comte de Guines, linked him – as well as d'Eon and Morande – to a gang of stock exchange speculators who approached him for inside information during the Anglo-Spanish crisis of 1770.[156] Vignoles was a keen freemason, and in the 1760s headed the French lodge of *L'Immortalité de l'Ordre*, in which d'Eon served as a secretary.[157] He also briefly served the Swedish legation in London.[158] Vignoles was a close ally of d'Eon in his disputes with Morande and Beaumarchais, and it was the latter's denunciation that cost him his position with the Swedes.[159]

Jacquet de Douai

Unlike the other *libellistes* discussed here, the corrupt police officer Jean-Claude Jacquet de Douai was never based in London, but made several clandestine visits while running an international *libelle* network from Paris.[160] Manuel, in *La Police de Paris dévoilée* [*The Paris Police Unveiled*] (1791), a document-based *exposé* prepared from official police archives while its author was *procureur de la commune de Paris*,[161] reveals that Jacquet came from a well-connected legal family, and was a *procureur du roi* at Lons-le-Saulnier in the Franche-Comté before becoming a police agent and inspector in the book trade.[162] Arrested in October 1781, Jacquet was transferred to the abbey at Charenton, an institution for insane prisoners, and freed only in early 1789. Manuel says that on his release he applied for his old job with the police, but his plans were thwarted by the overthrow of the *ancien régime*.[163]

Serres de La Tour

La Tour, who served as the comtesse de La Motte's ghost-writer in 1788, was born to a 'good' family in about 1740 and served briefly in the military before gravitating towards Paris, where he married and tried to establish himself in a literary career.[164] He then passed into the service of Pierre-Farrand Guerrier de Bésance, master of requests at Versailles, who felt an obligation towards La Tour, who had lost money in Bésance's father-in-law's bankruptcy.[165] In 1771, La Tour paid Bésance back by absconding to London with his wife.[166] In 1776, he became founding editor and one-third stakeholder in the *Courier de l'Europe*. Launched on the eve of the American revolution, the paper caught the imagination of Europe, and soon had 5,000 subscribers.[167] La Tour, a confirmed cynic, was astounded by his success and boasted of earning more money in a year than Rousseau made in a life-time.[168] After La Tour was ousted from the paper in 1783, he never knew such prosperity again. His dreams of establishing a journal and cultural institution in partnership with Brissot fell through, and a series of short-lived journalistic ventures failed.[169]

La Tour survived on the profits from a quack remedy whose recipe he owned.[170] By 1787, when he became involved with the La Mottes, he was struggling financially.[171] He kept afloat with loans from Calonne, who was living in self-imposed exile in London and hoped to return to favour by securing the suppression of the La Mottes' work. When Calonne refused further subventions, La Tour sued him in desperation.[172] When he lost the case, he published a savage pamphlet attack on Calonne. He probably returned to Paris in early 1790, and shortly thereafter disappears from view. His last known pamphlet, a *Lettre à M. de Calonne*, was published in Paris in 1790; his last periodical, *Le Gazettin*, in 1790–91.

MacMahon

Joseph Parkyns MacMahon, who preceded La Tour as the comtesse de La Motte's ghost-writer, was like Vignoles a former clergyman. Of Irish Jacobite descent, he was according to his obituary in the *Gentleman's Magazine* the nephew of Lord Macklethwaite, earl of Portarlington, and had served from childhood in the French army's Irish brigade. The latter is probably a care-fully constructed falsehood.[173] Until about 1771, when he fled to London with a young *penitente*, whom he later married, MacMahon was *vicaire* of a parish near Rouen. In London, he turned to journalism, working as a sub-editor for the *Courier de l'Europe* and *Morning Herald*. Manuel asserts he wrote almost all the scandalous anecdotes and calumnies in the English papers.[174] When La Tour proposed that MacMahon collaborate on their proposed journal, Brissot replied revealingly:

> Il peut connaître l'Opèra et les filles. Mais nous ne bornons pas à un concert, et nous n'avons pas besoin d'un sérial. . . . je sais le métier qu'il fait, et ce métier est scandaleux, abominable. [He may know about the Opera and prostitutes. But we are not limiting ourselves to concerts, and we have no need of a harem. . . . I know what profession he follows, and that profession is scandalous, abominable.][175]

MacMahon was probably the journalist whom Brissot depicts gloating with Morande over spoils fleeced from, among others, a merchant who wished him to traduce a competitor and an actress-courtesan desperate to conceal the nocturnal encounter that left her pregnant.[176]

The degree of MacMahon's association with blackmailing pamphlets is unclear. However, he did publish several sensational works in translation, including an abridgement of Louis Sébastien Mercier's *Tableau de Paris* and one of Cagliostro's trial briefs relating to the diamond necklace affair. Robiquet suggests that he was closely associated with Boissière.[177] However, his only proven involvement in blackmail-pamphleteering is his association with the La Mottes. The MacMahons were involved with the La Mottes almost from the moment the comtesse escaped, and it was Madame MacMahon who fetched her from the Low Countries. MacMahon's involvement in the comtesse's project was cut short by his death on 14 January 1788, and her *Mémoires* appear to have been primarily the work of La Tour.

The *libellistes* in profile

The time has come to measure all sixteen *libellistes* against the Darntonian model, assessing the extent to which their backgrounds, experiences, and eventual fates share common features. Here, a distinction should perhaps be made between those *libellistes* who plied their trade on a repeat basis or in a quasi-professional manner, targeting the monarchy for large financial stakes, and those who resorted to blackmail through circumstance, in support of trifling financial demands, political or commercial favours, personal vendettas, or non-financial requests. The 'professional' category includes Fauques, d'Eon, Morande, Pelleport, Jacquet, the La Mottes, MacMahon, La Tour, and, presumably, Dom Louis, Campagnol, and Vignoles. The other category, *libellistes de circonstance*, includes La Bussière, Vergy, Linsing, and Linguet.

The career backgrounds and gender balance of this sample are immediately striking. The presence of three women in the 'professional' group is particularly remarkable. This proportion far exceeds the percentage of women in the overall eighteenth-century literary population.[178] Moreover, after d'Eon's gender change, contemporaries considered him a woman, too, and a distinguished one. Perhaps the prevalence of women indicates a lack of options open to female adventuresses, authors, and ageing women of easy virtue; or maybe intelligent and beautiful women had greater access to scandalous knowledge? However, the sample is too small to generalise. The presence in the 'professional' category of three defrocked clergymen – Dom Louis, Vignoles, and MacMahon – together with a lapsed nun, Fauques, is perhaps a little less surprising, as a significant proportion of the French exile community were refugee monks or priests.[179] Well educated, frequently well connected, and stripped of their usual means of support, they perhaps found *libelles* an attractive option. Nor, perhaps, is it a surprise to find a sizeable contingent of ex-military men – d'Eon, La Motte, La Tour, Linsing, Morande, Pelleport – among our sixteen literary adventurers. Given that *libellistes* exploited and tested the limits of the English law, it is also unsurprising that four of the most persistent of them – d'Eon, Jacquet, Linguet, Morande – had a legal training.

Equally striking is the prevalence of nobles. Four *libellistes* – d'Eon, Pelleport, Linsing, and the comtesse de La Motte – definitely had noble backgrounds. MacMahon also had blue blood; and six more, La Bussière, Jacquet, La Tour, Campagnol, Fauques, and Vergy, claimed to be noble, perhaps with reason. Morande made fraudulent claims to noble status, as did the comte de La Motte. Vignoles used the particle 'de', indicating authentic or usurped nobility. Linguet was born a commoner but elevated to the Austrian nobility. Bearing in mind that the final *libelliste*, Dom Louis, belonged to the first estate (clergy), none of the *libellistes* identified exclusively with the Third Estate. Even if all the potentially spurious claims to noble status are ignored, under half the sample were full-blooded *roturiers* [commoners].

Established criminality is another common theme. This is not surprising, since French subjects seldom settled in England without good reason. Nevertheless, the extent of the *libellistes*' previous criminal activity is striking. Several left France having committed crimes, among them Morande, the La Mottes, and Linsing. Pelleport was also probably involved with petty crime, gambling, and prostitution. Vergy apparently fled France because of debts, and either was involved in a criminal conspiracy to poison d'Eon as he claimed, or was a perjuror. Moreover, at least four *libellistes* abandoned France in sexually scandalous circumstances. Vignoles and MacMahon both absconded with young *penitentes*; La Tour fled with the wife of his employer; Linguet was accompanied by a married mistress. All such elopements and seductions were considered criminal.

Pressing financial circumstances are known to have driven several *libellistes*. Morande and d'Eon needed to clear serious debts, while Pelleport travelled to London to repair an ailing fortune. La Tour's periodical was in serious financial trouble when he became involved with the La Mottes; Linsing was ruined by his military service and imprisonment; La Bussière was shipwrecked and destitute. The La Mottes, whose fabulous ill-gotten gains were frittered and gambled away or confiscated by the French government, needed to appease English creditors. Those *libellistes* whose lives remain shrouded in mystery may well also have been weighed down by debts incurred through extravagant and, not infrequently, debauched living. Seasoned criminals and adventurers, many, probably most, *libellistes* descended into 'Grub Street' through circumstances of their own making, rather than, as Darnton would have it, frustrated literary ambitions.

While it is dangerous to speculate about psychological motivations, several of the *libellistes* also seem to have been driven by a strong sense of personal entitlement. Linsing based his claims more on princely status than on military service. D'Eon justified his behaviour by past service and the expenses associated with his espionage mission. Madame de La Motte was probably convinced of her Valois ancestry, which had been recognised by royal heralds, and thus felt entitled to rewards from the family that had sup-planted and spurned her own. Linguet, too, fits into this category: he was obsessed by his struggle for justice against a regime that had stripped him of his livelihood as a lawyer and threatened his living as a journalist. Likewise, La Bussière felt that his misfortunes deserved generous treatment, and if there was any truth in his tales, Vergy must have felt bitterly betrayed and cheated by Guerchy.

Many of the *libellistes* were involved in trading information. Several became involved in espionage, including d'Eon, Morande, Pelleport, Jacquet, and perhaps, in a less formal sense, Vergy and the comte de La Motte. A number were also involved in journalism, notably Linguet, La Tour, MacMahon, Vignoles, Pelleport, and Morande. Such work could be lucrative: La Tour's share in the *Courier de l'Europe* made him wealthy, but as its salaried editor, Morande was also well paid, and his underlings earned a solid professional salary. D'Eon was a respected author who wrote vari-ously on many topics; Fauques wrote novels. Several *libellistes* thus made adequate incomes from writing, and some became rich or famous from their pens. It is hard to see them as the literary failures that Darnton's model would suggest, although Vergy, La Tour, MacMahon, and Vignoles might be characterised as hired hacks.

Nor, contrary to the expectations of the 'Grub Street' model, did the *libel-listes* tend towards Jacobin republicanism. Taking Darnton's arguments to their logical extent, Peter Wagner asks 'whether the [prerevolutionary Grub Street] pamphleteers were present' when Marie-Antoinette's favourite, the princesse de Lamballe, whom pornographers portrayed as her lesbian lover, was (allegedly) gang-raped, murdered, and beheaded in the September mas-sacres and, according to some reports, her heart was roasted, and her head carried to the queen's prison by a mob for her to kiss one last time?[180] The answer is somewhat surprising. Among those *libellistes* who dealt in sexual slander and whose political trajectory is known, Morande and Pelleport had embraced counter-revolution, and even the La Mottes may have been chas-tened. This is hardly a large sample group, but as it incorporates the most cel-ebrated scandalmongers among the *libellistes*, it has to be taken as indicative.

Among those blackmailers who eschewed sexual scandal, a similar trend is identifiable. D'Eon turned against the revolution, and Linguet, a long-time apologist for absolutism, retired from the national scene and was executed in the Terror. In sum, those *libellistes* whose political affiliations are discernible appear to have been reformist *patriotes*, strongly opposed to ministerial despotism and clandestine court politics. They were, nonetheless, strong proponents of regenerated monarchy. When the revolution lurched too far to the left, they rejected it.

Thus the London *libellistes* bear little resemblance to the model derived from Darnton's work. They were not failed writers, frustrated hacks, hate-filled nihilists, or Jacobins *avant la lettre*: those who did not write against ministers through opportunism apparently did so as reformist patriots. If some were masterless men and women, the most successful necessarily had good contacts and sources in the establishment, and most were minor or fallen nobles or hailed from France's professional elites. Their attempts at blackmail may thus be considered an extreme form of the traditional noble art of prising favours and rewards out of the monarchy. In a society where provincial *parvenus* like the Polignac clan, favourites of the queen, could enrich themselves shamelessly from the royal treasury in less than a generation, it would hardly be surprising if others used every resource at their disposal to acquire wealth. Some, including Linsing, Linguet, d'Eon, and probably the comtesse de La Motte, felt morally justified in doing so.

Notes

1 In closely defining 'London's French *libellistes*', I excluded Goupil because his association with London is uncertain; Goëzman and Beaumarchais because their collaboration is unproven; Goudar, Fini, and Lallemand because they apparently never tried to sell their silence; St Julien and Angelucci because their existence is doubtful; the ghost-writer Peter Stuart because he was British; and Brissot because accusations against him were false. Boissière was an entrepreneur rather than an author, and so is treated in chapter two.

2 'Fauques' is preferred to 'Falques', because the author used this spelling herself in Add. MS 35,365 fo. 365, Fauques to C. Yorke, London, 26 March 1760.

3 *Dictionnaire de biographie française* (Paris: Letouzey et Ané, 1933–present), XIII, 551. Although just one paragraph long, this entry indicates that it may be factually unreliable.

4 Her known works include: *Le Triomphe de l'amitié*, 2 vols (1751); *Abbasaï, histoire orientale*, 3 vols (1753); *Contes du sérail* (1753); *Les Prejugés trop bravés et trop suivis* (1755); *La Dernière Guerre des bêtes* (1758); *Le Danger des préjugés* (1774); *The Vizirs or the Enchanted Labyrinth* (1775); *Dialogues moraux et amusantes*, 2nd edition (London, 1784).

5 See editor's 'Notice' in Fauques, *L'Histoire de Madame la marquise de Pompadour* (Paris: Le Moniteur du bibliophile, 1879), pp. 6–7, 13; Agnani, 'Libelles et diplomatie', p. 61.

6 See below, chapters two and three.

7 Add. MS 35,365 fo. 365, Fauques to C. Yorke, London, 26 March 1760.

8 MD France 1351 fos 96–7, Mme Hervé to Mme Geoffrin, London, 20 January 1759 (extrait). The 'Notice' in Fauques, *Histoire de Pompadour*, 1879 edition, p. 12, notes that Nivernais said her collaborator was female.

9 However, Voltaire and the Goncourts distinguished some truth among Fauques's falsehoods. See 'Notice' in Fauques, *Histoire de Pompadour*, 1879 edition, p. 13.

10 ADCO, 2E26/4, Etat civil, Arnay-le-Duc. The main biographical sources are Paul Robiquet, *Théveneau de Morande: étude sur le XVIIIe siècle* (Paris: Quantin, 1882); *BCE*; Burrows, 'Literary low-life'.

11 ADCO, 2E26/4–7, Etat civil, Arnay-le-Duc.

12 Morande, *Réplique à Brissot*, p. 7; César Lavirotte, 'Notice sur M. de Morande' (private archive). I wish to thank Bernard Leblanc for sending me a transcribed copy of this manuscript, which was uncovered by Claude Guyot (1890–1965) in papers belonging to Lavirotte's descendants. Morande's regiment is confirmed in Arsenal, MS 12,247 fo. 302.

13 Morande, *Réplique à Brissot*, p. 7; *Public Advertiser*, 5 September 1776 and 6 September 1776. Both newspaper articles were probably placed by d'Eon. For cuttings see Add. MS 11,340 fos 21–2.

14 The versions of his duelling and other activities in Morande, *Réplique à Brissot*, pp. 8–11, and Lavirotte, 'Notice sur M. de Morande' (private archive), differ in detail. Arsenal, MS 12,345 fo. 136, Juliot to Sartine, undated [May 1768], confirms details concerning Morande's arrests.

15 Arsenal, MS 12,247 fos 303–4, La Janière to [Sartine], 17 February 1765; fo. 309, [Sartine] to Saint-Florentin, 24 January 1765; fos 313–14, La Saule to Sartine, 18 February 1765; fo. 320, [Sartine] to Saint-Florentin, 14 March 1765.

16 Arsenal, MS 12,345 fos 128–9, Flesselles to Sartine, [undated, c. 11 May 1768]; fos 134–5, Mlle Danezy to Sartine, 25 May 1768; fo. 136, Juliot to Sartine, [undated]; fos 137–8, Louis Théveneau's power of attorney, Arnay-le-Duc, 27 January 1768 (copy).

17 Arsenal, MS 12,247 fos 307–8, Morande to Sartine, Fort l'Evêque, 17 February 1765; fos 315–16, La Saule to Sartine, 3 March 1765.

18 Arsenal, MS 12,345 fo. 164, Antoine Durand to Sartine, [undated; received 19 July 1768]; fos 198–9, Morande to Sartine, 4 August 1769; see also MS 12,247 fos 315–16, La Saule to Sartine, 3 March 1765; fo. 305, Sartine to la Jannière, 20 February 1765. Arsenal, MS 12,345 fos 143–4, Bethune to Sartine, 2 July 1768, petitions for Morande's release, as a family friend, apparently unaware that Louis Théveneau supported the *lettre de cachet*.

19 Arsenal, MS 12,345 fos 132–3, Marais to Sartine, 17 May 1768, links Morande with la Beauchamp, a brothel-keeper; la petite Desmares, who fled his violence; la Doppy; la Souville, mistress to M. de Bourgogne; and Mademoiselle Lacour, mistress to the prince de Lamballe.

20 See Charles-Claude Théveneau de Morande, *Le Gazetier cuirassé* (London: n. p., 1771), esp. part III, 1–35. See also Morande (attrib.), *La Gazette noire* ([London]: n. p., 1784), 97–106; Morande (attrib.), *Le Portefeuille de Madame Gourdan* ([London]: n. p., 1783). There are problems with both these attributions. The former, with its Rousseauist rhetoric and praise of Linguet, may well have emanated from Pelleport's circle. Nineteenth-century bibliographers habitually attributed *libelles* to Morande.

54   *Blackmail, scandal, and revolution*

21 Morande, *Réplique à Brissot*, pp. 13, 15–17.
22 Arsenal, MS 12,345 fos 183–4, Croquison to Sartine, Armentières, 4 May 1769; fo. 187, Juliot to Sartine, [undated, June 1769]; fos 194–5, Croquison to Sartine, Armentières, 17 July 1769. The first and last of these letters have been published in François Ravaisson (ed.), *Archives de la Bastille*, 19 vols (Paris: Durand et Pedone-Lauriel, 1866–1904), XII, 485.
23 Arsenal, MS 12,345 fos 204–5, Chenu to Sartine, 8 December 1769; [Sartine] to Saint-Florentin, [undated, 'bon pour l'ordre', 29 December 1769].
24 Arsenal, MS 12,345 fos 210–11, Narbens to Sartine, 13 May 1770; Morande, *Réplique à Brissot*, 17–18. CPA 502 fos 177–9.
25 City of Westminster Archives, parish of St George, Hanover Square, marriage registers, vol. 16, no. 155.
26 Morande, *Réplique à Brissot*, p. 19.
27 Anne-Gédeon de La Fite de Pelleport, *Le Diable dans un bénitier* (London: n. p., 1783), p. 62; *MSB*, 9 February 1774; Manuel, *Police*, II, 252; CPA 518 fos 78–90, [d'Eon], 'Le Mandrin littéraire ou anecdotes du *Gazetier cuirassé*'; AN, 446AP/3, 'Mémoire pour J. -P. Brissot', fo. 36; Beaumarchais to [?], Paris, 24 January 1781, published in *BCE*, I, 111–15.
28 On the Goëzman affair see Maza, *Private Lives*, and the principal biographies of Beaumarchais cited in the bibliography. For Beaumarchais's trial briefs, see his *Mémoires de Beaumarchais dans l'affaire Goëzman* (Paris: Garnier, n. d.).
29 PRO, SP78/300 fos 210–11, Stormont to Weymouth, Fontainebleau, 6 November 1776; Morande, *Réplique à Brissot*, p. 23. An article entitled 'M. Demorande' in *Biographical Anecdotes of the Founders of the French Republic* (London: R. Philips, 1797), pp. 131–2, suggests that Morande received a pension of £200–300 as compensation for leaving London.
30 On Morande's espionage services see Burrows, 'Literary low-life', pp. 82–5; *BCE*, document 516, [Morande] to Montmorin, 28 April 1788. For his earliest surviving spy reports, dating from 25 December 1786 to 3 October 1787, see CPA supplément 28. *BCE* reproduces some subsequent reports, which span CPA 562–77. His last report (CPA 577 fos 122–3) is dated 8 April 1791.
31 See chapters two to four below and Burrows, 'Innocence of Brissot', pp. 854–60.
32 Pelleport, *Diable*, p. 34; Manuel, *Police*, II, 253; CPA 523 fos 203–4, Tort to Raynach, 6 June 1777; ULBC, file 3 fos 253–6, d'Eon to Drouet, 25 April 1777.
33 See LMA, G1/1, accounts of surveyors of highways, Great Stanmore. Morande's name first appears in these accounts in 1778 and disappears after 1782–83. Land tax returns (LMA, MR/PLT 1418–20) confirm that Morande's residence was vacant in 1784, and valued at less than forty-five other properties in the parish.
34 See PRO, TS11/793 file 2 and TS11/1116; *Public Advertiser*, 8, 11, 12 January and 16, 27, 28 July 1781; *Morning Chronicle* 8, 11, 12 January, and 16, 28, 30 July 1781; *Morning Herald*, 9, 10, 11 January and 16 July 1781; *St James Chronicle*, 4–6 January and 14–17 July 1781; *Annual Register* 24 (1781), 184–6; *Courier de l'Europe*, 17, 31 July 1781. *BCE*, I, 116, misleadingly implies that this last newpaper contains allegations against Morande.
35 The charge first appears in ULBC, file 3 pp. 253–6, d'Eon to Drouet, 25 April 1777, but is absent from his subsequent denunciations of Morande and

Beaumarchais (pp. 268–85, d'Eon to Louis XVI, 28 May; pp. 303–6, d'Eon to Vergennes, 1 July 1777). However, CPA 523 fos 203–4, Tort to Raynach, 6 June 1777, insists it was Tort who first denounced Morande and Beaumarchais some months previously. The most likely scenario is that Tort, who was closely connected with d'Eon, was d'Eon's front-man. If so Louis and Vergennes were not fooled. Beaumarchais remained in favour.

36 See *BCE*.

37 On Morande's journalism, see Burrows, 'Literary low-life', pp. 85–9; Simon Burrows, 'The cosmopolitan press' in Barker and Burrows (eds), *Press, Politics and the Public Sphere*, pp. 29–30, 36, 37; *BCE*, I, 180–96 and *passim*.

38 See Burrows, 'Literary low-life', and below, chapter six.

39 ULBC, file 7, 'Mémoire pour servir de Preface' (1794), p. 36; AN, 446AP/7, Manuel to Brissot, June 1791.

40 On Morande's arrest see AN, F[7] 4774[51] dossier 3; W251 dossier 27.

41 See the list of suspects drawn up on 7 April 1793 and published in Jules Parthiot, *Episodes de le révolution dans les baillage et district d'Arnay-le-Duc* (Dijon: Venot, 1901), p. 48. I thank Bernard Leblanc for this reference.

42 See AN, W292 dossier 204, 3e partie, piece 6, Siessel [?] fils to Fouquier Tinville, 17 brumaire [1793].

43 ADCO, 2E26/15.

44 Robiquet, *Théveneau de Morande*, p. 307; Wagner, *Eros Revived*, p. 98; Gary Kates, *Monsieur d'Eon is a Woman: A Tale of Political Intrigue and Sexual Masquerade* (New York: Basic Books, 1995), p. 214.

45 See *BCE*, I, 112–15 and *passim*.

46 See Manuel, *Police*, II, 28–9.

47 CPA 542 fos 285–9, Receveur's 'Compte rendu', 22 May 1783; *Intermédiaire des chercheurs et des curieux* 61 (1910), column 137. I thank Paul Agnani for this reference.

48 Louis Charpentier et al., *La Bastille dévoilée*, 9 'livraisons' (Paris: Desenne, 1789–90), 3rd livraison, pp. 66–7. On his early life and career, see also Manuel, *Police*, II, 28–9.

49 Ibid., 235–6. On d'Hémery's files, see Darnton, 'Police inspector'.

50 Robert Darnton, 'J.-P. Brissot and the Société typographique de Neuchâtel (1779–1787)', *SVEC* 2001:10 (Oxford: Voltaire Foundation, 2001), pp. 8, 10–11; letters of Brissot to Pelleport, dated 31 August 1779, [1779], and 5 October 1779, and Brissot to STN, Paris, 11 October 1779 in *CBW*, letters 1–2 and 4–5.

51 Charpentier, *Bastille dévoilée*, 3rd livraison, pp. 66–7; Darnton, 'Brissot and the Société typographique de Neuchâtel', p. 11. Her full name appears on a *lettre de change* from 1779, BPUN, MS 1190 fo. 138. Manuel, *Police*, II, 29, ridicules the romantic notions about Pelleport entertained by Leynard [*sic*].

52 Charpentier, *Bastille dévoilée*, 3rd livraison, pp. 66–7.

53 CPA 542 fos 285–9, Receveur to d'Adhémar, 'Compte rendu', London, 22 May 1783.

54 Manuel, *Police*, II, 256.

55 Jacques-Pierre Brissot de Warville, *Réplique de J. P. Brissot à Charles Théveneau Morande* (Paris: de l'imprimerie du *Patriote françois*, 1791), p. 26; AN, 446AP/2 'Mémoire pour Brissot', fos 2–3. Brissot, *Mémoires*, II, p. 192, says Pelleport refused these offers.

56 AN, 446AP/2, 'Deuxième interrogatoire de Brissot', fos 2, 10; 446AP/3, 'Mémoire contre Desforges', fo. 80; Brissot, *Mémoires*, II, p. 192. J. Dybikowski, *On Burning Ground: An Examination of the Ideas, Projects and Life of David Williams*, SVEC 307 (Oxford: Voltaire Foundation, 1993), p. 310, notes that advertisements for the third edition of David Williams's *Letters on Political Liberty* (London, 1782) name Pelleport as the translator.

57 AN, 446AP/3, 'Mémoire contre Desforges', fos 65, 68–9; Brissot, *Mémoires*, II, 305–6.

58 On Desforges's relations with Brissot see Burrows, 'Innocence of Brissot', pp. 849–53.

59 AN, 446AP/3, 'Mémoire contre Desforges', fo. 31; Brissot, *Mémoires*, II, 299, 317.

60 On the conspiracy to ensnare Pelleport, see CPA 549 fos 56–7, d'Adhémar to Vergennes, 22 June 1784; fos 80–1, d'Adhémar to Vergennes, 1 July 1784; CPA 552 fos 20–1, Buard to Vergennes, 10 January 1785.

61 AN, F^7 4445^2 dossier 3, pieces 17, 18, 23, letters of [comtesse de La Motte] to [comte de La Motte], dated respectively ce Samedi 19 ja [? or ju], [1789 or 1790]; 12 Feb 1790; 19 October 1790. Eventually the comtesse turned against Pelleport: see piece 19 bis, [comtesse] to [comte de La Motte], ce vendredi 23 juillet [1790?].

62 Charpentier, *Bastille dévoilée*, 3rd livraison, pp. 68–9. See also Manuel, *Police*, II, 29–30.

63 Charpentier, *Bastille dévoilée*, 3rd livraison, pp. 69–70. The incident is also recorded in a painting attributed to Charles Thévenin in the Musée Carnavalet, Paris (inv. P. 267), and an engraving by Janinet preserved in the Bibliothèque nationale.

64 AN, F^7 4445^2 dossier 3, piece 6, abbé Pfaff to the comtesse de La Motte, 9 January 1790.

65 Olivier Blanc, *Les Espions de la révolution et de l'Empire* (Paris: Perrin, 1995), pp. 293, 306.

66 *Archives parlementaires de 1787–1860. Série 1, 1787–1799*, edited by J. Mavidal, E. Laurent, et al., 100 vols (Paris: Dupont et al., 1867–2000), XXXVIII, 507–8, 521–6, 545–6, 584–90.

67 AN, F^7 4224/46, Pelleport to Fouché, Hamburg, 1 February 1801; F^7 4336^1; Blanc, *Espions*, p. 293.

68 See *Intermédiaire des chercheurs et des curieux* 61 (1910), column 137.

69 See Louis XVI to Vergennes, 16 August 1785, in *Louis XVI and the comte de Vergennes: Correspondence*, edited by John Hardman and Munro Price, *SVEC* 364 (Oxford: Voltaire Foundation, 1998), p. 376. J. L. H. Campan, *Mémoires (inédits) de Madame Campan*, 3 vols (Paris: J. Tastu, 1822), II, 24.

70 See AN, F^7 4445^2 dossier 2, 'Mémoire instructif sur la connoissance de Mme la comtesse de La Motte avec M. Bohmer et Bassange'.

71 For the the traditional version see: Frances Mossiker, *The Queen's Necklace* (London: Victor Gollancz, 1961), 130–46; Jones, *Great Nation*, pp. 336–48; Maza, *Private Lives*, pp. 183–5. On the story's inconsistencies see Munro Price, *Preserving the Monarchy: The Comte de Vergennes, 1774–1787* (Cambridge: Cambridge University Press, 1995), pp. 180–2.

72 On the trial briefs see Maza, *Private Lives*, pp. 190–205.

73 Letter of Charles de Rohan to *The Times*, 19 January 1959, reproduced in Mossiker, *Queen's Necklace*, p. 611.
74 Evelyne Lever, *L'Affaire du collier* (Paris: Fayard, 2004), pp. 98–102, 304–5; Jeanne de La Motte, *Memoirs*, pp. 46–7. Lever notes that Michelet and Louis Blanc both suggested that the queen connived in d'Oliva's meeting with Rohan, as did Louis Hastier's *La Vérité sur l'affaire du collier* (1955).
75 See below, chapter four.
76 On this point see also Maza, 'Diamond necklace affair' and Gruder, 'Question of Marie-Antoinette', p. 277.
77 The fullest account of her childhood is in La Motte, *Life*, I, 1–117. Cf. the hostile anonymous *Authentic Adventures of the Celebrated Countess de la Motte* (London: E. Johnson, 1787), pp. 5–63, and the probably spuriously attributed La Motte, *Second Mémoire*, pp. 7–20. For documents relating to family titles, pension, etc., see AN, F⁷ 4445² *passim*.
78 La Motte, *Life*, I, 129–45.
79 Frantz Funck-Brentano, *L'Affaire du collier*, 12th edition (Paris: Hachette, 1926), p. 74. La Motte, *Life*, I, 143–5, explains that she used her pregnancy to gain her relatives' consent for the marriage.
80 AN, F⁷ 4445² dossier 1, 'Extrait des registres du Conseil du Roi', 10 October 1783, mentions three 'fausses couches' [miscarriages].
81 Funck-Brentano, *Affaire du collier*, pp. 74–5.
82 Ibid., p. 83.
83 AN, F⁷ 4445² dossier 1 reveals their debts and attempts to gain suspensions of payment.
84 The La Mottes' activities can be reconstructed from witness statements and interrogations in AN, K 162; financial and legal documents in AN, F⁷ 4445² dossier 1; and Target's notes for Rohan's defence in BHVP, MS 691, which contains a note from the cardinal (fos 170–9) confirming that he met the comtesse in September 1781.
85 MO, MS 1423/3 pp. 11, 35.
86 Iain McCalman, 'Queen of the gutter: the lives and fictions of Jeanne de La Motte' in John Docker and Gerhard Fischer (eds), *Adventures in Identity: European Multicultural Perspectives* (Tübingen: Stauffenburg-Verlag, 2001), pp. 111–27.
87 Frantz Funck-Brentano, *Cagliostro and Company*, transl. George Maidment (London: Greening, 1910), pp. 165–8.
88 Marc de La Motte, *Mémoires inédits*, pp. 264–81.
89 Ibid., p. 314; Funck-Brentano, *Cagliostro and Company*, pp. 217–18.
90 Marc de La Motte, *Mémoires inédits*, p. 354.
91 Funck-Brentano, *Cagliostro and Company*, pp. 218–22; Mossiker, *Queen's Necklace*, pp. 587–9.
92 Funck-Brentano, *Cagliostro and Company*, p. 224.
93 Ibid., p. 249.
94 Among numerous studies of Linguet, see: Daniel Baruch, *Simon-Nicolas-Henri Linguet ou l'irrécupérable* (Paris: Bourin, 1991); Darline Gay Levy, *The Ideas and Careers of Simon-Nicolas-Henri Linguet: A Study in Eighteenth-Century French Politics* (Urbana, IL: University of Illinois Press, 1980); Jean Cruppi, *Un Avocat-journaliste au XVIIIe siècle: Linguet* (Paris: Hachette, 1895). On Linguet's journalism see Jeremy D. Popkin, 'The prerevolutionary origins of

political journalism' in Baker (ed.), *Political Culture of the Old Regime* and 'The business of political enlightenment in France, 1770–1800' in John Brewer and Roy Porter (eds), *Consumption and the World of Goods* (London: Routledge, 1993).

95 Levy, *Linguet*, p. 9. The following account of Linguet's life and ideology draws heavily on this work.

96 See CPA 522 fo. 37, Vergennes to Noailles, dated 7 March 1777. Vergennes says he was unaware that Linguet was Panckoucke's editor at the time of the complaint.

97 Levy, *Linguet*, p. 174.

98 Popkin, 'Business of political enlightenment', argues that Linguet was a better example of a Grub Street hack than most of Darnton's representative figures.

99 However, Kates, *Monsieur d'Eon*, p. 212, notes that d'Eon 'dabbled in political muckraking', and Alexandre Stroev, *Les Aventuriers des lumières* (Paris: Presses universitaires de France, 1997), considers him an adventurer. My outline of d'Eon's life draws on Kates's account. Kates lists forty-two other non-fiction works on d'Eon plus twelve fictional ones. Subsequent studies include: Anna Clark, 'The chevalier d'Eon and Wilkes: masculinity and politics in the eighteenth century', *Eighteenth-Century Studies*, 32:1 (1998); Nathalie Grzesiak, *Le Chevalier d'Eon: tout pour le roi* (Paris: Acropole, 2000) which ignores Kates's work; and Jonathan Conlin, 'Wilkes, the chevalier d'Eon and "the dregs of liberty": an Anglo-French perspective on ministerial despotism, 1762–1771', *English Historical Review* 120:5 (2005).

100 Kates, *Monsieur d'Eon*, p. 47.

101 See Patricia Kennedy Grimsted, *The Foreign Ministers of Alexander I: Political Attitudes and the Conduct of Foreign Policy 1801–1825* (Berkeley, CA: University of California Press, 1969), pp. 181–3.

102 D'Eon, *Pièces relatives aux Lettres, mémoires et négociations particulières du chevalier d'Eon* (London: Dixwell, 1764), p. 15; ULBC, file 9 pp. 216–17; file 24 p. 13; file 69 pp. 8, 59; multiple references in d'Eon, *Lettres, mémoires et négociations*; and Ange Goudar's response, *Examen des Lettres, mémoires et négociations particulières du chevalier d'Eon* (London: Becket and de Hondt, 1764) reprinted in d'Eon, *Pièces rélatives*, p. 117.

103 See CPA 541 fos 255–6, d'Eon to Guerchy, 22 September 1763; fos 268–71, d'Eon to Guerchy, 25 September 1763; ULBC, file 23, Nivernais to d'Eon, Paris, 11 September 1763. For d'Eon's accounts for work on Guerchy's house, see d'Eon, *Lettres, mémoires et négociations*, pp. 174–218. The French lacked fixed embassies at this time, so ambassadors purchased their own residences.

104 See below, chapter three.

105 Ibid.

106 Kates, *Monsieur d'Eon*, pp. 182–8.

107 Ibid., pp. 191–2.

108 For the trial, see ULBC, file 27.

109 See ULBC, file 60 p. 201, undated, unidentified newspaper cutting.

110 Kates, *Monsieur d'Eon, passim*.

111 D'Eon's 'Transaction' with Beaumarchais was signed on 4 November 1775 but backdated to 5 October. For copies see CPA supplément 16 fos 436–42; ULBC, file 3 pp. 43–6 (extrait); BMT, R7; Gaillardet, *Mémoires du chevalier d'Eon*, pp. 326–32.

112 See, for example *CSP*, IV, 125–31; Ange Goudar, *L'Espion françois à Londres*, 2 vols (London: aux depens de l'auteur, 1780 [original edition, 1779]), I, 203–40; and the newspaper cuttings in Add. MS 11,340.

113 Add. MS 11,340 fos 8–9 and *passim*; CPA supplément 17 fos 7–17.

114 Add. MS 11,340 contains the offending articles and judgement.

115 ULBC, file 67, d'Eon to Barthelemy, 11 February 1791.

116 Ibid., d'Adhémar [?] to Vergennes, 24 December 1784 (copy).

117 ULBC, file 65 p. 316.

118 ULBC, file 67, Mémoire of d'Eon to Montmorin [undated. Early February 1788].

119 ULBC, file 18 fos 63–4.

120 ULBC, file 67, Delessart to Kirsinger, Paris, 27 January 1792; Kirsinger to Delessart, London, 31 January 1792.

121 ULBC, file 52 p. 203, undated note of Richardson, received 29 November 1804.

122 Kates, *Monsieur d'Eon*, pp. xi–xiii. His biological masculinity was confirmed by four surgeons: see *Courier de Londres*, 25 May 1810.

123 *Patriote françois*, 13 June 1792; *Gazette universelle*, 13 June 1792. For cuttings see ULBC, file 49.

124 Kates, *Monsieur d'Eon*, pp. 272–3.

125 ULBC, file 18 fos 63–4, notes for d'Eon's autobiography.

126 For d'Eon's antipathy towards the revolution see the 'Epître préliminaire' to his unpublished memoirs in ULBC, file 7.

127 Blanc, *Espions*, p. 15.

128 ULBC, file 22, loose page numbered 86.

129 See ULBC, file 72, *Adresse . . . à la nation angloise*, January 1799, p. 3.

130 ULBC, file 58 p. 36; file 27 pp. 261–83, 'Lettre du chevalier d'Eon aux courtiers souscripteurs de polices sur son sexe', at p. 271. On Goudar's involvement with Guerchy and d'Eon see Jean-Claude Hauc, *Ange Goudar: un aventurier des lumières* (Paris: Honoré Champion, 2005), pp. 97–102.

131 See CPA 502 fos 177–9, d'Eon to Broglie, London, 13 July 1773; Morande's correspondence with d'Eon in AN, 277AP/1.

132 CPA 502 fos 177–9, d'Eon to [Broglie], London, 13 July 1773.

133 See CPA 474 fos 286–7, Vergy to Guerchy, 12 August 1767, enclosing the first canto of the *Guerchiade* (fos 288–91).

134 See PRO, SP78/259 fo. 171, Halifax to Guerchy, St James, 21 December 1763; Pierre-Henri Treyssac de Vergy, 'Seconde lettre à Monseigneur le duc de Choiseul' in Charles-Geneviève-Louise-Auguste-André-Timothée d'Eon de Beaumont, *Suite des pièces relatives aux Lettres, mémoires et négociations particulières du Chevalier d'Eon* (London: Dixwell, 1764), pp. 19–62, at pp. 51–5.

135 *Lettre de Mademoiselle Le Bac de Saint-Amant à Monsieur de la M**** (London, 1763), pp. 3–4. This 'letter', which emanated from d'Eon, is dated both 29 and 30 December 1763. A copy is in ULBC, file 58, between pp. 4 and 5. Vergy, 'Seconde lettre à Choiseul', p. 56, mentions his request to Guerchy.

136 A flier published by act of parliament, 4 February 1775, in the ULBC's unique 'extra illustrated' edition of Ernest Alfred Vizetelly, *The True Story of the Chevalier d'Eon*, 2 vols (London: Tylston and Edwards and A. P. Marsden, 1895), which is rebound in seven folio volumes with 900 original documents and prints, reveals (vol. III, p. 160) that Vergy gave his testimony before the Court of King's Bench to John Wilmot and Mr Yates on 12 and 27 November 1764 respectively.

137 CPA 474 fos 286–7, Vergy to Guerchy, 12 August 1767. A further letter dated 19 August (CPA 474 fos 323–4) attempted to create a bidding war by suggesting that d'Eon would pay to publish the manuscript.

138 'Note remise à Guerchy' in d'Eon, *Pièces rélatives*, pp. 21–5, 42.

139 *London Evening Post*, 1–4 October 1774 and 11–14 October 1774. Cuttings in ULBC, file 58 pp. 79, 81.

140 Ibid., 2–4 March 1775. Cutting in ULBC, file 58 p. 91.

141 Ibid., CPA 508 fo. 284, Lenoir to Vergennes, 18 February 1775; fos 323–4, Vergennes to Lenoir, 22 February 1775.

142 For a translation of one such article, in Vergy's hand, dated 13 September 1763, see CPA 451 fo. 238.

143 ULBC, file 22, undated fragment in folder marked 'papiers qui peuvent servir à la vie de Mlle d'Eon, 1805–6'; CPA 474 fos 288–91, *La Guerchiade*, canto 1. Kates, *Monsieur d'Eon*, p. 316, n. 8, assumed that no copies survive because Guerchy suppressed it.

144 CPA 518 fo. 122, Lenoir de La Bussière to [Garnier], London, 16 September 1776.

145 Paul-Philippe Gudin de La Brenellerie, *Histoire de Beaumarchais*, edited by Maurice Tourneux (Paris: Plon, 1888), p. 165.

146 ULBC, file 65 p. 153.

147 Jeanne de La Motte, *Memoirs*, p. 180; Marc de La Motte, *Mémoires inédits*, p. 116.

148 CPA 542 fo. 358, [Receveur], note of 4 June 1783.

149 No pamphlet with this title seems to exist. However, the Bibliothèque nationale holds two copies of the similarly titled *Le Ciel ouvert à tout l'univers, par J. J.* (1782), which Barbier attributes to Dom Louis. A manuscript copy survives in the Bibliothèque municipale at Rouen.

150 On Dom Louis, see Manuel, *Police*, II, 262–3; CPA 542 fo. 358, [Receveur], note of 4 June 1783.

151 Arsenal, MS 12,433 fos 219–313.

152 CPA 515 fos 189–90, Garnier to Vergennes, 18 March 1776; *BCE*, document 20, Beaumarchais to Vergennes, 19 April 1776.

153 CPA 516 fos 422–3, Garnier to Vergennes, 28 June 1776; ULBC, file 65 pp. 164–5, entries for 5 and 6 July 1776.

154 CPA 518 fos 186–7, Garnier to Vergennes, 27 September 1776.

155 *CSB*, II, 40n.; Kates, *Monsieur d'Eon*, p. 220.

156 See CPA 526 fos 408–11, 'Projet d'accord proposé au Sr Tort par la dame de Moriencourt de la part du Sr Salvador', at fo. 410.

157 W. J. Chetwode Crawley, *The Chevalier d'Eon: J. W. of Lodge 376 Grand Lodge of England (Moderns)* (n. pl., n. d.). A copy of this rare pamphlet is in ULBC, Vizetelly, *Story of d'Eon*, extra illustrated edition, vol. VI.

158 CPA 518 fos 267–9, Vignoles to Vergennes, London, 14 October 1776 (copy).

159 *BCE*, document 6, Vergennes to Beaumarchais, 21 June 1775, including n. 6.

160 MO, MS 1422 p. 54.

161 This elective post, whose holder was charged with defending the interests of the community, has no precise English equivalent.

162 Manuel, *Police*, I, 256.

163 Ibid., 259; Arsenal, MS 12,453 fos 41–2.

164 Robert Granderoute, 'Serres de La Tour' in Jean Sgard (ed.), *Dictionnaire de*

journalistes, 1600–1789, 2nd edition, 2 vols (Oxford: Voltaire Foundation, 1999), II, 917–20.

165 Manuel, *Police*, II, 234.

166 CPA 497 fo. 95, Sartine to d'Aiguillon, Paris, 19 July 1771. The elopement was notorious: see *CSCV*, I, 503–4, letter dated 15 September 1782. This letter's assertion that Madame de Bésance became a *marchande des modes* in Edinburgh is clearly inaccurate. She was still living with La Tour in 1788.

167 On the paper's early history see *BCE*, esp. I, 15–103. On its ownership, see Burrows, *French Exile Journalism*, p. 231.

168 AN, 446AP/3, 'Mémoire pour J. -P. Brissot' fo. 28; Brissot, *Mémoires*, II, 160–7.

169 AN, 446AP/1, 'Minute d'une lettre de Brissot' [to La Tour], dated 28 fr [?] [Feb.] 1783; Granderoute, 'Serres de La Tour'.

170 Manuel, *Police*, II, 234. *Courier de l'Europe*, 12 June 1789, advertises his 'Dragées de la Mecque' as a remedy for stomach complaints.

171 Proschwitz, *BCE*, document 473, La Tour to Beaumarchais, London, 15 September 1786, records his recent bankruptcy and hopes that Madame de Bésance would soon receive her parents' legacy. PRO, FO95/631/263B–264, La Tour to Calonne, Walcot Place, 22 July 1788, dates the bankruptcy to 1784 and reveals that La Tour was still awaiting the legacy.

172 See see PRO, C12/1389/27 and chapter four below.

173 *Gentleman's Magazine*, vol. 58:1 (1788), p. 85.

174 Manuel, *Police*, II, 248.

175 AN, 446AP/1, 'Minute d'une lettre de Brissot' [to La Tour], dated 28 fr [?] [February] 1783. MacMahon's identity is clear although he is only named as 'Mac- Irlandais'.

176 AN, 446AP/3, 'Mémoire pour J. -P. Brissot' folio K (inserted between fos 38 and 39).

177 Robiquet, *Théveneau de Morande*, pp. 60–1. Manuel is not explicit on this point.

178 Only sixteen out of 359 (i.e. under 4.5 per cent) of the 'active writers' in France identified by d'Hémery's survey were women. See Darnton, 'Police inspector', p. 154.

179 At least five of the thirty-nine men on Manuel's list of London exiles (i.e. over 12.8 per cent) were former clergymen. See Manuel, *Police*, II, 232–69.

180 Wagner, *Eros Revived*, p. 98.

2

Peddling *libelles*

If the *libellistes* were not the alienated literary hacks of classic 'Grub Street' theory, it is necessary to reassess the operations of the London *libelle* industry and importance of its products. Consequently, this chapter examines the ways and means by which *libelles* were produced, advertised, disseminated, and received, in order to assess the validity of three key assumptions arising from the historical literature. First, late eighteenth-century London has generally been seen as a backwater in the French cosmopolitan print and publishing trades. This view has been reinforced, *inter alia*, by awareness of Linguet's remark that no London printers were familiar with French and his decision to self-publish.[1] Hence French publishing in the period has been ignored by scholars. Second, Darnton's early work implies that the most subversive political pamphleteers, especially writers outside France, operated independently and outside established patronage networks. Finally, the work of Darnton and the pornographic school suggests that subversive political *libelles* sold like hot cakes, particularly scathing attacks on mistresses, favourites, and ministers. Such attacks, they suggest, began the desacralisation of the monarchy under Louis XV and had by 1789 critically undermined the position of Louis XVI's monarchy and particularly Marie-Antoinette. Almost all these assumptions, on closer examination, need considerable revision.

London's French publishing and book trades in the period covered by this book have been neglected by historians for both historical and historiographical reasons.[2] Linguet's remarks have played a part, as doubtless has Darnton's revelation that the third edition of the *Encyclopédie* sold almost as many copies in Dublin as in London.[3] Yet in fact the French book trade was surprisingly extensive, for as one recent article observed, 'for the period [from 1500] up to 1800 . . . French books represent one out of every ninety editions printed in London'.[4] Nevertheless, demand for French books probably stagnated in the mid-eighteenth century, once Britain's *huguenot* exile community had been assimilated. In 1770, Samuel Roulet, an insider to the trade, told the Société typographique de Neuchâtel that in London the 'peu de consommation pour les livres françois, italiens, allemans &c porte obstacle à la vente des livres dont vous cherchés a désposer' ['low level of demand for books in French, Italian, German etc is an obstacle to the sale of the books you wish to dispose of']. Likewise, one minister plenipotentiary, the comte de Moustier, reported that the most successful French works sold at most 500 copies per year in London, and French periodicals found at most 300 subscribers.[5]

Nevertheless, French publishing in London remained significant, partly because many books produced there were popular illegal works for export. Unfortunately, identifying such works is problematic. 'London' was ofen falsely used as a place of publication in clandestine works, and imprint details are sometimes deliberately misleading. Take the case of the *Mémoires secrets*, part of the so-called Mairobert corpus, named after its putative author Mathieu-François Pidansat de Mairobert, which is probably the most influential group of clandestine pamphlets of the period. They appeared as a manuscript newsletter before being published between 1777 and 1787 by 'John Adamson' in London.[6] It is widely believed that John Adamson was a false name, as the only editions published under it belong to the Mairobert corpus or similar genres, and the name is missing from English sources concerning the publishing trade.[7] If this assumption is correct, who did publish the *Mémoires secrets*? If it was produced in London, the most likely candidate is Boissière, the major player in the illegal trade, who certainly dealt in several of Mairobert's works. Although Boissière himself was Genevan, this theory might fit Horace Walpole's assertion that the *Mémoires secrets* were produced in London by 'the excrement of Paris'.[8] This attribution would, however, be mere speculation. The provenance of many less celebrated works is more doubtful still.

Sufficient individuals involved in the French book trade can be identified to suggest an extensive industry. Boissière, who founded his business in St James Street about 1770, and by 1782 was described as the 'principal libraire français de Londres' ['main French bookseller in London'], was one of the most important.[9] According to Goëzman, who was in London as a police agent between 1781 and 1783, Boissière's Société typographique de Saint-James was both a publishing house and a bookshop, but not a printer.[10] Hints of the scale of Boissière's business are found in legal documents from 1783, when Linguet sued him for printing and distributing 'many thousands' of counterfeit copies of his *Mémoires sur la Bastille*. Although Boissière pleaded ignorance and innocence on the printing charge, he admitted receiving 100 copies of Linguet's work in a large consignment of books from the Netherlands.[11] Clearly, Boissière's was a substantial commercial operation.

The *English Short Title Catalogue* gives further indications of the scale of the publishing side of Boissière's business. Between 1772 and 1785, it lists twenty-six editions of seventeen different works carrying his various imprints, which include 'chez Boissière', 'à Londres: chez la Société typographique', 'à Londres, chez M. Boissière à la Société typographique', and, for his earliest known publication, Voltaire's *Le Tocsin des rois* [*The Kings' Alarm Bell*] (1772), the transparently fictitious 'Imprimé à Constantinople: l'an de l'Egire 1168. Se trouve à Londres chez Boissière'

['Printed at Constantinople, year 1168 of the Hegira. Available in London at Boissière's shop']. In addition, Pelleport published his *Petits Soupers* with Boissière in 1782. A further six works list Boissière's Société typographique as a retail outlet. A handful of these editions are probably foreign counterfeit imprints, particularly later editions of Helvétius's materialist bestseller, *De L'Homme* [*Of Man*], the original edition of which was published by Boissière in 1773. However, the majority of works carrying his imprints are doubtless genuine.[12]

For French readers, Boissière's titles often reeked of the exotic, the illegal, or political or religious taboo, including his *Fragment de l'histoire de l'Indostan, avec une rélation de la religion ancienne de ses peuples et des Brahmines* [*Fragment on the History of Hindustan, with an Account of the Former Religion of her Peoples and the Brahmins*]; *Ouvrages politiques et philosophiques d'un anonyme* [*Philosophical and Political Works of an Anonymous Person*]; and Jean-Frédéric Bernard's *Eloge d'Enfer* [*In Praise of Hell*]. In addition, Boissière published some more conventional religious works and critiques of British policy. Clearly he ran a substantial legitimate publishing house specialising in works that could not be published inside France, but sought to supplement his income with suppression fees. His first known client for this side-line, in 1772, was Morande, but they fell out when Morande refused to share his hush-money.[13]

D'Eon's account books reinforce these impressions of Boissière's retail business. His six known purchases from Boissière include three scandalous works, notably *L'Espion anglois* [*The English Spy*] and Mirabeau's *Erotika biblion*. They also include the anti-religious tract *De La Cruauté réligieuse* and more conventional works, including *La Vie et les lettres de Pape Clement* [*Life and Letters of Pope Clement*], and a subscription to Linguet's *Annales*. Between January and August 1787, d'Eon bought books from Boissière on seven occasions, spending over nine guineas on one visit, a figure which suggests that Boissière's stock was substantial and included much more than scandalous or irreligious works.[14] Thus, Goëzman's assertion that Boissière hid his disreputable business behind a respectable façade seems indisputable.[15]

Many other booksellers also sold French works as a specialism or sideline. Despite his pessimistic view of the trade, Roulet identified seven 'principal' dealers in foreign books in London: James Robson in New Bond Street; Thomas Davies in Great Russell Street; Thomas Payne in Castle Street; and in the Strand, Millar, Elmsley, Nource [Jean Nourse], and Becket & de Hondt.[16] In addition, D'Eon purchased books from M. de Lorme of Dover Street, Piccadilly, at whose stock sales in 1773 he bought several volumes, including materialist tracts by Helvetius, La Mettrie, and d'Holbach, Leclerc's *L'Incredulité de la réligion* [*The Unbelievability of Religion*], and two scandalous works, *L'Observateur françois à Londres* and *Lettres de Madame de Pompadour*.[17] Primarily a printer-bookseller, from about 1776 to 1782, Lorme also ran a circulating library.[18] D'Eon also did business with the *huguenot* bookseller Paul Vaillant (c. 1715–1802), a correspondent and agent of Voltaire, who became master of the Stationers' Company and sheriff of London, but apparently retired from the book trade by the mid-1770s.[19] Other dealers' names appear on title pages or in newspaper advertisements. My copy of Mouffle d'Angerville's *Vie privée de Louis XV* [*The Private Life of Louis XV*] was published by John Peter Lyton in 1781. In 1789, the *Courier de Londres* was sold by its publisher, Henry Brookes, stationer, in Coventry Street; Garrett in Panton Street; Shepperson and Reynolds in Oxford Street; and Axtell of Finch Lane, who also traded by the Stock Exchange.[20] Most of these dealers also sold other French works and periodicals. The names of several other booksellers, mostly small-time merchants who operated from boutiques or peddled their wares direct to the British aristocracy, appear in the archives of the Société typographique de Neuchâtel. It was in correspondence with Jean-Baptiste Arnal from 1781 to 1783; Huguenin du Mitand between 1782 and 1784; Edward Lyde in the late 1770s; and James de Winter in 1785. None were long-term clients and most seem to have gone out of business quickly.[21]

The years around 1770 also saw the opening of John Boosey's bookshop and lending library, which specialised in foreign publications. In the 1790s Boosey's business became a significant bookseller-publisher serving the émigré community, before branching into music publishing in about 1813. It survives today as the music publisher and musical instrument supplier Boosey and Hawkes.[22] By 1786, the Swiss bookseller Joseph de Boffe was also established in London. By November 1788 he was trading in Soho at 7 Gerard Street.[23] He, too, grew fat on the émigré book trade, before merging his business with A. B. Dulau and company, the other leading player in the early nineteenth-century French book trade. Their London business survived until 1940, when a German bomb hit its premises. Thereafter, the company traded in Oxford for several years.[24]

In the 1770s and 1780s, a new group of specialised French publishers and printers emerged. Besides Boissière, they included Edward Cox and his heirs at 75 Great Queen Street, who printed the *Courier de l'Europe*,[25] and Thomas Spilsbury, who took over William Strahan's printshop in Snow Hill about 1780. Spilsbury produced many of Calonne's pamphlets, La Tour's *Azile*, Linguet's *Annales* and *Mémoires sur la Bastille*, and some native British pornography.[26] In 1786 de Boffe also entered the publishing trade, and three years later he published La Tour's short-lived *Journal de l'Europe*.[27] In addition, several English printers and publishers dabbled in French books. Elmsley, a substantial player in the London book trade, devoted perhaps 40 per cent of his publishing enterprise to foreign works.[28] Between the late 1750s and mid-1760s, when there were possibly no specialist French publishers in London, Samuel Hooper in the Strand published at least four English editions of Fauques's *History of Pompadour*, while several of d'Eon's works were published by Jacques Dixwell.[29] Both these publishers had wide catalogues of English works. Between about 1761 and

1787, Dixwell was associated with almost 100 editions, while between 1754 and 1793, Hooper produced over 350.[30] The comtesse de La Motte published with the radical Whig publisher James Ridgway and the bookseller-publisher John Bew, whose prolific output between 1774 and 1793 included a handful of French editions.[31]

Not all *libellistes* employed others to publish their works. Several considered it safer to print on their own premises. Linguet installed presses in his London house to print several works.[32] Morande purchased two presses for a secret printshop, probably in his own home, to produce the *Mémoires secrets d'une femme publique*.[33] Yet even clandestine printing presses depended on finding specialist type-setters and printers. The comte de La Motte bought a press, characters, and paper, supposedly with funds advanced by Calonne, and MacMahon procured him workers and a print foreman who spoke good French.[34] La Motte made them swear not to leave his house until his wife's *Mémoires* were complete, but later, fearing they were in Calonne's pay, sacked them and hired new staff.[35] He had grounds for such fears, as French agents suborned print workers on several occasions. In 1753, they smashed a Dutch *libelle* network by infiltrating the publishing houses; in 1777, a print-worker was bribed to procure one of Linguet's pamphlets; and in 1784, a type-setter named Lion provided (false) testimony against Brissot.[36] The habit of clandestine printing died hard. As late as March 1790, the French ambassador, La Luzerne, announced that Calonne was using a secret press in his London house to produce political pamphlets for distribution in France.[37]

In London, the *libellistes* found ready-made support, advice, and social and literary networks in at least three distinct exile *milieux*: the social networks connected with d'Eon; the journalistic *milieu* of the *Courier de l'Europe*; and Boissière's literary and intellectual circle. D'Eon was an important contact for many exiles: his reputation for exploiting British liberty and the press drew budding *libellistes* to him for advice. This also allowed d'Eon to gather intelligence from the exile community, some of which he reported to the French government. Nevertheless, d'Eon kept much back. For example, in the early 1770s, although he initially tried to keep Morande at arm's length, the two men were more intimate than d'Eon admitted in his correspondence with the court, and Morande sent him private bulletins full of scandalous anecdotes and stories.[38] D'Eon visited Morande's home well before Broglie instructed him to do so, and he developed a strong regard for Morande's wife. D'Eon played an ambiguous role when Morande consulted him during negotiations for the suppression of the *Mémoires secrets d'une femme publique*, and lent him books while he researched a subsequent pamphlet.[39] When they were reconciled after a ten-year rift in 1786, they quickly resumed their friendship.[40]

D'Eon's account books show that he was also on familiar terms with several other *libellistes*, including Vignoles, Linsing, Campagnol, Linguet, and possibly MacMahon and La Tour. Indeed, on 28 December 1775 d'Eon

Lenain sc. A.Quantin Imp.Edit.

THEVENEAU DE MORANDE

4 Charles-Claude Théveneau de Morande

threw a banquet for Morande, Campagnol, and Vignoles, which must have witnessed some interesting table-talk: Beaumarchais had bought off three of the diners in the previous two years, and the fourth, Campagnol, was paid off several months later.[41] D'Eon was also a useful contact because of his experience of English law and legal process, and his acquaintances in publishing, politics, and the upper echelons of British society. His contacts included Lord Chief Justice Mansfield and Sir John Fielding, the magistrate charged with policing the metropolis; while his solicitor, Peter Fountain, numbered Louis-Mathieu Bertin, marquis de Fratteaux, the author of a scandalous manuscript, among his previous clients.[42] D'Eon also knew the prince of Wales, with whom he shared a passion for sword-collecting. Moreover, until the early 1790s, he dined regularly with diplomatic staff from London's major embassies.[43]

The *Courier de l'Europe* was a second important means of support. It had a larger staff than most eighteenth-century newspapers, and at various times employed La Tour, Morande, MacMahon, Brissot, and Pelleport. Other exiles were associated with it in a less formal capacity. Swinton paid Morande six guineas per week to edit the paper, and this seems to have remained the editorial salary for ever afterwards. This was a significant income: £200–£300 per annum supported a modest gentleman's lifestyle in London, the world's most expensive city. Sub-editors and proof-readers tended to earn a guinea per week, about twice the income of a skilled artisan, but far less annually than the average *libelle* suppression fee. Thus individuals like MacMahon and Pelleport who obtained a basic income from the *Courier de l'Europe* were likely to have grander aspirations. The paper also offered other money-making opportunities: some of Morande's personal campaigns in the paper doubtless aimed to extort suppression fees or bribes.

The third focal point was the circle of pamphleteers and miscellaneous scoundrels around Boissière. Like many of his associates, Boissière was almost certainly a criminal. Manuel recounts that for seven or eight years Boissière served as a lackey to an adventurer and card-sharp called Matousky. Alexandre Stroev has convincingly identified Matousky as the Russian courtier, privy councillor, and chamberlain Dmitri Mikhaïlovitch Matiouchkine (or Matuchkine) (1725–1800), a 'professional' gambler who travelled extensively in Europe. Matiouchkine left Russia in 1762 and was absent from St Petersburg in 1766 when Casanova visited, but it remains unclear where or when Boissière entered his service.[44] However, Manuel reveals that during a stay in Lübeck, Boissière was accused of theft by 'Matousky' and escaped hanging only because of lack of evidence. Thereafter, Boissière fled to Britain and established his business.[45] Receveur, suspecting his identity, reported that Boissière turned pale when 'Matousky' was mentioned.[46] Boissière held regular meetings of a so-called 'Société littéraire' at his premises.[47] This veritable *salon* for French malcontents was presided over by the geographer de La Rochette, an ally of d'Eon and former French *commissaire des prisonniers*, who turned coat when his pension was cut.[48] Its other members included another turncoat, Goëzman; some of the staff of the *Courier de l'Europe*; and Ange Goudar.[49] They were joined by the abbé Séchamp, a journalist, suspected poisoner, and former chaplain to the duc de Deux-Ponts (Zweibrücken);[50] Joly de Saint-Valier, an author, military officer, and *soi-disant* Burgundian gentleman, who besieged ministers with ridiculous schemes and spied for the British in the Netherlands;[51] and the chevalier Réda, who probably helped finance Pelleport's *Diable dans un bénitier* and, in 1784, played host to Mirabeau, the most celebrated refugee of all.[52] Manuel accused several of these men of collaboration with Boissière and Pelleport, including Séchamp, Réda, Goudar, and Goëzman.[53] Other exiles who intervened in Pelleport's negotiation may also have belonged to Boissière's gang, notably the chevalier Joubert; the duplicitous soldier-of-fortune the Baron de Navan; and the Swiss language teacher Lamblet [*sic*] (presumably the same Lambelet who carried Pelleport's messages in 1792).[54]

Libellistes, Paul Agnani notes, rarely appear in isolation in eighteenth-century sources. Indeed, they congregated in numerous hang-outs in the capital, including the Spring Gardens and Prince of Orange coffee-houses and an illegal gambling den run by Swinton.[55] Nor was d'Eon the only exile to act as a magnet for others. By the 1780s, Morande's home had become a port of call for French visitors to London, including Madame Roland.[56] It was even represented in fiction: the heroine of the patriot novel *Julie philosophe* (1791) called on Morande, only to be seduced, parted from her money, and unceremoniously abandoned.[57] Likewise, the comte de La Motte chose Linguet and later MacMahon as counsellors when he arrived in London,[58] while Brissot went to see La Tour. In 1788, La Tour published a visitor's guide to London, so it is probable that his house in Brompton provided a focal point for some exiles, although Brissot says he was a recluse.[59]

Effective *libellistes* needed sources or connections to provide raw materials for their works and, if they were not suppressed, to facilitate their distribution inside France. Lenoir, who knew more about the *libellistes* than almost anyone, believed that they were 'servi par des relations en France, et à la Cour' ['assisted by contacts inside France and at court'].[60] He was convinced that illegal pamphleteers operated within traditional networks of power and patronage and hence most scandalous political pamphlets were produced by, or for, powerful individuals at court or in the *parlements*.[61] Jeremy Popkin's revealing case study of the Lemaître affair of 1785–86 supports Lenoir's conviction. Pierre-Jacques Lemaître, a prosperous lawyer and venal office-holder, was arrested in December 1785 while trying to smuggle the type-set 'form' for a clandestine pamphlet into Paris. His interrogation revealed that he belonged to a long-established propaganda network, involving powerful members of the *parti Janseniste* and the Paris *Parlement*, which had produced many of the most influential pamphlets against the ministries of Maupeou (1770–74), Necker (1777–81), and Calonne (1783–87). Popkin contends that such propaganda could be published and distributed inside France only by well-connected individuals capable of evading police surveillance. It came from insiders, not outsiders to the establishment. Indeed, Lemaître's associates were so powerful – they included royal ministers and *protégés* of the queen – that the affair was eventually covered up.[62] The clandestine output of more obscure scribblers, including several of the future revolutionaries whom Darnton considers to be Grub Street hacks – Carra, Gorsas, Brissot, and Mirabeau – was likewise written for wealthy patrons including, according to Lenoir, the police and government ministers.[63]

There is little doubt, too, that the earliest rumours, songs, poems, and manuscript pamphlets against Marie-Antoinette originated in court circles, and were usually confined to them. Many were undoubtedly manufactured in the coterie of Provence, who, as heir apparent, had most to lose should the queen produce a son. His malice and resentment were notorious and public. During the baptism of Louis XVI's first child, he even interrupted the officiating grand almoner (Rohan!) with the malign insinuation that 'the ritual prescribes above all that you ask the name and quality of the mother and father of the child'. The Orléanist and Conti branches of the royal family also helped confect and spread scandalous rumours and materials, as did the king's maiden aunts and, according to Vincent Cronin, Louis XVI's youngest brother, the comte d'Artois, despite his public affection for the queen.[64] Frederick the Great also seems to have encouraged underground *nouvellistes* to spread rumours about the queen's behaviour, doubtless in the hope of weakening the Franco-Austrian alliance.[65] Thus, far from being autonomous agents, as Darnton's early publications imply, many individual scandalmongers had close links to powerful interests.

Did such patronage links extend to London-based *libellistes*, as Lenoir believed? Certainly Beaumarchais's correspondence with Lenoir's predecessor, Sartine, promoted the suppression of a series of *libelles* by suggesting that they did. Beaumarchais asserted that Campagnol was 'charged' to publish her *libelle* by correspondents in Paris; the *Guerlichon femelle* was designed to provoke disharmony among the royal family; Vignoles's journal was composed by anti-ministerial figures in Paris; and the madman Linsing was 'une marionette que des fils cachés font mouvoir en France' ['a puppet moved by hidden strings from France'].[66] However, Beaumarchais's testimony was clearly self-serving, and it is not inconceivable that he and his subaltern Morande acted in league with some of the authors whose works he denounced. Moreover, the *libellistes'* willingness to accept suppression fees suggests their loyalty to faction or patrons was limited. Several leading *libellistes*, including d'Eon, Morande, and Pelleport, nevertheless had connections at court, although it is often difficult to prove a patron–client relationship.

The sole *libelliste* whose patrons at court are well documented is d'Eon. His dismissal and descent into blackmail were precipitated by the fall of his protector, Broglie, following which, in his *libelles*, d'Eon launched a furious attack on the rival faction that he blamed publicly for his and Broglie's misfortunes.[67] In contrast, Morande's *Gazetier cuirassé*, written during the Maupeou crisis ministry, appears to show Choiseulist and *parlementaire* sympathies, although it is a deeply ambiguous document. While Morande's only known connection at court was a mysterious Burgundian *grande dame* named Madame de Courcelle – who also had close links to d'Eon – much of his material on Madame du Barry probably came from the Choiseulists.[68] According to Mairobert, the Choiseuls, abetted by Sartine, at that time *lieutenant de police*, were behind most early pamphlets and songs directed against her.[69] Madame de Courcelle and the Choiseulists were probably not Morande's only sources for his biography of du Barry. D'Eon suspected he was assisted by a secretary in the embassy of Spain, the Choiseulists' natural ally, and a government clerk at Versailles. Manuel believed his work was sponsored by court grandees.[70] Perhaps d'Eon himself also provided Morande with materials, wittingly or unwittingly.

Morande also drew on his own experience as a pimp, gambler, *roué*, and confidence trickster in the 1760s for anecdotes for the *Gazetier cuirassé* and material for his blackmail campaigns. In this Morande resembled many other *libellistes*, including Linguet, the La Mottes, Linsing, Vergy, and d'Eon, who embroidered their own stories, presenting real or fictionalised personal experience as parables with which to attack French ministers or personal enemies. Later, Morande acquired other patrons, including Beaumarchais and, it was rumoured, Marie-Antoinette and Louis XVI, who reputedly commissioned him to write *La Vie privée ou apologie du tres-sérénissime prince Monseigneur le duc de Chartres* [*The Private Life or Apology of the Most Serene Prince Monseigneur the Duke of Chartres*], a *libelle* which, as its name suggests, attacked Chartres, who on the death of his father in 1785 became duc d'Orléans.[71] Pelleport's family association with Provence's household is highly suspicious given Provence's links to manuscript *libelles* against Marie-Antoinette. Indeed, Goëzman asserted that Pelleport's threatened *La Naissance du dauphin dévoilée* [*The Dauphin's Birth Unveiled*] was the fruit of a court intrigue.[72] In addition, Pelleport doubtless gleaned insider knowledge working for La Vauguyon at The Hague while Jacquet gained it as a police insider. Given such a plethora of contacts, French ministers and diplomats naturally associated the *libellistes'* activities with intrigues among courtiers or *parlementaires*.

The *libellistes'* publications reached the public by a variety of routes. In London, they were usually distributed openly, often through Boissière's shop, although from early 1783 he became more cautious. Morande made no secret of his authorship of the *Gazetier cuirassé*, which he hawked round London's most fashionable houses at a guinea a time. He reputedly made a profit of 800 guineas from it.[73] Several copies were carried by English travellers to Paris, where they passed furtively from hand to hand. Consequently, the French police resorted to searching travellers to contain the contagion, and the ambassador at The Hague was alerted, lest copies arrive via Dutch channels. Similar measures were used in 1783 to prevent infiltration by Boissière's productions and in 1789 to intercept Madame de La Motte's *Mémoires*.[74]

Book trade channels through the Dutch and Austrian Netherlands were a major route for distribution on the continent. Morande says that when his *Mémoires secrets d'une femme publique* was suppressed, crates full of copies were waiting to be despatched to Michel Rey in Amsterdam, as well as booksellers in Brussels, Rouen, and Paris.[75] British legal documents confirm police suspicions that Boissière's principal outlet for mainland Europe was Pierre

Gosse (Gosse *fils*) in The Hague.[76] Receveur suspected that Pelleport, too, used Gosse, having made his acquaintance during his sojourn in the Netherlands.[77] Although it is unlikely that he collaborated in its production, Brissot also acted as a middleman in the distribution of Pelleport's *Diable dans un bénitier*. Evidence from Brissot's Bastille interrogations, corroborated by apparently authentic documents published by Morande, indicates that he forwarded 100 copies intended for the bookseller Métra in Cologne and 125 to Villebon in Brussels in crates containing his *Journal du Lycée*. On Pelleport's instructions, Brissot's agent Vingtain also sent six copies to the bookseller Lacroix at Bourges.[78] However, although Brissot, Pelleport, and Goëzman were all current or former clients, the Société typographique de Neuchâtel did not receive any London-produced *libelles* direct from London correspondents or Dutch publishing contacts.[79] The editions of the *Diable* and the *Gazetier cuirassé* that they sold were probably counterfeit editions, some of them produced, in all likelihood, at the ducal printworks in Deux-Ponts.[80] Several pirate editions of Madame de La Motte's *Mémoires* also circulated, including one available in the Netherlands within days of the first edition's publication.[81]

Illegal works were smuggled into France in the myriad colourful ways described by Robert Darnton, their pages 'married' (interleaved) with legal works; hidden under false covers and title pages; or sneaked through Swiss mountain passes.[82] It was a risky business, and sometimes whole consignments of books were confiscated, including, supposedly, the entire first edition of Pelleport's *Petits Soupers* in June 1782.[83] Despite the risks involved, individual books and small consignments were sometimes entrusted to the regular post, including, apparently, the six aforementioned copies of the *Diable dans un bénitier* sent to Bourges. Books and pamphlets which reached their destination were either sold under the counter by booksellers or peddled by *colporteurs* [street hawkers], who were often illiterate and unaware of what they sold.[84] The *colporteurs* were prime targets during police crackdowns on illegal books. Between 1774 and 1785 several spent spells in the Bastille, where, Lenoir later lamented, they lived in comparative luxury and saved nest-eggs from their generous daily allowances.[85]

Booksellers and *colporteurs* were both victims and beneficiaries of a system of permits, publishing licences, *tolérations*, and bans so extensive and arcane that even the police were unsure what was legal or illegal. However, everyone agreed that London-produced *libelles* traducing the royal family were among the most toxic of banned books, and large consignments of them ended up under Lenoir's seal in the secret *dépôt* in the Bastille.[86] There were persistent rumours that many *libelles* circulated with the connivance of police officers, who conducted a lucrative trade in confiscated titles siphoned off during police raids. D'Hémery was said to have built up a magnificent library of banned books, which he later sold to the court financier Beaujon for 40,000 *livres*. Brissot alleged that d'Hémery's successor, Pierre-Etienne-Auguste Goupil, who was later himself arrested for producing *libelles*, let him escape arrest in return for a manuscript and some banned books.[87] It is possible that Lenoir set up the Bastille *dépôt* precisely because he feared his officers could not be trusted.

Initial print-runs of London-produced *libelles* often considerably exceeded 1,000 copies, a standard size for an eighteenth-century first edition. At Marylebone in April 1774, the funeral pyre for Morande's *Mémoires secrets d'une femme publique* contained 3,000 sets (6,000 volumes), suggesting that Morande was confident of his market.[88] This level of demand was consistent with that for French editions of Fauques's *Histoire de Pompadour*, three of which were published in 1759. The publishers of the *Guerlichon femelle* expected similar sales: their initial print-run was 1,000, but they threatened to print 2,000 more unless the work was suppressed.[89] According to Goëzman, Boissière, too, anticipated a print-run of 3,000 for the *Naissance du dauphin*.[90] Such numbers exceeded print-runs for many illegal works published clandestinely inside France: when Manuel was arrested for peddling a collection of tracts on the diamond necklace affair in 1786, police searches revealed that its printers had produced 1,500 copies.[91] However, not everyone was so ambitious. According to Brissot, Pelleport's original print-run for the *Diable dans un bénitier* was a modest 500.[92] In contrast, the comtesse de La Motte aspired to greater sales. In 1789, she produced 5,000 copies of the French edition of her *Mémoires* and 3,000 of the English version.[93] Two years later, she printed 4,000 copies of a single-volume edition of her revised autobiography destined for export to Paris, while two-volume editions in French and English destined for Britain would each run to a further 1,000 copies.[94] However, sexually scandalous works such as La Motte's *Mémoires* were probably not the best-selling genre of illegal material. D'Eon had an avid audience for his *Lettres, mémoires et négociations*. In a letter written a month after the work's publication, d'Eon claims he had sold 600 copies in the previous ten days, although his assertion that total sales reached 36,000 copies is doubtless an exaggeration.[95] Yet even if he had trebled the actual figure, d'Eon's work probably outsold any of the London *libellistes*' sexual-political works.

The *libellistes*' works were sufficiently lucrative that publishers and speculators were often willing to advance money against future sales. In 1790 and early 1791, Madame de La Motte lived on about £170 borrowed from her bookseller, Bew, but the cost of producing her *Life*, including living expenses, was over £1,000. In addition, she owed around £120 to a perfumier called Warren, who had been in league with the La Mottes for several years and contributed to her upkeep.[96] Warren pressed her to distribute her work and ignore efforts by royalist agents to suppress it.[97] Since the French edition was worth five shillings and British editions were priced at fourteen shillings, her backers hoped to recoup a healthy £2,400 from their investment.[98] Boissière, too, advanced funds to authors, including Morande. Still, some print-runs may have been overly optimistic. In May 1789, the Bond Street hatter Coup, business partner and creditor of the La Mottes, seized and sold their property after an altercation. Among the goods he auctioned were 600 copies of the comtesse's *Mémoires*, published four months earlier, which, Morande asserted, would scarcely fetch their value as pulp.[99] Nevertheless, the *Mémoires* ran to at least five editions, including pirate printings produced in Dublin and the Netherlands, and were translated into German. The comtesse's 1791 *Life* was reprinted in Dublin and Paris. Demand was also buoyant for Morande's *Gazetier cuirassé*, which was republished in 1772, 1777, and 1785, mainly in pirated editions, complete with inferior copies of the famous frontispiece (see plate 9), and Fauques's *Histoire de Pompadour*, which ran to at least eleven editions in three different languages.[100]

These figures might appear proof of the 'pornographic school's' assertions that the London blackmail industry was pumping highly subversive political pornography into France. However, on closer examination it becomes clear that this was not the case. The blackmail works which were actually published by the London's *libellistes* before the revolution tended to deal with political affairs, such as d'Eon's *Lettres, mémoires et négociations* or Pelleport's *Diable dans un bénitier*, which was reported circulating in its hundreds among *le monde* [high society] even before it was pirated.[101] Those scandalous texts that did discuss the sexual lives of important figures either concentrated on aristocrats and minor royalty, like Pelleport's *Petits Soupers*, or focused on the dead king, Louis XV, and his mistresses, rather than Louis XVI and his wife. This pattern supports Vivian Gruder's contention that the 'pornographic school' has significantly exaggerated the circulation and importance of prerevolutionary attacks on the queen.[102]

In fact, a combination of suppressions and arrests prevented the widespread circulation of printed pornographic attacks against Marie-Antoinette until the very eve of the revolution. Chapter five presents evidence that few, if any, copies of prerevolutionary *libelles* against the queen escaped government agents and that several infamous *libelles* were almost certainly never published. Thus the first scandalous *libelle* against Marie-Antoinette to have a wide circulation was Madame de La Motte's *Mémoires*, which was published on the eve of the revolution and had an impressive circulation, probably totaling well over 10,000 when pirate editions are taken into account.[103]

Despite the scale of sales of those *libelles* and scandalous texts which did appear, it is important not to exaggerate their place in late eighteenth-century French print culture. Indeed, the most sensational best-seller of the early 1780s was not a scandalous work but essentially an accountant's report on the state of French finances, Necker's celebrated *Compte rendu*, which ran to at least seventeen editions and sold an estimated 40,000–100,000 copies.[104] A decade later, in April 1790, a further set of accounts, the notorious *Livre rouge* [Red Book], which chronicled the king's secret expenditure, allegedly sold over 2,000 copies within hours of going on sale.[105] In early 1789, even sales of La Motte's *Mémoires* failed to match the hottest political pamphlets of the day, especially the abbé Siéyès's *Qu'est-ce que le tiers état* [*What is the Third Estate?*] and the comte d'Antraigues's *Mémoires sur les États-généraux, leurs droits et la manière de les convoquer* [*Memoirs on the Estates-General, their Rights, and how they should be Convened*], whose sales outstripped them several times over. Moreover, the prerevolutionary crisis and *de facto* collapse of state censorship apparatus precipitated an explosion of print. An estimated 1,500 to 2,200 pamphlets appeared between the beginning of 1787 and end of January 1789.[106] This was a massive increase on the previous period: the Bibliothèque nationale's vast, if not comprehensive, *Catalogue de l'histoire de France* lists 312 pamphlets for the entire period 1774–86; 217 from 1787; 819 from 1788, and 3,305 from 1789. In all, the catalogue lists over 12,000 titles for the years 1789–99.[107] By contrast, the entire corpus of clandestine literature from 1769–89 identifiable through Darnton's extensive sampling of police, customs, and publishing trade sources comprises just 720 illegal titles across all genres. His analysis of the 457 works which feature in his extensive sampling of the book orders received by the Société typographique de Neuchâtel, if representative of the whole illegal sector, suggests that only a quarter of the clandestine trade in this period comprised topical political works, 'libels and court satires', or *chroniques scandaleuses*.[108] Hardly any of this material attacked Louis XVI or his queen. Moreover, even the publication of the comtesse de La Motte's *Mémoires* did not open the floodgates to other scandalous *libelles* against the queen immediately: other pamphlets in the genre probably only appeared after the fall of the Bastille. They represent a very small part of the total output of revolutionary pamphlets.

Several inferences follow from these observations. First, the French government's policy of containment worked. Attacks on the queen, smutty or otherwise, were almost literally unobtainable before 1789. Second, before the revolution, there was little demand for anti-Marie-Antoinette pamphlets, even among vendors of illegal literature. Few buyers existed, the genre was not profitable, and publishers preferred to sell their product to the French government, often for relatively modest prices. Moreover, after 1783, when the court stopped paying suppression fees, several *libelles* with which they had been threatened never eventuated, and they enjoyed almost four blackmail-free years. This quiet period ended only when the de La Mottes appeared on the scene. Third, the comtesse de La Motte's *Mémoires*, the first sexually salacious pamphlet against the queen to reach a large public, set the main precedent for the genre, in combination with suppressed works liberated from the Bastille's secret *dépôt*. In the revolutionary turmoil, however, a heady brew of politics, salacious interest, and suspicions caused by the sudden availability of forbidden works created a more receptive climate for anti-Marie-Antoinette materials. Nevertheless, even the most popular anti-Marie-Antoinette pamphlets were certainly not the best-selling political works of the era.

In contrast to the anti-Marie-Antoinette pamphlets, material aimed against Louis XV and Madame du Barry ranks prominently in Darnton's statistics of the Société typographique de Neuchâtel's book trade between 1769 and 1789. Between them, orders for the three best-selling attacks on the king total around 800, and the three leading works against his favourite about 1,300. Together they account for some 7.5 per cent of his sample of the Société's clandestine trade. However, despite a few pithy blue passages in Morande's *Gazetier cuirassé*, which circulated in Louis XV's lifetime, the significant attacks on both king and his mistress were published after his death in May 1774. This has hitherto been overlooked by historians for three reasons. First, Darnton published several of the most piquant extracts from the *Gazetier* in his famous article 'The high enlightenment and the low-life of literature'. Second, two other biographies of the favourite from Louis's lifetime are discussed in Mairobert's *Anecdotes sur Madame la comtesse du Barry*. However, one of these appears to be misdated, and was actually published after Louis XV's death: the other is Morande's *Mémoires secrets d'une femme publique*, which was suppressed.[109] Thirdly, although Mairobert's *Anecdotes* appeared only in 1775, it is usually associated with the large volume of 'Maupeouiana' he published in 1771–74. Thus major anti-du Barry pamphlets circulated widely only after her fall. The same pattern appears to apply, to a lesser extent, to Madame de Pompadour. The one notable exception is Fauques's scandalous life, which the Goncourt brothers described as 'la seule histoire véritable de Pompadour, écrite de son vivant' ['The only genuine history of Pompadour written in her lifetime'].[110] Tellingly, French editions of this work are considerably rarer than English and German ones, suggesting that the main demand came from outside France. Moreover, by the time Fauques's work appeared, the king's sexual relationship with Pompadour was over and hence she appeared vulnerable. As for Louis XV, he appeared in a handful of *romans à clef* from the middle of his reign, most notably *Les Amours de Zeokinizul, roi des kofirans*, which is sometimes attributed to Crébillon, *fils*, and was published in 1745. However, since they described the identities of persons, places, and institutions with anagrams, analogies, and codes, they were all but impervious, even to the initiated, who debated their meaning at length.[111] Serious, transparent, popularly accessible critiques had to await the king's death.

It thus appears that even Gruder's radical revaluation of late eighteenth-century French 'political pornography' does not go far enough. While a particular regime maintained a firm grip on power, deeply ingrained habits of respect or fear, together with effective policing, combined to prevent the circulation of written sexual *libelles* beyond a tiny court-based elite. Scandalmongering *libelles* should not therefore be seen as political weapons against a regime at the height of its power. Instead, following the death of a king, the demise of a mistress, or the eclipse of the absolute monarchy, libellous works about them proliferated and probably served three functions. They were parables about the abuses of power; weapons to prevent the resurgence of the eclipsed regime's practices and personnel, or, in the case of the Marie-Antoinette *libelles*, to destroy them totally; and a means of conferring legitimacy on the new regime, by making an implicit contrast with that which had preceded it. The primary function of scandalmongering pamphlets and political pornography has thus been misread. Far from sapping support from an existing regime, they consecrated the demise of a collapsed power and provided buttressing and a moral compass for its successor.

The fragmentary evidence concerning audience reception of the London *libellistes'* works before the revolution offers tentative support to many of these conclusions. Naturally such evidence is problematic, both because reader response is a highly controversial and little-understood area, and because much of the evidence comes from semi-official, elite, published, or partisan sources. Nevertheless, the existing material is consistent enough to suggest a few generalisations. The *Encyclopédie's* article on *libelles*, penned by Louis de Jaucourt, although it makes the case for greater press freedom, is representative of a standard view that *libelles* attacking the probity, reputation, or honour of individuals 'méritent l'opprobrium des sages' ['deserve the opprobrium of the wise'].[112] Such views were echoed by Madame Hervé in her scathing and dismissive assessment of Fauques's *Histoire de Pompadour*:

> Elle a confondû mille sottes histoires qu'elle a entendû à Paris parmi le peuple et son invention a supplée a ce quelle croyoit qui y manquoit. Enfin il n'y a de plus méchante que cette femme et son livre, et quoique le titre l'a donné du cours d'abord, tout le monde l'a trouvé exécrable et on ne le lit plus. [She has mixed together a thousand stupid tales that she has heard among the people of Paris and her imagination has supplied whatever she believed to be lacking. Thus there is nothing more wicked than this woman and her book, and although the title helped to sell it at first, everyone found it execrable and it is no longer read.][113]

Similar sentiments are also expressed by Voltaire, who described Morande's *Gazetier cuirassé* in 1772 as:

> un de ces ouvrages de ténèbres, où, depuis le monarque jusqu'au dernier citoyen, tout le monde est insulté avec fureur, où la calomnie la plus atroce et la plus absurde distille un poison affreux sur tout ce qu'on respecte et qu'on aime. [one of those works of darkness, where, from the monarch to the last citizen, everyone is insulted with fury, where the most atrocious and absurd calumny distils a frightful poison over all which is respected and loved.]

Such works, he contended, were doubly offensive because they provoked official hostility to all books.[114] D'Eon, too, argued that the *Gazetier* should be understood first and foremost as a work of insult, and to emphasise the point produced a bilingual alphabetical index of 256 names of 'Princes, princesses, lords, ladies and others . . . insulted and abused in [the] *Gazetier cuirassé*'.[115] The *Mémoires secrets*, in contrast, praised the freshness of Morande's anecdotes, while describing it as 'très informe et fort méchante' ['well-informed and very wicked'].[116] Métra's underground *Correspondance secrète*, written primarily for circulation outside France, described the *Gazetier* as 'sale et monstrueux' ['sordid and monstrous'], but this description is juxtaposed against a puff praising the tone and alleged veracity of Mairobert's sensational, scandalous, and best-selling *Anecdotes sur Madame du Barry*.[117]

The comments of Métra and the *Mémoires secrets* imply that perceived credibility was a key factor in the reception of *libelles*. Likewise, Morande attributed the success of Madame de La Motte's *Mémoires* to public credulity. He claimed to find the demand for her work unbelievable, especially from French travellers. On reading La Motte's account of an amorous affair between the queen and Rohan, and the fabricated love-letters that accompanied it, even *gens du monde* [members of high society] were credulously remarking that they contained nothing to prove them false.[118] Edmund Burke was convinced that the *Mémoires* had greatly harmed the queen's reputation, and his celebrated passage on Marie-Antoinette in the *Reflections* was probably intended as a response to the comtesse's libels.[119] His concern may have been justified. If the anonymous author of a manuscript newsletter published by M. de Lescure is representative, the judgement of normally judicious contemporaries was eventually polluted by a corrosive tidal wave of revolutionary mudslinging. Lescure's *nouvelliste* is perspicacious in his judgement of the diamond necklace affair and in February 1789 considered La Motte's *Mémoires* 'un horrible *libelle* contre une personne auguste qui a les plus grands droits à notre amour et notre vénération' ['a horrible libel on an august person who has the greatest right to our love and veneration'].[120] However, by 1792 the scandalmongers' poisons had taken their toll, and he readily accepted many of their allegations. When the princesse de Lamballe was butchered and dismembered, he recalled that, on arrival at Versailles, she was 'instruite d'un libertinage honteux' ['instructed in a shameful libertinism'] and regretted that she would not be able to testify during the queen's judicial examination.[121] However, this response was the product of three years of revolutionary turmoil, scandalmongering, and rumours of court conspiracies.

Before the revolution, audiences responded in a very different way to scandalous attacks on the monarchy. The general pattern was disgust mixed with interest in those passages which might just be true or provide piquant anecdotes. This position is reflected in Voltaire's comments on Fauques's *Histoire de Pompadour*: 'La moitié de l'ouvrage est un tissu de calomnies, mais ce qu'il y a de vrai fera passer ce qu'il y a de faux à la posterité' ['Half the work is a tissue of calumnies, but the truth it contains will ensure that the falsehoods pass to posterity'].[122] The same attitude is seen in a review of Pelleport's *Diable dans un bénitier* in the *Correspondance secrète*, which hastened to condemn pornographic *libelles* against the queen, while hinting at their salacious interest. It suggested that Pelleport's account of police missions to suppress *libelles* against Marie-Antoinette:

passe trop rapidement sur ces pamphlets abominables . . . qui ne doivent le jour qu'au souffle empoisonné de l'infernale envie contre une princesse dont les graces, l'esprit et les qualités du coeur doivent la faire chérir de toute la nation dont elle est la souveraine. [passes too rapidly over those abominable pamphlets . . . which owe their existence only to the poisonous murmurs of infernal envy against a princess whose graces, and qualities of heart and mind ought to make her dear to the whole nation of which she is queen].[123]

At the same time the reviewer approved of the political aspect of Pelleport's work, describing it as one of those:

ouvrages piquans qui dévoilent les tyrannies, les injustices et les persécutions qu'exercent le chef et les subalternes de l'inquisition françoise, contre ceux qui osent élever la voix pour se plaindre des intrigues de quelques gens en place et de leur despotisme. [piquant works which unmask the tyrannies, injustices and persecutions practised by the chief and subalterns of the French inquisition against those who dare to raise their voices to complain against the intrigues of a handful of men in place and their despotism.][124]

Finally, the reviewer also approved of the work's literary qualities, finding that its satire offered 'des tableaux dont le coloris fait plaisir' ['scenes whose colouring gives pleasure'].[125]

All three assumptions listed at the opening of this chapter thus appear invalid. London's French book trade and publishing industry have proved far more extensive and dynamic in our period than was previously supposed. This industry had strong links to the continent, especially through several of the larger Dutch French-language publishing houses. Similarly, enough *libellistes* seem to have had informants and patrons in high places to call into question Darnton's depiction of them as autonomous individuals. Nevertheless, such patronage links remain hazy and were, necessarily, ambiguous. Finally, contrary to expectations aroused by Darnton and his followers, there is overwhelming evidence that before the revolution – and especially under Louis XVI – sexually salacious pamphlet attacks on a ruling monarch or his consort were published rarely, aroused widespread disgust, and did not enjoy a popular market. A pornographic interpretation of the revolution's origins is thus unsustainable, although some evidence suggests that political pornography played a subordinate role in the revolution's progress.

Nevertheless, other sorts of scandalous material, attacking lesser individuals, did circulate before 1789, as well as salacious *chroniques scandaleuses* concerning the delinquencies and peccadilloes of previous ministries, monarchs, and mistresses. These appear to have been parables about abuse of power, a means of legitimising the current regime, and weapons in intra-elite power struggles. Thus scandalous *libelles* need to be interpreted within traditional frameworks as denunciations of scandal and Biblical-style warnings of the consequences of corruption in high places. However, until the revolution began to demolish absolute authority, few writers envisaged attacking that fount of all power, the Bourbon monarchy. Yet at the same time, *libelles* containing denunciations of abuses or the arbitrary actions of ministers found an increasingly receptive audience among at least some sections of the public. These texts, as chapters six and seven reveal, played important and ambiguous roles in shaping political attitudes in both France and Britain.

Notes

1 Eisenstein, *Grub Street Abroad*, p. 39. However, Eisenstein points to Robiquet's *Théveneau de Morande* as evidence that Linguet's assertion is questionable.

2 The standard reference work, Ian Maxted, *The London Book Trades, 1775–1800: A Preliminary Checklist of Members* (Woking: Dawson, 1977), is silent, while David J. Shaw, 'French émigrés in the London book trade to 1850' in Robin Myers, Michael Harris, and Giles Mandelbrote (eds), *The London Book Trade: Topographies of Print in the Metropolis from the Sixteenth Century* (London: British Library, 2003), 127–43, has nothing on our period. The *BBTI*, which covers 'people working in printing, bookselling and other book-related trades in England and Wales to 1851', currently contains some of the people mentioned here.

3 BPUN, MS 1212 fos 30–1, Roulet to STN, London, 27 February 1770; Robert Darnton, *The Business of Enlightenment: A Publishing History of the Encyclopédie* (Cambridge, MA: Harvard University Press, 1979), p. 309. However, Darnton expresses some caveats. On the French book trade in Ireland see Máire Kennedy, *French Books in Eighteenth-Century Ireland*, SVEC 2001:7 (Oxford: Voltaire Foundation, 2001).

4 David J. Shaw, 'French-language publishing in London to 1900', in Barry Taylor (ed.), *Foreign Language Printing in London 1500–1900* (Boston Spa and London: British Library, 2002), 101–22, at p. 101.

5 CPA 542 fos 37–42, Moustier, 'Moyens simples et efficaces pour prévenir la recedive d'attentats semblables à celui de Boissière'. Morande apparently prepared this document. The figures appear to be underestimates: in November 1778 the *Courier de l'Europe*'s British edition was printing 700 copies. See also Burrows, *French Exile Journalism*, pp. 80–1.

6 On the Mairobert corpus see Jeremy D. Popkin and Bernadette Fort (eds), *The Mémoires secrets and the Culture of Publicity in Pre-Revolutionary France* (Oxford: Voltaire Foundation, 1998). Although it is seen as part of the Mairobert corpus, the history of the authorship of the *Mémoires secrets* is obscure and complex. The main editorial role probably passed from Louis Petit de Bachaumont (to whom the work is usually attributed in catalogues and bibliographies) to Mairobert and finally to B.-F.-J. Mouffle d'Angerville.

7 Jeremy D. Popkin, 'The *Mémoires secrets* and the reading of the enlightenment' in Popkin and Fort (eds), *The Mémoires secrets*, pp. 17, 21.

8 Walpole to William Mason, 4 August 1777 in Horace Walpole, *Correspondence*, edited by W. S. Lewis, 48 vols (New Haven, CT: Yale University Press, 1937–83), XXVIII, 323–6. Quote at p. 324. Another manuscript newsletter printed by 'John Adamson', CSP, V, 142, claims (30 August 1777) that the *Mémoires secrets* were printed in Holland.

9 BPUN, MS 1114, Arnal to STN, London, 5 February 1782. Boissière does not appear on Roulet's list of French booksellers in 1770, but was involved with Morande by 1772.

10 CPA 541 fos 346–9, Goëzman to Vergennes, London, 4 April 1783.

11 PRO, C12/2002/26.

12 The *ESTC* lists an anonymous *Satire sur les prétendus magistrats* from 1789 and a 1792 edition of Helvétius, *De L'Homme*, both carrying Boissière's imprints, as do five earlier editions of *De L'Homme*. As other evidence of Boissière's business disappears after 1787, subsequent imprints may be false. His name does not appear in émigré sources.

13 CPA 541 fos 346–9, Goëzman to Vergennes, London, 4 April 1783.

14 On d'Eon's business with Boissière, see ULBC, file 65 pp. 174, 177, 179, 184, 187, 341, 343–7. Their final transaction was on 28 May 1787. CPA 541 fos 346–9, Goëzman to Vergennes, London 4 April 1783, reveals that Boissière also stocked *L'Aretin* and [Voltaire's] *La Pucelle* [*d'Orléans*].

15 See CPA 542 fos 177–8, Goëzman to Vergennes, London, 2 May 1783.

16 BPUN, MS 1212 fos 30–1, Samuel Roulet to STN, London, 27 February 1770. The *BBTI* reveals that Thomas Becket and Peter Abraham de Hondt were trading by 1760 and were partners by 1767; de Hondt went bankrupt in 1776, but the business still existed in 1815. James Robson (1733–1806) was in the publishing and bookselling trades from 1759 until his death; Thomas Payne and his son, heir, and namesake traded from 1739 at least until 1806. Peter Elmsley, who published Gibbon's *Decline and Fall of the Roman Empire*, traded from the late 1760s until 1802. Goulemot, *Forbidden Texts*, pp. 86, 103, reveals that Nourse published pornographic novels.

17 ULBC, file 65 pp. 102–4.

18 *BBTI*.

19 Paul Vaillant to Escalier, in ULBC, Vizetelly, *Story of d'Eon*, extra illustrated edition, VII, fo. 1; Sainte-Foy to d'Eon, Versailles, 19 June 1763, in d'Eon, *Lettres, mémoires et négociations*, p. 317; Walpole to Mann, Strawberry Hill, 7 May 1760, in Walpole, *Correspondence*, XXI, 394–404; Voltaire, *Correspondence*, edited by Theodore Besterman, 107 vols (Geneva: Institut et musée Voltaire, 1953–65), vols LII–LIV, documents 10,434, 10,729, 10,782, 10,844, 10,856, 10,871; CPA 525 fo. 316, Lenoir to Amelot, 7 November 1777. *BBTI* entries claim that Vaillant inherited the business from his uncle Isaac (died 1753) and left it to his son Paul. However, the dates given for the two Paul Vaillants imply that they are the same person. On the Vaillant family see also Shaw, 'French émigrés in the London book trade', pp. 134–5.

20 Brookes, Axtell, Garrett, and Shepperson and Reynolds all appear in the *BBTI*.

21 BPUN, MSS 1114, 1168, 1176, and 1230. Lyde, who traded in and around the Strand between 1772 and 1781, was the largest of these dealers, ordering over 1,500 books between March 1778 and October 1779. On Lyde see also the *BBTI*.

22 For a brief outline history, see Jeremy Boosey and Ernst Roth, *Boosey and Hawkes 150th Anniversary* (London: Boosey and Hawkes, 1966). I thank Paula Rainsborough of Boosey and Hawkes for supplying a copy.

23 ULBC, file 65 pp. 353–4, records that d'Eon bought books from him in February and November 1788. One imprint (from three) from 1786 in the *ESTC* gives his address as 10 Princes Street.

24 Margery Weiner, *The French Exiles, 1789–1815* (London: John Murray, 1960), p. 114; Shaw, 'French émigrés in the London book trade', pp. 138–41. On Boosey, de Boffe, and Dulau see also Burrows, *French Exile Journalism*, pp. 61–2, 66–8.

25 Ibid., pp. 66, 233.

26 Apart from a leaflet from 1772, presumably printed on a hired press, Spilsbury's earliest extant publication dates from 1780; on his death, in 1795, Spilsbury's business passed to his heir Charles Spilsbury and operated until the Napoleonic period. Spilsbury's pornographic output includes Richard Knight's *An Account of the Remains of the Worship of Priapus*. I thank Jenny Skipp for this reference. See also Julie Peakman, *Mighty Lewd Books: The Development of Pornography in Eighteenth-Century Britain* (London: Palgrave Macmillan, 2003).

27 Burrows, *French Exile Journalism*, p. 66.

28 Of forty editions bearing Elmsley's name in the BL catalogue, thirteen are French-language works. Two others are in Latin and one in Spanish.

29 Bills from Dixwell dated 13 March 1764 and 8 June 1769, preserved in ULBC, Vizetelly, *Story of d'Eon*, extra illustrated edition, VII, fos 1 and 3, show that d'Eon paid Dixwell to print a *Lettre de Mlle le Bac de Saint-Amant* in 1763 and 1,000 prospectuses for an unspecified work by Vergy in 1764.

30 Figures and dates are from imprint and keyword searches of the *ESTC*. The *BBTI* reveals that Dixwell was apprenticed in 1744 and died in 1788.

31 The *BBTI* reveals that Bew went bankrupt in 1790 and died in 1793.

32 Levy, *Linguet*, p. 178.

33 CPA 502 fos 182–3, d'Eon to Broglie, London, 15 July 1773. D'Eon's account of seeing printed pages on every floor of Morande's house (CPA 504 fos 20–1), implies that they were printed and assembled there. CPA 516 fos 219–28, d'Eon to Vergennes, 27 May 1776, says that Morande also printed an annotated edition of Beaumarchais's judicial *Mémoires* (against Goëzman) in his 'secret printshop', and was storing it at a secret location prior to distribution in France.

34 Marc de La Motte, *Mémoires inédits*, pp. 135–6. CPA 569 fos 225–6, Morande to Montmorin, 11 May 1789, instead asserts that the press and printers were funded by the La Motte's business partner, Coup.

35 Marc de La Motte, *Mémoires inédits*, p. 144.

36 Geneviève Aclocque, *Un Épisode de la presse clandestine au temps de Madame de Pompadour* (privately printed: Impressions du Carré, 1963); CPA 524 fo. 335, abbé Bassinet to Vergennes, 18 August 1777; AN, 446AP/2, 'Interrogatoire de Brissot de Warville à la Bastille', 3 August 1784, fo. 1; 'Deuxième interrogatoire du Sr Brissot de Warville', 21 August 1784, fos 6–7.

37 CPA 572 fos 307–11, La Luzerne to Montmorin, London, 23 March 1790.

38 See Morande's correspondence with d'Eon in AN, 277AP/1. Agnani, 'Libelles et diplomatie', p. 126, suggests that d'Eon was the 'Mentor' addressed by Morande in the dedicatory epistle to the second part of the *Gazetier cuirassé*.

39 See d'Eon's correspondence with Broglie and Morande's letters to d'Eon in CPA 502–3, esp. CPA 502 fos 177–9, d'Eon to Broglie, London 13 July 1773; fos 182–3, d'Eon to Broglie, London, 15 July 1773; CPA 503 fos 308–10, Morande to d'Eon, undated letter, received 21 December 1773 (copy). Note also the tone of Morande's letters in AN, 277AP/1.

40 Private archive, Morande–Beaumarchais correspondence fos 252–3, Morande to Beaumarchais, 14 March 1786. D'Eon's account books (ULBC, files 55 and 65) record several social and business interactions between 1787 and 1791.

41 ULBC, file 65 pp. 153, 164–5, 170, 343.

42 On Fountain see ULBC, file 65 p. 117; comte d'H***, *Histoire de Mr. Bertin, marquis de Fratteaux* (Paris: aux depens de l'auteur, 1753), pp. 86, 108, 141, 202. On d'Eon and Mansfield (who secretly disliked him) see Kates, *Monsieur d'Eon*, pp. 23, 247. ULBC, file 65 pp. 116, 117, 120, indicates that Fielding and d'Eon socialised several times in 1774. Fratteaux's activities and fate are discussed below, chapter three.

43 See ULBC, files 55 and 65 *passim*.

44 Alexandre Stroev, private communication (to Simon Davies), 14 February 2004. I thank the recipient and its author for this document and permission to cite it.

45 Manuel, *Police*, II, 237.

46 CPA 541 fos 309–10, Moustier to Vergennes, 31 March 1783.

47 CPA 542 fos 10–13, Moustier to Vergennes, London, 11 April 1783, at fo. 11.

48 Manuel, *Police*, II, 245–7.

49 Ibid., 236.

50 Ibid., 244–5.

51 Ibid., 238–9; Boissière published two works by Joly de Saint Valier: *Mémoire du Sieur Joly de Saint-Valier* (1780) and *Exposé ou examen des operations des ministres en Angleterre* (1781). Both ran to two editions.

52 Manuel, *Police*, II, 236; AN, 446AP/2 fos 6–7 'Deuxième interrogatoire du Sr Brissot'; [René Nicolas Dufriche Desgenettes], *Souvenirs de la fin du XVIIIe siècle et du commencement du XIXe siècle, ou mémoires de R. D. G.*, 2 vols (Paris: Firmin-Didot, 1835), I, 125.

53 Manuel, *Police*, II, 236, 244–5, and *passim*.

54 Ibid., 255–6, 266–7. On Lambelet see chapter one above.

55 See Agnani, 'Libelles et diplomatie', pp. 45–6, 170; Hauc, *Ange Goudar*, pp. 89, 92, 166; Pelleport, *Diable*, p. 145; *Westminster Gazette*, 31 August–3 September 1776, cutting in Add. MS 11,340 fo. 17.

56 See, for example, Jeanne-Marie Phlipon Roland, *The Works of Jeanne-Marie Phlipon Roland*, edited by L. A. Champagneux (London: J. Johnson, 1800), p. 218.

57 André-Robert Andrea de Nerciat (attrib.), *Julie philosophe, ou le bon patriote*, 2 vols (Paris: Le Coffret des Bibliophiles, 1910 [original edition, 1791]), II, 6–11.

58 Jeanne de La Motte, *Memoirs*, pp. 157–8 and *Life*, II, 204–20.

59 Brissot, *Mémoires*, II, 160–7.

60 CPA 541 fos 280–1, Lenoir to Vergennes, 27 March 1783.

61 See Simon Burrows, 'Police and political pamphleteering in pre-revolutionary France: the testimony of J. -P. Lenoir, lieutenant-général of police of Paris' in David J. Adams and Adrian Armstrong (eds), *Print and power in France and England, 1500–1800* (Aldershot: Ashgate, 2006).

62 Popkin, 'Pamphlet journalism'.

63 Burrows, 'Police and pamphleteering'.

64 D'Almeras, *Marie-Antoinette et les pamphlets*, pp. 45–6, 188–91 223, 236–40, quote at p. 238; Vincent Cronin, *Louis and Antoinette* (London: Collins, 1974), pp. 197, 402–5. *CSMT*, III, 458–9, suggests that in 1780 d'Artois was in

correspondence with *nouvellistes* who denigrated the queen and falsely attributed anti-French sentiments to the emperor's coterie.

65 Ibid., III, 14–15, 16–17, 21.

66 Beaumarchais to Louis XVI, 27 April (extrait) and 15 December 1775; Beaumarchais to Sartine, London, 14 October 1776, in Jacques Donvez, *La Politique de Beaumarchais* (Leiden: IDC, 1980), pp. 411–15, 415–19, 422–5.

67 See below, chapter three.

68 CPA 502 fos 177–9, d'Eon to [de Broglie], London, 13 July 1773. This document reveals that Monsieur and Madame Courcelle were in London while Morande wrote the *Gazetier cuirassé*, but by 1773 were living in the Faubourg St Germain. BMT, d'Eon manuscripts J62–3 and J154–67, suggest that the Courcelles served as intermediaries between d'Eon and Versailles. On d'Eon and the Courcelles, see also ULBC, file 65, 82–6. ULBC, Vizetelly, *Story of d'Eon*, extra illustrated edition, V, fo. 273 reveals that Monsieur Courcelle probably befriended d'Eon while in London on parole as a prisoner of war.

69 Mathieu-François Pidansat de Mairobert (attrib.), *Anecdotes sur Madame la comtesse du Barry* (London: n. p., 1775), pp. 158–61.

70 CPA 502 fos 182–3, d'Eon to Broglie, London, 15 July 1773; Manuel, *Police*, II, 251. On Morande's political contacts see also Agnani, 'Libelles et diplomatie', p. 77.

71 See Robiquet, *Théveneau de Morande*, pp. 211–12; Marcellin Pellet, *Variétés révolutionnaires* (Paris: Félix-Alcan, 1885), ch. 3, 'Théveneau de Morande', p. 49.

72 CPA 541 fos 132–3, Göezman to Baudouin, London, 7 March 1783.

73 *MSB*, 15 August 1771; CPA 502 fos 182–3, d'Eon to Broglie, London, 15 July 1773.

74 CPA 497 fos 111–13, Marin to d'Aiguillon, 3 August 1771; Vergennes to Lenoir, 12 June 1783 in Manuel, *Police*, I, 153–5; *The Times*, 18 June 1789. I have not found Vergennes's letter in the AAE.

75 Morande, *Réplique à Brissot*, p. 21.

76 See Manuel, *Police*, II, 237; PRO, C12/2002/26. The *ESTC* lists two works bearing Boissière's imprint 'Londres: chez la Société typographique' which name 'Gosse *fils*' as their continental distributor. Similarly, two 'Pierre-Frédéric Gosse' imprints advertise their availability at the Société typographique in London. This has led bibliographers to conclude erroneously that 'Londres: chez la Société typographique' was invariably a Dutch false imprint.

77 CPA 542 fos 285–9, 'Compte rendu' of Receveur, at fo. 289.

78 AN, 446AP/2, 'Interrogatoire de Brissot', fos 5, 12; AN, 446AP/2, 'Mémoire pour Brissot', fos 3–4; Morande, *Réplique à Brissot*, pp. 106–7. François Dupont to Brissot, Ostende, 14 May 1783, in Jacques-Pierre Brissot de Warville, *Correspondance et papiers*, edited by C. Perroud (Paris: Picard, 1912), pp. 54–5, shows that Vingtain regularly undertook commissions for Brissot. On these documents' authenticity see Burrows, 'Innocence of Brissot', pp. 859–60.

79 This statement is based on documents from the STN archives: the correspondence of every London-based correspondent identified in BPUN, MS 1000, plus Göezman (MS 1159 fos 93–200), Pelleport (MS 1190 fos 138–40), Brissot (MS 1128 fos 26–253), and Pierre Gosse (MS 1159 fos 86–111); STN inventories from 1781 and 1787 (MSS 1003–7 and 1009); and itemised accounts labelled 'Journal C' (MS 1028).

80 The London *libellistes* had contacts with the duchy of Deux-Ponts in the 1770s and 1780s via Beaumarchais and Maximilien de Radix de Sainte-Foy, former treasurer to the navy, and from 1785 to 1788 proprietor of the *Courier de l'Europe*, probably as a front-man for the navy who wanted to provide cover for Morande's intelligence-gathering activities. Despite a reputation as a *roué* (Madame du Barry numbered among his former mistresses), Sainte-Foy was appointed as the duc's diplomatic representative in London. See *MSB*, 17 January 1785; Burrows, *French Exile Journalism*, p. 231. BPUN, MS 1006 fo. 41, records that the STN bought twenty-six copies of the *Diable* from a supplier named Serini on 26 July 1784.

81 Marc de La Motte, *Mémoires inédits*, p. 163.

82 See, for example, Robert Darnton, 'Trade in the taboo: the life of a clandestine book dealer in prerevolutionary France' in Paul J. Korshin (ed.), *The Widening Circle: Essays on the Circulation of Literature in Eighteenth-Century Europe* (n. pl.: University of Pennsylvania Press, 1976), 13–83.

83 Advice to subscribers in the 1783 edition of Pelleport's *Petits Soupers*, pp. 5–7. The alleged 'confiscation' could have been a device to boost sales.

84 See Louis Sébastien Mercier, *Parallèle de Paris et de Londres*, edited by Claude Bruneteau and B. Cottret (Paris: Didier érudition, 1982), p. 138.

85 MO, MS 1422 pp. 253–4, 310–11.

86 See appendix.

87 Brissot, *Mémoires*, I, 166–8.

88 See CPA 505 fo. 207, 'Indenture between Joshua Van Neck and Morande', 29 April 1774. French translations of this document speak ambiguously of 6,000 copies. See also Louis Dutens, *Mémoires d'un voyageur qui se repose*, 3 vols (London: Dulau, 1806), II, 40. CPA 503 fos 308–10, Morande to d'Eon, undated, received 21 December 1773, makes clear that it was a two-volume work.

89 CPA 528 fo. 93, 'Humanity' to Forth, 15 January 1778.

90 CPA 541 fos 346–9, Goëzman to Vergennes, 4 April 1783. The *libelle*'s identity is evident only from context and description.

91 AN, W 295 fos 246, 'Affaire Manuel' [1793]. This dossier, especially pieces 14–16, shows that Darnton's assertion ('Grub Street', pp. 319–20) that Manuel was arrested for peddling pornography is erroneous. The police found twenty-one copies of Mirabeau's *Ma Conversion, ou le libertin de qualité* among his stock, but their primary concern was political tracts relating to the diamond necklace affair.

92 AN, 446AP/2, 'Mémoire pour Brissot', [1784], fo. 3. Brissot's wording implies uncertainty about this figure, but since he prepared this document while in the Bastille, he would not have wanted to appear too knowledgeable. One pirate edition circulating around Troyes in 1784 was probably produced by a certain Jacques Mallet. See BPUN, MS 1129 fos 149–50, Mauvelain to STN, Troyes, 10 August 1784; fos 163–4, Mauvelain to STN, 29 October 1784. See also Darnton, 'Trade in taboo', esp. p. 27.

93 La Motte, *Life*, II, 230.

94 AN, F^7 4445^2 dossier 3, piece 42, Bertrand to Du Bu de Longchamp, 14 June 1791.

95 CPA supplément 13 fos 169–72, d'Eon to Broglie, 20 April 1764 (copy); CPA supplément 16 fos 17–18, Tercier to d'Eon, Broglie, 18 February 1763 (extract), footnote annotation at fo. 18 (probably added c. 1775).

96 AN, F⁷ 4445² dossier 3, piece 42, Bertrand to Du Bu de Longchamp, 14 June 1791. See also piece 28, Warren to the comte de La Motte, London, 14 June 1791.

97 AN, F⁷ 4445², dossier3, piece 43, Bertrand to Du Bu de Longchamp, 17 June 1791; piece 28, Warren to the comte de La Motte, London, 14 June 1791.

98 The prices are from AN, F⁷ 4445² dossier 3, piece 42, Bertrand to Du Bu de Longchamp, 14 June 1791. 4,000 copies × 5 shillings = £1,000; 2,000 × 14 shillings = £1,400.

99 CPA 569 fos 225–6, Morande to Montmorin, 11 May 1789; *The Times*, 20 May 1789.

100 The first English edition of Fauques's work dates from 1758, and a 'fourth edition', with the narrative extended to Pompadour's death appeared in 1766; I have discovered three French and two German editions from 1759 and another German edition from 1760. A (fourth) German edition from 1766 is mentioned in the introductory notice to the French reimpression of 1879. The page decoration of the eighteenth-century French and German editions seems to confirm the BL catalogue's assertion that they were produced in the Netherlands. The 'Advertisement' to the 1766 English edition claims that Fauques's work was translated into 'most European languages' and the first German edition was reprinted fourteen times.

101 *CSP*, XVI, 97. This figure may have been hyperbole.

102 Gruder, 'Question of Marie-Antoinette'.

103 In her *Life*, II, 235, the comtesse claims to still have 800 French and 300 English copies of her *Mémoires* left: thus by 1791, her sales presumably totalled 6,900. See also Henry Vizetelly, *The Story of the Diamond Necklace*, 2 vols (London: Tinsley, 1887), II, 211–14.

104 Michael Kwass, *Privilege and the Politics of Taxation in Eighteenth-Century France: Liberté, Egalité, Fiscalité* (Cambridge: Cambridge University Press, 2000), p. 214.

105 Nicolas Ruault, *Gazette d'un parisien sous la révolution: lettres à son frère: 1783–1796*, edited by Christiane Rimbaud and Anne Vassal (Paris: Perrin, 1976), p. 193.

106 Gruder, 'Question of Marie-Antoinette', p. 297, n. 94.

107 De Baecque, 'Pamphlets', p. 165.

108 Darnton classifies forty-five titles as topical political works, forty-five as libels and court satires, and seventeen as *chroniques scandaleuses*. They account for 26 per cent of orders in his sample. See Darnton, *Corpus*, pp. 201–3. However, several of these titles were probably never published.

109 Mairobert (attrib.), *Anecdotes*, pp. 238–9 and Darnton, *Corpus*, p. 116, date the *Mémoires authentiques de Madame la comtesse Dubarri* to 1772. Darnton reveals that the STN received 109 orders for this work, a respectable number (Morande's *Gazetier cuirassé* received 135 orders). However, the earliest copies I have located date from 1775, and Darnton's dateable evidence all comes from the period 1775–81.

110 Quoted in editor's 'Notice' to Fauques, *Histoire de Pompadour*, 1879 edition, p. 13. Fauques's work is the only pamphlet published in the favourite's lifetime cited in Thomas E. Kaiser, 'Madame de Pompadour and the theaters of power', *French Historical Studies* 19:4 (1996). However, Ange Goudar (attrib.), *Mémoires pour servir à l'histoire de la marquise de Pompadour* (London:

Samuel Hooper, 1763) apparently appeared in the final months of Pompadour's life. The imprint may be false.

111 See Robert Darnton, 'Mademoiselle Bonafon et la vie privée de Louis XV', *Dix-huitième siècle* 35:2 (2003).

112 *Encyclopédie, ou dictionnaire raisonné des sciences, des arts et des métiers*, 3rd edition, 17 vols (Livourne: Imprimerie des éditeurs, 1770–75), IX, 415–16. The author's initials ('D. J.') are decoded in John Lough, *Contributors to the Encyclopédie* (London: Grant and Cutler, 1973), p. 84.

113 MD France 1351 fos 96–7, Madame Hervé to Madame Geoffrin, London, 20 January 1759 (extract).

114 Voltaire, *Questions sur l'Encyclopédie*, nouvelle édition, 9 vols (n. pl., 1771–72), IX, 224. Desgenettes, *Souvenirs*, I, 92, also uses the phrase 'ouvrages de ténèbres' to describe Charles-Claude Théveneau de Morande (attrib.), *La Vie privée ou apologie du tres-sérénissime prince Monseigneur le duc de Chartres* (London: n. p., 1784).

115 CPA 513 fos 439–43.

116 *MSB*, 15 August 1771.

117 *CSP*, II, 314. Madame du Deffand praises the veracity of the *Anecdotes* in a letter of 25 February 1776: see Marie du Deffand, *Lettres de la marquise du Deffand à Horace Walpole (1766–1780)*, edited by Mrs Paget Toynbee, 3 vols (London: Methuen, 1912), III, 176.

118 CPA 568 fos 276–7, [Morande] to Montmorin, 3 March 1789.

119 See Edmund Burke, *Reflections on the Revolution in France* (Harmondsworth: Penguin, 1969), pp. 168–70; Iain McCalman, 'Mad Lord George and Madame de La Motte: riot and sexuality in the genesis of Burke's *Reflections on the Revolution in France*', *Journal of British Studies* 35:3 (1996), p. 364.

120 *CSCV*, II, 333.

121 Ibid., 621.

122 Voltaire to Bertrand, 7 January 1760, in Voltaire, *Correspondence*, XLI, 18–19, quote at p. 18.

123 *CSP*, XVI, 96.

124 Ibid., 94.

125 Ibid., 97.

3

The policing and politics of *libelles*, 1758–78

Between 1758 and 1792, *libellistes* based in London proved a constant thorn in the side to French policy makers and diplomats. The French government took them seriously – probably too seriously – because of their perceived potential to damage the honour and reputation of private individuals, the French state, and the royal family. This chapter and the next outline the *libellistes'* activities, the political damage they inflicted, and the attempts of the French authorities to control them. They reveal how successive French ministries vacillated between using draconian force and suppression fees to prevent the appearance of key *libelles*. These twin policies were remarkably successful in preventing the appearance of the most significant scandalous texts. However, as the number of suppressions grew, and several former *libellistes* were recruited as French agents, the government gradually became convinced that they were best ignored. From 1783, when they began scorning the *libellistes'* demands, they ceased to be troubled by them. Unfortunately, this policy came unstuck on the eve of the revolution.

The task of restraining the *libellistes* often fell to French diplomats. In the late eighteenth century, the post of ambassador to the court of St James was among the most prestigious offices in the Bourbon diplomatic service. It was also taxing, risky, and treacherous. Ambassadors had both to deal with the manoeuvres of France's greatest rival and come to grips with the subtleties of Britain's representative system of government and its handmaiden, the press. Unable to grasp the concept of a loyal opposition, many French diplomats and politicians misunderstood British politics, and most found the press exasperating and often dangerous. Of the five ambassadors who served in London between 1758 and 1789, two were ruined by accusations made against them in print. Guerchy's career, health, and reputation were permanently destroyed by d'Eon's accusations, while Guines was dogged by allegations that he speculated on the stock exchange using insider knowledge. A third, Jean Balthazar, comte d'Adhémar, risked disgrace in his pursuit of *libellistes*, and the marquis de Noailles considered his entanglement with Linguet the worst incident of his embassy.[1] Foreign ministers were not spared either. Praslin was unmasked as the *deus ex machina* of plots against d'Eon; d'Aiguillon suffered sustained exposure; and Vergennes was denounced for despotic tendencies. With the exception of the Guines affair, the involvement of exiled French *libellistes* was a common strand in all these incidents.

French diplomats and politicians showed differing levels of sensitivity to printed poisons. D'Aiguillon was particularly thin-skinned, having experienced concerted political and pamphlet attacks during the Brittany affair. He was savaged again during the Maupeou crisis, but his sensitivity was probably aggravated by his unwavering devotion to Madame du Barry, a favourite target for salacious pamphleteers. In contrast, the insouciance of d'Aiguillon's uncle, Maurepas, towards pamphlet attacks was notorious. Maurepas was an avid collector of songs and epigrams against himself, and took pleasure in quoting them.[2] In 1749 he had been dismissed from Louis XV's service reputedly for circulating scurrilous verses about Pompadour.[3] Nevertheless, there were limits to his tolerance, and paradoxically his ministry (May 1774 to November 1781) witnessed more concessions to *libellistes* than any other. Maurepas considered the *Guerlichon femelle*, the pamphlet discussed in the prologue, intolerable owing to its defamation of members of the ruling dynasty. He found its title alone 'si horrible qu'il n'y a personne qui ne doive s'y intéresser' ['so horrible that everyone should be concerned about it'],[4] and added: 'les libelles m'a paru scandaleuse et je m'y trouve singulièrement blasphemé; mais gens qui valent mieux que moy y sont aussi et je n'ai rien a dire au surplus.' ['I found the defamations scandalous and I am singularly blasphemed by them; but persons of greater worth than me are also [blasphemed] and so I will say nothing more.']⁵ Vergennes shared Maurepas's position, remarking: 'Je serois bien plus froid, et même totalement passif, si ces vipères vouloient se contenter de ne mordre que les ministres; nous sommes faits pour souffrir' ['I would remain far cooler, even totally passive, if these vipers contented themselves with biting only ministers; we were created to suffer'].[6] On learning that d'Adhémar intended to advise Louis XVI to scorn *libelles* concerning the paternity of Marie-Antoinette's children, Vergennes's response was curt. He informed d'Adhémar that *libelles* should indeed be despised, but not when they threatened crowned heads.[7]

Thus ministers assessed the threat of *libelles* according to hierarchical gradations. Maurepas and Vergennes were willing to tolerate attacks on individuals, even themselves, as a corollary of political life. However, slanders against the monarch or his spouse were an affair of state and a different issue entirely. The monarchy, France's most enduring political institution, was permanent and irremovable. It merited undiluted respect to maintain its dignity and ensure obedience. Sexual slanders, especially concerning the chastity of the queen, which *in extremis* might undermine the succession and internal stability of the realm, were a particular threat. After defamations of the monarchy itself, French ministers tended to consider attacks on diplomatic staff the most culpable form of *libelle*, since their authority was a manifestation of royal power, and their credit with host courts necessitated an unsullied reputation.

Ministerial responses to *libelles* were also influenced by experience and the conviction that many *libelles* were emanations of factional conflict among the political elite. Nevertheless, French policy makers considered the London *libellistes* a distinctive phenomenon, whose origins could, according to the keeper of the seals, Miromesnil, and *chargé d'affaires*, Garnier, be traced back to d'Eon.[8] However, even before d'Eon, Louis XV's government sought to suppress libellous material published abroad. In April 1752, the marquis de Fratteaux, who had sent a manuscript *libelle* 'of the greatest violence against the king and royal family' to 100 leading courtiers, was seized in London by French agents abetted by a bailiff named Blaisdell.[9] The following year, an agent involved in Fratteaux's kidnapping, Dagès Desouchard, infiltrated the Dutch *libelle* industry. In August 1753, he identified the chevalier de La Roche-Gérault as the author of *libelles* against Pompadour and Louis XV. Immediately, the French ambassador to The Hague secured the seizure of the work and La Roche-Gerault's arrest and extradition. Such energetic persecution by the Dutch authorities was unprecedented and reflected the decline of Dutch power and the demise of the United Provinces as the leading centre for anti-Bourbon publishing.[10] Thereafter, that mantle was assumed by London, where the laws offered much greater protection. In 1757, when Britain and France were at war, French diplomats were horrified by British press comment on Damiens's attempted assassination of Louis XV, which appeared to justify regicide.[11] They also worried about attacks on Louis XV's private life, and according to Morande, Pompadour paid 100,000 *livres* (over £4,000) to suppress a libellous work.[12] This was probably the French edition of Fauques's *Histoire de Pompadour*, which certainly worried Pompadour. She ordered the original English edition of 1758 to be translated by the dramatist La Place,[13] and in consequence, Louis XV ordered the French ambassador to the Netherlands, the comte d'Affry, to suppress the French edition. Although payments were made on two separate occasions, this policy failed:[14] by the end of 1759, several French- and German-language editions were in circulation.

Thus d'Eon was not the first blackmailer-*libelliste*. His contribution was to demonstrate that *libellistes* could act with impunity by exploiting British press laws and the zeal of the London mob.[15] Thereafter, complained Garnier, licence had become common in the British press, and he presciently warned his government not to rely on the British to repress future outrages in print.[16] It was thus the public aspect of d'Eon's activities which made him a pivotal figure. As we have seen, d'Eon resorted to blackmail to extort payment of expenses incurred during his service as a spy. On 23 March 1764, the very day he published his *Lettres, mémoires et négociations*, he imposed a one-month deadline for Louis XV and Broglie to settle his dispute with Guerchy. Otherwise he would sell his papers – including his secret orders – to British opposition politicians. This, d'Eon asserted, would provoke war.[17]

In his *Lettres, mémoires et négociations*, and a series of pamphlets and

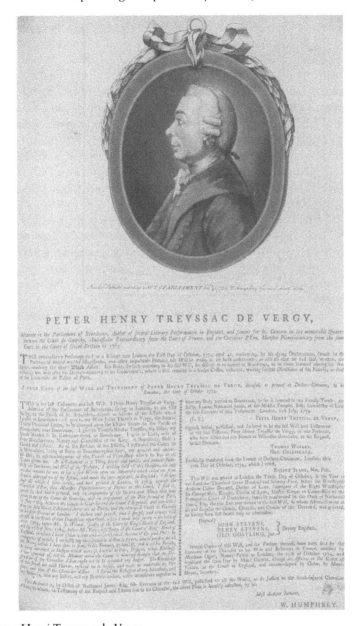

5 Pierre-Henri Treyssac de Vergy

newspaper articles, d'Eon savaged his personal enemies, and reiterated claims that Guerchy had poisoned him and incited Vergy to assassinate him.[18] D'Eon linked Guerchy's actions to a powerful clique at court, headed by Praslin, Pompadour, and Choiseul.[19] D'Eon claimed, and may have believed, that this pro-Austrian faction would stop at nothing to marginalise the advocates of a traditional anti-Habsburg policy. He asserted that they arranged the sudden deaths of two of his allies at court, Lebel and Tercier, as well as Broglie's dismissal.[20]

The truth of d'Eon's allegations against Guerchy is hard to ascertain. According to d'Eon, Guerchy's 'master of horse', Stephen Chazell, administered opium to him in a glass of wine while he dined at the embassy on 28 October 1763. The poison made him ill, but having refused assistance and a carriage from the ambassador's staff, he managed to return home, thwarting attempts to capture him.[21] D'Eon's testimony is problematic both because it is self-interested, and because other guests also fell ill.[22] However, in October 1764, his claims were corroborated by Vergy's testimony that Guerchy and Praslin employed him to assassinate d'Eon. After Vergy's confession, d'Eon asserts, Chazell fled to Naples, despite being newly wed. This is no evidence of his guilt, however, for Chazell was excessively violent towards his wife, and other criminal motives probably determined his flight.[23] Moreover, many details of Vergy's testimony were clearly fabricated. Vergy claimed that he was recruited by d'Argental; told by Praslin that d'Eon must be destroyed; and ordered to assassinate him by Guerchy after Chazell's poison failed.[24] The first two assertions appear false. The first cannot be credited because before Vergy turned against Guerchy, d'Eon himself revealed that Vergy had been chased from d'Argental's home.[25] Likewise, although Vergy met Praslin before leaving Paris, their subsequent correspondence makes clear that his account of their interview is a fabrication.[26] His assertions that the plot originated in July 1763, at least six weeks before problems emerged between d'Eon and Guerchy, also look suspect.[27] Nevertheless, d'Eon grew so suspicious of Vergy's intentions in the run-up to the poisoning incident in October 1763 that he challenged him to a duel.[28] On balance, there may have been a grain of truth somewhere in Vergy's allegations, especially as they involved huge personal cost for little gain, but most of the details were fabricated to suit d'Eon's purposes.[29] Nevertheless, his tale did untold damage to Guerchy and the reputation of the French government.

Following Vergy's confession, the attorney-general considered the evidence against Guerchy strong enough to lodge a bill of indictment against him for hiring Vergy to 'kill and assassinate d'Eon', and an Old Bailey grand jury found against the ambassador.[30] This embarrassed the British government: in absolutist France, where justice flowed directly from the monarch, instigating proceedings against an ambassador would be tantamount to declaring war. Ministers pressurised the attorney-general to suppress the case by means of a *noli prosequi*, but without success. The jury's decision vindicated d'Eon, and effectively neutralised a libel conviction that Guerchy had won against him. The government responded by transferring the case against Guerchy to the Court of King's Bench, where it remained in limbo.[31] The dispute broke Guerchy. He was recalled in 1767, was snubbed at Versailles, and died within weeks.[32]

If the poison allegation remains unproven, documentary evidence confirms that the French ministry considered abducting d'Eon. Choiseul and Praslin sent an agent to London to investigate the possibility just before Guerchy's arrival,[33] and Guerchy himself proposed a kidnap to the British.[34] They replied that 'selon les loix de ce Royaume, on ne pourroit aucunement justifier la saisie ni de la personne, ni des papiers de cet infortuné' ['the laws of this kingdom cannot justify the seizure of either the person or papers of this unfortunate'].[35] In April 1764, Louis XV authorised a three-pronged approach: if the British refused to extradite or deport d'Eon, Guerchy could bring his libel prosecution. Failing that, Praslin was to proceed with kidnap plans anyway.[36] The extradition request was duly refused, even though Guerchy's demand for a 'prompt and proportionate satisfaction' for d'Eon's violation of the 'droit des gens' ['law of nations'], together with new legislation to prevent a recurrence, was formally backed by the ambassadors of other powers.[37]

Nevertheless, George III and his ministers deeply disapproved of d'Eon's conduct and investigated their options carefully. The prime minister, Grenville, favoured expelling him if indisputable legal means existed, but government lawyers proved divided on this point. In cabinet on 30 March 1764, the duke of Bedford proposed introducing legislation to facilitate d'Eon's expulsion, but Grenville and the lord chancellor sensed that many 'inconveniences' might arise from appearing to yield to French demands, and Bedford withdrew the suggestion.[38] Likewise, government lawyers informed Grenville that it might be unlawful for Fielding to seize d'Eon's papers. Grenville concluded that it would provoke 'great clamour and uneasiness' and vetoed the idea.[39] In consequence, the British repeated that under English law no-one could be arrested, not even foreigners, unless they had committed a crime.[40] British ministers would reiterate this position over subsequent decades whenever French governments complained about exile writers. Their attitude astonished the French, who could scarcely conceive that the rule of law could take precedence over the will of a legitimate sovereign, and on occasion it severely embittered relations between the two countries and caused serious misunderstandings.[41]

Throughout the summer of 1764 the British press repeated rumours that French agents were in London to kidnap d'Eon: it was even suggested that the government intended to exchange him for the radical British politician John Wilkes, who had fled to France to avoid prosecution for libel.[42] Wilkites drew parallels between the persecution of Wilkes and d'Eon, but opposition leaders had other reasons to cultivate d'Eon. They hoped that his diplomatic correspondence would confirm that ministers had been bribed to betray Britain's interests, and hence bring down the government. Their suspicions related to territorial concessions made by Britain after the Seven Years' War in the vain hope that magnanimity in victory would prevent future French aggression.[43] Thus they wooed d'Eon assiduously, and reputedly offered to pay £40,000 for his papers.[44] They also guarded him against kidnap,[45] organised an escort, and orchestrated protective mobs, which on one occasion stoned Guerchy's carriage.[46]

Although the French failed to meet d'Eon's deadline, he did not deliver his papers to the British. Doubtless he hesitated to burn bridges. Perhaps he had been informed also that, unknown to Praslin, Louis XV intended to send a secret agent named Nort to negotiate with him.[47] However, Nort's departure was delayed by wrangling, allowing the dispute to escalate. Ironically, d'Eon's quarrel with the French foreign ministry facilitated a reconciliation with the king, because it gave him increased access to British politicians and convinced them that he was a renegade. As a result, by mid-1765 Broglie had persuaded the king of d'Eon's continued utility as a spy, and so, on 1 April 1766, Louis XV granted d'Eon a pension of 12,000 *livres* (£500) until a post could be found for him.[48] In return d'Eon would spy for Broglie, stay in exile while Praslin and Choiseul remained in government, and surrender his diplomatic papers. However, this did not prove a final settlement. Although d'Eon returned the king's secret order, he concealed many other sensitive papers.[49] He sold further papers in 1775, when he hastened negotiations by hiring Vignoles to prepare a second volume of *Lettres, mémoires et négociations*.[50] The agreement brokered by Beaumarchais prevented this work appearing, but during their subsequent pamphleteering battles, details of their transaction became widely publicised, and doubtless inspired other *libellistes*, including Vergy.[51]

From the French government's perspective, d'Eon differed from later *libellistes* in several significant ways. Above all, he possessed genuinely explosive material. Broglie thought publication of d'Eon's secret order would provoke war. Louis XV was less pessimistic, but feared that the entire French diplomatic corps would be compromised. Equally, d'Eon could be genuinely useful. Ignoring him was not an option. Once he published the *Lettres, mémoires et négociations*, Louis XV saw no alternative but to silence him by force, legal proceedings, or capitulation. In pursuing all routes simultaneously, Louis set an important precedent.

By publishing his correspondence, d'Eon had revealed the potential for disgruntled diplomatic staff to exploit British press liberties. He thus helped to broaden the arena for public discussion of foreign affairs, chipping away at the area of policy formerly considered 'the king's secret'. However, d'Eon was not the first to publish diplomatic documents. Across the eighteenth century, newspapers with an international audience – especially French-language gazettes published in the Netherlands – enjoyed a symbiotic relationship with governments, as public authorities began to recognise the increasing ability of an elite public to influence policy discussions. Policy makers and institutional bodies began attempting to influence 'public opinion', especially in foreign states, by communicating manifestos, treaties, remonstrances, and other key documents to the press. Simultaneously, continental governments tried to control the content of the international gazettes, and most forbade newspapers produced on their territories to give domestic political news. The most powerful governments were able to suppress much hostile coverage by domestic censorship, diplomatic complaints, and threatening to ban individual papers from their soil. When the Maupoeu crisis broke in January 1771, the Dutch gazettes published a flurry of *parlementaire* remonstrances, but from late March, after sustained French pressure, they printed no further material from the *parlementaire* opposition. Moreover, until the late 1760s, international gazettes carried no editorial comment: they served as a *dépôt* for materials to support discussion, rather than a forum for debate.[52] In this world of closely controlled, officially sanctioned knowledge, d'Eon's publication was a bombshell, laying bare the workings of the diplomatic machine and the thinking of its operatives, while accusing several of them of homicidal skulduggery. Europe's educated elite were fascinated by his revelations, which were widely discussed. While many readers were scandalised that d'Eon had defied his recall and betrayed his master's confidences,[53] he had given the public an unprecedented glimpse of the diplomatic world. Thereafter it proved impossible to prevent London exiles from discussing ambassadorial activity.

The legal case between Guerchy's successor, Guines, and his former secretary, Tort, illustrates just how problematic the exposure of diplomatic documents could become. Although the case gave rise to several sensational pamphlets, most of them published in Paris, Tort was no blackmailer. Nevertheless, as the case lasted for seven years, threatened the reputation of the French diplomatic service, and allowed Tort to pose as the little man struggling against a corrupt political system, it merits investigation here.[54]

The Tort–Guines case began as a simple allegation of corruption. On 28 April 1771, Tort was thrown into the Bastille, accused by Guines of having communicated diplomatic secrets to London speculators earlier that year, when Britain and Spain were at loggerheads over the Falkland Islands and war seemed likely. However, when Tort failed to predict the French mediation that ended the crisis, his associates made massive losses. To evade their wrath, Tort fled to Paris, where he was arrested. At first Tort was just a mild embarrassment to Guines and the French government, but after several months' incarceration he announced that he had acted on Guines's behalf and accused him of calumny. With Tort's English creditors clamouring for money, the affair could not be hushed up, and so, alarmed for the integrity of the French diplomatic corps, the interim foreign minister, La Vrillière, allowed Tort to bring a case against Guines. Shortly afterwards he was released from gaol for lack of evidence. Guines alleged that Tort had been incited to make his accusations by d'Aiguillon, who shortly afterwards replaced his uncle, La Vrillière, at the foreign ministry.[55] Guines's patron was d'Aiguillon's rival, Choiseul, and hence he enjoyed the backing of an unholy alliance combining Choiseulists, Marie-Antoinette, and the pro-Austrian party with the *patriote* and *parlementaire* opposition to Maupeou, d'Aiguillon, and Terray.

By the time the case was judged in June 1775; the political balance had tipped strongly in Guines's favour. Following Louis XV's death, d'Aiguillon was disgraced, the old *parlements* were restored, and Marie-Antoinette became queen. Munro Price has uncovered evidence that she and the Choiseulists attempted to use the affair to secure the dismissal of Maurepas and Vergennes, who in January 1776 persuaded Louis XVI to recall Guines, ostensibly on the ground of incompetence.[56] As a result, many *parlementaires* began to have doubts, and thus the Paris *Parlement*'s judgement by seven votes to six, confirmed on appeal in March 1777, did not entirely favour Guines. While the ambassador was cleared, Tort's sentence was light, and Guines had to contribute one-sixth of the costs.

The Tort case was problematic because, to establish his innocence, Guines needed to present diplomatic documents to the court, and Tort therefore also claimed the right to access and quote them.[57] As the allegations were public, each party also demanded the right to publish its justifications. As high-profile litigants customarily published their legal briefs, and equity required that both protagonists be allowed to speak freely, this demand was hard to resist. The affair was also widely debated in Britain, and caused misunderstandings in the press and Parliament, where it was erroneously stated that the ambassador had 'advanced facts contrary to the truth'.[58] Appraised of these circumstances, Vergennes wrote a deeply ambiguous letter to Guines on Louis XVI's behalf. It acknowledged that his defence necessitated revelations Vergennes would prefer to avoid, but ordered him to publish nothing from his official correspondence without prior permission.[59] On another occasion, Vergennes suppressed one of Guines's judicial memoirs through lack of respect for the monarch, and Tort faced similar reprimands.[60] Thus the case brought the requirements of justice and equity into conflict with the need for secrecy, especially once Vergennes sensed the queen's hostile intentions towards him.[61] Ultimately, the government was forced to concede the right to publish extensive documentary evidence to all major parties, including d'Aiguillon. However, the zeal with which ministers, particularly Vergennes, subsequently clamped down on journalists, news-mongers, and the underground press can also probably be attributed in part to their alarm at the way in which a minor criminal scandal had come to threaten the ministry itself.[62]

Before the Tort case ended, the French government had to deal with several other *libellistes*, starting with Morande. He first came to their attention in August 1771, when his *Gazetier cuirassé* was denounced for containing 'des horreurs contre les personnes les plus respectables et . . . même le roi' ['horrors against the most respectable people and . . . even the king'].[63] However, he became a serious problem only from early 1772, when he threatened to publish his biography of du Barry, *Les Mémoires secrets d'une femme publique*, and in the process amplify the *Gazetier*'s attacks on the royal mistress and Maupeou ministry.

Informed of Morande's intentions and terms by an intermediary called Benevent, d'Aiguillon approached the British ambassador, Harcourt, demanding action and asking whether writing threatening letters was a hanging offence in England.[64] Harcourt confirmed that it was, but only if the recipient was a resident. Nevertheless, he told the secretary of state for the Southern Department,[65] Lord Rochford, that he had assured d'Aiguillon that Rochford was 'very desirous of doing anything in *your power* to oblige him'.[66] Such promises amounted to little until April 1774, when Morande was summoned to a private interview with Fielding in a last-ditch effort to dissuade him from publication by emphasising the risks he ran.[67]

Fielding's admonitions probably amused Morande, who had already over-come many dangers: d'Aiguillon and the comte du Barry, the favourite's brother-in-law, former lover, and pimp, had sent a succession of secret agents to London, intent on silencing him. Until late 1773, their missions remain shadowy, but it seems that, while they never stopped negotiating with Morande, d'Aiguillon and du Barry preferred more sinister methods. Perhaps, too, d'Aiguillon mistook Harcourt's promise of support for tacit permission to employ discreet clandestine means, for usually well-informed French underground newsletters allege that the British gave permission to seize Morande quietly.[68] In fact, Harcourt was concerned to prevent such action and in July 1772 warned about a possible kidnap. His suspicions centred on the chevalier de Fontaine, a notorious 'sharper', gaolbird, and father of the comte du Barry's mistress, who had just set out for London.[69] Details of Fontaine's mission are sketchy: the only certainty is that on his arrival in London, Boissière took him to negotiate with Morande.[70] However, the ambassador's suspicions are corroborated by a chance remark from Morande, who eighteen months later described encountering other would-be kidnappers, 'qui ont l'air aussi ingenu que cher Fontaine quoiqu'ils n'ayent pas la même grosseur epaisseur &c.' ['who seemed as artless as dear Fontaine, though without the same massive bulk'].[71]

After the failure of Fontaine's mission, negotiations stalled until mid-1773, when Broglie was asked to sound out d'Eon as a possible go-between.[72] D'Eon responded positively, confirming that he could acquire Morande's manuscript for £800.[73] Louis XV referred the idea to Madame du Barry,[74] who declined the offer on d'Aiguillon's advice. He persuaded her to appoint another intermediary, fearing lest d'Eon's success increase Broglie's credit. However, the favourite delayed notifying Broglie for several weeks, and by the time d'Eon learned of her decision, he had ingratiated himself with Morande.[75] Broglie, reluctant to abandon his efforts, gained Louis's permis-sion for d'Eon to observe developments.[76] The arrival of a new negotiator, Marie-Félix Guerrier de Lormoy, in October, only confused matters. Although almost certainly d'Aiguillon's agent, Lormoy claimed to represent the duc de Deux-Ponts and had, he asserted, authority to pay up to £5,000 for the *libelle*.[77] He met Morande several times, but nothing was concluded. Lormoy probably negotiated in bad faith, for he consulted d'Eon about kid-napping Morande, or arranging to have him convicted of libel, transported, and thrown overboard *en route*. D'Eon replied that kidnapping would be dangerous and libellers were not transported. By early December 1773, Lormoy's negotiation had ended in farce, after Morande refused to accept his promissory notes.[78] Thereafter, Morande informed d'Eon that 'Enfin, tout va être resolu ce fois et mon ouvrage paroîtra' ['this time at last all will be resolved and my work will appear']. D'Eon wrote immediately to Broglie, to scotch any suspicion that he had obstructed Lormoy.[79]

Meanwhile, the court accepted the offer of a Sr Bellanger to kidnap Morande.[80] Unlike Fontaine, Bellanger was provided with 6,000 *livres* of advances and a posse of police officers, including Receveur.[81] Unfortunately, Morande was tipped off about their mission, possibly by correspondents at court, but also by Anne de La Touche de Gotteville, a roving *femme galante*, pamphleteer, and blackmailer in whom the agents confided while at Dover.[82] When they arrived in London, two of the agents met Morande in a tavern, where, after some discussion, they lent him thirty guineas.[83] However, before they could have him seized for debt, their quarry turned the tables on them. While still in the tavern, he repeated what they had said at Dover; told them that he had smashed chairs over adventurers who believed 'que ma peau se vendrait cher à Paris' ['that my hide would fetch a good price in Paris']; and spoke of 'pistolets' [duelling pistols] and 'Tyburn'.[84] He then contacted several newspapers, alerting them to the officers' presence, and incited a mob against them in the city's taverns and coffee-houses.[85] The officers fled in fear for their lives. According to rumour, some were lynched and Receveur lost his mind.[86] Morande, exultant, at once wrote to d'Eon, 'je vous annonce que j'ai fait, ce qu'on appelle en termes de Grenadiers, foutre le camp à deux exempts, quatre archers et un vaisseau qui les attendait dans la Tamise' ['I can inform you that I have, in soldiers' language, forced two [police] exempts, four archers, and a ship waiting for them on the Thames to bugger off'].[87] Thereafter, he announced defiantly:

> Je me fous du poison et du poignard, si je meurs de cette façon. Je ne serai pas pendu et cela déshonorera uniquement mes empoisonneurs ou mes assassins. Vous pouvez marquer si vous voulez au Duc d'Aiguillon et à toute sa clique que je me fous et me contre fous de lui, de toute la cour et de toute l'armée. [I don't give a fuck about poison and daggers, if I die thus. I will not have been hanged and it will dishonour only my poisoners or assassins. If you like, you can tell the duc d'Aiguillon and his whole clique that I really couldn't give a flying fuck about him, the whole court, and the entire army.][88]

Morande's references to poison and daggers are probably not coincidental.[89] The former was presumably an allusion to d'Eon's allegations against Guerchy, while mention of daggers probably relates to an attempt on Morande's life recounted in a neglected manuscript biography. It tells how two assailants attempted to stab or strangle him in a carriage. Morande, a very large man, fought them off. This tale is probably true, for the manuscript's author, César Lavirotte (1773–1865), was a resident of Morande's home town, a distinguished *savant* and local historian, who had befriended the elderly *libelliste* in his youth.[90] The story does not appear in any published source, so presumably came from Morande himself.

Thus, by early January 1774, Morande had survived several kidnap attempts, and possibly assassins too, but the *Mémoires secrets d'une femme publique* were ready. When d'Eon reported seeing stacks of freshly printed sheets throughout Morande's house, the court knew time had run out. Broglie thus pressed for d'Eon to be permitted to conclude his negotiations.[91] The court had other ideas, however, and in March charged Beaumarchais to travel to London and arrange a pay-off through the London banker Joshua Van Neck.[92] A deal concluded, the books were taken by cart to Marylebone, then a village on the outskirts of London, and burned in a brick kiln.[93]

The legal contracts by which Beaumarchais secured the suppression of Morande's work and his future good behaviour were a model of their type. By a contract with Van Neck, Morande bound himself to deliver his entire print-run for burning and never again to libel the French monarch, ministers, or court. In return, his debts of 32,000 *livres* (approximately £ 1,400) were paid and he received a life-long annuity of 4,000 *livres*.[94] Morande also insisted on a clause stating that in the event of his death, a reduced annuity should be paid to his English wife and children, apparently because he feared assassination.[95] By a second contract, Morande guaranteed to pay 32,000 *livres* to one of his former victims, Lauraguais, should a court of law ever find him to have written further *libelles* against the French court or monarchy.[96]

Previous historians, aware of the first contract but ignorant of the second, have usually concluded that Morande abandoned blackmail after 1774 because, following the sudden death of Louis XV only days after the contracts were signed, the court no longer offered rich pickings. In fact, the years 1774 to 1781 witnessed a series of further suppressions or concessions to *libellistes*. Indeed, within weeks of Louis XVI's accession, Beaumarchais informed Sartine that a new *libelle*, the *Avis à la branche espagnole sur ses droits à la couronne de France, à défaut d'héritiers* [*Advice to the Spanish Branch on its Rights to the Crown of France in the Absence of Heirs*], was being prepared in London.[97]

This new pamphlet claimed that Louis XVI was impotent and Marie-Antoinette was taking lovers to produce an heir. It demanded she be isolated from the pro-Austrian party, banned from corresponding with Vienna, and kept under close surveillance.[98] The pamphlet appeared to be designed to undermine the queen's position, by casting doubts on the legitimacy of her future children and encouraging Louis XVI to repudiate her. In consequence, it tended to cement Provence's influence as heir apparent and undermine the Austrian alliance. A decision was taken to suppress it and Beaumarchais again dispatched to London, despite Louis XVI's reservations about him. On Sartine's orders, he suppressed a further *libelle* entitled *Epître à Louis XVI* for a mere eighty guineas,[99] before reporting that the *Avis à la branche espagnole* was being produced by Guillaume Angelucci, alias William Hatkinson [*sic*], an elusive Venetian Jew. Thereafter, Beaumarchais's tale, as recounted by Gudin de La Brenellerie and in Beaumarchais's letters to Louis XVI and Sartine, becomes increasingly bizarre and improbable.[100] There are also substantial discrepancies between these accounts, which differ also from reports that Beaumarchais produced for the Austrian authorities.[101]

Beaumarchais and Gudin record that after Beaumarchais suppressed and burned 4,000 copies of Angelucci's pamphlet outside London, the two men travelled separately to Amsterdam, where a continental edition was also suppressed. Having paid Angelucci £1,400 (35,600 *livres*), Beaumarchais learned that he had fled to Nuremberg with a copy of the pamphlet, and intended to print further editions. Beaumarchais took a mail coach and set off in pursuit.[102] As his coach approached Neustadt, Beaumarchais spied Angelucci in the distance, riding on a pony. Seeing him coming, Angelucci rode into a wood, whereupon Beaumarchais told the coachman that he needed to answer a call of nature, descended, and gave chase. He caught Angelucci and, holding him at gunpoint, retrieved the *libelle*. However, Beaumarchais was then set upon by two brigands, who were soon joined by more, and after a frantic struggle, in which he was wounded in the arm and chin, his enemies were put to flight by the sound of the coachman's horn.[103] Using his valet as an interpreter, Beaumarchais told the incredulous coachman what had happened, but refused to see a doctor or report the incident to the authorities until they reached Nuremberg, some twenty leagues away.[104]

Having made his deposition, Beaumarchais disobeyed his orders and travelled to Vienna, where he requested an audience with Maria-Theresia. He read her the *libelle* and requested permission to prepare and print a single copy of a bowdlerised version to present to Louis XVI, stripped of references that might damage Marie-Antoinette's marriage. Beaumarchais asserted that the French would never discover this petty deception because he possessed the only copy. When this suggestion was rejected, Beaumarchais contradicted himself, insisting that Angelucci must be apprehended and searches made at Nuremberg for a new edition. His inconsistencies aroused suspicions, and he was placed under house arrest, while the Austrians made enquiries to Sartine. Sartine confirmed that Beaumarchais was a French agent and insisted that his only offence was an excessive zeal to please the empress. Beaumarchais was released and allowed to return to Paris, where he presented the *libelle* to Sartine.[105]

Many details of this extraordinary saga are transparently fabricated, including Beaumarchais's inconsistent accounts of his encounter with the sylvan brigands. In one version, his attackers called one another 'Hatkinson' and 'Angelucci', which not only alters his assailants' identity, but suggests that Hatkinson was a separate person.[106] Significantly, his postillion, Georges Dratz, did not believe a word of Beaumarchais's tales, having never encountered brigands on that stretch of road, nor seen Angelucci. He believed Beaumarchais's wounds were self-inflicted and concluded that he was either mad or intent on harming the local economy. Thus, barely three hours after the supposed incident, he made a declaration to the police outlining his suspicions.[107] Moreover, despite extensive searches by the authorities, no trace of the brigands, the *libelle*, or Angelucci was ever found.[108]

All the evidence suggests that Beaumarchais's excursion to Vienna via Amsterdam and Nuremberg was a premeditated attempt to win Maria-Theresia's favour. There was no continental edition, no betrayal by Angelucci. The 'encounter' with brigands was faked as a pretext for travelling to Vienna. This would explain why Beaumarchais employed a German-speaking servant for his mission and requested a letter of authority only after he arrived in London, when the suppression was already settled.[109] It also explains why Beaumarchais, who bound Morande in a web of contracts, did not make similar arrangements with Angelucci, assuming that he existed.[110]

Were the Austrians correct therefore to conclude that Beaumarchais also helped produce the *Avis à la branche espagnole*? Biographers tend to exonerate him, explicitly or implicitly, on the grounds of his character; the *libelle*'s attacks on his political allies; the difficulty of producing a *libelle* in secret in London; or lack of evidence.[111] These objections are far from compelling.[112] The *Avis* appears to have been part of a plot hatched by Morande and Beaumarchais to squeeze a final suppression payment from the French government while increasing Beaumarchais's credit. Morande had the means to produce a *libelle* in secrecy, for he had a printing press in his house. As he faced massive financial losses if his involvement was discovered, owing to his bond to Lauraguais, Beaumarchais could depend on his silence. Moreover, as Paul Huot pointed out, the *Avis*, which survives in manuscript form, was calculated perfectly to serve Beaumarchais's interests. Its main targets, Marie-Antoinette, Louis XVI, Sartine, Maria-Theresia, and the Austrian chancellor, Kaunitz, were probably the only people who would ever read it, and the very people whose favour he sought. Its subsidiary attacks on Beaumarchais's allies and patrons, Choiseul and Maupeou, its eulogy of his enemy d'Aiguillon, and the disingenuous initials 'G. A.' on the cover were carefully contrived red herrings.[113] Moreover, some passages in the pamphlet clearly post-date Beaumarchais's departure for London on 26 June 1774, notably a reference to the successful vaccination of the king and royal family against smallpox. They were inoculated on 18 June 1774, but the procedure's success was not known until about a week later.[114] Since Beaumarchais claimed to have destroyed the pamphlet on 23 July and then set off for Holland, it must have been completed rapidly.[115] The obvious inference is that Beaumarchais colluded in the pamphlet's production with Morande, his only pre-existing and secure contact among the *libellistes*. This suspicion is reinforced by Sartine's admission that Beaumarchais himself revealed the pamphlet's existence and Beaumarchais's hints that he learned of it from Morande, his avowed spy among the *libellistes*.[116] This theory also explains why Morande was subsequently able to blackmail Beaumarchais repeatedly with threats to implicate him in the production of *libelles*.[117] Finally, the laxity of Beaumarchais's arrangement with 'Angelucci' suggests that he was convinced that the pamphlet would not be reprinted.

6 Pierre-Augustin Caron de Beaumarchais

The Angelucci affair did little harm to Beaumarchais's credit. After a brief investigation, Sartine concluded that the pamphlet emanated from the d'Aiguillon camp. Beaumarchais was cleared of all suspicion and reimbursed for itemised expenses totalling 72,000 *livres* (2,983 guineas).[118] By April 1775 he was back in London, where he suppressed Vignoles's journal and, eighteen months later, Madame Campagnol's *Considérations sur les moeurs de mon siècle*, which he described as 'un ouvrage politique contre toute l'administration actuelle' ['a political work against all the current government'].[119] Soon afterwards, the French government employed him to channel money and supplies to the insurgents in Britain's rebel American colonies. Yet according to Mercy-Argenteau, the Austrian ambassador to France, Sartine soon eliminated all other suspects and was tormented by suspicions that Beaumarchais was culpable.[120] Huot speculated that Sartine finally concluded that Beaumarchais was guilty, but instigated a cover-up, possibly calculating that such a man could be useful.[121]

Suspicions that Beaumarchais was a *libelliste* are echoed by Sartine's contemporaries. His enemies d'Eon and Tort both produced inconsistent and non-specific allegations that Beaumarchais collaborated with Morande to produce pamphlets for suppression.[122] The long-serving minister Malesherbes, Mercy-Argenteau, and Lenoir all believed that Beaumarchais produced calumnious verses and anti-court *libelles*, and Lenoir suspected he carried the manuscript and engravings for a notorious poetic *libelle*, *Les Amours de Charlot et Toinette*, to London.[123] Gruder has suggested that Beaumarchais was its author, citing its literary quality.[124] On the balance of probabilities, it appears almost certain that Beaumarchais was an accomplice of the *libellistes*, but the nature of his collaboration remains uncertain. Most commentators believe that the *Avis à la branche espagnole* has insufficient verve to have emanated from his pen, but Beaumarchais's desire to re-edit the text in Vienna suggests he feared it would betray his involvement.[125] Morande or another collaborator probably did the actual writing.[126] Perhaps the author really was called Angelucci for, although no works have been attributed to his pen, the name appears in a list of writers requesting pensions from the Calonne ministry.[127] If the signatures on deeds suppressing the *Avis* are discounted, it is the only independent evidence for his existence.[128]

Between 1774 and 1776, Beaumarchais was involved in the suppression of five *libelles*, just two of which cost the French treasury over 144,000 *livres* (approximately £6,000).[129] These suppressions inspired further *libelle* threats, ranging from professional blackmail attempts to the amateur and *ad hoc*. Among the latter is the tragi-comic case of Linsing, who, on arrival in London in February 1775, began bad-mouthing France; attacked the Rohan-Chabot brothers in print; and attempted to extort compensation for 150,000 *livres* he had spent during twenty-three years' service in the French army.[130] He demanded a trial to clear his reputation concerning events before his *embastillement*; a 300 *Louis* gratuity; the removal of a retention on his pension of 1,000 *écus* (3,000 *livres*); the brevet of a retired officer; and either permission to return to France or a position in Austrian service.[131] Vergennes, a close ally of the Rohans, hoped that Linsing might be bought off by a position in a Hanoverian regiment, but the British rejected this request.[132] Meanwhile Guines, perhaps influenced by his experience with Tort, advised capitulation: throughout August and September he spent several hours daily trying to mollify Linsing.[133]

Guines pressed Linsing's case strongly, but Vergennes and Louis XVI were reluctant to make significant concessions, fearing lest 'les fols et les fripons, croiroient qu'il suffiseroit s'émigrer en Angleterre et de menacer de la diffamation, quelques personnes principales pour se faire acheter chèrement' ['madmen and scoundrels believe that it is sufficient to emigrate to England and threaten to defame several important persons in order to be bought off at great cost'].[134] Thus Linsing remained a nuisance, plaguing Guines and Vergennes with his demands. Finally, in January 1776, Guines offered Linsing 300 *Louis* (6,000 *livres*) and a pension of 3,000 *livres* (approximately £120), though he stressed that the king was not behind the initiative.[135] This is clearly true, though the source of the money remains a mystery. Linsing refused the offer, and in newspaper articles, private letters, and pamphlets distributed at London theatres unleashed a sustained barrage of abuse against Sartine, whom he blamed for the refusal of a public judgement and right to return to France. Faced with this 'abominable scandal',[136] Guines delivered Linsing an ultimatum to take up his offer and sign a good behaviour bond, which he accepted. Guines boasted that this was a cheap victory: without humiliation and for a mere 'bagatelle', he had ended 'le plus grande scandale que ce pais-ci ait jamais produit' ['the greatest scandal this country has ever produced'].[137] Vergennes, who had just sent Guines his letter of recall, felt otherwise, for before news of the agreement reached Versailles he informed Guines that Louis XVI and his council considered Linsing's 'pretensions' unworthy of attention and buying his silence inappropriate.[138]

The Linsing episode was followed by the pitiful menaces of the ship-wrecked Lenoir de La Bussière to appeal to the British public and expose Garnier in print.[139] Garnier immediately alerted Vergennes and informed La Bussière that he had not known he was still in London, that his family ought to help him, and that he would forward his letter to the court.[140] La Bussière immediately came to his senses and requested a free passage from Dover to Calais and half a guinea to help him reach his point of embarkation.[141] Faced with such a modest demand, Garnier immediately complied.[142] Several days later, Garnier received Vergennes's gratifying response that the best approach to La Bussière would be to pay for his journey.[143] This trivial incident reveals that extortion, however modest the complaint or sum involved, had become a natural resort among the French expatriate community. Intriguingly, La Bussière said he abandoned his petty blackmail because it would be humiliating to make a public appeal, not because it was criminal.

Linguet, the next *libelliste* to trouble the French administration, was a rather more formidable opponent. Unusually, he did not demand money:

SIMON NICOLAS HENRI LINGUET

7 Simon-Nicolas-Henri Linguet

instead he hoped to obtain permission for his *Annales* to circulate inside France, his initial application having failed. Thus, on 1 April 1777, he sent ministers a list of seven items that he would publish if the ban was upheld. These included *exposés* of Miromesnil, Maurepas, and d'Aiguillon, including a history of his role in the Guines case, and a treatment of d'Eon's affairs.[144] Subsequently, he threatened to publish an *Aiguillonade*, or *Aiguilloniana*, which he printed but apparently suppressed. The entire edition ended up in the secret *dépôt* in the Bastille.[145] Linguet told the new ambassador, Noailles, that such threats were forced upon him by the obstinacy, blindness, and violence of ministers, who had 'reduit un homme né bon, simple, sensible, passioné pour la paix, à prendre le ton de méchanceté, à passer la vie dans les convulsions du desespoir et les angoisses de la haine' ['reduced a man born good, unaffected, sensitive, passionate for peace, to take a wicked tone, to spend his life in the convulsions of despair and anguish of hatred']. He added that he never acted without first warning the ministry, and, to prove it, threatened to publish his letters to d'Aiguillon, Vergennes, and Noailles. Rather than seeking justice, however, he merely wished for a 'cessation d'outrages' against him.[146]

Linguet's actions embarrassed Noailles, who feared damage to his own reputation. When Linguet asked him to forward his *Lettre à Vergennes* to the foreign minister, Noailles included a justificatory letter in which he explained that he had informed Lord Suffolk, secretary of state for the Northern Department, about Linguet's threats, but told him that he did not want to lodge a ministerial complaint, because 'l'offense est trop grave pour que je voulusse en poursuivre inutilement la reparation' ['the offence is too serious for me to wish to pursue a remedy unsuccessfully']. Suffolk responded by offering some 'paroles obligeantes' ['obliging words'], but as Noailles remarked, they could neither remedy the present evil nor prevent its repetition. Like other ministers before and after him, Noailles was exasperated with English laws. He commented:

> Il est etrange que les loix d'Angleterre se taisent sur de semblables délits. Qu'on dise que la liberté de la presse est de l'essence du gouvernement d'Angleterre, j'y consens. Le Roi d'Angleterre, ses ministres, les representans de la nation seront en butte aux traits les plus noirs de la satyre, tout qu'on voudra. Mais qu'à de commun la constitution d'Angleterre avec le respect qui est du aux autres sociétés politiques? L'empire britannique est donc un monde tout à fait à part, qui ne veut prendre aucune connoissance de ce qui peut offenser la dignité des autres pays. [It is strange that the laws of England remain silent over such offences. I accept that liberty of the press is the essence of English government. I accept that the king of England, his ministers, the representatives of the nation, should be targets for the darkest sorts of satire. But what does the English constitution have to do with the respect due to other political societies? The British Empire is thus a world on its own, which does not wish to give any consideration to whatever could offend the dignity of other countries.][147]

Vergennes, although personally implicated, stood firm in the face of Linguet's threats, at least superficially. His response to Linguet's *Lettre à Vergennes* was disdainful. It dishonoured the English to harbour 'vipères', who clamoured about the French tyranny despite having been left at liberty to travel. As for Linguet's personal attacks, Vergennes declared, 'J'y suis assez indifférent . . . ma conscience repousse de pareille outrages, et mon ame est assez forte pour ne s'en pas affectuer.' ['I am totally indifferent . . . my conscience rejects such outrages, and my spirit is strong enough not to be affected by them'.][148] Vergennes accepted, too, that little could be done to contain Linguet, since 'les loix d'ang^re [Angleterre] sont si favorables a ces sortes de fripons qu'il faut renoncer a leur faire rendre gorge.' ['The laws of England are so favourable to such rogues that we must abandon hope of having them hanged.'] Nevertheless, he saw that British obstructions might be used as bargaining chips in cases where they asked for French co-operation.[149] Vergennes's

attitudes were largely shared by Maurepas and Miromesnil. Maurepas recommended disdain, dismissing Linguet as a rabid dog and pondering whether
the British might expel him.[150] Miromesnil offered similar counsel, remarking that d'Eon 'eut ete oublié, si on l'avait meprisé. Que faire à Linguet?
Serait-il sage de lui donner la meme celebrité?' [would have been forgotten if
he had been disdained. What should be done about Linguet? Is it wise to give
him the same celebrity?'] He felt that it degraded ministers to reply to *libellistes* and seemed to accredit their lies. Perhaps, he added mordantly, Linguet
was right to blame his outrages on the French authorities: they should have
gaoled him for life after his first offence.[151]

Yet despite ministerial irritation, policy towards Linguet was fudged, and
the ban on his journal was not absolute. In response to his 'insolent' memoir,
Vergennes instructed Noailles to inform Linguet verbally that his journal
would be neither banned nor permitted: instead subscribers would have to
make their own arrangements.[152] This amounted to a *permission tacite* for
Linguet's journal to circulate, but prevented his using the *bureaux des
gazettes étrangères*, which usually received subscriptions and distributed
papers free of charge through the postal system. This briefly placated
Linguet, who promised not to publish his letters to the ambassador and tem-
porarily suspended printing his *Aiguilloniana*.[153] Despite further threats and
bluster, by late August 1777 Linguet's Parisian agent Lequesne had secured
permission to circulate the *Annales* through the post, with Lenoir as a sym-
pathetic censor.[154]

What occasioned ministerial leniency? By not formally banning his
Annales, Vergennes, Maurepas, and Miromesnil probably wished to deny
Linguet opportunity for further complaint, while by granting partial access
to the French market they hoped to gain leverage over him. Since 1759
Bourbon policy allowed foreign-based journals to enter France precisely
because fear of losing this privilege was a powerful incentive to editorial self-
censorship. French ministers also underestimated Linguet's appeal. Maurepas
believed he would find few readers, while Vergennes was confident that he
could not harm Noailles's reputation.[155] In addition, attitudes towards
Linguet in the ministry and royal family were divided. According to
Vergennes, Maurepas was amused by the *Aiguilloniana*, particularly passages
attacking himself and Miromesnil. Vergennes, however, was not amused:
'pour moi, je n'en ris pas car je me propose bien de ne lire des mechancetés
de cet enragé que ce qui trait à moi.' ['As for me, I do not laugh, because I
propose to read only the slanders of that madman that refer to me'.][156] In
contrast, a manuscript newsletter reported that the *Annales* were Louis XVI's
favourite reading, and hence the minister Amelot refused to propose their
interdiction when approached by the Académie.[157] Linguet also had powerful allies in the clergy and *dévot* party because of his journalistic attacks on
the *philosophes*, and in the queen owing to her dislike of d'Aiguillon.[158]
Possibly Vergennes also hoped to employ Linguet, the self-proclaimed patriot
and champion of absolute monarchy, as a propagandist.[159]

Linguet's activities were tolerated because he refrained from attacking the royal family and might be useful, but the same could not be said of two *libelles* denounced in 1777, Saint-Julien's *Vie et anecdotes des maitresses du roi de France, et des ministres de ce royaume* [*Lives and Anecdotes of the Mistresses of the King of France and the Ministers of that Kingdom*] and the anonymous *Guerlichon femelle*. The first of these works was chimerical. A letter to a Parisian book dealer offered to sell the manuscript for 2,800 *livres*, but ambassadorial research revealed that the bookseller Vaillant, whom it named as a contact, had retired years previously. It therefore appears to have been a hoax, malicious denunciation, or device to test French interest in suppressing *libelles*.[160] Vergennes, having been tricked too often, was growing reluctant to pay suppression fees, save for the most serious offences. He instructed Noailles to search for the *libelle* and take steps to prevent it by non-official means, but he was not to buy the manuscript, since the author or bookseller would probably keep copies and break any agreement.[161] Vergennes and Maurepas took a very different line with the *Guerlichon femelle*, the *libelle* described in the prologue, because, in its full version, its very title defamed Marie-Antoinette.

The first explicit reference to the *Guerlichon* appears in a letter by Vergennes dated 7 June 1777. It reveals that a London printer had announced the imminent publication of *La Reine des Welches et sa surintendante ou les deux amans femelles* [*The Queen of the Welches and her [female] Superintendent or the Two Female Lovers*]. Since 'Welches' was a synonym for the French in scandalous texts, informed readers would recognise that the title referred to Marie-Antoinette and the princesse de Lamballe, who in September 1775 had been appointed *surintendante de la maison de la reine*. It was, therefore, the earliest pamphlet to accuse Marie-Antoinette of lesbianism. Vergennes did not mince words in instructing Noailles:

> Quelles horreurs nos têtes scelerats enfantent et que Londres reflechit! Je ne pense pas qu'il fut possible d'obtenir du gouvernement anglois le moindre assistance pour arreter la publication de ce scandaleux ecrit, mais il n'en est pas moins important de le faire supprimer et d'y adopter tous les moyens possibles. [What horrors are born of the minds of our scoundrels and reflected in London. I don't think it would be possible to obtain the least assistance from the English government to prevent this scandalous publication, but it is no less important to have it suppressed and to adopt all possible means to do so.][162]

Vergennes argued that if the work existed, it would be necessary to buy up the entire edition and original manuscript as cheaply as possible, without allowing any copy to escape. In return, the vendor must sign a binding legal contract, enforceable under English law, so that any breach of the agreement could be punished. Noailles should not appear to be personally involved, but should do all that he could pour prevenir un scandale qui ne prendroit que trop dans un tems ou les têtes exaltées semblent accueillir avec avidité les mechancetés les plus atroces et les calomnies les plus indignes [to prevent a scandal which will spread all too much in a time when [even] exalted persons seem to welcome the most atrocious malignities and unworthy calumnies with eagerness].[163]

When Noailles discovered nothing,[164] the search was entrusted to Forth, who at Maurepas's request had been attached to the British embassy as a special envoy. Forth acted as a go-between for the British ambassador, Lord Stormont, and Maurepas, who disliked each other, allowing Maurepas to by-pass the supposedly more bellicose Vergennes, who was probably ignorant of Forth's search.[165] Forth's expense account shows that he and his servant Quin were hunting the *libelle* as early as 18 June 1777. By August, Quin had identified *l'Imprimeur* ['the Printer'] – the pamphlet's pseudonymous author – and was making small loans and gifts to him and his wife. By December he had discovered *l'Imprimeur*'s residence and the location of a trunk containing the finished pamphlets.[166]

Maurepas spent December and early January trying to persuade Forth to help suppress the pamphlet, even hinting that its allegations might cause his own downfall and the accession of a more hawkish ministry. Stormont, desperate to postpone a rupture, eventually secured Forth's agreement to Maurepas's request, and so Forth set off for London.[167] He arrived on Sunday 11 January 1778 and quickly won promises of support from Lord North. On 15 January he received letters signed 'Humanity' and '*l'Imprimeur*' outlining the *libellistes*' demands and enclosing the advertising handbill quoted in the prologue. Forth could buy the entire edition, now retitled *La Guerlichion femelle ou la reine chaude et sa surintendante*, for 500 guineas. Forth should apply to Mr Thomas Smith in Silver Street, Blackfriars, who had seized all 1,000 copies of the work because *l'Imprimeur* owed him 300 guineas. However, Forth must hurry, because a certain Mr Shaw had offered 500 guineas for them and printed the handbill. He intended to sell them the following Tuesday, after the opening of Parliament, a traditional moment for releasing political tracts. The notes gave Forth a *rendez-vous* and deadline for Monday morning.[168] Forth immediately wrote for instructions to Maurepas, although he could not expect a reply before the deadline, and on learning that *l'Imprimeur* had gone to Oxford, he sent Stormont's secretary, Thomas Jeans, to drag him back.[169] On Tuesday 20 January, Maurepas replied that Forth should not hesitate to pay the sum requested or solicit help from British ministers, even though the publication of the handbill seemed a 'mauvais pronostic' ['bad omen'] and indicated that the blackmailers might hold back a copy and reprint the work.[170]

Maurepas's fears of double-dealing were justified, for on the night of 30 January Smith began to prevaricate, and instead of delivering the trunk containing the *libelles* sent *l'Imprimeur* to Forth's house with his apologies.

Forth, who was waiting with John Robinson, first secretary to the Treasury, and other dignitaries assembled to witness the placing of seals on the trunk, reacted with characteristic decisiveness. He sent his servant to collect Smith, who, after 'mille tours et quelques coups de cannes' ['a thousand tergiversions and several blows with a cane'] from Forth, promised to release the trunk in return for a further 100 guineas.[171] Forth also extracted a signed statement from *l'Imprimeur*, promising to pay 1,000 guineas if he were ever convicted of writing another *libelle*.[172] A week later, Forth was in Paris, where he surrendered the *libelle* and presented an expense account, totalling £859 05s ½d.[173] It reveals that the payments to *l'Imprimeur* and Smith – who almost certainly wrote the letter signed 'Humanity' – were made by Robinson, on behalf of Maurepas, and thus mark a high-point in Anglo-French co-operation over *libellistes*.

Forth never revealed *l'Imprimeur*'s identity, not even to his diary. His biographer, Marion Ward, asserts that Morande, collaborating with Beaumarchais, was almost certainly both Angelucci and *l'Imprimeur*. She asserts that by 1777 Maurepas had rumbled their cosy arrangement, and employed Forth for this reason.[174] Had Ward known that in October 1775 Beaumarchais had reported that an illustrated *libelle* against the princesse de Lamballe – undoubtedly the *Guerlichon* – was being prepared in Oxford, and over the next year repeatedly urged its suppression, she would have been even more convinced.[175] There are, however, compelling reasons for doubting that Morande was *l'Imprimeur*. First, Morande had avoided using middlemen in his negotiations since falling out with Boissière in 1772. Second, the handwriting of *l'Imprimeur* differs from Morande's scrawl in several consistent and important respects. Although *l'Imprimeur*'s letter may have used a disguised hand and apparently deliberately misspelt words to appear Alsatian, German, or Swiss, it is unlikely that Morande wrote it.[176] Thirdly, it is probable that Forth knew of Morande's contract with Lauraguais, for the latter was an old friend who shared Forth's passion for horseracing.[177] Thus, if Morande were *l'Imprimeur*, Forth could have silenced him by threatening him with the clause in the contract whereby Morande would forfeit 32,000 *livres* to Lauraguais if he were convicted of writing further *libelles* against the French court. Invoking the clause would also surely have resulted in Morande's being imprisoned for debt.

However, the most significant problem with Ward's attribution concerns British reasons for withholding *l'Imprimeur*'s identity. Among three conceivable motives, none apply to Morande. If Quin and Forth did not name *l'Imprimeur* because they knew him only by sight, he cannot have been Morande, a notorious *libelliste* and prime suspect, whose address Quin could have discovered in hours rather than months. Equally, there is no reason to suppose that exposing Morande as *l'Imprimeur* would embarrass either the British or the supposedly doveish Maurepas. Finally, if the British concealed *l'Imprimeur*'s identity in order to gain a hold over him, it is again unlikely that he was Morande. Morande may well have made a useful British agent as he was a known correspondent of Beaumarchais, whom they knew to be gun-running to the rebel American colonists with Vergennes's blessing.[178] However, the British would have gained still more by exposing Morande as the author of the *Guerlichon*, since this would wreck the credit of Beaumarchais, who was known to be Morande's patron.[179] Conceivably, Vergennes might not survive the fallout of such a revelation, and the French hawks would suffer a serious blow. Furthermore, when war broke out, the British ordered Morande to leave London for its duration – clear proof that he was not their double agent.[180]

A more likely author is the corrupt Parisian police officer Goupil. Although existing sources are contradictory and none exactly matches the facts recounted above, it is intriguing that Goupil, who was allegedly responsible for an unnamed pamphlet whose description resembles the *Guerlichon*, was arrested just one month after the *Guerlichon* was suppressed.[181] Moreover, Goupil's accomplice, Poultier alias Delmotte, who was said to have written pamphlets that Goupil used in his intrigues, was, like *l'Imprimeur*, married and lived in London for a while with his wife.[182] Both Lenoir and Marie-Antoinette's lady-in-waiting, Madame Campan, report that Goupil produced and partially printed a *libelle* against Marie-Antoinette and the princesse de Lamballe, which he 'discovered' and later suppressed for cash.[183] However, their accounts imply that these events occurred in 1775 or 1776. The *Bastille dévoilée* correctly dates Goupil's arrest to 9 March 1778, and alleges that he had returned from the Low Countries with the entire edition of the *libelle* in question just weeks earlier.[184] Manuel's *La Police de Paris dévoilée* offers yet another version, asserting that Goupil boasted of suppressing an 'infamous brochure against the queen' [i.e. the *Guerlichon*], unaware that the whole edition had been sent from London to the Bastille under Lord North's seal.[185] If this is true, Goupil's knowledge of the *Guerlichon* is highly suspicious, since the police were not involved in the suppression. Taken together, these sources hint that Goupil was behind the production of the *Guerlichon*, but lost control over the manuscript before it was suppressed.

There is, however, one final piece to the jigsaw: for the sources also suggest a credible motive for British reticence to identify *l'Imprimeur*, who was presumably Goupil's printer or the owner of his manuscript. Lenoir, Manuel, and the *Bastille dévoilée* concur that Goupil's actions earned him the protection of the princesse de Lamballe, who nominated his wife for the vacant position of *lectrice* (reader) to Marie-Antoinette.[186] Perhaps, then, the British hoped to use the threat of exposure as leverage on Goupil, a rising star in the Paris police whose wife served the queen, to coerce him into becoming their agent. If so, the plan failed. Goupil was arrested and died in prison at Vincennes on 28 April 1780. His wife and Poultier were also incarcerated.[187] Over the next few years several other *libellistes* suffered similar fates. Their heyday was drawing to a close.

Notes

1 CPA 522 fos 292–3, Noailles to Vergennes, 1 April 1777.
2 MO, MS 1422 p. 306. For his manuscript song collection, the 'Chansonnier Maurepas', see BN, Manuscrits français 12,616–12,659.
3 John Hardman, *Louis XVI* (New Haven and London: Yale University Press, 1993), p. 28.
4 CPA 528 fos 136–7, [Maurepas] to Forth, 2 January 1778.
5 CPA 528 fo. 168, Maurepas to Forth, 26 January 1778.
6 CPA 523 fos 217–18, Vergennes to Noailles, Versailles, 7 June 1777. Another copy is at fos 223–4.
7 CPA 542 fos 320–1, Vergennes to d'Adhémar, 29 May 1783. See also CPA 545 fos 170–1, Vergennes to d'Adhémar, 16 October 1783.
8 CPA 497 fos 176–82, Garnier to d'Aiguillon, London, 31 August 1771; CPA 522 fo. 357, [Miromesnil] to [Maurepas?], 6 April 1777.
9 Comte d'H***, *Histoire de Bertin*, esp. pp. 108, 137–76. See also ULBC, file 58 pp. 14, 23–4, 30, cuttings from *Gazetteer*, 28 June 1764; *Public Advertiser*, 29 June and 4 July 1764. Quote from Darnton, 'Police inspector', p. 178.
10 See Aclocque, *Presse clandestine*. Goulemot, *Forbidden texts*, pp. 15–16, notes the successful French pursuit of Dutch-based French pornographers at around this time. On the Netherlands' role in European publishing, see G. C. Gibbs, 'The role of the Dutch Republic as the intellectual entrepôt of Europe in the seventeenth and eighteenth centuries', *Bijdragen en mededelingen betreffende de geschiedenis der Nederlanden* 86:3 (1971).
11 CPA 441 fos 72–4, 'Traduction d'une pièce de vers Anglois' [from the *London Chronicle*, 30 June 1757]; fos 96–7, anonymous letter [to the comte d'Affry?], 28 July 1757.
12 PRO, SP78/285 fos 210–11, Morande to Benevent, undated [1772].
13 The 'Notice' in Fauques, *Histoire de Pompadour*, 1879 edition, notes (pp. 9–10) that La Harpe and La Porte both identify La Place as the translator, and that his manuscript was recovered from Marigny on Louis XVI's orders in March 1782. It survives, with annotations confirming this story, in MD France 150, and differs from the published translation.
14 'Notice' in Fauques, *Histoire de Pompadour*, 1879 edition, pp. 6, 10, 13. See also the 'Advertisement' in Hooper's 1766 English edition.
15 CPA 522 fo. 357, [Miromesnil] to [Maurepas?], 6 April 1777.
16 CPA 497 fos 176–82, Garnier to d'Aiguillon, London, 31 August 1771.
17 D'Eon to Tercier, 23 March 1764, in *CSI*, I, 313–16.
18 See esp. d'Eon's *Lettres, mémoires et négociations*, pp. xxx–xxxi, 148–56, 174–218, and passim; *Letter Sent to His Excellency, Claude-Louis-François Regnier, Comte de Guerchy* (London: Dixwell, 1763), reprinted (in French) in d'Eon, *Pièces relatives*, pp. 3–21; *Dernière Lettre du chevalier d'Eon de Beaumont à Monsieur le comte de Guerchy* (London: n. p., 1767).
19 See CPA 511 fos 115–20, d'Eon to [Vergennes?], 14 July 1775, at fo. 118; ULBC, file 19 fos 42–3, 45; file 58 fo. 91, cutting from *London Evening Post*, 18–20 April 1775.
20 CPA supplément 16 fos 111–12, annotation of d'Eon on Tercier to d'Eon, 27 December 1763 (copy).

21 The allegation first appears in d'Eon to Broglie and Louis XV, London, 18 November 1763, in Gaillardet, *Mémoires du chevalier d'Eon*, pp. 199–205. Chazell's role is identified in CPA supplément 16 fos 113–14, 'Note de M. d'Eon' and ULBC, file 2 pp. 87–95, 'Extrait de la lettre de . . . d'Eon à . . . d'Autichamp', at p. 91; file 19 fo. 43, unpublished memoir drafts (1805); *Political Register*, October 1768, p. 367 (copy in ULBC, file 58, between pp. 62 and 63).

22 D'Eon to Broglie and Louis XV, London, 18 November 1763, in Gaillardet, *Mémoires du chevalier d'Eon*, pp. 199–205, at pp. 200–1.

23 D'Eon to Guerchy, 5 August 1767, in *Political Register*, October 1767, p. 377 (offprint at ULBC, file 58, bound in pp. 62–3). PRO, SP78/262 fos 85–97 and 131–7 show that on 15 June 1764 a warrant was issued for Chazell's arrest for threatening to burn down his mother-in-law's house, where his wife had taken refuge. Six days later, three officers attempted to arrest him at Guerchy's house. Guerchy intervened, throttled one of the officers, tore up their warrant, imprisoned them briefly, and protested that they had violated diplomatic immunity. Fos 138, 146, 149, 151, and 202 reveal that the British government tried desperately to placate the French rather than let the affair go to court, where, given Chazell's crime and the ambassador's 'highly improper and illegal' behaviour, Guerchy would probably have lost. ULBC, file 69 pp. 7–8 records that Chazell secured a place in the Lazaroni regiment through the vicomte de Choiseul, French ambassador to Naples, but fled when d'Eon's complaints reached Italy. He joined the Polish *confédérés*, and was killed by Russian forces.

24 Vergy, 'Seconde lettre à Choiseul'; PRO, SP78/264 fo. 59, Treyssac de Vergy to Choiseul, 15 November 1764.

25 'Note remise à Guerchy' in d'Eon, *Pieces relatives*, pp. 21–5, 42.

26 CPA 451 fo. 237, Vergy to [Praslin], London, 16 September 1763, refers to Vergy's presentation to Praslin by d'Argental, and begs for employment. Praslin annotated the letter 'point de reponse', the standard phrase when no reply was to be given.

27 CPA 507 fos 46–8, will of Pierre-Henri Treyssac de Vergy, 24 July 1774, at fo. 47.

28 See CPA 451 fo. 468, d'Eon to Lord Sandwich and Lord Halifax, 26 October 1763; fo. 469, Vergy to d'Eon, 27 October 1763; fos 470–1, note of d'Eon, 27 October 1763; CPA supplément 16 fos 113–14, 'Note de M. d'Eon'; d'Eon, *Letter to Guerchy*.

29 Indeed, Morande claims that d'Eon and Vergy fabricated Vergy's affidavits: see Add. MS 11,340 fos 8 and 34, cuttings from *Westminster Gazette*, 20–4 August and 10–14 September 1776.

30 See cuttings from the *Gazette britannique*, 8 March 1765; *London Chronicle*, 29 September – 1 October 1767; *Political Register*, September 1767, in ULBC file 58.

31 Kates, *Monsieur d'Eon*, pp. 133–6.

32 CPA 474 fos 143–5, Guerchy to Choiseul, 7 July 1767; *Political Register*, September 1767, p. 295.

33 *CSB*, I, 238n.

34 CPA supplément 13 fos 132–3, Guerchy to Louis XV, London, 6 November 1763 (copy).

35 PRO, SP78/259 fo. 39, Halifax to Guerchy, St James, 24 November 1763.

36 Louis XV to Tercier, 10 April 1764, in *CSI*, I, 320. PRO, SP78/261 fo. 54, Hertford to Halifax, Paris, 11 April 1764, confirms that Praslin applied diplomatic pressure.

37 See PRO, SP78/261 fos 206–7, memorial delivered by Guerchy, 17 May 1764.

38 See Henley to Grenville, 31 March 1764; Grenville to Henley, Downing Street, 31 March 1764; both in *The Grenville Papers*, edited by William James Smith, 4 vols (London: John Murray, 1852–53), II, 280, 281–4.

39 Grenville to George III, Downing Street, 4 April 1764, in *The Grenville Papers*, II, 285–7.

40 See Kates, *Monsieur d'Eon*, pp. 128–9.

41 See, for example, Praslin's heated views in PRO, SP78/259 fos 82–5, Hertford to Halifax, Paris, 30 November 1763, or Choiseul's comments reported in SP78/273 fo. 264, Rochford to Shelburne, Paris, 10 December 1767. Simon Burrows, 'Culture and misperception: the law and the press in the outbreak of war in 1803', *International History Review* 18:4 (1996), contends that disputes over the press embittered relations between Britain and Napoleonic France and precipitated a war neither side wanted.

42 See below, chapter seven.

43 Linda Colley, *Britons: Forging the Nation* (New Haven, CT: Yale University Press, 1993), p. 101; d'Eon to Tercier, 23 March 1764, in *CSI*, I, 313–16; Kates, *Monsieur d'Eon*, pp. 123–6. D'Eon later refuted in court, allegations on this point published in 1769 by the MP, Dr Musgrave.

44 ULBC, file 8, 'Etat des services', [1777?], pp. 5–6; CPA 16 supplément fos 24–53, 'Etat abregé des services militaires et politiques de Mlle d'Eon', at fo. 29.

45 D'Eon to Tercier, 23 March 1764, in *CSI*, I, 313–16.

46 ULBC, file 58 pp. 23–4, cutting from *Public Advertiser*, 4 July 1764; Kates, *Monsieur d'Eon*, p. 134.

47 See Broglie to Louis XV, 10 April 1764 in *CSB*, I, 218–19.

48 For the royal decree conferring this pension, which exists in multiple copies, see Kates, *Monsieur d'Eon*, p. 137.

49 CPA supplément 16 fos 241–2, d'Eon to Louis XV, 16 July 1766; fos 268–70, 'Etat des papiers que le chevalier d'Eon a remis à M. le Baron de Breteuil'; ULBC, file 3 pp. 83–136, 'Double de l'inventaire de la correspondance secrète du Chevalier d'Eon'.

50 Kates, *Monsieur d'Eon*, p. 220.

51 For contemporary references to d'Eon's payments, see for example, *Westminster Gazette*, 20–4 August 1776 (cutting at Add. MS 11,340 fo. 8); *CSP*, IV, 127. On d'Eon's dispute with Beaumarchais see above, chapter one.

52 See Burrows, 'Cosmopolitan press'.

53 Kates, *Monsieur d'Eon*, pp. 119–21.

54 On the Guines affair, see CPA 496–526 *passim*, and CPA supplément 28. The only major study is Pierrette Girault de Coursac, *Marie-Antoinette et le Scandale de Guines* (Paris: Gallimard, 1962), but see also Price, *Preserving the Monarchy*, pp. 30–41; Maza *Private Lives*, pp. 156–65; Lucien Laugier, *Le Duc d'Aiguillon* (Paris: Editions Albatros, n. d.), pp. 250–8; Christophe Dehaudt, 'Le Duc de Guines: un courtisan entre service du roi et affaires au temps des lumières' (unpublished doctoral thesis: University of Paris IV, 1998), esp. pp. 322–30. I thank Paul Agnani for the final reference.

55 Commentators are divided about d'Aiguillon's role. Price, *Preserving the Monarchy*, pp. 30–1, finds some evidence to support Guines's allegations; Maza, *Private Lives*, p. 158, accepts them at face value; and Girault de Coursac, *Scandale de Guines*, pp. 130–46, contends that d'Aiguillon tried to exacerbate the dispute. Laugier, *D'Aiguillon*, pp. 253–8, contends that he acted with impartiality throughout. Dehaudt, 'Guines', pp. 321–2, is reluctant to pronounce.

56 Price, *Preserving the Monarchy*, pp. 30–41. Price's version is more credible than Coursac's contention that Vergennes manipulated the affair to have d'Aiguillon exiled from court, aided by the Austrian ambassador, Mercy-Argenteau, who wished d'Aiguillon's disgrace to appear a result of the queen's influence. While her description of their motives is credible, the idea of a conspiracy between Vergennes and Mercy is far-fetched, given Vergennes's affiliation to the anti-Austrian faction.

57 See, for example, CPA 509 fos 123–9, Guines to Louis XVI, 16 March 1775; fo. 343, Tort to Vergennes, 17 April 1775; fos 356–7, Tort to Vergennes, 20 April 1775.

58 CPA 508 fos 161–2, Guines to Rochford, 2 February 1775 (copy).

59 CPA 508 fo. 163, Vergennes to Guines, Versailles, 2 February 1775.

60 CPA 510 fos 85–6, Arrêt du Conseil, 16 May 1775, suppressing Guines's judicial memoir; fo. 162, abbé Aubert to Vergennes, 30 May 1775; fo. 206, La Vrillière to Vergennes, 4 June 1775.

61 See Price, *Preserving the Monarchy*, pp. 30–41, esp. pp. 39–40.

62 On these attempts see Nina Rattner Gelbart, *Feminine and Opposition Journalism in Old Regime France* (Berkeley and Los Angeles: University of California Press, 1987), pp. 232–47; Jeremy D. Popkin, *News and Politics in the Age of Revolution: Jean Luzac's Gazette de Leyde* (Ithaca, NY, and London: Cornell University Press, 1989), pp. 72–3, 149–57; Maza, *Private Lives*, p. 175; Burrows, 'Cosmopolitan press', p. 33.

63 CPA 497 fos 111–13, Marin to d'Aiguillon, Paris, 3 August 1771.

64 See the undated letters of Morande to Benevent in PRO, SP78/285 fos 207–8, 209, 210–11, and fos 205–6, Harcourt to Rochford, 20 May 1772.

65 Until 1782, British foreign policy was conducted by two separate offices, the Northern and Southern departments, each responsible for a different geographical area of Europe.

66 PRO, SP78/285 fos 205–6, Harcourt to Rochford, 20 May 1772, quote at fo. 206 (emphasis in original).

67 CPA 505 fos 154–8, Garnier to d'Aiguillon, London, 12 April 1774.

68 *MSB*, 19 February 1774.

69 PRO, SP78/285 fo. 293, Harcourt to Rochford, Compiègne, 16 July 1772.

70 CPA 541 fos 346–9, Göezman to Vergennes, 4 April 1783. This incident may explain Morande's alienation from Boissière and refusal to share his pay-off.

71 CPA 503 fos 374–5, Morande to d'Eon, [undated] numbered 134 [attributed to 1773 but misdated. Internal evidence dates it to the night of 3–4 January 1774].

72 AN, K 157, Broglie to Louis XV, Compiègne, 29 July 1773, published in *CSI*, II, 361. Mairobert (attrib.), *Anecdotes*, p. 315, suggests that Préaudeau de Chemilly, the treasurer of the *Maréchaussée*, may have conducted negotiations during this time.

73 CPA 502 fos 177–9, d'Eon to Broglie, London, 13 July 1773; fos 182–3, d'Eon to Broglie, London, 15 July 1773.

74 See Louis XV's handwritten comments on AN, K 157, Broglie to Louis XV, Compiègne, 29 July 1773.

75 MD France 540 bis fos 168–9, Broglie to Louis XV, Ruffec, 18 November 1773, published in *CSB*, II, 464–6.

76 A summary of d'Eon's instructions is given in *CSB*, II, 425n. According to Didier Ozanan and Michel Antoine the original document is in the Broglie family archives.

77 The duc de Deux-Ponts probably played an intermediary role, as a document relating to the negotiation survives in the ducal archives. See Bayerisches Haupstaatsarchiv, Munich, Politische Korrespondenz des Herzogs von Pfalz-Zweibrücken, Kasten blau 405/34.

78 AN, 277AP/1 fos 148–9, Morande to d'Eon, undated, received 17 November 1773, and mostly transcribed in CPA 503 fos 258–62, d'Eon to Broglie, Stanton Harold, 12 December 1773. CPA 503 fos 31–2, Lauraguais to M. le comte [de Garnier?], 9 March 1774, states that d'Aiguillon would prefer to kidnap Morande.

79 CPA 503 fos 258–62, d'Eon to Broglie, Stanton Harold, 12 December 1773 (copy). For Lormoy's account, see MD France 1398 fos 176–81, Lormoy to Louis XVI, 1 July 1784.

80 *MSB*, 5 February 1774; Mairobert (attrib.), *Anecdotes*, p. 315.

81 CPA 503 fo. 289, 'Soumission du S. (inconnu) [Sr Bellanger?], entre les mains de M. Le D[uc d'Aiguillon]', Versailles, 18 December 1773.

82 On Gotteville (or Godeville) see: Frantz Funck-Brentano, *Lettres de cachet à Paris* (Paris: Imprimerie Nationale, 1903), pp. 405–6; Charpentier, *Bastille dévoilée*, 7th livraison, pp. 99–108, 8th livraison, pp. 136–7. See also Pierre-Augustin Caron de Beaumarchais, *Lettres à Madame de Godeville, 1777–1779*, edited by Maxime Formont (Paris, Lemerre, 1928); I have not yet consulted a new edition of this correspondence published as this book was nearing completion: *Les Lettres galantes de Beaumarchais à Madame de Godeville*, ed. Maurice Lever (Paris: Fayard, 2004). Beaumarchais and Gotteville, who became lovers, were probably introduced by Morande. Mme Latouche de Gotteville, *Voyage d'une françoise à Londres ou la calomnie détruite par la vérité des faits* (London: Mesplet, 1774), denies involvement with Morande or (pp. 9–10) producing *libelles* of her own. However, in May 1780, she was extradited from Holland and imprisoned in the Bastille after blackmailing the duc de Richelieu and libelling La Vauguyon's mistress.

83 *MSB*, 19 February 1774; Mairobert (attrib.), *Anecdotes*, p. 315.

84 CPA 503 fos 374–5, letter of Morande to d'Eon, numbered 134 [3 or 4 January 1774].

85 *MSB*, 5 February 1774. I have not found the relevant edition of the *Morning Post*, but traces of the alert survive in two papers which refused to publish Morande's allegations: see *Morning Chronicle*, 5 January 1774; *Public Advertiser*, 6 January 1774. Pelleport, *Diable*, claims instead (pp. 30–1) that Morande bribed his valet to swear a false oath against the agents. This contradicts all earlier sources.

86 *MSB*, 5 February 1774.

87 AN, 277AP/1 fo. 145, Morande to d'Eon, 4 January 1774 at 11 p.m. There is a copy at CPA 504 fo. 20. 'Exempts' and 'Archers' were both police ranks.

88 CPA 504 fos 20–1, note of d'Eon [January 1774].

89 A purported letter of Morande in Gotteville, *Voyage d'une françoise*, p. 60, also refers to 'daggers and poison'.

90 Lavirotte, 'Notice sur M. de Morande' (private archive).

91 AN, K 159, Broglie to Louis XV, Ruffec, 23 January 1774, published in *CSI*, II, 369–73 and *CSB*, II, 474–8.

92 *BCE*, I, 7.

93 On the burning, see CPA 517 fos 239–43, d'Eon to Morande, 8 April 1776 (copies, in French and English). Contemporary printed accounts are discussed in chapter seven below.

94 Copies of the contract, dated 29 April 1774, can be found in CPA 504 fos 197–200 and CPA 505 fos 208–11. An English version is at CPA 505 fo. 207.

95 CPA 503 fos 308–10, Morande to d'Eon, undated, received 21 December 1773, at fo. 308.

96 This contract, dated 29 April 1774 is in CPA 505 fos 205–6. On Morande and Lauraguais see Robiquet, *Théveneau de Morande*, pp. 35–7.

97 Beaumarchais to Sartine and Louis XVI, 20 June 1774, in Beaumarchais, *Correspondance*, II, 49–51; Paul Huot, *Beaumarchais en Allemagne, révélations tirées des archives de l'Autriche* (Paris: Librairie internationale, 1869), p. 182; René Pomeau, *Beaumarchais ou la bizarre destinée* (Paris: PUF, 1987), p. 87.

98 My description of the *libelle* draws on extensive extracts published in Maurice Lever, *Pierre-Augustin Caron de Beaumarchais*, 3 vols (Paris: Fayard, 1999–2004), II, 421–4n; Jacques Donvez, *La Politique de Beaumarchais*, pp. 257–72. I have not seen the original manuscript.

99 Sartine to Beaumarchais, 11 July 1774, ibid., pp. 273–4; ibid., pp. 401–5 reproduces Beaumarchais's expense account, as does Lever, *Beaumarchais*, II, 432–4n.

100 See Gudin, *Histoire de Beaumarchais*, pp. 125–41; Beaumarchais's letters in Loménie, *Beaumarchais*, I, 389–403; Beaumarchais, *Correspondance*, II, 54–118 *passim*.

101 For the key documents, see Alfred von Arneth, *Beaumarchais und Sonnenfels* (Vienna: Wilhelm Braumüller, 1868), pp. 65–107; Huot, *Beaumarchais en Allemagne*; Donvez, *Politique de Beaumarchais*, pp. 274–387. See also Beaumarchais, *Correspondance*, II, 50–118.

102 Gudin, *Histoire de Beaumarchais*, pp. 127–33; Beaumarchais to Sartine, [early August 1774], in Beaumarchais, *Correspondance*, II, 66.

103 Gudin, *Histoire de Beaumarchais*, pp. 133–5.

104 For his depositions on 15 August 1774, consult Donvez, *Politique de Beaumarchais*, pp. 301–5; Lever, *Beaumarchais*, II, 428–9n.

105 On these events see Arneth, *Beaumarchais und Sonnenfels*; Huot, *Beaumarchais en Allemagne*. See *CSMT*, II, 224–7, 230–5, 239, 244, 254, for correspondence between Maria-Theresia, her ambassor Mercy-Argenteau, and Marie-Antoinette concerning Beaumarchais and the *Avis*. Beaumarchais to Maria-Theresia, Vienna, 23 August 1774, and Beaumarchais to Seilern, Vienna, 24 August 1774, in Beaumarchais, *Correspondance*, pp. 92–7, 98–9, show how his story changed.

106 Huot, *Beaumarchais en Allemagne*, pp. 60–4. A further version of the encounter, in Beaumarchais to 'M. R.', 15 August 1774, in Beaumarchais, *Correspondance*, II, 66–74, says they were German highwaymen and does not mention Angelucci.

107 For Dratz's statement, dated Neustadt, 14 August 1774 'after' 6.30 p.m., see Arneth, *Beaumarchais und Sonnenfels*, pp. 65–8; Beaumarchais, *Correspondance*, II, 75–7. A French translation appears in Donvez, *Politique de Beaumarchais*, pp. 296–300; Huot, *Beaumarchais en Allemagne,* pp. 69–75; Lever, *Beaumarchais*, II, 430–1n.

108 Huot, *Beaumarchais en Allemagne*, p. 74; Arneth, *Beaumarchais und Sonnenfels*, p. 68. See also the letter of the burgermaster of Nuremberg to Maria-Theresia, 10 September 1774, in Donvez, *Politique de Beaumarchais*, pp. 335–8.

109 This argument follows Huot, *Beaumarchais en Allemagne*, pp. 84–5.

110 'Hatkinson's' signed statement, dated 22 July, agreeing that if the *libelle* ever appeared, he would submit 'à toutes les peines des lois d'Angleterre contre les libellistes' ['to the full weight of English laws against libelers'] was, if genuine, clearly meaningless, especially as he was about to leave the country. On this document see n. 115 below. Eugène Lintilhac, *Beaumarchais et ses oeuvres* (Paris: Hachette, 1887), pp. 63–4, insists that Angelucci existed, and hence Beaumarchais was above reproach, because Beaumarchais discussed Angelucci in letters to a dame Fabia. Since 'Fabia' was actually a codename for Sartine, Lintilhac's argument collapses.

111 See esp. Pomeau, *Beaumarchais*, pp. 78–83; Lever, *Beaumarchais*, II, 50–2, 56–8. Biographers before Arneth and Huot had little reason to doubt that Beaumarchais was an innocent victim. Among other subsequent authorities cited here, Lintilhac, Donvez, and Gudin's editor, Tourneux, acquit Beaumarchais; Gunnar and Mavis von Proschwitz do not question his behaviour; and Marcel Pollitzer, *Beaumarchais: Le Père de Figaro* (Paris: La Colombe, 1957) attributes his actions to 'mythomanie'.

112 The most credible theory in Beaumarchais's defence (see, for example, Donvez, *Politique de Beaumarchais*, p. 273n.) suggests he dreamed up his Vienna jaunt only when he first read the *libelle* in London on about 2–3 July.

113 On the manuscript text, see above, n. 98. This analysis draws on Huot, *Beaumarchais en Allemagne*, p. 184. Strangely, Huot does not mention Sartine here.

114 Ibid., pp. 103–5. This point was first noted by Kaunitz. Huot discovered reports of the innoculation in the *Gazette de France*, 19 June 1774.

115 Agreements between Beaumarchais and 'Hatkinson'/'Angelucci' suppressing the *Avis*, dated London, 22–23 July, and Amsterdam, 4 August 1774, are reproduced in Donvez, *Politique de Beaumarchais*, pp. 274–9, 284–5; Lever, *Beaumarchais*, II, 425–7n. Some commentators believe that Beaumarchais forged these documents. French scholars also overlook the improbability of the name 'Hatkinson', even as an alias.

116 Huot, *Beaumarchais en Allemagne*, p. 182; Beaumarchais to Sartine and Louis XVI, 20 June 1774, in Beaumarchais, *Correspondance*, II, 49–51. Recent historians indulgent to Beaumarchais seem to overlook these facts, though Donvez and Lever mention them.

117 See Beaumarchais's letter to an unknown correspondent, Paris, 24 January 1781, in *BCE*, II, 112–15. Although Beaumarchais feigns innocence, he admits paying Morande for a packet of incriminating documents.

118 His account is reproduced in Donvez, *Politique de Beaumarchais*, pp. 401–5, and Lever, *Beaumarchais*, II, 432–3n., which discusses it at pp. 56–8. *CSMT*,

II, 239, reveals that the Austrian ambassador Mercy also suspected that d'Aiguillon was behind writings against the government and the queen.

119 Gudin, *Histoire de Beaumarchais*, pp. 164–5; Beaumarchais to Sartine, London, 14 October 1776, in Donvez, *Politique de Beaumarchais*, pp. 422–5, quote at p. 424. See also Vergennes to Louis XVI, 23 February 1776, in *BCE*, document 17, and *Louis XVI and Vergennes: Correspondence*, pp. 221–2. See also Pomeau, *Beaumarchais*, p. 87. On Vignoles's journal's content see Beaumarchais to Louis XVI, 27 April 1775 (extrait) in Donvez, *Politique de Beaumarchais*, pp. 411–15.

120 Mercy to Kaunitz, 7 October 1774, cited in Huot, *Beaumarchais en Allemagne*, pp. 193–4.

121 Ibid., p. 194.

122 CPA 526 fos 416–17, Tort's 'List of points to discuss with Vergennes' [1777]. Tort's testimony is suspect as he gave no evidence, worked closely with d'Eon, and cited *Le Lever de l'Aurore* [*The Rising of the Sun*], which could not have been produced in London by Morande, or subject to a negotiation, as it appeared in Versailles rapidly after the events it described. On *Le Lever de l'Aurore*, see Campan, *Mémoires*, I, 93.

123 *CSMT*, II, 420; MO, MS 1422 pp. 308–10. Manuel, *Police*, II, 236–7, also insinuates that there was a connection between Beaumarchais and this pamphlet.

124 Gruder, 'Question of Marie-Antoinette', p. 276.

125 However, Huot, *Beaumarchais en Allemagne*, p. 178, found the pamphlet reminiscent of Beaumarchais, though he relied on Arneth's account. A. Gaston, 'Beaumarchais en Allemagne', *Revue critique* (1870), no. 27, also thought this possible. Tourneux in Gudin, *Histoire de Beaumarchais*, p. 131n. counters that nothing is more 'lourd . . . banal . . . soporifique' ['leaden . . . ordinary . . . soporific'] than the published extracts of the pamphlet.

126 Agnani, 'Libelles et diplomatie', p. 100n., wonders whether Angelucci was a playful soubriquet for Ange Goudar, but this is improbable since he was in Italy in 1774.

127 Gudin, *Histoire de Beaumarchais*, pp. 130–1n.

128 See n. 115 above.

129 This total includes the redemption value for Morande's annuity, half of which was liquidated for 20,000 *livres* by a contract between Morande and Beaumarchais dated 31 October 1775 (CPA 512 fos 183–4).

130 On Linsing see Arsenal, MS 12,433 fos 219–313; ULBC, file 65 pp. 164–5, entries for 5 and 6 July 1776; CPA 509–18 *passim*, esp. CPA 513 fos 8–9, Linsing to Vergennes, London, 24 November 1775. His arrival is noted in CPA 509 fo. 20, Garnier to Vergennes, London, 3 March 1775. Garnier's dispatch of 31 May (CPA 510 fo. 177) contains the earliest reference to his *libelles* in the press, referring to an (unnamed) gazette of the same date.

131 CPA 511 fos 382–3, Guines to Vergennes, London, 10 September 1775.

132 CPA 511 fo. 343, Vergennes to Guines, Versailles, 3 September 1775; fo. 344, [?] to Vergennes, undated letter; fos 362–3, Guines to Vergennes, London, 8 September 1775.

133 CPA 511 fos 362–3, Guines to Vergennes, London, 8 September 1775.

134 CPA 511 fo. 409, Vergennes to Guines, Versailles, 18 September 1775.

135 CPA 514 fo. 74 Linsing to Guines, London, 16 January 1776 (copy); fo. 75, Guines to Linsing, 17 January [1776].

136 CPA 514 fos 95–6, Guines to Vergennes, London, 19 January 1776.
137 CPA 514 fo. 153, Guines to Vergennes, London, 26 January 1776.
138 CPA 514 fo. 217, Vergennes to Guines, Versailles, 1 February 1776.
139 CPA 518 fo. 122, Lenoir de La Bussière to [Garnier], London, 16 September 1776.
140 CPA 518 fo. 123, Garnier to Lenoir de La Bussière, London, 19 September 1776; fos 136–47, Garnier to Vergennes, London, 20 September 1776, at fo. 147.
141 CPA 518 fo 133, Lenoir de La Bussière to Garnier, London, 20 September 1776.
142 CPA 518 fos 165–9, Garnier to Vergennes, London, 24 September 1776, at fo. 169.
143 CPA 518 fos 195–8, Vergennes to Garnier, Versailles, 28 September 1776.
144 CPA 522 fos 294–5, Linguet to Noailles, 1 April 1777; fos 296–7, Linguet's 'Mémoire' for ministers. CPA 522 fos 115–16, Vergennes to Noailles, Versailles, 21 March 1777, confirms that Linguet's journal was not to be permitted.
145 See appendix. As Levy notes, a dossier concerning the suppression negotiation, which Jean Cruppi claimed to have seen in the AAE, seems not to have survived.
146 CPA 522 fos 294–5, Linguet to Noailles, London, 1 April 1777. See also fos 358–9, Linguet to Noailles, 6 April 1777. For the threat to Noailles, see CPA 522 fos 368–9, Noailles to Vergennes, 8 April 1777 or the copy at CPA 520 fo. 284.
147 CPA 521 fos 364–5, Noailles to Vergennes, London, 28 February 1777.
148 CPA 522 fo. 37, Vergennes to Noailles, Versailles, 7 March 1777.
149 CPA 522 fos 352–3, Vergennes to Noailles, Versailles, 5 April 1777.
150 CPA 522 fo. 408, Maurepas to Noailles, Versailles, 15 April 1777.
151 CPA 522 fo. 357, [Miromesnil] to [Maurepas?], 6 April 1777.
152 CPA 522 fos 360–1, Vergennes to Noailles, Versailles, 7 April 1777.
153 CPA 522 fo. 427, Noailles to Vergennes, London, 18 April 1777.
154 For Linguet's continued threats see CPA 523, fos 331–2, Linguet to Vergennes, 30 June 1777; fos 333–4, Linguet to Noailles, 30 June 1777. On Lequesne's role and negotiations, see Levy, *Linguet*, pp. 190–1.
155 CPA 522 fo. 502, Maurepas to Vergennes, 28 April 1777; fo. 452, Vergennes to Noailles, Versailles, 19 April 1777.
156 CPA 523 fos 436–7, Vergennes to Noailles, Versailles, 12 July 1777, quotes at fo. 436.
157 CPA 522 fos 115–16, Vergennes to Noailles, 21 March 1777; CPA 525 fos 131–2, Vergennes to Noailles, 18 October 1777; CSCV, I, 133, 212, 237, 249, 320. CSCV, I, 141, reports that Lenoir told Miromesnil he would only ban the paper if he received an explicit order from the king. The *Academiciens'* complaint concerned *Annales* no. 18.
158 Levy, *Linguet*, p. 193; CSCV, I, 133.
159 See Frances Acomb, *Mallet du Pan (1749–1800): A Career in Political Journalism* (Durham, NC: Duke University Press, 1973), pp. 113–14; Levy, *Linguet*, p. 193.
160 CPA 525 fo. 316, Lenoir to Amelot, 7 November 1777; CPA 526 fos 7–20, Noailles to Vergennes, 21 November 1777, at fo. 7. No pamphlet with this or a similar title exists in British or French library research collections. Beaumarchais to Sartine, London, 'ce dimanche juillet 1774' [*sic*] in Beaumarchais, *Correspondance*, II, 59–64, reveals that Beaumarchais sent

an agent called Vaillant from London to Versailles while negotiating with 'Angelucci'. Thus Paul Vaillant was possibly involved in previous suppression negotiations.

161 CPA 525 fos 356–7, Vergennes to Noailles, 12 November 1777.

162 CPA 523 fos 217–18, Vergennes to Noailles, Versailles, 7 June 1777 (copy at fos 223–4).

163 Ibid.

164 CPA 523 fos 277–8, Noailles to Vergennes, London, 20 June 1777 (copy at CPA 520 fos 362–3).

165 See Ward, *Forth*, pp. 9–25. Forth's letters to Maurepas or his secretary Le Cler were apparently deposited in the AAE after the event. Price's and Hardman's introduction to *Louis XVI and Vergennes: Correspondence* notes that little of Maurepas's correspondence survives from this period, making it difficult to discern whether he was genuinely pacific.

166 CPA 528 fo. 389, 'Depenses faites . . . pour empecher la publication d'un libel a Londres'.

167 Ward, *Forth*, pp. 42–3.

168 CPA 528 fos 93 and 94, pseudonymous notes signed 'Humanity' and 'l'Imprimeur', addressed to Forth, both dated Thursday 15 January 1778; fo. 117, Forth to Le Cler, 16 January 1778; fo. 118, Forth to Maurepas, 16 January 1778.

169 CPA 528 fo. 389, 'Depenses faites . . . pour empecher la publication d'un libel a Londres'.

170 CPA 528 fos 136–7, [Maurepas] to Forth, 20 January 1778.

171 CPA 528 fos 202–3, Forth to Maurepas, London, 'midnight', Friday 30 January 1778.

172 Ward, *Forth*, p. 46. Her source for this statement is Forth's diary, which is in private hands. I have not seen this document.

173 CPA 528 fo. 389, 'Depenses faites . . . pour empecher la publication d'un libel a Londres'.

174 Ward, *Forth*, pp. 41–2.

175 Beaumarchais to Louis XVI, 15 December 1775 and Beaumarchais to Sartine, 14 October 1776, in Donvez, *Politique de Beaumarchais*, pp. 415–19, 422–5. Donvez's belief that the *libelle* against Lamballe was Campagnol's *Considérations sur les moeurs de mon siècle* is erroneous: Beaumarchais's letter of 14 October 1776 draws a clear distinction between the two *libelles* and their authors.

176 *L'Imprimeur* repeatedly uses the letter 'f' in place of 'v' or 'ph', whereas Morande's spelling is impeccable. Both use characteristically French letter shapes. *L'Imprimeur*'s letters are formed slowly and deliberately, whereas Morande scrawled rapidly. Both have slightly forward-sloping letters. However, there are key differences. *L'Imprimeur*'s writing lacks Morande's characteristic long 'S' and his open 'E' at the starts of words. Only *l'Imprimeur* uses a loop on the second leg of his 'h' and a capital 'R' shape in the lower case. There are also significant and consistent differences in shaping the numbers '3', '7', and '8'. It is unlikely that so many differences would have been consistently applied in a disguised sample.

177 See Ward, *Forth*, pp. 5–6, 33.

178 PRO, SP78/300 fos 210–11, Stormont to Weymouth, Fontainebleau, 6 November 1776.

179 Beaumarchais's use of Morande as agent in his quarrel with d'Eon was revealed in numerous publications and newsletters in 1776 and 1777.
180 See above, chapter one.
181 Charpentier, *Bastille dévoilée*, 4th livraison, p. 17. Unfortunately, Goupil's Bastille dossier (Arsenal, MS 10,028) sheds no light on the *Guerlichon* issue. I thank Paul Agnani for inspecting this dossier for me.
182 Charpentier, *Bastille dévoilée*, 5th livraison, pp. 64–5; Funck-Brentano, *Lettres de cachet*, p. 402, entries 5073–4.
183 Campan, *Mémoires*, I, 134.; MO, MS 1422 p. 47. Lenoir reveals that Goupil denounced the *libelle* to M. Albert, lieutenant of police between 14 May 1775 and 13 June 1776, but implies that the suppression occurred under his own administration. He links Goupil's arrest to a conspiracy to denounce an imaginery ministerial intrigue, rather than involvement with *libelles*. On Goupil, see d'Almeras, *Marie-Antoinette et les pamphlets*, pp. 208–14.
184 Charpentier, *Bastille dévoilée*, 5th livraison, pp. 60–4.
185 Manuel, *Police*, I, 262.
186 MO, MS 1422 pp. 47–8; Manuel, *Police*, I, 262; Charpentier, *Bastille dévoilée*, 5th livraison, p. 61. *MSB*, 11 May 1778, describes Goupil's wife as *femme de chambre* [maid] to the queen. Lenoir claims Maurepas eventually rescinded the appointment.
187 Manuel, *Police*, I, 262; Charpentier, *Bastille dévoilée*, 5th livraison, p. 63.

4

The policing and politics of *libelles*, 1778–92

The outbreak of war between Britain and France in July 1778 disrupted the *libellistes'* operations, as it became dangerous and difficult for French agents to communicate with Versailles and French diplomats were no longer on hand to oversee negotiations. Between March 1778 and mid-1781 it appears that the London *libellistes* fell silent and there were no missions against them. This is not certain, however, because, during the war, French secret agents in Britain were directed by the spy-master Baudouin, who worked for the naval ministry and whose correspondence has not survived.[1] However, in mid-June 1781, an adventurer named Baxon denounced a new *libelle*, Baudouin referred the matter to Vergennes, and subsequent correspondence concerning *libellistes* passed through foreign ministry files.[2] This new *libelle*, the scurrilous poem *Les Amours de Charlot et Toinette*,[3] was particularly worrying because it was to be accompanied by pornographic engravings of the queen.[4] This intelligence placed Vergennes and Baudouin in a quandary. They were deeply suspicious of Baxon, and had spurned his previous offers to procure secret intelligence if paid in advance.[5] However, they had few alternatives, following the destruction of Henri de La Motte's espionage network in January 1781. Moreover, the British decision to make an example of La Motte while allowing his accomplices to testify and escape scot-free, had sown terror and distrust among would-be spies. When the *chargé d'affaires* François Barthélemy was instructed to re-establish an espionage machine in the late 1780s, he complained that potential recruits remained terrified, making his task impossible.[6] Although Baudouin eventually recruited Morande to replace La Motte, he apparently did not wish him to deal with *libellistes*. Instead the task was assigned to the disgraced and ruined Goëzman, who like earlier agents, including d'Eon, Beaumarchais, and Lauraguais, accepted employment in the hope of restoring his fortunes.[7]

In the summer of 1781, Goëzman was despatched to London masquerading as a German baron under the alias de Thurne.[8] There, he negotiated the suppression of the *libelle* with Boissière, acquiring the whole edition including print blocks, which he smuggled back to France in a fishing boat.[9] Again, the fee was exorbitant: 15,000 *livres* for the *libelle*, plus a 3,600 *livre* gratuity demanded by Boissière at the last minute. The final fifty *Louis* (1,200 *livres*), which were unauthorised, came from Goëzman's own pocket.[10] On reaching

Versailles, Goëzman was given a personal interview with Vergennes, paid 2,400 *livres* expenses, and sent back to Britain on a monthly stipend of 1,000 *livres*. These measures were approved retrospectively by Louis XVI.[11]

Soon Goëzman complained of financial problems, but his nose for further scandalous works, notably *Les Rois de France dégénérés par les princesses de la Maison d'Autriche* [*The Kings of France Corrupted by the Princesses of the House of Austria*] and *Naissance du dauphin dévoilée*, became acute.[12] These titles almost certainly emanated from Pelleport, the star in Boissière's stable of *libellistes*, who had recently arrived in London and was already targeting the princesse de Bouillon. She initially refused to meet his price, but relented after the publication of the *Petits Soupers*.[13] Pelleport therefore decided that the French court offered better pickings, and announced the *Naissance du dauphin*, which contained 'des estampes qui tendent à déshonorer une reine, à vilipender son august époux, et à exciter le ressentiment dans un prince à peine né' ['prints which tend to dishonour a queen, vilify her august husband, and excite resentment in a prince who has hardly been born'].[14] When Lenoir learned of this new pamphlet in February 1783, he grew suspicious and remarked to Vergennes delicately that Goëzman's zeal might be inadvertently encouraging the manufacture of further *libelles* and prints. In fact, he feared both that Goëzman was in league with Boissière and that the British had blown his cover.[15] Lenoir proposed sending a police officer, Receveur, to acquire the plates and *libelles* and observe Goëzman. Vergennes immediately approved the idea, and ordered his minister plenipotentiary, Moustier, who was in London although a peace treaty had yet to be finalised, to support Receveur and provide introductions to British ministers and other useful contacts.[16]

Receveur, a man of private means and veteran of Bellanger's expedition against Morande, was selected because he was considered incorruptible.[17] Already, in late 1781, he had smashed Jacquet's clandestine publishing network. Jacquet and his collaborators produced manuscript *libelles* in Paris and printed them in Amsterdam, Brussels, and London, whereupon Jacquet would be sent to the Low Countries to suppress them.[18] According to Lenoir, their operation was rumbled by Morande, who denounced Jacquet's visits to London to a retired police inspector. Jacquet and his accomplices were arrested, and several packages of *libelles* were retrieved from Belgium and the Netherlands and deposited in the Bastille's secret *dépôt*.[19]

Receveur arrived in London on 13 March 1783 and rapidly concluded that Goëzman 'paroit jouer les deux partis' ['appears to play both ends against the middle']. He had suspicious links with the Chathamite Lord Shelburne, who had just resigned as prime minister, and the darling of the Whigs, Charles James Fox, who was about to be reappointed foreign secretary.[20] At the suggestion of Moustier, Receveur also hired Morande, hoping to benefit from his local and specialist knowledge.[21] Meanwhile, Moustier consulted English lawyers, hoping to find means of legal redress against writers or distributors of *libelles*, including Linguet, who had just published his *Mémoires sur la Bastille*.[22] Their advice was not encouraging: they advised against pursuing Boissière for extortion or conspiracy and concluded that none of the possible means of bringing a libel action was likely to be effective. To get a criminal information brought in King's Bench would take over a year; getting sworn affidavits from foreigners would be almost impossible; and non-resident aliens would be unable to bring a civil case.[23]

Receveur's arrival caused panic in the French exile community. Rumours and disinformation flew, encouraged by the *libellistes* and malice. Brissot, busy establishing his *Lycée*, was among those who feared being denounced. Encouraged by other refugees, he wrote to Moustier to deny involvement with *libellistes*. The ambassador and Receveur had heard no such rumours and were mystified. Receveur concluded that Brissot was involved, and only gradually realised his error.[24]

Receveur had authority to pay 200 *Louis* for the *Naissance du dauphin dévoilée* and 150 *Louis* for the *Petits Soupers*, and began negotiating their suppression with Boissière and Pelleport.[25] However, Pelleport, who claimed to be only a middleman, demanded 700 *Louis* and grew uneasy about Receveur's intentions. On 7 April, he circulated a broadside entitled *An Alarm-Bell against French Spies*, denouncing Receveur and alleging that secure carriages were being built to carry kidnapped Frenchmen to Dover. It also announced the imminent appearance of *Les Amours et aventures du Vizir Vergennes* [*The Love-Life and Adventures of Vizir Vergennes*] and *Les Passe-tems d'Antoinette* [*Antoinette's Amusements*], the latter of which Pelleport immediately offered to suppress.[26] Receveur was unnerved by the broadside and complained to the new ambassador, d'Adhémar, that his life was in danger.[27] Meanwhile, Boissière refused to deal with anyone but Goëzman and, it was reported, started carrying a pistol.[28] In these circumstances, Receveur was forced to negotiate through the increasingly suspect Goëzman. Six weeks later, he gave up and returned to France.[29] Having failed to check the *libelles* at source, the French government now tightened its control over imported books. An order of 12 June 1783 required that all consignments entering the country must be inspected by the Paris booksellers' guild, rather than customs officials in the provinces, who were often bribed. This added to delays and import costs, and made smuggling much more difficult: foreign publishing houses like the Société typographique de Neuchâtel considered it a disaster, and for a while the illegal trade was seriously disrupted.[30]

Furious to see his plans and his cosy relationship with Boissière and Goëzman disrupted, Pelleport retaliated by publishing *Le Diable dans un bénitier*, which exposed Morande as a police agent and spy, and accused the French ministry of corruption.[31] These revelations incensed Morande and upset d'Adhémar, who encouraged him to bring a libel case, apparently with the support of Fox, who felt that his mistress had also been mistreated.[32] However, Vergennes vetoed the idea, arguing that since crowned heads were not libelled, it was not for the French government to pursue the matter.[33] Morande apparently dragged Pelleport before the courts anyway and

Le Plénipot... reçoit l'abjuration de Charlot
et R.....r lui donne la croix de St André

8 Frontispiece woodcut from Anne-Gédeon de La Fite de Pelleport, *Le Diable dans un bénitier* (London, 1783) (this print is explained above, p. viii)

organised his creditors to pursue him.[34] However, his most spectacular revenge on Pelleport and his friend Brissot was yet to come.

In June 1784, desperate to find funds for his *Lycée* and break his partnership with Desforges, Brissot travelled to France. There, on 12 July, he was arrested for helping to compose the *Diable dans un bénitier*, on the basis of

Morande's denunciation and fabricated evidence.[35] Pelleport had been arrested the previous day, after Buard, d'Adhémar, Morande, and Swinton lured him to Boulogne in a plot approved by Vergennes.[36] Both men were taken to the Bastille for questioning. Under interrogation, Lenoir claimed that Pelleport 'n'avoit pu disconvenir qu'il avoit composé et fait imprimer un seul de beaucoup de libelles que les autres lui attribuoient' ['was unable to deny that he composed and printed a single one of the many *libelles* that others attributed to him']. Although his interrogation records do not survive, documents in his Bastille dossier imply he admitted producing the *Diable*,[37] and he seems to have refuted allegations that Brissot colluded in producing *libelles*.[38] Meanwhile, Brissot convinced even the hardened Bastille interrogators of his innocence.[39] In September, after a concerted campaign by powerful protectors, including the duc d'Orléans, he was released, but emerged to find his business and dreams in tatters.[40] Goëzman, although deeply implicated, was more fortunate: conclusive evidence of his complicity was never discovered. Following Receveur's departure, he continued negotiating with Boissière until ordered to return to France in July 1783.[41] He was received coldly, and requests for further payments and reimbursement of the fifty *Louis* he had paid Boissière in 1781 proved fruitless.[42]

A final associate of Pelleport, Jean-Claude Fini, alias comte Hyppolite Chamorand, was arrested in France in November 1785, after he fled London with the proceeds of a promissory note extorted at knife-point. Morande claimed to have seen manuscript *libelles* in Fini's possession, and this was corroborated when several were discovered on his person.[43] Under interrogation, he admitted writing some, and attributed others to a French refugee called Lallemand.[44] Possibly some were prepared in collaboration with Pelleport, for in the Bastille, Fini and Pelleport made accusations against each other.[45] Despite British extradition requests, Fini was sent to the Bicêtre, a prison for common criminals, and the French refused to return the stolen funds.[46] Among Pelleport's closest associates, only Boissière got away scot-free.

Despite contrary advice from d'Adhémar, Morande, Moustier, Receveur, Goudar, and their own barristers, the French government had always intended to pay Pelleport's ransom if legal remedies could not be found.[47] Even after Receveur's mission, Vergennes rejected d'Adhémar's advice to kidnap Pelleport and spurned Navan's offers to seize him, arguing that it was too risky and offered little gain. *Libellistes* needed salutary examples, but kidnapping must needs be kept secret. Besides, he noted, such remedies had been tried before without success.[48] Instead, his preferred solution was legal reform, by act of Parliament, as he was confident that the French could control the circulation of *libelles* inside France.[49] Thus the years 1782–84 witnessed concerted efforts both to persuade the British to introduce new legislation and to find remedies within existing laws.

A memoir in the hand of Rayneval, secretary to the foreign ministry, but doubtless containing Vergennes's thoughts, is particularly instructive, revealing French frustrations and the strongest arguments they could muster. It argued that the British were not adequately committed to the principle of reciprocity, because the English idea of liberty 'est contraire à tout ce qui a même l'apparence de la plus legère restriction' ['is opposed to everything which appears to offer even the least restriction'] and thus 'on aime mieux tolérer les abus que de penser à la sûreté de la société' ['they prefer to tolerate abuses rather than consider the security of society']. This was a vicious approach, for 'la sûreté doit être le premier effet de la liberté, et il est demontré que la liberté ne sauroit exister sans la sûreté: c'est là le principe de toutes les loix de police.' ['Security ought to be the main effect of liberty, and it is demonstrable that liberty would not exist without security: this is the principle of all police regimes'.] Surely, the British recognised that inadequate support for this principle could cause crimes through expectation of impunity? Thus the memorialist called for the British to legislate for an extradition treaty, or, failing that, to agree to the right of courts in each country to judge fugitive criminals from the other. Any legislation should include the crimes of *lèse majesté*, murders, robberies, and also *libelles*. A nation might grant by its constitution the right to censure its own government, but not to defame others and publish with impunity 'toutes les atrocités qu'une imagination déreglée peut enfanter' ['all the atrocities to which an unrestrained imagination might give birth']. Here the principle of reciprocity applied, for the British would find it unacceptable if France flooded Europe with *libelles* against George III. They might legitimately argue that press liberty was the most efficacious restriction on royal and ministerial authority, but *libelles* against foreign sovereigns were a matter of indifference to the British constitution. If all else failed, Rayneval suggested, the British should be urged to grant foreigners the same rights as British subjects to pursue *libellistes* before the courts. This surely would without inconvenience prevent London's remaining the source of sordid attacks on every crowned head in Europe.[50]

Because of the weakness of existing laws on *libelles*, other legal expedients were also considered. Moustier consulted the lawyer Thomas Evans to discuss whether the husband of Perrine Buttet, Linguet's long-term mistress, should be encouraged to sue him for adultery.[51] Moustier also supported a suggestion of the barrister Edward Bearcroft, who thought a legal victory against Boissière unlikely, but believed that the bookseller might be ruined if two of the less illustrious victims of the *Petits Soupers*, dame Bours and the chevalier Jerningham, brought separate cases. Should Boissière be awarded costs, they could abscond to France.[52] But the French were also aware of the dangers of a trial. Moustier noted that British aristocrats often preferred not to bring libel cases, fearing derision in court.[53] Moreover, as Evans noted, defeat could encourage new *libelles*, by demonstrating impunity.[54]

The failure of Receveur's mission was not absolute, for it appears that none of the new *libelles* threatened by Boissière ever appeared and, as Lenoir noted, following Pelleport's arrest, no further such pamphlets appeared for a considerable time.[55] However, the French government was soon troubled by a new problem: British newspaper articles concerning an alleged affair between Colonel Conway, a British army officer, and the French queen, which appeared in December 1784. The most outspoken of the Conway libels appeared in the *Morning Post* on 11 December 1784 and provoked an immediate diplomatic complaint.[56] It spoke of Conway's adventures and the sexual frustrations of the French queen, a crucial mistake. According to Lord Mansfield, by identifying Marie-Antoinette explicitly, the editor opened himself to legal action.[57] Mansfield also cited the precedent of an *ex officio* prosecution brought by the British Crown on behalf of the Russian government in January 1781, after John Bew's *General Evening Post* suggested that its ambassador, Simolin, had been implicated as a 'common spy' by members of Henri de La Motte's espionage ring.[58] *Ex officio* procedures, which were permissible in cases affecting the good order and peace of the realm, were useful in such instances because the attorney-general brought the case for the Crown, so there was no need to identify a complainant. Vergennes and the king therefore authorised d'Adhémar to ask for a charge to be brought, provided that Louis XVI be not named.[59] The British government agreed and began *ex officio* proceedings against Peter Stuart, at that time editor of the *Morning Post*, and J. S. Barr of the *Morning Herald*, for insinuating that Conway, Colonel Whitworth, and the British ambassador, the Duke of Dorset, had all enjoyed the queen's favours.[60]

The French also seized the opportunity to press for new libel legislation. However, d'Adhémar rightly doubted that this would result in any action. Although all 'honnêtes gens' ['men of honour'] in Britain agreed on the need to repress 'des abus aussi revoltans et aussi dangereux' ['such revolting and dangerous abuses'], none dared introduce a bill before Parliament: 'C'est le Conseil des Rats; aucun ne veut attacher le grelot, ou craindroit le lendemain d'avoir sa maison brulée. C'est ce qui est arrivé à Lord Mansfield dont la sévère intégrité fut punie par le feu dans le soulevement incendiaire de 1780.' ['It is the Council of Rats: none wishes to bell the cat, for fear of having their house burned down the next day. That is what happened to Lord Mansfield, whose stern integrity was punished by fire during the incendiary rising of 1780 [i.e. the anti-Catholic Gordon riots]'.][61] Whether or not d'Adhémar's explanation of ministerial reticence was correct, new legislation was not forthcoming until Fox's libel act of 1792. Nevertheless, in 1787 French complaints secured the prosecution and imprisonment, for libels against d'Adhémar, Barthélemy, and Marie-Antoinette, of Lord George Gordon, the noble hothead who, as elected leader of the Protestant Association, incited the 'incendiary rising' of 1780.[62] These libels related to France's treatment of the magician Cagliostro following the diamond necklace affair.

Cagliostro was an innocent victim in the diamond necklace affair, implicated only by the mendacious testimony of the comtesse de La Motte, who asserted that he had taken the necklace, and his own absurd claims to be able to manufacture diamonds.[63] Having been found innocent, Cagliostro and his wife were nevertheless expelled from France and sought refuge in England. There, he published pamphlets attacking Breteuil and accusing the governor of the Bastille, de Launay, of pilfering 100,000 *livres* of his property. He demanded justice and instructed his lawyer to bring a complaint before the Châtelet.

Cagliostro's allegations were merely bluster and self-promotion, and Breteuil persuaded Louis XVI to call his bluff.[64] A commission of councillors of state was appointed to investigate,[65] and on 21 August 1786, Barthélemy received Cagliostro at the embassy and read him a letter from Breteuil granting permission to return to France to bring his case. Cagliostro, who arrived accompanied by Gordon, replied by demanding a safe conduct signed by Louis XVI, a request that Barthélemy forwarded.[66] However, when Gordon published an account of the meeting in the *Public Advertiser*, he insinuated that Breteuil's invitation was a trap:

> Will any friend to liberty blame Count de Cagliostro, after ten months imprisonment in a dungeon, for having his friends near him, when insidious proposals are made to him by the faction of Breteuil and the supporters of the Bastille? Men who have already sought his destruction after his innocence was declared by the Parliament of Paris, embezzled a great part of his fortune and exiled him from France?

Gordon's article also suggested that d'Adhémar and Barthélemy were instruments of the queen's faction; Louis XVI was being imposed upon; and Breteuil's behaviour was 'a very base proceeding indeed . . . and brings contempt and reproach upon all concerned in it.' Two days later, a yet more outspoken article asserted that 'a gang of French spies, who are linked in with Mr De Morand [*sic*], and the Sieurs Barthelemy, Dazimar [d'Adhémar], Combise [de Cambis] and the queen's Bastille party at Paris, are using the most insidious arts to entrap the Count and Countess [de Cagliostro], and have the effrontery and audaciousness to persecute them publicly in this free country, where these noble strangers are come to seek protection in the arms of a generous people.' Cagliostro was suffering the 'perfidious cruelties of a tyrannical government' because he had warned Rohan that the queen and comtesse were plotting against him. Meanwhile, the true history of the scandal remained untold because 'It would discover too much of the base arts practiced to destroy Prince Louis [i.e. the cardinal] and involve in guilt persons not safe to name in an arbitrary kingdom [i.e. France].'[67]

On learning of these passages, Barthélemy immediately sent his lawyer to the newspaper's publisher, Henry Woodfall, to learn who their author was, and consulted the barrister Thomas Erskine. Erskine replied that the articles were clearly libels. The only question was how to prosecute the culprits. Naturally, he advised an *ex officio* prosecution. This would upset the British populace, but seemed unavoidable, since Barthélemy was in Britain in a public capacity, and the libels attacked people of the highest rank in France.[68] The government agreed to procede, but had ulterior motives: when

Gordon appeared before the Court of King's Bench, he was also charged with libelling the British government in a pamphlet distributed to prisoners, concerning proposals to transport them to Botany Bay.[69] The British ministry clearly considered the libel against Marie-Antoinette primarily a means of ensuring the conviction and exemplary punishment of a dangerous firebrand.

When his case reached court, Gordon played to the gallery, claiming that he could not have libelled a queen who was already 'vilified in all the streets of Paris'. When upbraided for such comments, he declared that Marie-Antoinette was 'as great a whore as the Empress of Russia [i.e. Catherine the Great]'. The attorney-general retorted that Gordon was unworthy to be called an Englishman.[70] The jury found Gordon guilty, but he absconded after the trial. The Protestant champion was eventually found in Birmingham, dressed as a Jew, having apparently embraced Judaism.[71] He was sentenced to two years' imprisonment for libelling Marie-Antoinette and three more for libelling the British government.[72] He died, still in prison, in 1793.

Cagliostro, too, was soon discredited. Using evidence possibly provided by Paris police contacts, Morande published Cagliostro's biography in the *Courier de l'Europe*, revealing that the *soi-disant* immortal witness of the crucifixion was actually a Neapolitan charlatan called Guiseppe Balsamo.[73] Cagliostro, whose syphilis-ravaged mind probably believed his own propaganda, responded with an extraordinary challenge, designed to prove his powers. He invited Morande to banquet at his home on a sucking pig fattened with arsenic by Cagliostro's secret method. Morande would carve and serve, and they would wager 5,000 guineas on the outcome. Cagliostro bet that come the morning he would be alive and Morande dead. Morande accepted the challenge, subject to three conditions: the banquet must be public; Cagliostro must deposit 5,000 guineas with a neutral third party in advance; and a carnivorous animal must serve as Morande's substitute.[74] Unable to meet these conditions, exposed as a fraud, and ridiculed in the British press, which closely followed Morande's lead, Cagliostro watched helplessly as his supporters abandoned him. When Morande began organising his creditors to pursue him for debt, Cagliostro renounced plans to found a masonic lodge, and fled England.[75]

Another refugee from the diamond necklace affair, the comte de La Motte, arrived in Britain on 22 August 1785 and spent the next nine months traversing England, Wales, Ireland, and Scotland on the run from agents of the French police and the Rohan faction. During his travels, he asserts, he survived an assassination attempt in a London hansom cab and poison administered to him in Ireland. Thereafter, in the spring of 1786, Vergennes, d'Adhémar, and the new lieutenant of police, Louis Thiroux de Crosne, plotted to snatch him from South Shields, probably so that he might testify at the necklace trial. The scheme was orchestrated in partnership with Morande's old associate Benevent, who, by suspicious coincidence, had befriended La Motte in Scotland and travelled with him to England. Police agents were sent to Newcastle, but after several delays La Motte rumbled the plot and conspired with Benevent to extract 'advances' on the 10,000 guinea reward for his capture.[76] Eventually, La Motte informed d'Adhémar that he was willing to return to France if given immunity from arrest. D'Adhémar, a member of the queen's inner circle, wrote to Vergennes on 30 May to suggest that Marie-Antoinette would be delighted if judgement could be delayed to allow the comte to be heard, but the verdict was passed before his letter even arrived.[77]

Vergennes's most recent biographer sees the kidnap attempt as part of the foreign minister's efforts to ensure that Rohan was exonerated by rounding up key players who had fled abroad.[78] However, it seems that Vergennes actually feared that the comte's evidence would favour the queen: it was Marie-Antoinette who desired the comte's return.[79] In March 1786, when Benevent offered to deliver La Motte,[80] d'Adhémar wrote to her directly, thus outflanking Vergennes, perhaps unintentionally. When Marie-Antoinette forwarded the letter to Vergennes, he had little alternative but to concur with the king's desires and order the kidnap.[81] However, circumstantial evidence suggests that Vergennes tried to sabotage the mission, by causing delays and giving police officers opaque orders and a complex plan.[82] He was certainly dissembling when he announced Rohan's acquital to d'Adhémar, remarking: 'On en est généralement surpris et moi autant que personne' ['People are surprised generally, and me as much as anyone'].[83] Thereafter, the French government lost interest in repatriating La Motte, but continued to keep him under surveillance.[84]

La Motte now turned his hand to blackmail. In October and November 1786, his agents sent the queen's favourite, the duchesse de Polignac, a series of letters,[85] and on 13 December the *Morning Chronicle* published an anonymous 'letter from Canterbury' claiming that the comte intended to reveal 'the truth' behind the affair.[86] It soon transpired that one of the paper's editors, a Frenchman called Damecy, was in league with La Motte, and had already informed the embassy that La Motte had letters from Marie-Antoinette and Breteuil in his possession, which he offered to acquire.[87] Finally, on 29 December, the *Morning Chronicle* published a letter from La Motte himself, declaring his intention to publish a pamphlet. Thereafter the embassy began hearing carefully released rumours about the letters.[88]

The response of Vergennes, whom the comte de La Motte threatened to compromise, shows that ministerial policy towards *libellistes* who attacked the royal family had been reversed. In a letter to d'Adhémar, he expressed characteristic disdain for *libelles* and disgust with the English press. *Libelles* were a 'mal sans remède' ['evil without remedy']: the only option was to prevent their dissemination in France.[89] When on 9 January 1787 the embassy received a letter instructing them to send an emissary to the Bull and Gate Inn in Holborn to negotiate the suppression of the comte's *libelle* with his associate, Mr Warren, nothing was done. The letter arrived too late to be acted upon, but the embassy made no attempt to follow it up.[90] Nevertheless, nothing was published until late February, when d'Adhémar announced the appearance of a *libelle*, which was apparently just a newspaper article.[91] He found it absurd and disgusting and doubted that anyone would read it. The queen would be indignant at the mere suggestion that such works could upset her. He therefore advised ignoring the *libellistes*, and recommended punishing only those who 'par la publication de semblables écrits troublent l'ordre public et manquent de respect aux objets de culte et de la vénération des françois' ['by the publication of such writings disturb the public order and lack respect for objects of adoration and veneration for the French']. Casting the net any wider would be maladroit, as it made the *libellistes* seem important. So did the police surveillance of La Motte and his associates, which d'Adhémar recommended abandoning for the same reason.[92] He also assured the new foreign minister, Montmorin, that until the British government chose to punish such publications, the only solution was to despise them, adding, 'La liberté, la licence de la presse sont des choses si chères à la populace anglaise que le ministère entreprendrait tout plutôt que de porter la main à cela.' ['Freedom, licence of the press are things so dear to the English populace that the ministry will do everything to avoid raising a hand against it'.][93] On 25 March, Montmorin replied: he agreed that *libelles* should be scorned.[94]

Although d'Adhémar had carried his point, the queen's convictions are less clear. When the public learned of the comtesse de La Motte's spectacular escape from the Saltpetrière in June 1787, usually well-informed sources reported that it was the 'fruit' of a negotiation at Bath the previous month between her husband and the queen's favourites, the duchesse de Polignac and the comte de Vaudreuil. In return for suppressing his pamphlet and surrendering thirteen letters written by the queen and Breteuil, La Motte was supposedly promised his wife's freedom and 4,000 *Louis*.[95] It is almost certain that the comtesse had internal assistance for her escape: but if the comte received any money it was rapidly dissipated. The comtesse reached London in August 1787.[96] Once there, she claims, she wrote to Breteuil to announce her 'intention of doing what I am now compelled to' – that is publishing her memoirs. According to her own testimony, a negotiation followed, but faltered – perhaps because the queen was reluctant to make a pay-off.[97] Finally, on 20 December 1787, newspaper advertisements announced that the comtesse intended to publish memoirs containing an amorous correspondence between Rohan and the queen.[98] Clearly she hoped both to negotiate a large suppression fee and to whet the public appetite.

By now the La Mottes had abandoned hope of extorting payments directly from the Crown.[99] Instead, they targeted Calonne, who had retired to England following his dismissal, which had been largely orchestrated by the queen. Desperate to return to favour, he hoped to prove his devotion by succeeding where Breteuil had failed.[100] He proved a sitting duck for the blackmailers. Within hours of the advertisement's appearance, Calonne was visited by La Tour, who knew London's publishing industry and exile community inside out and had close connections with the La Mottes' host and ghost-writer MacMahon.

La Tour's visit to Calonne was arranged through their mutual publisher, Spilsbury, ostensibly to ask Calonne to subscribe to La Tour's new journal, *L'Azile*, which had recently praised Calonne. However, the timing of *L'Azile*'s article, the newspaper advertisement, and the visit strongly suggest that La Tour was involved in a sting. Immediately the conversation turned to the comtesse's *libelle*, he offered himself as a negotiator. Calonne instantly engaged him to discover the nature of the correspondence the La Mottes claimed to possess, and the following day lent him £120 to cover the costs of *L'Azile*.

Within ten days, La Tour had provided written statements from the La Mottes confirming that they had numerous letters, but would be willing to suppress them and the memoirs and promise eternal silence if indemnified for the losses that they claimed to have suffered. Calonne told the La Mottes to contact his banker, Charles Herries, who would guarantee any settlement.[101] On 31 December 1787, Calonne sent the queen a package of documents and a letter explaining these terms via the duke of Dorset. It was returned, unopened, with orders to send it to Louis XVI, together with instructions to open it in Marie-Antoinette's presence. Calonne did as instructed, but on 21 February received a reply that 'leurs majestés pensoient l'une et l'autre qu'on devoit se dispenser de tout sort de pareilles ecritures' ['their Majesties both believe that one should ignore all such writings']. He therefore informed La Tour that the La Mottes' proposals merited contempt and the letters were undoubtedly false.[102]

The negotiation might have ended there had Calonne's fabulously wealthy mistress, Madame de Harvelay, not agreed to marry him. The wedding, in Bath on 3 June 1788, increased Calonne's revenues by 230,000 *livres* (nearly £10,000). Even before the ceremony, Calonne was planning to use this money to win royal favour. In mid-May, La Tour, who had succeeded MacMahon as the La Mottes' ghost-writer, sent Calonne a description of the memoirs. Calonne, in turn, wrote to the duchesse de Polignac offering to suppress them using his betrothed's money. He would grant the La Mottes a pension of 10,000–12,000 *livres* and they would retire to the United States.[103] Several weeks later, on his return from Bath, he found a letter from La Tour enclosing fragmentary notes prepared by MacMahon. Calonne sent them to the queen and entreated the duchesse de Polignac to persuade her to accept his offer.[104] On 19 July he received a letter from the queen containing a further rebuff. She despised anything the La Mottes might write and ordered him to remain inactive.[105]

By this time, La Tour had presented Calonne with a draft manuscript, which Calonne corrected in a clandestine meeting, in order, he said, to smooth the style and remove those passages that would most revolt the queen.[106] Calonne lived to regret this action. Within months, La Tour and the La Mottes had used it to vilify him, accusing him of both commission-ing the manuscript and, once the queen rejected his proposals, editing it to maximise its impact.[107] A manuscript copy of the memoirs apparently reached the queen, and according to Madame Campan, it was the original bearing Calonne's annotations.[108] If so, she again scorned the *libellistes'* demands and returned the manuscript, for it is now in Britain's National Archives.[109]

Despite the queen's second refusal, Calonne continued to lend money to Serres de La Tour until October, hoping he could be useful. When La Tour's demands became too exorbitant, Calonne refused them, La Tour became insolent, and Calonne broke with him. Still hoping to milk the situation, La Tour launched his absurd legal complaint before the Court of Chancery on 5 December 1788, claiming that Calonne had promised him large sums and the loans were a salary.[110] The case and negotiation gave rise to a series of sensational pamphlets, notably La Tour's *Appel au bon sens* and the comtesse's *Address to the Public* and *Detection, or a Scourge for Calonne*, both partially ghost-written by Peter Stuart.[111] Morande, too, joined the attack in the *Courier de l'Europe*, probably hoping for a pay-off.[112]

Calonne's behaviour was certainly naïve, but it is extremely improbable that the *libellistes'* allegations against him are true. The annotations on the manuscript in his hand are mostly stylistic: they certainly neither aggravated the comtesse's attacks on the queen nor corrected erroneous facts as the *libel-listes* and Madame Campan asserted. The most significant amendments tone down what was said against Calonne's rival Breteuil; remove an indiscreet reference to the queen's favourite, Axel Fersen; and delete a passage where cardinal Rohan describes the queen as a whore. Although the relevant passage is nearly illegible, Rohan then appears to add that her vulva is so flaccid that he always makes love to her from behind.[113] They thus bear out Calonne's claims that he removed phrases 'too gross and obscene' to lay before the queen.[114]

These disputes delayed publication of the comtesse's *Mémoires* until mid-February 1789.[115] Their reception, together with pressure from her cred-itors, encouraged the comtesse to produce further versions of her life-story, above all a revised autobiography, the *Vie de Jeanne de Saint-Rémy de Valois*, which she prepared in conjunction with Peter Stuart. Once again, she hoped to negotiate a lucrative suppression deal. Once again, her offers were spurned.

The comte de La Motte left England in April 1789. In August, he returned to Paris, where he attempted to secure a retrial for his wife, encouraged and fêted by the Orléanist faction. A letter from Mirabeau to the court, written on 12 November 1789, asserts that the Orléanists intend to propose royal divorce proceedings in the Assembly as soon as the judgement is overturned and the comtesse's mendacious accounts recognised as truth by a court of law. This would leave Louis XVI with little alternative but to abdicate and accept a regency under d'Orléans. Mirabeau therefore suggested keeping the comtesse under surveillance and trying to discover and hinder her plans.[116] Incredibly, the royalists achieved this by pursuading the comte to appoint the head of their secret service, Jacques Marivaux, as his lawyer.[117] In early 1791, Marivaux learned that the comtesse's *Vie* was nearing completion and, in a last-minute effort to suppress it, sent an agent called Bertrand to London.

Before Bertrand arrived, disaster struck. Throughout 1790 and 1791 the comtesse had resisted her husband's invitations to Paris, fearing the machinations of her enemies and revolutionary factions. Meanwhile, her debts to her publisher, Bew, and the perfumier, Warren, mounted, and they pushed her to publish and seized her work as it was printed. Under such pressures, she grew suspicious of those closest to her. She was tortured by reports of her husband's infidelities and indignantly rejected generous overtures from her sister, Marie-Anne, who, after four failed suicide attempts, invited her to renounce her memoirs and retire with her to Italy or Switzerland.[118] In mid-June 1791, bailiffs arrived at the comtesse's lodgings. Fearing that they were acting for her enemies, she plied them with drink, sent her servant to find someone to act as a bond, and suddenly fled her apartment. She ran into a neighbouring building and barricaded herself in an upper room. As her pursuers pounded at the door, she leaped from a window, collided with a tree, and suffered terrible injuries. Succoured by Warren, she rallied for nine weeks. However, on 23 August she suffered fatal haemorrhaging, precipitated, said contemporary reports, by eating a bowl of mulberries.[119]

The comtesse's death did not prevent publication of her new autobiography, since Warren and Bew were desperate to recover their money, and Bertrand's backers were unable to pay a suppression fee owing to the king's suspension following his abortive flight in June 1791. When the comte de La Motte failed to respond to Warren's requests for reimbursement, Bew put the English edition on sale in London. He also dispatched all 4,000 copies of the French edition to the Paris bookseller Gueffier, who placed them in a secret warehouse. Once again, there were attempts at blackmail. Madame Campan was offered the entire edition for 1,000 *Louis*. Marie-Antoinette rejected the offer, remarking that if she paid, the Jacobins would learn of her actions, reprint the *libelle*, and render it more dangerous by informing the public of the attempted suppression.[120] When separate overtures were made to Louis XVI in May 1792, he proved more flexible.[121] Fearing for the queen, especially as France was now at war with Austria, he ordered his close friend Arnaud de La Porte, intendant of the civil list, to suppress the edition. La Porte arranged for an intriguer named Ristron to purchase the books and transport them to the porcelain works at Sèvres for burning.

Ristron's arrival at Sèvres on the evening of 26 May accompanied by two wagons packed with mysterious crates intrigued the factory's workforce, as did his strange *auto-da-fé* the following day. It was denounced to the Municipality of Saint-Cloud, which informed the *comité de surveillance* of the Legislative Assembly on 28 May. The deputies François Chabot and

Antoine Merlin de Thionville proposed that the burned papers probably belonged to the (mythical) Austrian Committee, which was said to control French foreign policy, and fellow Jacobins seized upon the incident to whip up suspicions against the monarchy. An investigation was ordered, and La Porte, Ristron, and their assistants were summoned before the Assembly, where they admitted their actions. According to Madame Campan, the queen, when informed, immediately asked her husband what he knew of the affair. Louis XVI lowered his head, then confessed that he had ordered the suppression. The queen, touched by his shame and concern for her, concealed her mortification.[122]

The book-burning, one contemporary commentator remarked, was yet another 'imprudence' at a moment when nothing should have been done that might 'faire soupçonner un grand secret' ['create suspicions of a big secret'].[123] Eleven weeks later, on 10 August 1792, the monarchy was overthrown, and many of its key supporters arrested. Among them was La Porte, who was executed on 24 August. A surviving copy of Madame de La Motte's *Vie* was found among his papers and, as Marie-Antoinette had feared, the Committee of Public Safety ordered it to be published, complete with a preface explaining that: 'The lengths to which the court has gone to prevent publication of this work clearly prove how greatly the monarchy feared its publication, how many facts it contains which the royalist party would have preferred to keep from public knowledge.'[124]

At her trial, on 14 October 1793, Marie-Antoinette was asked about the books burned at Sèvres. She responded, 'I believe it was a libel. I was not, however, consulted on the matter . . . Had I been consulted, I should have opposed the burning of any writing which was against me.'[125] Nevertheless, Madame de La Motte's spurious charges and those found in other revolutionary *libelles* could not be dismissed so easily, and many were cited by the prosecution. Indeed, the prosecution's accusations mimic the language of the anti-Marie-Antoinette pamphlets described in chapter five, describing her as a 'Messalina', '[Catherine de] Medici', and 'new Agrippina'. The extent to which tales of the queen's promiscuity and perversions had entered revolutionary folklore was exemplified by a decision to allow Hébert and Antoine Simon, the dauphin's gaoler, to present concocted 'evidence' that she had sexually abused her own son.

The inclusion of this evidence was a tactical miscalculation. Marie-Antoinette responded by indignantly asking the mothers in the audience whether they could credit such a charge, and her prosecutors were alarmed by the murmurs of sympathy this provoked.[126] The absurdity of the charge and the queen's innocence of all sexual allegations made no difference.[127] The trial was political and its result predictable: Marie-Antoinette was condemned and executed. However, the inevitability of the outcome should not obscure the novelty of a queen-consort, who could never enjoy power in her own right, standing trial at all. Lynn Hunt explains the spectacle by placing the queen's trial at the centre of the revolutionary gender-drama, arguing that the queen was tried as a representative political woman: a corrupter of public life, a bad mother, and a dissembler (a type that contemporaries associated with women), whose presence in the political sphere was illegitimate. In the process, she uncovers a link between pornography and politics that alone seems able to account for the otherwise inexplicable, sexualised, and supremely hostile rhetoric of her prosecutors.[128] By late 1793 the line between the *libellistes'* fantasies and political realities had disintegrated.

Even now, the Bourbons had not heard the last of the La Mottes' demands. In 1816, Provence, recently enthroned as Louis XVIII, sought out the comte de La Motte and asked him to write his memoirs. Presumably he wanted to clear the royal family of suspicion, although that cannot be certain given his hatred of his sister-in-law. The comte demanded a pension, a proposal that Louis XVIII found impudent, and the idea was shelved. In 1829, the comte reversed his tactics and said he would publish his memoirs unless he was given a modest pension and a place in the Hospice de Chaillot. This time, the government of Charles X (formerly d'Artois) agreed, encouraged by police predictions that 'In his state of decrepitude, the annuity should not have to be long continued.'[129] By the time La Motte died two years later, Charles X had himself been overthrown in another revolution. Twenty-seven years later, the comte's incomplete memoirs were edited and published by Louis Lacour. The London *libellistes'* last pamphlet had finally appeared.

From 1758 to 1792 and even beyond, the London *libellistes'* activities damaged the reputation of private individuals, diplomats, and political figures, and soured French views of the British government and constitution. At their most extreme, especially when encouraged by meddling politicians, they might even threaten ministers, the French diplomatic corps, the king's marriage, and the Austrian alliance. Hence successive French administrations and individual politicians had to choose between a variety of unpalatable expedients and tactics to contain *libellistes*. These included kidnap, entrapment, and, probably, assassination. *In extremis*, however, the government of Louis XV was prepared to pay for the *libellistes'* silence and, to a hitherto unsuspected degree, this practice continued under Louis XVI until 1783. Thereafter, the French government found that disdain combined with fear of prosecution or arrest made more effective deterrents. Until the appearance of the comtesse de La Motte's *Mémoires* on the eve of the revolution, these strategies generally contained those texts they most feared, and whose control they prioritised. However, some of the methods adopted to achieve this remarkable success proved problematic. Diplomatic pressure and clandestine means could not serve as deterrents if they remained covert, yet when they became public they could stir up hostility in both Britain and France. In contrast, pay-offs, unless they remained secret, had the predictable effect of encouraging new *libelles* and accrediting existing ones, with potentially disastrous consequences. Hence, the following chapters explore three main manifestations of these policy failures: the *libelles* they helped encourage; the explosive context in which pamphlet attacks on the queen became public; and the discourses which arose from the exposure of French clandestine methods.

Notes

1 No trace of Baudouin's correspondence remains in the Archives nationales or the naval ministry archives at Vincennes. I would like to thank the archivists at both institutions who assisted my search.
2 CPA 534 fo. 104, Baudouin to Vergennes, Paris, 16 June 1781; fos 105–7, Baxon to Baudouin, 16 June 1781. The date on the latter letter is probably the date of receipt.
3 The title is not given by Baxon, but Goëzman's correspondence reveals that it was the *Amours*. Although the first edition bears the date 1779, Lenoir (MO, MS 1422 pp. 309–10) confirms that this was the edition Goëzman suppressed in August 1781.
4 A print usually associated with this pamphlet, purportedly depicting d'Artois fondling Marie-Antoinette's genitalia, was not among these engravings. Gruder, 'Question of Marie-Antoinette', p. 282, reveals that it is actually a revolutionary caricature representation of Lafayette entitled 'Ma Constitution' which was pasted into a copy of the 1779 edition of the *Amours*. The engravings and plates for the London edition presumably perished in the Bastille.
5 See CPA 534 fos 80–1, Baxon to Vergennes, Courtray, 30 May 1781, enclosing fos 82–5, Baxon's proposals; fo. 93, Vergennes to Baudouin, Versailles, 7 June 1781; fo. 94, Vergennes to Baudouin, Versailles, 8 June 1781; fo. 101, Baudouin to Vergennes, Paris, 13 June 1781; fo. 103, Vergennes to Baudouin, Versailles, 14 June 1781. Baxon's duplicity was later confirmed: see CPA 534 fos 207–8, Baudouin to Vergennes, 23 September 1781.
6 CPA 563 fos 28–9, Barthélemy to Montmorin, 14 July 1787.
7 However, CPA 542 fos 322–3, Goëzman to Vergennes, 30 May 1783, reveals that hunting *libelles* was not Goëzman's original brief.
8 A series of letters signed 'Lerchenberg' but written in Goëzman's distinctive hand also survives, the first written within days of Goëzman's arrival in London on his second mission. Throughout these notes letters signed 'Goëzman', 'de Thurne', or 'Lerchenberg' are attributed directly to Goëzman.
9 CPA 534 fos 158–61, Goëzman to Vergennes, Ostende, 10 August 1781.
10 See CPA 534 fos 158–61, Goëzman to Vergennes, Ostende, 10 August 1781; fos 162–5, Goëzman to Louis XVI, 10 August 1781; fo. 303, Goëzman to Maurepas, Paris, 14 November 1781; fo. 315, Goëzman to Vergennes, 27 November 1781.
11 CPA 534 fo. 302, Goëzman's receipt for secret expenses; fo. 303, Goëzman to Maurepas, Paris, 14 November 1781; fo. 355, 'copie d'une décision du Roi de 5 decembre 1781'.
12 For Göezman's importuning, see his letters to Vergennes and Baudouin dated 14 May 1782, 2 August 1782, 13 August 1782, and 4 April 1783 at CPA 537 fo. 46, CPA 538 fos 8 and 31, and CPA 541 fos 346–9.
13 Pelleport, *Diable*, p. 72; CPA 542 fos 37–42, [Morande], 'Moyens . . . pour prévenir la récidive d'attentats semblable à celui de Boissière' at fo. 41; fos 43–6, 'Case for the Opinion of Mr. Bearcroft'.

14 CPA 541 fos 132–3, Göezman to Baudouin, London, 7 March 1783.

15 CPA 541 fo. 24, Baudouin to Vergennes, Paris, 19 February 1783; fos 50–1, [Lenoir] to [Vergennes], Paris, 24 February 1783; fo. 134, Baudouin to Vergennes, Paris, 7 March 1783.

16 CPA 541 fo. 61, Vergennes to Lenoir, Versailles, 25 February 1783; fo. 71, Vergennes to Moustier, 26 February 1783.

17 CPA 541 fos 50–1, [Lenoir] to [Vergennes], 24 February 1783.

18 Ibid. On Jacquet see MO, MS 1422 pp. 53–5; Arsenal, MS 12,453; Charpentier, *Bastille dévoilée*, 3rd livraison, pp. 36–9; Manuel, *Police*, I, 255–60; Pelleport, *Diable*, pp. 44–8; *MSB*, 22 December 1781, 26 January 1782, 7 February 1782.

19 MO, MS 1422 pp. 54–5. This was probably Morande's first service for the French police. See also *MSB*, 22 December 1781. Nine of the fifteen editions of *libelles* in the secret *dépôt* in the Bastille were produced by Jacquet: see appendix. The arrested accomplices were Costa, Marcenay de Ghuy, and Louis-Claude-César de Launay.

20 CPA 541 fo. 207, Moustier to Vergennes, London, 19 March 1783; fos 234–7, Moustier to Vergennes, London, 23 March 1783. Manuel, *Police*, II, 237–8 and CPA 541 fo. 305, Moustier to Vergennes, London 31 March 1783, suggest that Boissière introduced Goëzman to Shelburne via Shelburne's valet, and that he betrayed French secrets. However, Receveur's 'compte rendu', 22 May 1783 (CPA 542 fos 285–9), states that he was unable to discover concrete evidence of treason. CPA 542 fos 291–2, Lenoir to Vergennes, 23 May 1783, and fo. 295, Vergennes to d'Adhémar, 24 May 1783, show that Lenoir and Vergennes shared Receveur's suspicions. Goëzman's correspondence reeks of complicity with the *libellistes*, especially his letters to Vergennes dated 9 and 12 May 1783 (CPA 542 fos 217–20, 232–3).

21 CPA 541 fos 196–9, Moustier to Vergennes, London, 16 March 1783; fos 257–9, Vergennes to Moustier, 25 March 1783, approves the suggestion.

22 See CPA 541 fo. 224, [Lord Barrington] to [Moustier], Cavendish Square, 22 March 1783 [billet]; fos 234–7, Moustier to Vergennes, London 23 March 1783; fos 239–40, Moustier to Vergennes, London, 23 March 1783; fos 369–75, 'Opinion of Thomas Evans on Linguet's *Mémoires sur la Bastille* and the *Petits Soupers*', London, 7 April 1783; CPA 542 fos 43–6, 'Case for the Opinion of Mr. Bearcroft'.

23 See CPA 542 fos 37–42, Moustier, 'Moyens simples . . . pour prévenir . . . attentats semblable à celui de Boissière' [this document appears to have been ghost-written by Morande]; fos 43–6, 'Case for the Opinion of Mr. Bearcroft'.

24 CPA 542 fo. 81, billet [of Moustier for Vergennes], London, noon 21 [April 1783]; fos 187–8, Lenoir to Vergennes, Paris, 4 May 1783. Lenoir strongly suspected Pelleport, but doubted that Brissot was involved. See also Burrows, 'Innocence of Brissot'.

25 On Boissière's involvement see CPA 541–7 *passim*, esp. CPA 542 fos 285–9, 'Compte rendu' of Receveur, 22 May 1783.

26 CPA 541 fo. 378, 'An Alarm-Bell against French Spies'; CPA 542 fos 15–16, Pelleport to Moustier, Little Chelsea, 12 April 1783.

27 CPA 542 fos 285–9, 'Compte rendu' of Receveur, 22 May 1783; fos 373–5, d'Adhémar to Vergennes, London, 3 June 1783.

28 CPA 542 fo. 358, [Receveur], note of 4 June 1783; fos 217–20 [Goëzman], 'Mémoire concernant les libelles', 9 May 1783.

29 CPA 542 fos 285–9, 'Compte rendu' of Receveur, 22 May 1783.
30 See Darnton, 'Trade in taboo', pp. 19, 22.
31 See Pelleport, *Diable*, pp. 61–72, 95, and *passim*.
32 CPA 545 fo. 132, d'Adhémar to Vergennes, 4 October 1783.
33 CPA 545 fos 170–1, Vergennes to d'Adhémar, 16 October 1783. A draft version at fo. 167 expresses surprise that d'Adhémar recommends pursuing *libellistes* having previously advised disdain.
34 *BCE*, document 516, Morande to Montmorin, 28 April 1788.
35 For documents concerning Brissot's embastillement see AN, 446AP/2. See also Burrows, 'Innocence of Brissot'.
36 See above, chapter one.
37 MO, MS 1422 p. 56; Arsenal, MS 12,454. For further evidence of his guilt see CPA 542 fos 15–16, Pelleport to Moustier, 12 April 1783, offering to suppress the *Passe-tems*; fo. 81, Moustier to Vergennes, 21 [April] 1783, revealing that he also approached the Polignacs; fos 285–9, Receveur's 'Compte rendu', 22 May 1783, concluding that Pelleport was culpable. Manuel, *Police*, II, 28, names Pelleport as author of the *Diable*; ibid., p. 257, reports that he tried to hire a refugee named Doucet to copy the manuscript of the *Passe-tems*.
38 Brissot, *Réplique*, p. 25, and AN, 446AP/3, 'Mémoire contre Desforges', fo. 153, assert that Pelleport declared Brissot innocent. Nothing in the transcripts of Brissot's interrogation suggests that Pelleport gave evidence against him.
39 AN, 446AP/2, note [of Lenoir] 'pour le baron de Breteuil', 5 September 1784.
40 On his finances see Darnton, 'Brissot and the Société typographique de Neuchâtel'.
41 CPA 542 fo. 358, [Receveur], note of 4 June 1783.
42 CPA 552 fos 74–5, Goëzman to Vergennes, 23 January 1785.
43 On the crime of Fini [Chamorand]: *Gazetteer*, 31 October 1785, translated in Charpentier, *Bastille dévoilée*, 3rd livraison, p. 101–4. On Morande's role: *BCE*, document 516, Morande to Montmorin, 28 April 1788.
44 CPA 555 fos 214–15, Crosne to Vergennes, Paris, 24 February 1786.
45 Their Bastille dossiers are in Arsenal, MS 12,454. The exact nature of the charge made by Fini [Chamorand] against Pelleport is unclear. An undated letter (fos 10–11) admits that he performed several 'services considérables' for Pelleport.
46 Charpentier, *Bastille dévoilée*, 3rd livraison, p. 101, asserts that the *libelles* were only a pretext to refuse extradition. See also Manuel, *Police*, II, 51–2. For ambassadorial correspondence concerning Fini's extradition see CPA 555 fo. 209, Dorset to Vergennes, Paris, 20 February 1786; fo. 232, Vergennes to Dorset, Versailles, 3 March 1786; CPA 506 fo. 3, Dorset to Vergennes, Paris, 1 April 1786; fo. 16, Vergennes to Dorset, 4 April 1785. The refusal to return the money appears to have been in retaliation for French problems in recovering jewels from the diamond necklace from London.
47 CPA 541 fos 239–40, Moustier to Vergennes, 23 March 1783.
48 CPA 545 fos 134–8, d'Adhémar to Vergennes, London, 4 October 1783; fos 176–7 Moustier to Vergennes, Paris, 17 October 1783; fos 170–1, Vergennes to d'Adhémar, 16 October 1783.
49 CPA 545 fos 170–1, Vergennes to d'Adhémar, 16 October 1783.
50 CPA 541 fos 104–7, '[Mémoire] de la main de Rayneval', 1 March 1783.

51 CPA 541 fo. 377, Thomas Evans to Moustier, 7 April 1783. See also fos 369–75, 'Opinion of Thomas Evans'.

52 CPA 542 fos 43–6, 'Case for the Opinion of Mr. Bearcroft', 15 April 1783; fos 62–3, Moustier to Vergennes, 18 April 1783. CPA 541 fo. 224, Barrington to Moustier, 22 March 1783, insists that the princesse de Bouillon will not win damages for harm to reputation, because she is unknown in Britain.

53 CPA 541 fos 234–7, Moustier to Vergennes, 23 March 1783.

54 CPA 541 fos 369–75, 'Opinion of Thomas Evans'.

55 MO, MS 1422 p. 56.

56 For a copy and translation of the offending passage see CPA 550 fos 349–50. The same document contains articles from the *Gazetteer*, 11 December 1784 (fo. 348) and *Morning Post*, 14 December (fo. 350). Passages from the *Morning Herald* (19 December), *Public Advertiser* (17 December), and *Morning Post* (17 December) appear at fos 363–5.

57 CPA 550 fos 344–5; fos 346 and 352, letters of d'Adhémar to Vergennes, London, 14 December 1784; fos 362 and 366, d'Adhémar to Vergennes, 17 December 1784.

58 For the Crown's case, see PRO, TS11/506. The *Courier de l'Europe*, 6 July 1781, indicates that the proprietors of the *London Courant*, *Noon Gazette*, *Morning Herald*, *Gazetteer*, *St James Chronicle*, *Middlesex Journal*, and *Whitehall Evening Post*, among others, were also prosecuted successfully.

59 CPA 550 fo. 391, Vergennes to d'Adhémar, 27 December 1784.

60 See PRO, TS11/46, which contains copies of the *Morning Herald* (10 and 13 December 1784) and the *Morning Post* (11 and 13 December 1784).

61 CPA 552 fos 83–6, d'Adhémar to Vergennes, London, 25 January 1785, at fo. 83. See also CPA 552 fos 30–1, d'Adhémar's draft memoir on *libellistes*; fos 53–6 and 57, letters of Vergennes to d'Adhémar, 17 January 1785.

62 The judgement is recorded at CPA 560 fos 162–5.

63 See La Motte, *Mémoire pour Jeanne de Valois*.

64 CPA 557 fos 200–1, Barthélemy to Breteuil, London, 22 August 1786, argued that Cagliostro's imposture would be exposed when he refused to return to France.

65 Lever, *Affaire du collier*, p. 298.

66 CPA 557 fos 200–1, Barthélemy to Breteuil, London, 22 August 1786; PRO, TS11/388, 'Brief for the Prosecution', p. 1.

67 *Public Advertiser*, 22 and 24 August 1786, quoted at CPA 557 fos 202–3, 207. Gordon's handwritten drafts of the offending paragraphs, supplied by Woodfall as evidence, are in PRO, TS11/388.

68 CPA fos 212–14, 'Consultation of Thomas Erskine', London, 27 August 1786.

69 For documents concerning the case and a copy of Gordon's pamphlet, *The Prisoner's Complaint* (London, 1787), see PRO, TS11/388.

70 For his trial, see: *The Trial at Large of the Hon. George Gordon* (London: R. Randall, 1787); *The Whole Proceedings on the Trials of George Gordon* (London: M. Gurney, 1787); *Annual Register* 29 (1786), p. 246. These accounts do not repeat Gordon's exclamations, which according to the *London Chronicle* (5–7 June 1787) were 'too delicate to be repeated', so I have retranslated Barthélemy's version from CPA 560 fos 160–5.

71 McCalman, 'Mad Lord George'. For legal documents concerning Gordon's disappearance see PRO, KB33/5/13.

72 CPA 564 fo. 139, La Luzerne to Montmorin, London, 28 January 1788.

73 See esp. *Courier de l'Europe*, 1 and 5 September 1786. Morande's main campaign lasted from 22 August to 1 December 1786, with sporadic articles in early 1787. *Courier de l'Europe*, 8 September 1786, implies that Morande used police sources. However, MD France 1400 fo. 38, Crosne to Vergennes, 19 September 1786, states that searches of police files were ordered after, not before, Morande's initial revelations. CPA 559 fos 224–5 and 228–9, d'Adhémar to Montmorin, 13 March 1787, states that Morande wrote as a freelancer.

74 For Cagliostro's challenge see *Public Advertiser*, 5 September 1786. For Morande's reply: *Courier de l'Europe*, 5 September 1786. Their exchanges were widely republished in the London press.

75 Robiquet, *Théveneau de Morande*, pp. 194–205; Roberto Gervaso, *Cagliostro*, transl. Cormac O'Cuilleanáin (London: Gollancz, 1974), pp. 167–77; Iain McCalman, *The Seven Ordeals of Count Cagliostro* (London: Century, 2003), pp. 159–73.

76 Documents concerning the police mission are in MD France 1400. For the comte's version of his travels and intrigues see Jeanne de La Motte, *Memoirs*, pp. 146–92; Marc de La Motte, *Mémoires inédits*, pp. 66–125; AN, F^7 4445^2 dossier 3, pieces 14, 14 bis, and 14 tiers (apparently an early draft of the account in the comtesse's memoirs). The three narratives vary in minor details. A further proposal to kidnap the comte is mentioned in Vizetelly, *Story of the Necklace*, II, 128–30.

77 CPA 556 fo. 275, d'Adhémar to Vergennes, 30 May 1786.

78 Price, *Preserving the Monarchy*, pp. 178–80.

79 See CPA 556 fos 282–3, d'Adhémar to Vergennes, London, 1 June 1786.

80 MD France 1400 fos 75–6, Benevent to d'Adhémar, Edinburgh, 20 March 1786.

81 See MD France 1400 fos 89–90, Vergennes to d'Adhémar, Versailles, 4 April 1786.

82 See Burrows, 'Despotism', pp. 538–9.

83 CPA 556 fos 294–5, Vergennes to d'Adhémar, Versailles, 5 June 1786.

84 Louis XVI to Vergennes, 4 June 1786, *Louis XVI and Vergennes: Correspondence*, pp. 382–3; CPA 558 fo. 179, extract of letter of [the police officer] Longpré [to Crosne], 24 November 1786.

85 See MD France 1400 fo. 326, chevalier de Falguières-Troupel to [duchesse de Polignac], London, 6 October 1786; fo. 331, chevalier de Vaux-Landry to [duchesse de Polignac or princesse de Lamballe?], 9 November 1786. Both correspondents express a desire to silence La Motte, but were almost certainly his agents. The former was probably 'Falquier', who, with Benevent and La Motte, was under police surveillance: see: CPA 559 fo. 166, d'Adhémar to Crosne, London, 24 February 1787.

86 The letter is translated in CPA 558 fos 259–60.

87 CPA 558 fo. 315, Barthélemy to Vergennes, London, 26 December 1786.

88 CPA 559 fo. 12, Barthélemy to [Vergennes], London, 2 January 1787. La Motte's letter was first published in English. It was republished in French in the *Morning Chronicle*, 2 January 1787.

89 CPA 559 fo. 21, Vergennes to d'Adhémar, Versailles, 9 January 1787.

90 CPA 559 fo. 42, Barthélemy to Vergennes, 15 January 1787; fo. 43, anonymous billet to d'Adhémar or Barthélemy, 'ce mardi matin' [9 January 1787].

91 Despite rumours in Paris in June–July that the comte's memoir had appeared and inspired an English 'history of the necklace', no work from 1787 seems attributable to La Motte. For the rumours see CSCV, II, 164–6. CSCV, II, 221, reports that a *marchande de modes* was arrested in January 1788 for receiving pages from the comte's pamphlet in consignments of fabric.

92 CPA 559 fo. 166, d'Adhémar to Crosne, London, 24 February 1787.

93 CPA 559 fos 181–6, d'Adhémar to [Montmorin], London, 27 February 1787 at fo. 186.

94 CPA 559 fos 251–2, Montmorin to d'Adhémar, 25 March 1787.

95 CSCV, II, 140, 154–5, 161, 166–7; Vizetelly, *Story of the Necklace*, II, 159–60.

96 For the comtesse's narrative of her escape, see La Motte, *Life*, II, 154–220; *Morning Post*, 16 August 1787. The latter was reprinted in Anon., *Authentic Adventures*, pp. 153–63. Jean-François Georgel, *Mémoires pour servir à l'histoire de la fin du dix-huitième siècle*, 6 vols (Paris: Alexis Eymery, 1817–18), II, 208, concludes that the comtesse must have had 'ministerial' assistance. See also Funck-Brentano, *Cagliostro and Company*, pp. 101–7; Vizetelly, *Story of the Necklace*, II, 161–75.

97 Jeanne de Saint-Rémy de La Motte, *An Address to the Public* (London: Ridgway, 1789), pp. 7–10. Jean-François Georgel, *Mémoires*, II, 208–9, also speaks of a negotiation involving Breteuil and a pay-off made by Polignac on a trip to Bath. His chronology is clearly erroneous, and his statement based on speculation. Tales of a second Polignac mission surely stem from this mistake, as Vizetelly, *Story of the Necklace*, II, 181, noted.

98 Alphonse-Joseph de Serres de La Tour, *Appel au bon sens* (London: Kearsley, 1788), pp. 4–5: advertisements appeared in the *Morning Post* in late December 1787.

99 The comte claims (Marc de La Motte, *Mémoires inédits*, p. 147) that during Brienne's ministry (May 1787–August 1788), La Luzerne offered him 50,000 *livres* and a 10,000 *livre* pension, and that Necker withdrew the offer after Brienne's fall. This is not supported by documentary evidence. The court's attitude to Calonne's negotiation suggests it was hostile to the La Mottes' demands at that time.

100 Robert Lacour-Gayet, *Calonne: financier, réformateur, contre-révolutionnaire, 1734–1802* (Paris: Hachette, 1963), pp. 247–74, implies (p. 252) that Calonne picked up court rumours about Breteuil's negotiations.

101 PRO, C12/1389/27, 'La Tour versus de Callonne [sic]', 5 December 1788. See also Calonne's three drafts of his 'Exposé des faits' dated 9 December 1788 in PRO, FO95/631/247–9.

102 See Calonne's accounts in PRO, FO95/631/248 pp. 33–6; *The Times*, 2 February 1789. PRO, FO95/631/156, Calonne to duchesse de Polignac, 27 January [1788], and FO95/631/164, Calonne to duchesse de Polignac, 'pour vous seule', undated, confirm many of these details.

103 PRO, PC1/129/151, Calonne to duchesse de Polignac, London, 16 May [1788].

104 PRO, PC1/129/155, Calonne to duchesse de Polignac, London, 10 June 1788; PC1/129/157, Calonne to duchesse de Polignac, London, 8 June 1788; PRO, FO95/631/267; *The Times*, 2 February 1789.

105 PRO, FO95/631/248 p. 38.

106 Ibid., pp. 38–41.

107 See La Tour, *Appel au bon sens* and La Motte's *Address to the Public* and *Detection, or a Scourge for Calonne* (London: n. p., 1789).

108 Campan, *Mémoires*, II, 107–8.

109 PRO, FO95/631/245. The La Mottes later claimed that Calonne obtained the corrected manuscript from them by trickery.

110 For the complaint brought by La Tour and Calonne's response, see PRO, C12/1389/27. These documents seem to have been unknown to previous commentators. La Tour's claims seem improbable, especially as he signed for the advances made by Herries as loans.

111 La Motte, *Address to the Public*, p. 29; McCalman, 'Queen of the gutter', p. 116. Calonne's reply appeared in *The Times* on 2 February 1789.

112 Morande's correspondence with Montmorin in CPA 567–9 discusses his campaign against Calonne, which displeased Montmorin.

113 PRO, FO95/631/245, esp. corrections at fos 31, 50, 55, 63. Cf. claims in La Motte, *Address to the Public*, p. 14; Campan, *Mémoires*, II, 108.

114 *The Times*, 2 February 1789.

115 Although CPA 568 fos 144–5, Morande to Montmorin, 10 February 1789, refers to the 'atrocity of Madame de La Motte', the same day's *The Times* reports that the comtesse was still threatening publication to extort money. It did not announce the work until 13 February.

116 Mossiker, *Queen's Necklace*, pp. 536–7. Lever, *Affaire du collier*, p. 311, notes that many of La Fayette's supporters also hoped for a divorce, believing it would restore Louis XVI's authority.

117 Marc de La Motte, *Mémoires inédits*, p. 191, notes Marivaux's role.

118 On the comte's behaviour see AN, F⁷ 4445² dossier 3, piece 25, Anne-Marie de Saint-Rémy to comtesse de La Motte, Paris, 15 December [1789 or 1790]. The same dossier contains documents concerning the comtesse's relations with her sister, and (piece 16) a letter to Mme Seymour, presumably 'la belle impure Semour' ['the beautiful prostitute Semour'] who, according to CSCV, II, 481 (5 November 1790), was living openly with the comte.

119 La Motte, *Life*, II, supplement pp. 32–6.

120 Campan, *Mémoires*, II, 194–5.

121 Vizetelly, *Story of the Necklace*, II, 204–5, cites an autographed letter in a private collection from the comte de La Motte to Louis XVI, dated 5 May 1792, announcing that the *libelle* was in Gueffier's possession, offering terms, and citing a previous suppression negiotiation involving the royalist-leaning ex-minister of justice, Duport Dutertre.

122 Campan, *Mémoires*, II, 195–6; Antoine François Bertrand de Molleville, *Private Memoirs Relative to the Last Year of the Reign of Lewis the Sixteenth*, 3 vols (London: A. Strahan, 1797), II, 248–50; *Archives parlementaires*, XLIV, 191–204. Extracts of these sources are reproduced in d'Almeras, *Marie-Antoinette et les pamphlets*, pp. 377–88. See also Marc de La Motte, *Mémoires inédits*, pp. 237–43, 257–8; Mossiker, *Diamond Necklace*, pp. 560–7; Funck-Brentano, *Cagliostro and Company*, pp. 162–3; Vizetelly, *Story of the Necklace*, II, 204–10.

123 CSCV, II, 598.

124 Mossiker, *Queen's Necklace*, p. 565. The translation is Mossiker's own. I have not used this edition, published by Garnery in the rue Serpente. Mossiker says it appeared in 1792. This is an error. The Committee of Public Safety was

formed only on 1 January 1793 and was known as the Committee of General Defence until 26 March 1793.

125 Vizetelly, *Story of the Necklace*, II, 210.

126 Gérard Walter, *Actes du Tribunal révolutionnaire* (Paris: Mercure de France, 1968), pp. 96–7.

127 The public was unaware of details of Marie-Antoinette's one relationship that might have been adulterous: her friendship with Axel Fersen. Price, *Fall of Monarchy*, pp. 16–17, states that they were certainly 'in love', but if – despite the risks – the relationship was ever consummated, it was almost certainly only after 1789, when they had little to lose. Fersen's descendants tampered with his papers, so the truth is unknowable.

128 Hunt, 'Many bodies'.

129 Mossiker, *Queen's Necklace*, p. 588.

5

The scandalous history of
Marie-Antoinette

Since Marie-Antoinette is central to the pornographic interpretation of the revolution, this chapter examines two key questions. First, how many *libelles* against the queen circulated prior to the revolution, and in what quantities? Chapter two has already suggested that they were relatively few in number, since many such pamphlets were suppressed. This chapter goes one step further and contends that printed *libelles* directed primarily against the queen probably did not circulate before 1789, and certainly not in substantial numbers. As a result, it is also necessary to ask how, why, and when pamphlet attacks on Marie-Antoinette developed, and what the London *libellistes'* contribution was.

Even advocates of the 'pornographic interpretation' admit that the corpus of pornographic texts concerning the queen was not large. Lynn Hunt acknowledges that over 90 per cent of anti-Marie-Antoinette titles date from after 1789,[1] and this disparity would be magnified if she included obscene attacks in revolutionary newspapers.[2] Remarkably, just eight titles, all of them associated with London, comprehend all the major prerevolutionary anti-Marie-Antoinette *libelles* mentioned in secondary sources.[3] Six of these have already been encountered in chapters three and four. The other two, *Le Portefeuille d'un talon rouge* [Portfolio of a Dandy][4] and *Essai historique sur la vie de Marie-Antoinette d'Autriche* [Historical Essay on the Life of Marie-Antoinette of Austria] were produced by Jacquet's network and probably printed in London.[5]

Two of these eight pamphlets certainly never circulated. Beaumarchais suppressed and destroyed the entire edition of the *Avis à la branche espagnole*, if it was ever printed. Similarly, the *Guerlichon femelle* appears to have perished in the Bastille, presumably destroyed deliberately by Lenoir in 1785, or accidently in the fall of the fortress.

A further three titles, all associated with Pelleport, were probably never written. Lenoir's assertion that, after Receveur's mission to London in 1783, no new *libelles* appeared for several years implies that the *Passe-tems d'Antoinette*, *Naissance du dauphin dévoilée*, and *Les Rois de France dégénérés* were not published.[6] Morande says this explicitly,[7] while Brissot and Manuel claim that the *Passe-tems* was a chimera.[8] Despite the high survival rate for other *libelles*, no copies of these three titles are known.[9] This

Table 1 Copies of anti-Marie-Antoinette *libelles* in French and British research collections that possibly pre-date 1789.

Title	Pre-1789 copies in British libraries (*Copac*)	Pre-1789 copies in French libraries (CCF)	Total
Amours de Charlot et Toinette	0	8	8
Portefeuille d'un talon rouge	3	6	9
Essai historique sur la vie de Marie-Antoinette	0	0–3	0–3
All other known anti-Marie-Antoinette *libelles*	0	0	0
Total: all Marie-Antoinette *libelles*	3	14–17	17–20

Source: Figures were compiled from *Copac*, the collective catalogue databases for British research libraries, and its French equivalent, the *Catalogue collectif de France* (CCF).

is strong evidence that they were never published.[10] Moreover, although Darnton found two orders for the *Passe-tems* in the archives of the Société typographique de Neuchâtel, both came from the book dealer Bruzard de Mauvelain in Troyes, a specialist in scandalous works, who clearly learned of the pamphlet from the *Alarm-Bell against French Spies*, which was translated and published in several underground texts.[11] The Parisian bookseller Nicolas Ruault learned of the *Passe-tems* by the same means.[12] These orders offer no proof that the work actually existed. It seems, therefore, that Pelleport's protests that he never libeled the royal family were technically true: his *libelles* remained unwritten.[13]

This leaves just three *libelles* which might possibly have entered circulation: the *Essai historique*, the *Amours de Charlot et Toinette*, and the *Portefeuille d'un talon rouge*. There are good *prima facie* reasons to assume that they were familiar to *ancien régime* readers. All three were remanded in the Bastille, all three survive in library collections (see table 1), and the first two were ordered from the Société typographique de Neuchâtel. However, close analysis challenges this conclusion.

The most compelling evidence that these *libelles* circulated before 1789 is the fact that a handful of copies survive in libraries. Their rarity has traditionally not been seen as problematic, because *libelles* were considered dangerous to possess, clandestine, and ephemeral. On-line collective library databases make it possible to test these assumptions by conducting censuses of comparable texts. Table one reveals that, at most, twenty copies of pre-1789 editions of anti-Marie-Antoinette *libelles* survive in major British and French research collections. However, these figures may over-state numbers because library bibliographic data is not always sufficient to make a conclusive judgement, especially in the case of the *Essai historique*. As a standard for comparison or 'control', table two lists surviving copies of Morande's *Gazetier cuirassé* and Goudar's *Procès des trois rois* [*Trial of Three Kings*].

Table 2 'Control' *libelles* in French and British research collections.

Title	Pre-1789 copies in British libraries (*Copac*)	Pre-1789 copies in French libraries (CCF)	Total
Gazetier cuirassé	10	39	49
Procès des trois rois	14	45	59
Total control texts	24	84	108

Source: Figures were compiled from *Copac*, the collective catalogue databases for British research libraries, and its French equivalent, the *Catalogue collectif de France* (CCF).

Like the anti-Marie-Antoinette *libelles*, both these works were highly illegal, clandestine, and ephemeral. Both contained anti-Bourbon material and both were the subjects of zealous police and customs searches. In short, they might be expected to have survival rates similar to anti-Marie-Antoinette *libelles*. Revealingly, library evidence suggests that sales of each of the 'control' texts outstripped the entire corpus of anti-Marie-Antoinette texts (see table 2).

Moreover, we have a good idea of total sales of the *Gazetier* and the *Procès*. Both ran to five known prerevolutionary editions. Hence, to judge from the edition sizes given in chapter two, both presumably sold around 10,000–15,000 copies.[14] If anti-Marie-Antoinette texts were available before the revolution and survive in roughly similar proportions to the 'control texts', their total circulation, inside and outside France, was in the region of 3,000–5,000 copies.

However, it is likely that these works did not circulate at all before the revolution, and surviving copies came from the Bastille's secret *dépôt*.[15] For although Lenoir ordered the destruction of the works in the *dépôt* in 1785, he instructed that twenty copies of each be kept in the Bastille, and a further dozen distributed among high-ranking officials (see appendix). It is reasonable to suppose that several of these copies might have survived in libraries and archives, since in July 1789 municipal officials succeeded in retrieving many documents from the Bastille, and the libraries of *ancien régime* public figures were frequently confiscated for, or bequeathed to, the nation. The survival in the Bibliothèque nationale of two copies of another work liberated from the *dépôt*, Linguet's *Aiguilloniana*, although it had long lost its interest and topicality by 1789, bears out these observations. If surviving prerevolutionary copies of anti-Marie-Antoinette *libelles* came from the Bastille, we would expect greater proportions of them to survive in French collections than in British ones, and more copies to be located in Paris than in the provinces. Both these assumptions appear correct.[16] Library census data therefore does not disprove, and to some extent supports, the hypothesis that anti-Marie-Antoinette texts did not circulate before the revolution.

The inventory of the secret *dépôt* in 1785 given in the appendix provides strong further evidence that the *Portefeuille d'un talon rouge* and *Amours de Charlot et Toinette* did not circulate. It was said to contain the entire edition, or thereabouts, of the *Portefeuille* and the complete 1779 edition of the *Amours*, together with the plates for the engravings that were intended to accompany it. The plates were destroyed, but eight copies of this edition of the *Amours*, minus illustrations, survive in French research libraries. Tellingly, however, there are no copies of this edition in British research collections, suggesting that it did not circulate in London. More revealing still, the 1789 edition of the *Amours* both flaunts its provenance and insinuates that it had previously been unobtainable by claiming to be published 'à la Bastille'. Similarly, the *Portefeuille* does not feature in Darnton's listing of the corpus of prerevolutionary clandestine literature which, in addition to an extensive sampling of the orders of the Société typographique de Neuchâtel, draws on the records of ten police raids and a comprehensive listing of works seized by French customs between 1771 and 1789.[17] It seems fair to suggest that this is because, before the liberation of the Bastille, it was not in circulation and few people knew of its existence.

The evidence of the secret *dépôt* concerning the *Essai historique* is more problematic, since it was said to contain 534 copies of this work, rather than a complete edition. Understandably, Lynn Hunt took this as evidence of wide circulation, assuming this haul to be the fruit of multiple police confiscations.[18] However, it is much more probable that, along with the other incomplete editions attributed to Jacquet in the secret *dépôt*, they were the fruit of Receveur's mission to the Low Countries, especially as the *Essai* does not appear in Darnton's listings of works seized by the French police and customs. They may therefore represent all the copies that had been produced. Although clandestine newsletters discussed illegal works avidly, and the *Mémoires secrets* picked up rumours that the pamphlet caused Jacquet's arrest, its content is not described in any prerevolutionary source consulted for this study.[19] The only other allusions in the *Mémoires secrets* to the *Essai* relate to seizures of the work, its authors, and printer-booksellers before it could be introduced into France, and clearly reflect whispers concerning Receveur's mission.[20] It is thus conceivable, though unlikely, that several dozen copies of the *Essai* were in circulation, but it was certainly not widely known before the revolution. Indeed, a scene in *Bord[el] r[oyal]* [*The Royal Bordello*] (1789), in which Marie-Antoinette tells cardinal Rohan, 'On fait paraître à Paris ma vie, les Mémoires de la comtesse de La Motte' ['in Paris they're publishing my life-story, [and?] the memoirs of the comtesse de La Motte'] and asks him to gather up every copy, implies that scandalous biographies, and specifically, apparently, the *Essai historique* (which was also known as the *Vie d'Antoinette*), were not previously available.[21]

Finally, there is the evidence of orders received by the Société typographique de Neuchâtel, which is also deceptive, since the only correspondent among Darnton's sample to place orders for *Les Amours de Charlot et Toinette*, the *Essai historique*, and a *Vie d'Antoinette* (the last two of which were almost certainly the same thing) was Mauvelain.[22] His orders for anti-Marie-Antoinette *libelles* – the only ones in Darnton's entire sample – total just thirty-eight books among 28,212 copies of illegal works ordered from the Société by French book dealers between 1769 and 1789. This amounts to a risible 0.13 per cent of its clandestine trade.[23] Moreover, much to Mauvelain's chagrin, the Société did not dispatch a single copy of the *Passetems*, *Essai*, or *Amours* in the three consignments of books that it sent him.[24] None of these titles feature in stock inventories that it maintained during the period 1781–87, which survive mostly intact. Nor do any other specifically anti-Marie-Antoinette titles.[25] Mauvelain's orders thus offer no proof that either work circulated, particularly as he had contacts among or close to the London *libellistes*, above all Brissot.[26]

It thus seems probable that none of the major anti-Marie-Antoinette titles mentioned in the existing historical literature actually circulated before 1789. Nevertheless, Darnton's survey does supply proof that some printed material attacking the queen's sexual behaviour circulated prior to the definitive breakdown of royal censorship in September 1789. However, these attacks were either incidental or appeared late in the day, and relate to just two texts. In 1781 customs twice confiscated consignments of Goudar's *Procès des trois rois*, which in 198 pages contains two passing allusions to Louis XVI's impotence and the paternity of his children,[27] and in 1789 La Motte's *Mémoires* was confiscated four times.[28]

A few copies of Joseph Lanjuinais's *Supplément à l'Espion anglois* (1781), which, as the *Mémoires secrets* and Gruder note, contained two pages 'de mensonges et d'horreurs' ['of lies and horrors'] against the queen, also circulated, but the work is too obscure to feature in Darnton's figures and does not appear in the inventories of the Société typographique de Neuchâtel.[29] It accuses the queen of conspiring with the Austrians to bankrupt France by her lavish spending, but its only innuendo concerning her fidelity is so muted as almost to escape notice: 'la reine chérit autant le royaume de France que le Roi son auguste époux' ['the queen cherishes the kingdom as France as much as her august husband the king'].[30] In addition, clandestine manuscript newsletters mention three *libelles* so obscure that no copies are known to have survived. Given the survival rates for other *libelles*, it seems unlikely that they were ever printed, although they may have circulated in manuscript.[31] The sum total of French printed pamphlets circulating against Marie-Antoinette before 1789 was perhaps just two *libelles* that made passing aspersions concerning her marital chastity. The scores of hostile pamphlets required to justify a pornographic interpretation of the origins of the revolution simply did not exist.

In consequence, the history of scandalous pamphlets against Marie-Antoinette needs to be radically revised. Broadly speaking, it seems fair to suggest a three-stage chronology. During the first stage, until mid-February 1789, scandalous printed attacks on the queen were probably literally unavailable, if we ignore Lanjuinais's and Goudar's passing allusions. It appears that the odd manuscript *libelle* probably circulated among leading courtiers and that malicious rumours reached leading aristocrats across

Europe in gossipy *nouvelles à la main*. Occasionally, too, rumours escaped to a wider public about defamatory works that had been suppressed. Lewd songs, epigrams, withering *bons mots*, or *mauvais propos* perhaps also occasionally passed by word of mouth, but scandalous histories and sustained slander were unavailable.[32] A second stage, between February and August 1789, saw the publication of the foundational texts of the anti-Marie-Antoinette corpus, all prepared under the *ancien régime*. It began with the publication of the comtesse de La Motte's *Mémoires*, which was followed in July by the liberation and republication of texts from the Bastille's secret *dépôt*, especially the influential *Essai historique*. Finally, from August or September 1789, texts written after the commencement of the revolution, and hence under its influence, began to appear.[33] Together, these texts created a powerful mythology about *l'Autrichienne*. The rest of this chapter charts the contribution by the London *libellistes* of material and motifs to this legend.

The most potentially damaging *libelles* to come out of London were the corpus of texts associated with the comtesse de La Motte, commencing with her *Mémoires*, which contained thirty-two purported letters between the queen and Rohan.[34] As the first salacious *libelle* against Marie-Antoinette to enjoy a wide circulation, the *Mémoires* had a decisive influence on the genre and revolutionary political pornography. The *Mémoires* offer a mendacious history of the diamond necklace affair. They portray the otherwise feisty and resourceful comtesse as the incomprehensibly naïve tool and victim of a coldly duplicitous, libertine queen, who beguiled her in order to acquire the fabled diamond necklace. The nature of the comtesse's relationship with the queen is never explicitly spelt out, but a passage that appears only in the French edition, and that the comtesse later disavowed,[35] alludes obliquely to sexual intimacy:

> Cette seconde entrevue ne fut pas purement des affaires; j'y reçus l'explication de ce qu'avoit voulu me faire entendre le Cardinal lorsqu'il m'avoit parlé du *goût* et de *tournure* – Dieu! que la Reine est charmante! quelle affabilité, quelle effusion de bonté! en vérité je me crus aussi quelque chose de plus qu'une simple mortelle. [This second interview was not only a matter of business; I received there an understanding of what the cardinal wished me to understand when he spoke of the taste and inclinations [of the queen] – God! How charming the queen is! What affability, what an effusion of kindness! I honestly believed myself something more than a simple mortal.]

Thereafter, the comtesse had frequent assignations with the queen, involving shared 'momens d'ivresse que j'ose à peine retracer' ['moments of delirium that I can scarcely dare recall'].[36]

Having seduced the comtesse, Marie-Antoinette used her as a go-between with Rohan, who, she claimed, was both the queen's lover and an Austrian agent.[37] The queen's relationship with Rohan had nothing to do with love or passion. Her motives were cupidity, libertinism, and revenge. Having been

banned from buying the necklace by Louis XVI,[38] the queen hoped to manipulate Rohan into acquiring it secretly. She also wished to advance him into
the ministry, so that he might help Austria regain Lorraine from France.[39]
Nevertheless, Marie-Antoinette hated Rohan, because after she spurned his
advances during his embassy to Vienna, he had informed Maria-Theresia of
her youthful dalliances.[40] Once he outlived his usefulness, she intended to
destroy him. This, according to the comtesse, is exactly what she did when
Breteuil, informed by his spies of the necklace transaction and the cardinal's
financial difficulties, persuaded the jewellers to approach the queen.[41] Marie-
Antoinette denied any involvement. Her complicity was untraceable, for
although the jewellers had insisted on knowing the purchaser's identity, the
queen had asked the comtesse to have her signature forged on the contract
of sale. The comtesse, however, was heavily implicated, arrested, and warned
against implicating Marie-Antoinette on pain of death.[42]

The comtesse's memoirs appeared to illuminate other mysterious aspects
of the affair. The bizarre scene involving the swooning cardinal and young
prostitute in the Versailles gardens was, according to the comtesse, a ruse to
guage the cardinal's sincerity, and was observed secretly by Marie-
Antoinette.[43] The absurdity and inconsistency of La Motte's previous stories
– an earlier memoir had blamed Cagliostro for stealing the diamonds[44] –
were explained by her revelation that while in the Bastille she had been
coached on what to say under interrogation.[45] In return, the queen pledged
to protect her and arranged her escape from the Saltpêtrière.[46] Equally, the
comtesse's *Mémoires* contained her husband's account of his adventures
while on the run from French agents in Britain, telling how he had survived
sword-thrusts, poison, and a kidnap plot,[47] and how Vergennes, to prevent
him testifying against Rohan, had thwarted d'Adhémar's attempts to obtain
for him a safe conduct.[48]

Well-informed contemporaries realised that much of the story was fabricated. For example, the cardinal's embassy to Vienna occurred after Marie-
Antoinette left Austria. Some also recognised the *billets doux* of queen and
cardinal as crude forgeries. However, other parts of the tale had a loose
factual base, including the kidnap plot and factional machinations of
Breteuil and Vergennes. Moreover, in the heat of political crisis, other aspects
appeared credible, or anticipated familiar revolutionary motifs. Here,
already, is the fabled Austrian committee directing French foreign policy.
Here, too, is a convincing explanation of the queen's surreptitious acquisition of the necklace: the monarchy was already tightening its belt prior to
admitting the financial crisis. Here are ruthless ministers and courtiers prepared to stop at nothing in pursuit of riches and personal vendettas. Here,
too, are some key villains of the early revolution. They include the evil
favourite, the duchesse de Polignac, who maintains her influence by threatening to expose the full extent of the queen's munificence towards her, and
Breteuil, denounced as 'that thunderbearer of despotism'.[49] Above all, here
is corruption at court – political, sexual, and financial – centred on the

adulterous, lesbian, libertine queen. More literally than Pompadour and du Barry before her, Marie-Antoinette fuses together the three public roles played by women in the eighteenth century: queen, actress, and whore. As the only recognised political public woman under the *ancien régime* she serves as both prototype and stereotype of the revolutionary political public woman, corrupting everything she touches. She is the central player and villain of the tragedy. Hers is the will that moves France.

Jeanne de La Motte's *Mémoires* were not the final version of her story, which evolved further with the twists of the revolution. However, before she published again, the liberation of the secret *dépôt* in the Bastille added powerful new dimensions to the political pornography and mythology of the revolution. Most of the texts in the secret *dépôt* were effectively dead letters by 1789, pieces of political polemic or personal vitriol that had lost their relevance (see appendix). However, there were four texts which retained their resonance, and might attract attention from entrepreneurial revolutionary publishers. These works had much in common. All were *libelles* against the court, royal family, and queen, and all fleshed out Madame de La Motte's sketch of the degeneracy of the queen's circle. Three, the *Guerlichon femelle*, the *Essai historique*, and the *Portefeuille d'un talon rouge*, offered scandalous narratives about Marie-Antoinette and the court. The final title, *Les Amours de Charlot et Toinette*, was a lewd poem, the first work to provide graphic descriptions of Marie-Antoinette *in flagrante delicto* and place obscene language in her mouth.

All four embastilled texts were probably produced in London, but only three circulated in revolutionary Paris, since the entire edition of the *Guerlichon femelle* disappeared without trace in the bowels of the Bastille. Eighteenth-century copies of the *Portefeuille d'un talon rouge* are sufficiently rare that it is not entirely clear whether it was republished during the revolution. In contrast, the *Amours de Charlot et Toinette* was rapidly reprinted, and revolutionary editions of the *Essai historique* enjoyed a huge vogue. Patriot publishers reprinted it in multiple editions and different versions, and it survives in remarkable numbers.[50] In 1793 it was even translated into English.[51] Later editions of the *Essai* and *libelles* attributed to the comtesse de La Motte enter into a dialogue with revolutionary political-pornographic pamphlets and consciously reinforce one another. Revolutionary editions of the *Essai* refer to the comtesse's 'revelations', and she, in turn, responded to criticisms in other revolutionary texts. Thus, while anti-Marie-Antoinette folklore owed its genesis to blackmail *libelles* written in London before 1789, it was only forged into a final and popular form in the crucible of revolutionary Paris.

The *Essai historique* and *Portefeuille d'un talon rouge* share similarities that suggest common authorship or a common source. Both offer a near-identically structured narrative of Marie-Antoinette's life, favourites, and lovers, including the ubiquitous d'Artois, covering the same individuals in the same order and manner, sometimes using the same anecdotes. It therefore seems reasonable to accept Manuel's assertion that both *libelles* emanated from Jacquet's network, and conclude that although commissioned in Paris or the Low Countries, they were probably printed in London and shipped to the Austrian Netherlands and United Provinces before being seized or suppressed.[52] Indeed, the standard attribution of the *Essai* to Goupil must be erroneous, for he died before several of the events it described.[53]

The *Essai historique* is the more scathing pamphlet in its treatment of Marie-Antoinette. It opens with an extended comparison of the queen with du Barry, which stresses that both were dedicated to 'crapuleuse et dégoûtante débauche' ['crapulous and revolting debauch'] and deployed great skill 'tromper et d'avilir' ['to deceive and degrade'] a king.[54] The *Essai* argued that Marie-Antoinette had inherited Maria-Theresia's vices but not her virtues.[55] Her marriage to Louis XVI stemmed from an appalling political crime – the Franco-Austrian alliance – which Choiseul hoped would secure his political ascendancy over Louis XV.[56] There are hints, too, that Choiseul poisoned Louis XV's son, the dauphin, leaving the feeble Louis XVI to inherit the throne. However, Choiseul's rivals and successors were no better: the maréchal de Richelieu, d'Aiguillon, Maupeou, and their ilk were subalterns of the comtesse du Barry, a 'creature indigne de vivre' ['creature unworthy to live'].[57] Nor do the princes of the blood escape scrutiny: individually and collectively, they are presented as debauched nullities.[58] Their wives, too, save the virtuous duchesse de Chartres, are painted in unflattering terms, while the women of the court are, almost without exception, 'ou catins, ou tribades, ou joueuses, ou escrocs, et en général la plus mauvaise compagnie de l'Europe' ['either whores, or lesbians, or gamblers, or crooks, and in general the worst crowd in all Europe'].[59] Among such corrupt circles, infected with her mother's vices, and married to the dull and passionless Louis XVI, it was inevitable that Marie-Antoinette would fall into debaucherous promiscuity.[60]

Having set the scene, the *Essai historique* chronicles the queen's behaviour, favourites, and relations with the royal family, ministers, and lovers of both sexes. Recycling the darkest court gossip, it casts malicious aspersions on her friendships and innocent pleasures, whether walking in the Versailles gardens or watching the sunset or sunrise.[61] It recounts the excessive pecuniary favours lavished on the princesse de Lamballe – for whose benefit, it alleges, the economically prudent minister Turgot was sacrificed – and on the corrupt, grasping duchesse de Polignac, who, imitating Pompadour, traffics in state offices.[62] It also describes the role of the queen's 'society', composed of despicable, talentless debauchees such as d'Adhémar, Vaudreuil, the duc de Coigny, Edward Dillon, the duc de Polignac, the prince d'Hénin, the baron de Bezenval, and the abbé Vermond, under the direction of the duchesse de Polignac, the queen, Choiseul's sister, the duchesse de Grammont, and Madame Campan. This *comité femelle* makes and breaks ministers, dictates policy to the king, and intimidates his only independent minister, the wily Maurepas, into silence.[63]

Among the *Essai historique*'s most colourful passages are a letter from Marie-Theresia, advising her daughter to follow her example by taking a lover to sire a king, and a scene describing a game in which king, queen, and courtiers elect and enthrone a 'king of the ferns' in the Versailles gardens. This 'king' makes marriages between his 'subjects' and orders them to disperse and amuse themselves in their separate couples.[64] The doltish Louis XVI finds this an amusing pastime, the queen an unparalleled opportunity. However, Marie-Antoinette's pregnancies arose from other incidents: her daughter Marie-Thérèse-Charlotte, Madame Royale, was sired by Coigny during a masked ball at the Opera; the dauphin by the comte de Vaudreuil, whose regular lover, the duchesse de Polignac, loaned him for the purpose.[65] Unexpectedly, and despite allegations of impotence, the *Essai* also portrays Louis XVI conducting an affair, but with an artlessness that illustrates how the Bourbons have declined since the days of the legendary womaniser and warrior Henri IV.[66]

The *Essai historique* thus develops a number of key themes. A queen infected with foreign vices imports lesbianism into the already sexually and financially corrupt court of France. A feeble-minded, impotent king is dominated by a cabal of women who have instituted a reign of misrule and misappropriation, pillaging the state and replacing talented or disinterested ministers with their own cyphers. The royal line is polluted and there are suspicions of still deeper crimes of treason and murder. Amidst all this scurrilous invention and misrepresentation lie hints of genuine and deep discontent among the elite at rampant factionalism and lavish spending on a few favourites.

Not content with these tales, the editors of revolutionary editions of the *Essai* added an interpretative introduction and footnotes, which, *inter alia*, claimed that Marie-Antoinette should be contrasted with the Minotaur, Frédégonde, or Messalina, rather than warm-hearted whores like du Barry. Thus they call for her to retire to a convent, in accordance with the popular will, adding: 'nous ne voulons pas du sang, mais la cessation des maux' ['we do not wish for blood, but for the ending of ills']. Likewise, they called for the exile of Breteuil and the final disgrace of the Polignacs.[67] Since Breteuil and the Polignacs emigrated in the aftermath of the July days, the pamphlet must have appeared almost immediately the Bastille fell. Nor was this the final version of the text. Later in the year, Parisian publishers appended a more violent, more explicitly pornographic sequel to the original *Essai*, and consequently changed the title to read *Essais historiques*. In this second essay, narrated in the confessional first person, the queen 'reveals' that she murdered her elder son, who died on 4 June 1789, and extends her shocking life-story into the revolution.[68]

The *Portefeuille d'un talon rouge* is a more ambiguous text than the *Essai historique*, especially regarding Marie-Antoinette. It comprises two letters, the second of which declares, 'je me tais par respect sur ses moeurs; mais un roi aussi bon méritait d'être plus heureux.' ['I will remain silent through

respect regarding her morals; but so good a king deserves to be more fortunate.']⁶⁹ In contrast, the first letter purports to refute allegations against the
queen, and threatens to expose malicious courtiers who spread scandalous
gossip.[70] In the process of rebuttal, however, it recounts their tales of Marie-
Antoinette's nocturnal promenades and intimate friendships, and lesbianism
among the ladies of the court. Its narrative strategy might nevertheless be
read as a genuine defence of the queen and conscious refutation of charges
in the *Essai*. This may explain its lack of success during the revolution.

Because the *Portefeuille d'un talon rouge* traces the evolution of malicious
rumours and manuscript *libelles* against Marie-Antoinette, it has frequently
been used as a source by biographers. Its description of the networks of communication through which slanders supposedly circulated also provides the
empirical evidence for Darnton's circular model of information flows
between Versailles and the Parisian populace.[71] Whether a pamphleteer's
account of the transmission of gossip can bear the weight of such an interpretation is, as Gruder points out, a moot point, but the *Portefeuille* certainly
offers a plausible account of the central role of courtiers in the fabrication
of slander.[72] It describes courtiers as 'l'espèce la plus dangereuse qui soit dans
la terre' ['the most dangerous species on earth'].[73] But while the courtier is
portrayed as a malicious gossip and destroyer of reputations, the pamphlet
portrays the queen behaving similarly, making acerbic asides about court
ladies which permanently alienate much of the high nobility. This dangerous
mistake is compounded when she threatens to boycott Madame de Cossé's
ball if the princes of the blood, who had snubbed Marie-Antoinette's brother
Joseph II, are allowed to attend.[74] This anecdote, like tales of the queen's
exorbitant gambling debts and lavish gifts to the Polignacs, was based on
fact and explains much elite hostility to the queen.[75]

After the customary slurs against the princes, especially d'Artois and
Chartres, and key ministers, above all Sartine, the *Portefeuille d'un talon
rouge* concludes by summarising the situation of France under Louis XVI.

> La Cour de France, qu'on peignait sous la fin du règne de Louis XV comme
> abattue et plongée dans une débauche avilissante, est maintenant en proie aux
> petites intrigues de femmes ou de courtisans. Point d'énergie dans le maître; une
> indifférence entière dans le Mentor [Maurepas]; une crainte pusillanime dans le
> ministère; une reine colifichet, qui se mêle de tout, qui gâte tout, qui mettra
> bientôt toute la Cour en pantins, et qui décide tout. [The court of France, por-
> trayed towards the end of Louis XV's reign as despondent and plunged into
> degrading debauchery, is now prey to the petty intrigues of women and
> courtiers. There is no energy in the master; a complete indifference in his
> mentor; pusillanimous fear in the ministry; a trashy queen, who meddles in
> everything, ruins everything, will make fools soon of the whole court, and
> decides everything.][76]

This summary exemplifies many major tropes of the *libellistes'* mythology.
France was being bled by women and corrupt, incompetent, effeminate
courtiers, who exploited the king's weaknesses, systematically deceived him,

and marginalised him from government. Far from improving since the days of Louis XV, things were getting worse. From 1789, this caricature of reality entered mainstream public discourse, and was progressively absorbed into the revolutionary imaginery, where it underpinned much revolutionary rhetoric and empowered the creation of a masculinist state based around the cults of manly virtues, transparency, and public openness.

The final liberated text is explicit about matters that the other Bastille pamphlets treated coyly. *Les Amours de Charlot et Toinette*, a mellifluous, deeply ambiguous, 151-line poem, narrates how Toinette [Marie-Antoinette], disappointed by her husband's impotence, reluctantly turns to masturbation and finally to her brother-in-law d'Artois [Charlot]. Their lovemaking is described in considerable detail, but although the language used is often graphic, and the vocabulary coarse, the rhythmic, flowing sensuality of the poem is seductive, even enchanting. Although it is a tale of adultery, the tone evinces considerable affection for Marie-Antoinette. When she is first encountered, the queen is alone, naked, ravishing, warm, tactile, vulnerable:

> Tantôt mourant d'ennui au *milieu* d'un beau jour,
> Elle se trémoussoit toute seule en sa couche
> Ses tétons palpitans, ses beaux yeux et sa bouc [*sic*]
> Doucement hatelante, entrouverte à demi,
> Sembloit d'un fier fouteur inviter le défi.

> [Sometimes dying of boredom in the midst of a lovely day,
> She writhed all alone on her bed
> Her palpitating tits, her beauteous eyes and her mouth
> Gently panting, half opened,
> Appeared to invite the challenge of a proud shagger.][77]

Marie-Antoinette appears as a deserving, sensual woman with a human yearning for sexual fulfilment. She surrenders to d'Artois tentatively, but inevitably, and hence, it is insinuated, justifiably. The reader is invited to sympathise with the queen's predicament and condone her illicit liaison. If the poem is transgressive, it is less for depicting an unthinkable relationship than for daring to imbue the queen with normal mortal desires, for contemplating her naked charms and caresses, and for inviting the reader to experience her joyful romps with the manly Artois:

> Antoinette est divine et toute est charme en elle:
> La douce volupté dont elle prend sa part
> Semble encore lui donner une grace nouvelle:
> La plaisir l'embellit, l'amour est un grand fard.
> D'A . . . [Artois] la sait par coeur, et partout il la baise,
> Son membre est un tison, son coeur une fournaise;
> Il baise ses beaux bras, son joli petit con,
> Et tantôt une fesse, et tantôt un téton . . .
> Antoinette feignant d'éviter ce qu'elle aime,

Crainte de surprise, ne se prête qu'à moitié.
D'A . . . saisit l'instant, et Toinette vaincue
Sent enfin qu'il est doux d'être aussi bien foutue.

[Antoinette is divine and everything about her is enchanting:
The sweet voluptuousness of which she partakes
Seems to lend her a fresh charm:
Pleasure embellishes her, love is a great cosmetic.
D'Artois knows her by heart and kisses her all over,
His member is a firebrand, his heart a furnace;
He kisses her beautiful arms, her pretty little cunt,
And now a buttock, now a tit . . .
Antoinette, feigning to evade what she desires,
Afraid of the shock, only half surrenders.
D'Artois seizes the instant, and Toinette, vanquished,
At last knows how sweet it is to be so well fucked.][78]

Though graphic, the language of the poem lacks the violence of revolutionary political pornography. The queen is no rampaging sex-monster, and her fellow characters also lack the lurid depravity of those in later works. This point is best clarified by reviewing typical scenes from the revolutionary literature. In *L'Autrichienne en goguettes ou l'orgie royal* [*The Austrian Woman on the Rampage, or the Royal Orgy*] (1789) the duchesse de Polignac sits astride the slumbering, inebriated Louis XVI's back, kissing and fingering the queen, who is simultaneously sodomised and tupped from behind by d'Artois.[79] During an orgy scene in the *Bord[el] r[oyal]* involving stock aristocratic figures, Marie-Antoinette instructs a bishop to 'baptise my c***, wipe out the stain of original sin. Nothing is more salutary than this holy water.'[80] In *Le Godemiche royal* [*The Royal Dildo*] (1789), Juno [Marie-Antoinette], awaiting the return of Hebe [the duchesse de Polignac] with an army of well-hung, virile lovers, declares:

This lascivious twitching in my randy cunt,
This is my sole oracle; it must be heeded.
Fuck virtue, that's merely a chimera;
A really amorous cunt can fuck its own father.[81]

In contrast to these grotesque, transgressive, and blasphemous calumnies, the *Amours* appears more a masterpiece of erotic poetry than a crude sexual defamation. Nevertheless, its erotic charge depends primarily on its ambiguity, for it depicts a shocking, treasonous, unholy, adulterous love-affair. Yet in celebrating the joy of sexual union and implying that even a queen has a right to erotic fulfilment, it absolves its fantasy queen more than it condemns her. Instead it is the impotent, absent, cuckold King Louis XVI who is at fault, unable to control and satisfy his wife, because 'son allumette / N'est pas plus grosse qu'un fétu' ['his matchstick is no fatter than a straw'].[82] His alleged sexual impotence is a stark metaphor for political inadequacy. However, whereas many other *libelles* suggested that sexual impotence was endemic among royal and aristocratic males, in the *Amours* the problem is confined to the king himself.

Unlike revolutionary political pornography, the *Amours de Charlot et Toinette* is written with light-hearted humour. For example, the copulating lovers, irritated by the repeated interruptions of a page, eventually discover that the servants' bell-cord is caught between the cushions on which the queen reclines, so that every time d'Artois thrusts, they inadvertently summon an attendant.[83] Moreover, the poet, unlike later scandalmongers, insists on the lovers' constancy:

> Chaque jour plus heureux, devenant plus ardens,
> Ils offrent à Venus leurs feux toujours fidèles,
> Ils se foutent souvent; et l'amour et le tems,
> Pour ces heureux amans semblent n'avoir plus des ailes.

> [Each day more happy, growing more ardent,
> they offer to Venus their ever-faithful flame,
> They fuck each other often; and both love and time
> Seem to these happy lovers no longer to have wings.][84]

Thus the *Amours de Charlot et Toinette* stands apart from other *libelles*, and not merely in its literary quality. It differs from other prerevolutionary pamphlets because of its sexually graphic content, but also because it is an ambiguous and playful text, which fetishises and denigrates the queen in equal measure. This partial sympathy ensured that it remained unique, for in the hate- and tension-charged environment of revolutionary France, it was impossible to produce work of such delicate ambiguity, or perhaps even to appreciate this aspect of the *Amours*. Revolutionary readers and publishers probably seized upon it for its defamatory content, projecting their own hatred of the queen into a hostile reading of her purported adulteries and lasciviousness. Subsequent revolutionary pornographers were indebted to the *Amours* as the first truly pornographic portrayal of the queen, but their own texts are gross parodies of both the poem and its heroine.

Within weeks of the re-emergence of the *Amours de Charlot et Toinette*, *Essai historique* and *Portefeuille d'un talon rouge* from the Bastille, this debased revolutionary caricature of the queen was taking a more definitive shape in new publications, including two purported productions of the comtesse de La Motte: the *Lettre de la comtesse Valois de la Mothe à la reine de France* [*Letter from the Countess Valois de la Mothe to the Queen of France*] and *Second Mémoire justificatif de la comtesse de La Motte, écrit par elle-même* [*Second Justificatory Memoir of the Countess de La Motte, written by herself*], which she later disavowed.[85] The authorship of both texts remains problematic, although both conform to the comtesse's sentimental, melodramatic style. Since the *Lettre à la reine*, which is dated 18 October 1789, announces the imminent appearance of the *Second Mémoire*, they presumably share a common author, and the former was possibly written with hopes of extorting a suppression fee for the latter. Nevertheless, their authenticity is suspect. The autobiographical part of the *Second Mémoire* is derived from the anonymous but well-informed *Authentic Adventures of the Celebrated Countess de La Motte* (London, 1787), which gave an acute and unsympathetic account of the comtesse's youth and role in the diamond necklace affair. Moreover, the *Lettre à la reine* makes use of the variant 'La Mothe' spelling of the comtesse's name, is vague on questions of detail, and makes a rather incongruous, extended attack on Lenoir, who retired as lieutenant of police before the diamond necklace affair broke.[86] A passage in the *Second Mémoire* comparing the judgements in the diamond necklace case and a celebrated trial involving the maréchal-duc de Richelieu and marquise Saint-Vincent raises suspicions that both pamphlets, and perhaps the *Authentic Adventures*, were written by Benevent, who had been Saint-Vincent's lover and was embastilled for helping her forge money orders in the duc's name.[87] Benevent doubtless learned a great deal as the comte de La Motte's companion in 1785–86, and the La Mottes' correspondence hints that he wrote several pamphlets against them.[88] A vitriolic personal attack on the comte in the *Second Mémoire* supports this hypothesis, but as he deserted the comtesse in early 1789, she, too, had motives to abuse him.[89]

The continuations of the comtesse de La Motte's life-story, whether spurious or not, aimed at a radicalised revolutionary audience and promised to make explicit what her *Mémoires* had only implied. Her original *Mémoires* were reproached for being discreet, obscure, equivocal, and too lenient on Marie-Antoinette, explained the *Second Mémoire*, but now, at last, the veil would be torn from triumphant crime.[90] The 'comtesse' speaks out with the indignant voice of violated innocence against a despicable queen, a 'monstre sorti des enfers' ['monster from hell'].[91] Emboldened by the collapse of royal power, the 'comtesse' gloats in her *Lettre à la reine* that she can now write without fear of her cries being stifled by the Bastille.[92] As in her *Mémoires*, La Motte appears an unsuspecting outsider, seduced by the court's corrupting artifice and, above all, the queen's charms. When the queen accompanies a command with a kiss, the comtesse misses its sexual implication, but is enchanted and rapidly ensnared:

> Je n'eus bientôt aucun doute sur l'objet de tes impures caresses, et tu m'enseignas la pratique de ces plaisirs obscènes et revoltans qui ont tant d'empire sur les sens lascifs et corrompus. J'étois trop avancée pour reculer, et d'ailleurs je dois avouer aussi enchanteresse que Circée, séduisante que Calipso, aussi à craindre que Medée, en partageant ton délire, tu m'avois entièrement captivée par un contraste que le crime seul peut produire. [I soon had no doubt of the purpose of your impure caresses, and you taught me the art of those obscene and revolting pleasures which enjoy such dominion over corrupted and lascivious senses. I was too committed to recoil, and besides I must confess that enchanting as Circe, seductive as Calypso, and terrifying as Medea, in sharing your delight, you entirely captivated me by a contrast that crime alone can produce.][93]

The *Second Mémoire* recounts the comtesse's first amorous encounter with the queen in openly erotic language:

> La respect dont j'étois pénétrée l'affligeoit. Elle daigna m'enhardir par des caresses non équivoques et par les paroles les plus douces . . . Bientôt l'ingénieuse libertine parcourut avec des regards dévorants ce qu'elle vouloit bien appeler mes appas; sa bouche enflammée colla par-tout des baisers de feu, et je rougis en avouant que je fus satisfaite. [The respect I showed upset her. She deigned to embolden me by non-equivocal caresses and by the sweetest words. . . . Soon the ingenious libertine ran her devouring eyes over what she called my charms; her enflamed mouth pasted kisses of fire everywhere, and I blush to admit that I was sated.][94]

In these two pamphlets, for the first time, the comtesse or her imitator openly depicts the queen's lesbian lovemaking, imbuing the description with the authority and evocative power of the first-person narrative voice. This contrasts with pre-1789 pamphlets, which are voyeuristic, not confessional, in tone. As in the *Amours de Charlot et Toinette*, the queen's seductiveness is recognised, but there is a vital difference. In the *Amours*, the queen sought sexual satisfaction for its own sake, whereas now even the queen's 'unnatural' passions are artificial and subsidiary to corrupt and despicable ends. In contrast, the comtesse's only crime was participating in the queen's lesbian lovemaking, but she was rewarded by becoming the scapegoat for Marie-Antoinette's 'abominable' theft.[95]

In reality, the scapegoat of these pamphlets is Marie-Antoinette, whose repentance, retirement, or divorce is now touted as the only means for saving France.[96] The *Second Mémoire* lays the full range of revolutionary charges against her. She bears full responsibility for the abortive royal coups of July and October 1789, having 'tenté d'incendier et de submerger de sang tout un empire' ['attempted to torch an entire empire and submerge it in blood'].[97] She is also accused of numerous earlier crimes, some for the first time. She is accused of procuring the duchesse de Polignac to poison Maurepas,[98] and attempting to persuade the La Mottes to poison Vergennes.[99] It is even suggested that Marie-Antoinette conspired to kill Louis XVI.[100] The plots of the mythical Austrian committee are also described in greater detail than hitherto. For example, it was said to have employed Linguet to stir up the Belgian revolt against the emperor, hoping to provoke a war that a bankrupt France would inevitably lose.[101] The queen's fickleness and treachery are also implied by the now increasingly familiar ploy of listing of her supposed lovers, in this case ten women (viz., the comtesse de La Motte, [Mme?] Langeac, the duchesse de Polignac, the comtesse d'Ossun, the princesse de Lamballe, Madame Misery, the queen's dressmaker Rose Bertin, and three opera singers or dancers, Mademoiselles Guimard, Saint-Huberty, and Raucourt) together with a series of swains, including d'Artois, Fersen, the duc de Lauzun, the duc de Fronsac, Vaudreuil, Dillon, and the duc de Coigny.[102]

The *Lettre à la reine* fleshes out this picture, informing the queen that La Motte wishes to elaborate on the description of 'tes dépradations sans bornes, tes dissipations outrées, tes courses nocturnes et clandestines' ['your limitless depradations, your outrageous dissipations, your noctural and clandestine promenades'] given in her *Mémoires* and the *Essai historique*.[103] The 'comtesse' describes, for example, how, whenever Lenoir carried out the queen's 'terrible orders', she and Marie-Antoinette would drink to celebrate, just as Caligula drank his victims' blood from a human skull.[104] Marie-Antoinette was thus equated with the worst monsters of classical antiquity. In a particularly sinister turn, the pamphlet also incites public vengeance against Lenoir's agents, several of whom are named, including d'Hémery.[105] No longer does the 'comtesse' pretend to write in support of personal claims: she now speaks for the nation against its oppressor and her henchmen.

The themes of these works were taken up in further pamphlets, including *La Reine dévoilée, ou supplément au Mémoire de Mde la comtesse de La Motte* [*The Queen Unmasked, or Supplement to the Memoir of Madame la comtesse de La Motte*], which, despite its title, makes no claim to be written by the comtesse.[106] Nevertheless, it insists that the comtesse's *Mémoires* reveal the truth, and suggests that the queen sent assassins against her.[107] Such works reinforced the comtesse's self-presentation, describing her as 'aussi innocente que malheureuse' ['as innocent as unfortunate'] while the capricious, vindictive, pleasure-loving queen is 'un composé singulier de ce qui immortalisa Médicis et Messaline' ['a singular mixture of that which immortalised [Catherine de] Médici and Messalina'].[108] Marie-Antoinette's dominion over Louis XVI is described as infinite; her alleged affair with d'Artois and lesbian romps with the duchesse de Polignac, a favourite target of pamphleteers in 1789, are dredged up again.[109]

However, the main focus of *La Reine dévoilée* is not the diamond necklace affair, but the political intrigues of the queen's circle to prevent Necker reversing decisions made in the boudoir by Polignac and Marie-Antoinette. The narrative spans the period from the prerevolutionary crisis until the failure of the attempted royal coup in July 1789.[110] In effect, the pamphlet deploys the events of the diamond necklace affair and of July 1789 to illuminate each another, thereby insinuating the queen's culpability. This is most evident in a passage stating that Marie-Antoinette and her accomplices betrayed and silenced their secondary agents after the fall of the Bastille, paying lynch-mobs to assassinate Launay, Joseph Foulon, commander of Paris, and Flesselles, the *prévôt des marchands*.[111] This, the pamphlet asserted, was how princes repaid those who served them, just as the comtesse de La Motte had shown. Other pamphlets, too, cited the comtesse as a key authority. For example, the anonymous *Semonce à la reine* [*Reprimand to the Queen*] declares:

Le procès du Cardinal, et les Mémoires de la Lamotte attestent et divulguent que vous avez pris avec ce Pontife libertin et cette furie débordée des plaisirs odieux, qui révoltent l'amour et outrageant la nature. [The trial of the cardinal and the memoirs of the La Motte woman attest and reveal that you participated with that libertine Pontiff and that unbridled Fury in odious pleasures, which revolt love and outrage nature.][112]

However, in her reworked autobiography, the *Vie de Jeanne de Saint-Rémy de Valois*, first published in 1791, the comtesse renounced the continuations of her memoirs together with the description of her second interview with the queen in her *Mémoires*.[113] The Marie-Antoinette of this new work was passionate and haughty, but governed by the duplicitous duchesse de Polignac. This time there is no hint of lesbianism: Jeanne receives generous cash gifts rather than kisses in her interviews with the queen. Nevertheless, the comtesse's account of the diamond necklace affair and the queen's relations with Rohan remained almost word for word the same. The attack on the queen is less strident, but she remains a major villain, guilty of plotting the destruction of Rohan in cold blood and treating the comtesse unjustly.

The novelty of this new work lay in the comtesse's extended treatment of her early life; a detailed narrative account of Calonne's attempts to suppress her *Mémoire* and the aftermath of their publication; together with a smattering of attacks on the prerevolutionary police, prison system, and *lettres de cachet*.[114] This was mostly shadow-boxing, for the revolution had swept all these things away, as the comtesse acknowledged when she wrote: 'I see an august Senate dispensing freedom and happiness to a renovated Empire. I see them abolishing the absurd institutions that gave to one class of men the priviliege of oppressing another with impunity. I see the rights of the people clearly defined; and guarded against future encroachments.'[115] This was clearly a revolutionary text, for despite the back-pedalling concerning the queen, it both celebrated and legitimised the revolution. The revolutionary government understood this only too well and ordered it to be republished. Iain McCalman thus over-states his case when he claims that this new set of memoirs was aimed primarily at the British market and presents the queen as 'less the dissembling pervert, than an essentially good hearted woman who is over impulsive and naïvely susceptible to manipulation by scheming courtiers'.[116] The Committee of Public Safety recognised that La Motte's revised autobiography remained a potent propaganda weapon against the deposed Bourbons and readily republished it.

In conclusion, it appears that even Gruder probably over-estimates the prevalence of pornographic *libelle* attacks on the monarchy before 1789. Hence there is good reason to endorse D. M. G. Sutherland's recent observation that 'unfortunately for those who believe in the desacralization of the monarchy thesis, the revolution occurred under the reign of Louis XVI, not under the reign of his grandfather [Louis XV]'.[117] The hiatus between pamphlet attacks on du Barry and Marie-Antoinette was total, lasted for almost fifteen years, and did not come to an end until the revolutionary crisis was well underway. The connection between sexual corruption and political despotism, denounced in near-Biblical terms in anti-Maupeou literature, ended with the accession of Louis XVI, whose failings did not include a scandalous private life. While a few manuscript *libelles* may have circulated in aristocratic circles at Paris and Versailles, only the slenderest hints at the very possibility of queenly infidelity have been identified in printed texts available before the revolution. Only in 1789 did the mythical Austrian Messalina conjured up by the *libellistes*' darkest fantasies escape from the recesses of the comtesse de La Motte's mind and the dungeons of the Bastille, to rampage across the revolutionary imagination. The origins of hostility to Marie-Antoinette must therefore be sought not in prerevolutionary scandal-mongering but, as Thomas Kaiser has emphasised, in political causes, including deep-seated Austrophobia, resentment among courtiers, and suspicion of her family links both to the Habsburgs and the house of Lorraine.[118] Nevertheless, from 1789 the *libellistes*' pamphlets tapped, popularised, and amplified such sentiments and reinforced them with a powerful sexual and political mythology. There is little doubt that the 'revelations' of the comtesse de La Motte and the Bastille texts provided an empirical underpinning to prejudices against the queen, and that thereafter revolutionary pamphleteers fanned as well as reflected popular antipathy to Marie-Antoinette.

Notes

1 Hunt, 'Many bodies', p. 116.
2 The most notorious newspaper attacks were in Hébert's *Père Duchesne*: see Dena Goodman, 'Introduction' in Goodman (ed.), *Marie-Antoinette*, p. 20.
3 Nineteenth-century sources mention a handful of other untraceable titles. Fleischmann, *Pamphlets libertins*, p. 103, notes that an anonymous 1790 *Vie de Louis XVI* mentions a pamphlet entitled *Les Nuits d'Antoinette* produced at Angers early in Louis XVI's reign. As no copies survive, this title is probably apocryphal. Félix Rocquain, *L'Esprit révolutionnaire avant la révolution* (Paris: E. Plon, 1878), pp. 360–1, mentions three other untraceable *libelles* reputedly seized at source according to literary sources: *Les Amours de notre reine*, a scandalous *Almanach royal*, and *La Coquette et l'impuissant*. If these reports were true, the entire editions were presumably either destroyed or existed only in manuscript.
4 The term 'talon rouge' ['red heel'] denoted a fashionable young man-about-town.
5 See Manuel, *Police*, I, 257 and appendix below.
6 MO, MS 1422 p. 56.
7 *BCE*, document 516, Morande to Montmorin, 28 April 1788.
8 AN, 446AP/2, 'Mémoire pour Brissot', [1784], fo. 3; Manuel, *Police*, II, 29.
9 My research in on-line collective catalogues suggests that the ratio of copies of eighteenth-century *libelles* in British and French research libraries to original print-runs is approximately 1:200 to 1:300. If no copies of a work survive, it was probably never printed.
10 I will analyse library evidence further in a future work on scandalous lives of Marie-Antoinette.
11 Darnton, *Corpus*, p. 140. For the *Alarm-Bell* see *MSB*, 11 October 1784; *CSP*, XVI, 94–7; Pelleport, *Diable*, p. 78; Guillaume Imbert (attrib.), *Chronique*

scandaleuse ou mémoires pour servir à l'histoire de la génération présente, 3rd edition, 4 vols (Paris: n. p., 1788), I, 35. Mauvelain and Darnton both replicate the idiosyncratic rendering of the *Alarm-Bell* for all three titles that it mentioned, viz., *Les Passe-temps d'Antoinette*, *Les Amours et les Aventures du vizir Vergennes*, and *Les Petits-Soupers et les nuits de l'hôtel de Bouillon*; hence Mauvelain's source is beyond doubt. Nicolas Ruault (*Gazette d'un Parisien*, p. 23) transcribes the titles similarly. On Mauvelain's trade see Darnton, 'Trade in taboo'.

12 Ruault, *Gazette d'un Parisien*, p. 23.

13 For his protests see Arsenal, MS 12,454.

14 There were two editions of the *Procès des trois rois* in 1780 and three in 1781. At least two editions of the *Gazetier cuirassé* appeared in 1771; further editions date from 1772, 1777, and 1785.

15 The importance of the liberation of the secret *dépôt* was first raised by Gruder, 'Question of Marie-Antoinette', p. 276.

16 7–10 of the 14–17 anti-Marie-Antoinette *libelles* in French libraries (i.e. at least 50 per cent) are in the BN's collections (including the Arsenal). In comparison only 13 out of 45 copies (29 per cent) of the *Procès des trois rois* and 10 out of 39 copies (26 per cent) of the *Gazetier cuirassé* are in the BN. As table 2 shows, 24 out of 108 copies (22 per cent) of the 'control texts' are in British collections, as compared with 3 out of 17–20 anti-Marie-Antoinette *libelles* (see table 1).

17 Darnton, *Corpus*, esp. pp. 257–60 and *passim*.

18 Hunt, 'Many bodies', p. 117.

19 *MSB*, 26 January 1782. This source calls the pamphlet *La Vie d'Antoinette*, which formed part of the title of the *Essai historique*. No pamphlets entitled just *La Vie d'Antoinette* have been found.

20 *MSB*, 7 and 26 February 1782.

21 Translation from Thomas, *Wicked Queen*, pp. 217–27. It is unlikely that 'ma vie' refers here to La Motte's *Mémoires*, since they were not a biography of the queen.

22 This was first noted by Gruder, 'Question of Marie-Antoinette', p. 273.

23 Figures from Darnton, *Corpus*, pp. 15, 64, 184, 203.

24 BPUN, MS 1028, 'Journal C' fos 127, 213–15, and 231, lists the books sent to Mauvelain on 23 February, 26 July, and 18 August 1784. Darnton, 'Trade in taboo', pp. 74–5, itemises the shipment of 26 July.

25 BPUN, MSS 1003–7 and 1009.

26 Darnton, 'Trade in taboo'.

27 Goudar (attrib.), *Procès des trois rois*, pp. 145n., 171. On this work's success, see Hauc, *Ange Goudar*, p. 172.

28 Darnton, *Corpus*, pp. 118, 152; *CSCV*, I, 369. The STN also stocked a few copies of Goudar's *Procès des trois rois*, but as the only sales of this work recorded (BPUN, MS 1007 fo. 305) were to dealers based outside France, it does not appear in Darnton's figures.

29 *MSB*, 7 February 1782; Gruder, 'Question of Marie-Antoinette', p. 275n. Cf. Darnton, *Corpus* and the STN inventories BPUN, MSS 1003–7 and 1009. The *Mémoires secrets* suggest that the police seized most copies of Lanjuinais's work.

30 Joseph Lanjuinais (attrib.), *Supplément à l'Espion anglois* (London: John Adamson, 1781) pp. 19–21, 26, quote at p. 21.

31 Gruder, 'Question of Marie-Antoinette', p. 279, mentions *L'Histoire d'Aurore* (possibly a reworking of *Le Lever de l'Aurore*, a manuscript *libelle* in verse) and *Pour elle Messaline*. *CSCV*, I, 331 describes a third *libelle*, entitled *Le Pou* [*The Louse*]. It adds that a dozen copies are circulating in France and that police have been sent to Holland to apprehend the author and the 'brochure' [pamphlet]. However, it is not mentioned by Darnton, and searches of the *Catalogue collectif de France* and *Copac* (the collective catalogue for British academic and research libraries) found no printed versions.

32 Marie-Antoinette, Maria-Theresia, and Mercy-Argenteau express concern about all these media in *CSMT*, II, 235, 317, 403, 409, 416, 420, 438–9; III, 14–17, 295, 458–9. Much of the material they discuss is dismissed as 'insolent', and it is not clear whether any of it touched on the queen's chastity.

33 Goulemot, *Forbidden Texts*, p. 24, asserts that the proliferation in revolutionary pornography, including anti-Marie-Antoinette titles, occurred after decrees concerning press freedom on 4 and 24 August.

34 The letters are reproduced in Lever, *Affaire du collier*, pp. 342–73.

35 See below, n. 113.

36 Jeanne de La Motte, *Mémoires justificatifs*, p. 16.

37 Jeanne de La Motte, *Memoirs*, pp. 25–30, 33–4.

38 Ibid., p. 83.

39 Ibid., pp. 76–9, 86–7.

40 Ibid., pp. 30–2.

41 Ibid., pp. 134–7.

42 For Jeanne's account of negotiations for the necklace and its fate, see ibid., pp. 86–129.

43 Ibid., pp. 46–53.

44 See La Motte, *Mémoire pour Jeanne de Valois*.

45 Jeanne de La Motte, *Memoirs*, p. 230.

46 Ibid., pp. 219–20.

47 The comte's narrative covers ibid., pp. 146–213.

48 Ibid., pp. 180–90.

49 Ibid., pp. 62, 134.

50 The BN alone has eighteen copies under various variants of the title, and *Copac* lists another thirty. Of this total, barring cataloguing errors, only three undated copies (6 per cent) may pre-date 1789.The rest mostly date from 1789, with a handful from 1790 and 1791. I have consulted three French-language editions. The BL edition of 100 pages without date or place of publication is presumably the original. It is entitled *Essai historique sur la vie de Marie-Antoinette d'Autriche, reine de France, pour servir à l'histoire de cette princesse*. There are revolutionary editions of seventy-nine and eighty-three pages bearing (probably spurious) London imprints in the BL and Brotherton Library respectively. Both reproduce the original text but pluralise the title as *Essais historiques* and add identical editor's notes and introduction, which are lacking in the undated edition. My references are taken from the Brotherton edition. Later French editions modified and extended the text.

51 I uncovered this English translation (which does not identify its source) in Honoré-Gabriel de Riquetti, comte de Mirabeau, et al. (attrib.), *The Life and Death of Marie-Antoinette, Late Queen of France, from the French of Mirabeau and Others*, transl. W. S. Delome (London: W. S. Delome, n. d. [December

1793]), pp. 3–65. It includes the notes but not the editor's introduction from 1789 French editions.

52 Manuel, *Police*, I, 257; Charpentier, *Bastille dévoilée*, 3rd livraison, pp. 36–7, gives different examples of his titles and links their production and distribution to London, Brussels, and Amsterdam. See also appendix, below.

53 For example, the *Essais historiques* discuss Marie-Antoinette's second pregnancy, which led to the birth of the dauphin in October 1781. Goupil died in April 1780. The text of the *Portefeuille*, one of whose letters is dated 18 June 1779, thus appears to pre-date the *Essais historiques*.

54 Anon., *Essais historiques*, p. 2.

55 Ibid., pp. 3–4.

56 Ibid., pp. 4–5.

57 Ibid., pp. 5–6.

58 See esp. ibid., pp. 10–11, 17–19.

59 Ibid., pp. 11, 14–15.

60 Ibid., p. 11.

61 See, for example, ibid., pp. 13, 35–6.

62 Ibid., pp. 32, 45.

63 Ibid., pp. 53–63.

64 Ibid., pp. 20–1, 48–9.

65 Ibid., pp. 29, 52.

66 Ibid., pp. 50–1.

67 Ibid., pp. v–vi and p. 73, n. 1.

68 On this version see Hunt, 'Many bodies', pp. 118–20. It claimed spuriously to be published 'à Versailles, chez La Montensier, Hôtel des courtisannes' in 1789.

69 Anon., *Le Portefeuille d'un talon rouge* (Neuchâtel: Société des Bibliophiles cosmopolites, 1872), p. 32. The original edition claimed to be published in Paris at 'l'imprimerie du comte de Paradis, 178*', but was actually produced in London.

70 Ibid., pp. 24–6.

71 See esp. Robert Darnton, 'An early information society: news and the media in eighteenth-century Paris', *American Historical Review* 105:1 (2000), 1–35.

72 Gruder, 'Question of Marie-Antoinette', p. 286. The key passage in Anon., *Portefeuille d'un talon rouge*, is at p. 6.

73 Ibid., p. 22.

74 Ibid., pp. 14–19.

75 Ibid., pp. 22–3.

76 Ibid., p. 39.

77 Anon., *Les Amours de Charlot et Toinette* (Paris: 'à la Bastille', 1789), p. 3, lines 13–17. The text of this edition is almost the same as that of the original 1779 edition. The translations are my own. For a full English translation see Thomas, *Wicked Queen*, pp. 185–90. The French edition of Thomas's work reproduces the original 1779 text.

78 Anon., *Amours de Charlot*, p. 5, lines 60–7, 74–7.

79 This pamphlet is translated in Thomas, *Wicked Queen*, pp. 203–15, quote at p. 214.

80 This pamphlet is translated ibid., pp. 217–27, quote at p. 221.

81 This pamphlet is translated ibid., pp. 193–201, quote at pp. 200–1.

82 Anon., *Amours de Charlot*, p. 4, lines 29–30.

83 Ibid., pp. 6–7, lines 83–135.

84 Ibid., p. 7, lines 140–3.

85 La Motte, *Life*, I, pp. ix–x.

86 Jeanne de Saint-Rémy de La Motte (attrib.), *Lettre de la comtesse Valois de la Mothe à la reine de France* (Oxford: n. p., 1789), p. 8.

87 La Motte (attrib.), *Second Mémoire*, pp. 11–12. On Benevent's involvement in the Saint-Vincent affair see Mathieu-François Pidansat de Mairobert (attrib.), *L'Espion anglois, ou correspondance secrète entre Milord All'Eye et Milord All'Ear*, nouvelle édition revue, corrigée et consideralement augmentée, 10 vols (London: John Adamson, 1785), II, 14 (although early editions appeared under the title *L'Observateur anglois*, this work is usually referred to as *L'Espion anglois*); *MSB*, 23 August 1775; Maza, *Private Lives*, pp. 142–6. *MSB*, 10 February 1786, reveals that Benevent was also involved with Mirabeau.

88 See AN, F^7 4445^2 dossier 3, piece 17, [comtesse de La Motte] to [comte de La Motte], ce samedi 19 [?] Ja [?]. This letter suggests that Costa [Benevent] and 'les amis d'Angelique' (the comtesse's former confidante, cellmate, and servant) produced 'infames écrits' ['infamous writings'] wrongly attributed to Pelleport. Since Benevent met Angelique after the comtesse's escape, this cannot refer to Pelleport's earlier *libelles*. Although no month in 1790 contained a Saturday 19th, internal references prove that this letter post-dates the abbé Pfaff's letter to the comtesse of 9 January 1790.

89 La Motte (attrib.), *Second Mémoire*, p. 40.

90 Ibid., pp. 2–3. The editor's introduction to the 1789 reprintings of the *Essais historiques* also accuses Madame de La Motte's *Mémoires* of containing 'trop de ménagemens'.

91 La Motte (attrib.), *Lettre à la reine*, p. 10.

92 Ibid., p. 7.

93 Ibid., p. 10.

94 La Motte (attrib.), *Second Mémoire*, p. 32.

95 La Motte (attrib.), *Lettre à la reine*, p. 10.

96 La Motte (attrib.), *Second Mémoire*, pp. 4–5, 66.

97 Ibid., p. 27.

98 Ibid., pp. 57–9.

99 Ibid., p. 53–61.

100 Ibid., pp. 27, 66.

101 Ibid., pp. 51–2.

102 Ibid., p. 50. Cf. for example the comte de La Motte's list of five male lovers in Jeanne de La Motte, *Memoirs*, p. 188.

103 La Motte (attrib.), *Lettre à la reine*, p. 6. Note the disrespectful, familiar, egalitarian use of 'tes'.

104 Ibid., p. 8.

105 Ibid., p. 6.

106 Anon., *La Reine dévoilée, ou supplément au Mémoire de Mde la comtesse de La Motte* (London: n. p., 1789), p. 142.

107 Ibid., p. 34n., 106–7, 122.

108 Ibid., pp. 7, 12.

109 Ibid., pp. 26–7, 89–90, 91–2. The final reference highlights d'Artois's role as darling of the reactionaries and counter-revolutionaries.

110 Ibid., p. 52. On Polignac see esp. pp. 87–90, 105, 115n.

111 Ibid., pp. 139–40.
112 Anon., *Sémonce à la reine* (n. pl., n. d.), p. 3.
113 La Motte, *Life*, I, pp. vii–ix. She blamed the description of the second interview on La Tour and Calonne.
114 Ibid., I, 341; II, 128, 239–52.
115 Ibid., I, p. v.
116 See McCalman, 'Queen of the gutter', p. 118.
117 Sutherland, *Revolution and Empire*, p. 14.
118 See Thomas E. Kaiser's essays, 'From the Austrian committee to the foreign plot: Marie-Antoinette, austrophobia and the Terror', *French Historical Studies* 26:3 (2003); 'Who's afraid of Marie-Antoinette? Diplomacy, austrophobia and the queen', *French History* 14:3 (2000); 'Ambiguous identities'; and 'Nobles into aristocrats, or how an order became a conspiracy', unpublished chapter. I am grateful to Professor Kaiser for sending me a copy of this paper. On Austrophobia see also Gary Savage, 'Favier's heirs: the French revolution and the *Secret du roi*', *Historical Journal* 41:1 (1998).

6

The corpus of blackmail *libelles*, 1758–89

Although *libelles* against Marie-Antoinette were extremely rare and may not even have circulated before the revolution, the London *libellistes* did publish several other blackmail-related texts between 1758 and 1789. These texts, whether produced to extort a suppression payment or to help intimidate blackmail victims, are the subject of this chapter. Existing literature suggests that these blackmail *libelles* would possess certain key characteristics. They would tend to desacralise the monarchy by attacking its religious underpinning; contain scathing pornographic attacks on France's political and social elite; and offer a nihilistic, hate-driven critique of the monarchy and institutions of the *ancien régime*. Moreover, since they were written with the aim of extorting hush-money, they would presumably represent extreme forms of such material. In addition, feminist scholarship implies that they will contain an increasingly strident critique of female political influence. This chapter will argue that only this last expectation is supported by the evidence. Political pornography and attacks on religion were, in reality, marginal to *libelle* literature, and even the most violent *libelles* were reformist or factional attacks on alleged 'ministerial despotism' rather than proto-revolutionary attacks on the monarchy and social system. Nevertheless, discourses associated with the *libelles* had a powerful formative effect on revolutionary political culture.

Clearly, a focus on blackmail texts necessarily excludes a large proportion of the political or scandalous French texts published – or claiming to be published – in London during the late eighteenth century, including many political pamphlets and some works that Darnton describes as 'scandalous'. This excluded literature includes the *libellistes' exposés* of attempts of French police, spies, ambassadors, and ministers to control their activities, among which are Pelleport's *Diable dans un bénitier*: such works are discussed in the final chapter. It also includes the Mairobert texts published by 'John Adamson'; most of Linguet's *oeuvre*; the tracts published by Calonne and Mirabeau; and scandalous pamphlets such as the *Vie privée du duc de Chartres*; *Portefeuille de Madame Gourdan*; or *Gazette noire*. However, the approach adopted here has the advantage of providing a sharp focus on the texts that their authors or the French government considered most dangerous: those thought worthy or capable of extorting a suppression fee.

As so many *libelles* were suppressed, the corpus of known blackmail pamphlets published in London is not extensive. It comprises just five or six pamphlets: Fauques's *Histoire de Pompadour* (1759, first English edition 1758); d'Eon's *Lettres, mémoires et négociations* (1764); Morande's *Gazetier cuirassé* (1771); Linguet's *Lettre à Vergennes* (1777); Pelleport's *Petits Soupers* (1783); and, if it was ever published, Vergy's *Guerchiade* (1767). However, since this group contains influential examples of several genres of political pamphlet, it has a representative value. Fauques's scandalous biography of Pompadour was a model for a genre that included, among others, Mairobert's *Anecdotes sur Madame du Barry* and the *Essai historique*. Linguet's *Lettre à Vergennes* was both a polemical pamphlet and, in effect, a lawyer's brief: it contained autobiographical material, a manifesto, a rehearsal of the author's grievances, an advertisement for his *Annales*, and a pre-emptive warning against banning their circulation. The *Guerchiade* was an epic-comic poem relating the story of Guerchy's embassy to London and struggles with d'Eon, while the *Petits Soupers* was a sexually salacious prose tale of shenanigans involving aristocrats, minor royalty, and a government minister. D'Eon's *Lettres, mémoires et négociations* comprised a fifty-page justificatory memoir defending its author's reckless spending on Guerchy's embassy building and refusal to obey a letter of recall, to which were appended 400 pages of diplomatic correspondence. Finally, Morande's *Gazetier cuirassé*, the most misunderstood and complex text discussed here, was a collection of miscellaneous anecdotes about important figures at the French court, opera-girls, actresses, and occasionally churchmen or institutional bodies. It represents a genre that includes Guillaume Imbert's *Chronique scandaleuse* and the *Mémoires secrets*. The chronological range of these six texts is also representative of the *libelles* of the prerevolutionary period.

If, as Darnton suggests, the *libellistes* contributed to the desacralisation of the monarchy, their most scandalous pamphlets ought to contain sustained attacks on the Church and religious underpinnings of a sacralised monarchy. In fact, save for the odd anti-clerical sexual slander, religion is rarely treated in the blackmail pamphlets considered in this chapter. It is also absent from prerevolutionary anti-Marie-Antoinette *libelles*, save implicitly through the presence of cardinal Rohan in La Motte's *Mémoires*. The exceptions are Fauques's *Histoire de Pompadour* and Morande's *Gazetier cuirassé*, both of which use religion to reinforce political messages. Fauques offers a blistering attack on the Church's influence in French political life, combining utilitarian, deist, materialist, and secularist enlightenment critiques of Roman Catholicism. She ridicules the metaphysical debate between the Jansenists and the Jesuit-clerical establishment, comparing it unfavourably with the internecine dispute between big-endians and little-endians in Jonathan Swift's *Gulliver's Travels*.[1] Whereas the Lilliputian dilemma concerning the better end to crack an egg can be resolved, humanity can never know the right answer to the Jansenist issue, or derive a shred of material advantage from the solution.[2] Fauques nevertheless strongly prefers the Jansenists, since they seek to deliver the French people from the tyranny of the clergy. However, she upbraids their allies in the Paris *Parlement* for chasing shadows rather than focusing on material grievances such as taxation.[3] In contrast, she castigates the 'Jesuits and bigots', as murderers of common-sense. They give the king spiritual advisors who fill his mind with terrifying images of demons and hellfire, rather than emphasising the love of the 'Supreme Being', the true source of everything good in religion. Such 'impure' ideas give rise to the religious superstition, pointless ceremonies, and ridiculous practices that cause religious intolerance and persecution, things that God views with horror.[4]

Fauques's attack on the alliance between Catholic Church and Bourbon establishment was essential to her biography of Pompadour, since Louis XV's tender religious conscience was potentially the favourite's Achilles heel. Indeed, Louis had already repudiated one mistress, Madame de La Tournelle, when critically ill in 1744, in order to receive the sacrament.[5] However, after successfully transforming herself from royal lover to indispensable friend, Pompadour turns religion to her advantage. This transition allows her to survive the end of her sexual relationship with Louis, an event Fauques attributes to an unspecified gynaecological crisis.[6] Although Pompadour connives in Louis's subsequent sexual affairs, she remains jealous of any woman who receives the slightest favour.[7] Thus, she plays on Louis XV's conscience, hoping that he will repent, abandon his lecherous lifestyle, and be reconciled with the Church. To facilitate this process, she makes ostentatious overtures for a reconciliation with her husband, so that, once they are spurned, she can be welcomed back into the bosom of the Church.[8] Fauques implies that this was a calculated move, for Pompadour made a mockery of the sacraments in other circumstances.[9] Overall, Fauques adopts a Voltairean position as an enlightened secularist. She recognises the social and moral utility of religion and, apparently, the existence of God, but she rejects theological disputes as pointless, and abhors religious hypocrisy and the political influence of Roman Catholicism.

Like Fauques's *Histoire de Pompadour*, the *Gazetier cuirassé* contains bursts of anti-clericalism, drawing on established Jansenist themes. It repeatedly insinuates that Maupeou's secret motive for abolishing the *parlements* is the reintroduction of the Jesuits to France.[10] In one passage, Maupeou is caught *in flagrante* with Jesuits; in another the fictitious Jesuit-led *Parlement* of Trévoux offers a long-winded loyal address to the king.[11] Clearly Morande believes, like Fauques, that religious and political despotism go hand in hand. Morande also spices up his text with a sprinkling of traditional scandalous anti-clerical anecdotes featuring frolicsome nuns, lascivious monks, and fornicating, worldly bishops.[12] He mocks the Pope's claims to spiritual authority, argues that monks should be employed as soldiers, and jibes that the Virgin Mary was descended from four prostitutes.[13] However, these are isolated comments. Morande's treatment of the Roman Catholic

Church and Christianity may have scandalised the faithful and amused the irreverent, but it is mere sniping in comparison with the corrosive iconoclastic wit of Voltaire's *Philosophical Dictionary* (1764) or the atheistic materialism of d'Holbach, Diderot, and Helvétius. Taken as a whole, therefore, Fauques's and Morande's attacks on religion are subservient to their political aims. While they link religious and ministerial despotism, they do so within the context of the Jansenist–Jesuit debate and its aftermath. It is no coincidence, therefore, that religious motifs disappear from the London *libellistes*' works following the fall of the Jesuits and subsequent defeat of the *dévot*-backed Maupeou administration. The topos of linking corrupt politicians and Roman Catholic zealots was resurrected only in 1789, in the portrayal of a counter-revolutionary alliance of throne and altar. Attempts to link the London *libellistes* to a long-term process of desacralisation thus fail to account for political contingency.

Although several of the blackmail *libelles* discuss royal mistresses, it is difficult to characterise most of them as 'political pornography'. For example, Fauques's *Histoire de Pompadour* never mentions sex explicitly. It is a scandalous biography rather than 'political pornography': it lacks sustained erotic passages, explicit 'descriptions of sexual organs or activities with the . . . aim of producing sexual arousal', or even detailed accounts of venues or occasions for erotic encounters.[14] The same is true of most *libelles* penned before the revolution, including, surprisingly, the *Gazetier cuirassé*. In fact, the *Gazetier*'s raciest passages are an allegorical *double entendre* reporting the discovery of the lost royal sceptre of France 'sur la toilette d'une jolie femme apellée [*sic*] comtesse, qui s'en sert pour amuser son chat' ['on the dressing table of a pretty woman known as a countess, who uses it to amuse her cat/ pussy'],[15] and a passage describing how the king's attachment to du Barry comes from 'des efforts prodigieux, qu'elle lui fait faire, au möien d'un baptême ambré dont elle se parfume interieurement tous les jours' ['the prodigious efforts that she makes for him, by means of an amber douche with which she perfumes herself internally each day'] and 'un secret dont on ne se sert pas encore en bonne compagnie' ['a secret which is still not used in decent company'].[16] Thus, while Morande began to pry behind bedroom doors that Fauques discreetly refrained from opening, he nevertheless respected the privacy of the body of the king and other aristocratic characters. It is unlikely that he was so prurient in his next pamphlet, for its very title, *Mémoires secrets d'une femme publique, depuis son berceau jusqu'au lit d'honneur*, suggests more intimate revelations. As it was suppressed and burned, its content cannot be known, but Mairobert's best-selling and well-informed *Anecdotes sur Madame du Barry* assured readers that the *Gazetier* was 'eau rose' in comparison with its sequel.[17]

Intriguingly, Mairobert's *Anecdotes* contained several mildly erotic passages of their own concerning du Barry's amorous adventures, including a description of her first encounter with Louis XV in which readers are invited to imagine her 'secret charms', the 'monde nouveau de voluptés' ['new world of pleasure'], and the 'délices qu'il ignoroit' ['delights unknown to him'] that she offered her jaded lover.[18] Yet like other political *libelles* that circulated before the revolution, the *Anecdotes* left details of royal sexual encounters to the reader's imagination. This may not have been entirely true of ephemera such as popular songs and broadsheets, but at the level of books and pamphlets, there was a sea-change in erotic content from the start of the revolution.[19] Before 1789, the works that appeared (unlike at least one text safely locked in the Bastille's secret *dépôt*) titillated by erotic suggestion and by inviting readers to imagine amorous encounters for themselves. However, from 1789, as chapter five revealed, many *libelles* are graphic, explicit, and imbued with the crudest vocabulary. They often make their characters appear gross by the use of gutteral terms, the expression of deviant sexual practices or tastes, and extremes of transgressive behaviour, often involving a combination of incest, complex group sex, same-sex coupling, and mind-boggling levels of promiscuity. While these topoi feature occasionally in pornographic literature before 1789, they are not encountered in extreme forms in the slanderous political texts of the prerevolutionary period. The revolutionary crisis and the free market in printed products to which it gave rise thus seem to have precipitated the fusion of two hitherto distinct literary genres: politically slanderous *libelles* and pornography, in the conventional meaning of the term.

One partial exception to these observations is Pelleport's *Petits Soupers*, which in many ways foreshadowed revolutionary 'political pornography'. A tale of promiscuity, cuckoldry, and venereal disease in high places, it recounts the amorous adventures of the German-born princesse de Bouillon, her family and associates, and the mysterious suicide of her coachman. This unedifying story unfolds as a whispered dialogue between strangers at the Opéra. Written without verve, sophisticated humour, or literary merit, it was justifiably dismissed by Morande as 'mal écrite, si ordurière, si peu faite pour intéresser la curiosité' ['badly written, so foul, so little designed to interest curiosity'].[20] The paucity of surviving copies suggests that its scurrility, sensation, and obscenity found only a very limited market, despite the distress it caused many of its victims.

The cast of the *Petits Soupers* included important social and political figures, but not the king, queen, or their immediate family. Its most elevated victims were the duc de Chartres and the marquis de Castries, the naval minister. Chartres was accused of mere adultery, but Castries was charged with embezzling naval funds to finance his mistresses,[21] serial adulteries, whoring, and a penchant for 'les inclinations canoniques' [i.e. sodomy] with both sexes. The pamphlet's most scathing passage uses religious euphemism to explain how Madame Castries

> pour empêcher son august époux de s'abandonner à ses dépenses superflues, en portant ailleurs son hommage; lorsqu'il n'avoit pas de dévotion pour la chapelle ordinaire, elle le stiloit à visiter l'annexe. [to prevent her august spouse from resorting to unnecessary expenditure in taking his homage elsewhere, when he

had no reverence for the common chapel, used to entice him to visit the annexe.][22]

Moreover, a letter from the princesse de Bouillon to her preferred paramour, the parasitical, fickle, and worthless chevalier Jerningham, portrays Castries as a poor and brutal lover.[23]

Pelleport's characters of second rank include the princesse d'Henin; the duchesse de Lauzun; the prince de Guéménée; the chevalier de Coigny; the prince de Nassau; Jerningham; and the duc de Bouillon, a semi-autonomous prince, husband of the pamphlet's heroine, and maternal uncle of Guéménée.[24] All but the duc belong to the princesse's promiscuous set, and when a sexual infection strikes, following Jerningham's escapades and Castries's Holy Week whoring, few are spared.[25]

Predictably, Pelleport insinuates that his heroine is the product of an adulterous escapade. Her father, landgrave of Rothenbourg, was 'un peu entaché du goût Jésuitique' ['a little sullied by Jesuitical taste' – i.e. homosexuality],[26] so her mother enjoyed numerous adulterous intrigues with lackeys and monks. This both secured the dynasty and satisfied appetites so insatiable and diverse that:

> Nul n'a jamais violé celle-ci,
> Même à *Tarquin* elle eut dit grand merci.
>
> [No-one ever ravished her,
> She would even have said 'thank you very much' to Tarquin.][27]

Mother and daughter both bore illegitimate children.[28] The father of the princesse's child was a gardener, but thereafter the princesse enjoyed Guéménée, Chartres, and a succession of (unnamed) lovers, while her husband amused himself with minions and lackeys.[29] Eventually, abetted by Coigny, her regular pander, the princesse turned to Castries,[30] with whom she enjoyed frequent assignations at the house of 'la présidente Brisson'.[31]

When Castries entered the ministry, he feared that this arrangement might compromise him, so began visiting the princesse in her own home, aided by her attendant, dame Bours. Bours's lover, a young monk, was employed in the household and charged with secretly admitting Castries and escorting him to the princesse. Unfortunately, Bours's former lover, a coachman, observed his rival and attacked him in the street with a whip. A crowd gathered, and eventually the combatants were separated and taken before the authorities, where the monk swore he knew no reason for the assault. The princesse summoned the coachman, and threatened him with imprisonment. He then lost his head, shut himself in his room, wrote a memoir on the whole affair, and hanged himself. When servants found the memoir, the incident was hushed up by lavish payments to the coachman's widow, Bours, and the monk.[32]

In its dramatic style, sensational revelatory tone, and portrayal of impotent, debauched, and homosexual aristocratic males, the *Petits Soupers* is reminiscent of much revolutionary political pornography. It also contains hints of lesbianism: the princesse d'Hénin, who attended the princesse de Bouillon's intimate suppers, is described, on the authority of a defamatory song, as 'tribade et catin' ['lesbian and whore'].[33] But while the parallel between the defamations levelled against the German princess and the Austrian-born queen are intriguing, particularly the association with lesbian sex, it is hard to push the analogy further. Some of the individuals mentioned in the *Petits Soupers* had enjoyed the queen's favour, but none feature prominently in the anti-Marie-Antoinette literature. At base, the *Petits Soupers* is a salacious personal satire. Sordid and absurd, it is also self-consciously burlesque, especially in its closing pages, which concern the 'danse de l'ours' ['dance of the bear']. This erotocomic entertainment, designed by the monk to revive Castries's flagging libido, required Bours and the monk 'danser, *in naturalibus*, des bourrées' ['to dance *bourrées*, in the nude']. The monk ended the bear-dance, so called because of his hairy back, 'en *besognant* vigoureusement, sur le parquet, la vieille *Bours*; ou, au commandement, *court sus* à Monseigneur et lui donne *l'accolade*' ['in vigorously shagging the elderly Bours on the floorboards, or, on command, charging over to Monseigneur [Castries] and allowing him the honour'].[34] These, despite their absurdity, are the pamphlet's most sexually explicit passages. It is hard to believe that such puerile fantasy harmed either the reputations of their purported protagonists or the regime. Nor does the existence of this one relatively obscure pamphlet among the London *libellistes*' output suggest that the *ancien régime* drowned in a tidal wave of political smut.

This conclusion does not, however, dispose of the gossipy sexual slander in Morande's *Gazetier cuirassé*, which, according to Darnton, sets out to link the sexual depravity of the aristocracy to systematic corruption and incompetence in the French state. Retrospectively, Morande stated that it was intended as a critique of the abuses and morals of the court, but this comment is deeply ambiguous.[35] Was his scurrility intended or read as salacious gossip, designed to sell books? Or was it social commentary or even proto-revolutionary subversion of court and aristocracy? It is open to all three readings, although the last is problematic given that in 1771 no-one could foresee the revolution. However, readers of this and other *libelles* were probably strongly influenced by the deeply ingrained Judaeo-Christian tradition of conceiving sexual corruption as an ephemeral cause, consequence, or symbol of misrule, rather than proof that the whole system of government is illegitimate, especially as the *Gazetier* explicitly linked sexual corruption to government policy. News that a sexual infection is tearing like wildfire through the *filles* of the Opéra and society's upper echelons can be juxtaposed against allegations that Madame du Barry is protecting the brothels of Paris.[36] The message is clear: corruption and misrule are rife because a 'common prostitute'[37] occupies the royal bed and is in league with ministers who have side-lined the king and permit him only 'de coucher avec sa maitresse, de caresser ses chiens, et de signer des contrats de mariage' ['to sleep with his mistress, pet his dogs, and sign marriage contracts'].[38]

Morande's attempt to connect female influence with political corruption and misrule is typical of the *libellistes'* texts. The same trope can be found in the work of Fauques, d'Eon, Linguet, and Vergy, and prefigures the portrayal of the queen in the anti-Marie-Antoinette *libelles*. This is particularly noteworthy because Fauques's work predates the publication of Rousseau's ideas on the role of women, first expounded in *Julie, ou La Nouvelle Héloise* (1761) and *Emile* (1762), which recent historians tend to associate with the development of a more exclusively masculinist ideal of the state. As the only political biography among the *libelles* treated in this chapter, Fauques's treatment of Pompadour's seizure, use, and abuse of political power is thus particularly revealing.

Like the heroine of an eighteenth-century sentimental novel, Fauques's Pompadour consciously shapes her own destiny. Remarkably, her rise is presented without reference to factional politics and courtiers' jockeying for position. When she is checked, it is due to the intervention of the existing royal mistress, Madame de Mailly. The only outside help she receives is from a cousin who pleads her case with Louis XV.[39] However, Pompadour also transgresses against the emotional values of the sentimental genre, and to that extent is depicted as worthy of scorn. Fauques indicts her for abandoning her duty to an adoring husband to embrace a mercenary adultery with a man she does not love.[40] She also condemns her lack of tenderness towards her only child, whose untimely death Pompadour allegedly regretted only because having posterity helped to justify her cupidity.[41] Inured to the sufferings of the people, Pompadour only ever displayed compassion if it was expected of her.[42] As she was immune to true passion or love, her dominant personality traits were pride, greed, and vanity.[43] In effect, Pompadour was attacked for violating the new romantic ideal of woman's natural domesticity and family role, and turning her back on bourgeois virtues in pursuit of political power. Paradoxically, Fauques also displays more traditional prejudices, suggesting that Pompadour's lowly bourgeois status – which she exaggerates – was inappropriate for a royal mistress.[44] Indeed, Fauques dwells on Pompadour's origins as fruit of an adulterous relationship and speculations concerning her biological father's identity, especially the probability that he was Charles Lenormand de Tourneheim, the tax-farmer who paid for her education and helped arrange her marriage to his nephew, d'Estoilles. In Fauques's morality tale, Pompadour is conceived in sin and transgresses against both nature and the social order. Chaos is the inevitable result.

The ideal royal mistress, according to Fauques, was the aristocratic Madame de Mailly. She was beneficent to others, steered clear of politics, never asked anything on her own behalf, and thus died in debt.[45] She is the standard against which Pompadour is judged and condemned. Where Mailly was self-effacing and exercised restraint, Pompadour's rapacity knows no bounds.[46] She is deeply corrupt and sells state offices to the highest bidder.[47] Unlike previous mistresses, she also directs domestic and foreign policy, causing changes without rhyme or reason, the disgrace of ministers, and the sacking of France's most able generals.[48] The result is disorder and misrule, especially as Pompadour is unsuited to rule by background and governs by female ruses rather than 'male' and 'courageous' prudence.[49] Among numerous anecdotes supporting her allegations, Fauques reveals that the disastrous dismissal of the victorious maréchal d'Estrées resulted from Pompadour's grudge against his wife,[50] and that Maurepas was dismissed for remarking that he always knew that Pompadour would give the king 'fleurs blanches' ['white flowers'] – slang for venereal disease – after she presented Louis with a bunch of hyacinths.[51] Pompadour also overturns good order by establishing an absurd ceremonial,[52] but above all she is charged with reckless spending and despotic abuses of political power for petty or spiteful ends. She uses *lettres de cachet* to neutralise rivals, her husband, and an officer who composed a quatrain against her; and she 'tyrannically' despoils neighbouring landowners to extend her palace gardens.[53]

Yet Pompadour's policies are counter-productive. Her use of spies and banning of political discussion only feed false rumours.[54] Her refusal to adjudicate the religious dispute between the Jansenists and their enemies, for fear of jeopardising the voluntary contributions paid by the clergy in lieu of taxes, risks plunging the country into religious violence.[55] Moreover, Pompadour has dismissed or alienated France's traditional ruling families: persons of 'rank' and 'merit' are prevented from holding high office, or are unwilling to do so. State employment has thus fallen into the hands of toadies willing to sacrifice king and kingdom to Pompadour's caprices.[56]

Thus Fauques's biography of Pompadour introduces several recurrent tropes of later *libelle* literature concerning female power, including several that would be deployed against Marie-Antoinette. It is deeply hostile to female participation in politics and offers a fundamentally gendered view of public life and women's unfitness to participate in it. Success at court, particularly female success, is linked explicitly to an ability to dissemble, conspire, and deceive.[57] Pompadour is also directly associated with excessive taxation, the bleeding of state coffers, and misuse of royal prerogatives and *lettres de cachet*. Yet while she attacks the links between Church and state, sex and politics, Fauques targets an historically specific ministerial despotism, rather than condemning the monarchic system, *per se*.

While focusing on Pompadour, canto I of Vergy's *Guerchiade* (the only section to survive) also offers a scathing indictment of female political influence in general. Although male politicians, notably Praslin, d'Argental, and Choiseul, plot d'Eon's demise, Vergy emphasises that it is 'la belle marquise/ Qui pille cet etat de son dernier ecu' ['the beautiful marquise/Who pillages that kingdom of its last écu'] who has subverted their loyalty and imbued them with a topsy-turvy morality which denies any distinction between good and evil.[58] Hence Praslin explains to d'Argental that:

'J'aurois pû comme un autre acquitter le devoir
De mon poste élevé si l'on m'eût laissé faire,

Mais Pompadour prenant le soin de tout prévoir
Je n'avois qu'à signer, obëir et me taire.
De la confusion où l'état se trouvoit
Sous le gouvernement d'un ministre femelle
Le peuple injustement, amy, nous accusoit . . .'

['Like any other man, I would have been able to perform the duties
Of my elevated post had I been left alone to do so,
But Pompadour taking on the task of overseeing everything
I had only to sign, obey, and keep my silence.
The people, my friend, unjustly accuse us
Of the confusion in which the state finds itself
Under the government of a female minister . . .']⁵⁹

Similarly, Linguet's *Lettre á Vergennes*, in calling for membership of the Académie française to be determined by the 'suffrages de la nation', launches a full frontal assault on female influence. But unlike the earlier *libelles* of Fauques, Vergy, and Morande, which deplored the influence of a single royal mistress in government, Linguet's *libelle* detects a more pervasive and generalised female influence tending to systemic corruption. He claims that women 'peuvent faire, ou défaire, sans un danger bien instant, des *Ministres*, des *Généraux*, de *grands* ou *petits référendaires*, &c.' ['can, without any real risk to themselves, make or unmake ministers, generals, candidates great or small, etc.'] but adds that they are generally only

> des tirans en sous-ordre, ayant ordinairement un oracle caché, qui leur dicte ceux [*sic*] qu'elles prononcent un public, elles sont exposées à servir la haine et la rivalité, quand elles croyent n'obéir qu'à la tendresse. [sub-tyrants, having usually some hidden oracle which tells them what to say in public, they are likely to serve hatred and rivalry when that believe they serve only the dictates of tenderness.]

Thus, far from being autonomous agents like Fauques's Pompadour, women are viewed by Linguet as political puppets who act on behalf of concealed interests and bring despotism and prejudice to bear on political decisions that ought to be determined by reason and merit.⁶⁰ Thus, while Fauques confirms that discourses hostile to female influence in politics pre-date Rousseau and have multiple roots, Linguet's text suggests that by the late 1770s female corruption was coming to be perceived as a problem that spread well beyond the court and was harming many aspects of public life. Such a development does much to explain the perceived misogyny of the revolutionaries after 1789.

If the *libellistes* contributed to a powerful gender discourse which denied women a legitimate place in *ancien régime* political life, did they tend equally to delegitimise the *ancien régime* system of government? Certainly Darnton would argue that this was the case. According to his analysis, *libelles* like the *Gazetier cuirassé* were proto-revolutionary in intent and fundamentally undermined the monarchy. There is, however, a teleological flaw in this part of this argument, since, from the perspective or 1758, 1771, or 1783, the revolution of 1789 was unforeseen and, in form at least, unimaginable. The content of the *libelles* needs to be understood not from the standpoint of the revolution, but from that of the political context in which they were written, and which they hoped to shape. This approach yields a very different view of the *libelles'* purpose and significance. It suggests that prerevolutionary *libellistes'* aims and targets were limited to the removal of ministerial enemies, whom they invariably accused of despotism; to changes in policy direction; and to the reform of abuses, rather than the destruction of the monarchy, to which most professed loyalty.

Fauques's portrait of Louis XV offers a classic example of how criticism could be severe yet stop well short of questioning monarchic institutions. Her depiction of the king's character is certainly unflattering, but maintains a traditional respect for the monarch by blaming tyrannical and disastrous policies on Pompadour. Louis is weak, indolent, lascivious, inconstant, and ruled by pleasure. He is also miserly and mean-spirited. He refuses to reward his previous mistresses as befits a king and detests his grasping bastard children. He is generous to Pompadour only through feebleness,[61] but he is also her victim, duped by her flattery.[62] Surrounded by her cronies, he finds it almost impossible to get a clear picture of the state of his realm. Even when he encounters rioters protesting at high grain prices, she is able to persuade him that food is plentiful and cheap, and that the protestors are cynical opportunists, rather than starving unfortunates.[63] However, should the 'people's cries' be heard, it will be Pompadour's undoing.[64] Indeed, Fauques exalts that popular clamours and the 'vengeance d'un peuple, qui fait souvent la loi au pouvoir le plus despotique' ['vengeance of a people, who often dictate the law to the most despotic power'] have already brought down two of Pompadour's most zealous agents, the marquis de Paulmy and Antoine de Rouillé, and she laments their failure to punish the hand behind their despotic acts.[65] This came perilously close to asserting a right to rebel, but only with the immediate and limited aim of removing an unpopular favourite and her agents. There is nothing revolutionary about this: Fauques is advocating a traditional form of protest as a last-ditch attempt to communicate with an essentially benevolent and paternalistic monarchy when other means have failed.

The radicalism of d'Eon's *Lettres, mémoires et négociations* is similarly more apparent than real. It is above all a work of faction. While for d'Eon's contemporaries the spectacle of a diplomat publishing his public and private correspondence was a scandalous betrayal of royal trust, his actual revelations were cautious and, for many readers, disappointing. The *Monthly Review* commented that 'were they as interesting and important as they are minute and singular, they might prove a useful acquisition to the public in general, and an instructive lesson to all foreign ministers in particular'. Still, the reviewer believed d'Eon's work to be 'the most remarkable . . . of all [published] ministerial negotiations'. He concluded that d'Eon's book would amuse those who held 'the great' in disdain, by its exposure of ministers. Otherwise it was of interest only to those acquainted with its protagonists.[66]

The reviewer's comments on d'Eon's parochialism were not unjustified. D'Eon's targets are limited to personal enemies, especially Praslin and Guerchy, whom he accuses of despotism for refusing to reimburse his expenses and employing 'le verd et le sec' [literally 'the green and the dry', but metaphorically 'leaving no stone unturned'] to seize his person and papers.[67] Curiously, apart from this veiled allusion to poisoned wine, d'Eon is silent about the alleged attempt to murder him. However, he attributes plenty of 'despotic' ploys to his enemies. Guerchy is accused of surrounding d'Eon with spies, sending Vergy against him, and employing Goudar and Vergy to libel him.[68] D'Eon also asserts that Praslin and Guerchy fabricated his letter of recall, and accuses Guerchy and his entourage of abusing diplomatic privileges to flood London with contraband goods.[69] Alongside serious allegations are more trivial ones. D'Eon insists that Guerchy could barely read or write and accuses him of trying to isolate him from friends, family, and the diplomatic corps.[70] Against such courtier's intrigues, d'Eon juxtaposes his own 'masculine education' among rocks and mountains, insisting that he has no fear of death or telling the truth, since he is a soldier and lacks wife, children, or fortune.[71] Thus he feminises his enemies and the courtly arena with which he associates them, while stressing the manly and martial virtues which lie behind his own claims for advancement in the royal service.

Although d'Eon asserts that finances and factional rivalry lie behind his squabble with Praslin and Guerchy, he presents their behaviour as a part of a project to control French subjects residing in London.[72] Their ruses are destined to fail, however, because Guerchy is wrong to believe he could 'faire impunément, dans un pays libre, toutes les petites manoeuvres qui s'exécutent si souvent avec succès ailleurs, où tout plie sous le poids du despotisme des Satrapes' ['perform with impunity, in a free country, all the little manoeuvres which so often succeed elsewhere, where everything bends under the weight of the despotism of Satraps'].[73] D'Eon falls short here of suggesting that France is fundamentally despotic, but he implies that 'Satraps' are almost omnipresent and out of control. His juxtaposition of Britain as a 'free country' against France is deeply suggestive. Nevertheless, he stresses his loyalty to Louis XV, styling him as the best of kings and protector of innocence, and conflating his own personal enemies with those of the king.[74] D'Eon's critique of ministerial despotism is thus, like that of Fauques, couched in the language of loyalty.[75]

Linguet's *Lettre à Vergennes* also deploys the language of loyalty, although it blends the rhetoric of the loyal subject with that of the patriotic citizen. Stressing his love of 'patrie', he argues that both his own sufferings and France's woes stem from the same causes, and hence promises that 'en détestent la tyrannie ministérielle qui la subjugue et l'avilit, je n'en célébrerai pas moins ses vertus, sa noblesse, sa générousité' ['in detesting the tyranny that subjugates and demeans her, I will not celebrate her virtues, her nobility, her generosity any the less'].[76] He blames France's lack of military and diplomatic success on 'ce *Divan* corrompu, qui maîtrise le Trône et le rend inaccessible aux pleurs de ses sujets; . . . ce cahos de Bureaux, où l'argent seul est en honneur et la lâcheté seule favorisée' ['the corrupt *Divan*[77] which subjugates the Throne and makes it inaccessible to the tears of its subjects; . . . the chaos in government bureaux, where only money is honoured and baseness alone is viewed favourably'].[78] Linguet also hones in on specific ministerial targets. Vergennes is stigmatised for ordering Panckoucke to dismiss him from the *Journal de politique et de littérature*. Linguet asserts that this was a crime of *lèse majesté*, since Panckoucke's paper possessed a royal privilege. Such actions, he insists, would be anathema even in the Ottoman Empire, while in Britain they would be impossible because of laws ensuring that 'le nom de ministre n'est pas titre à impunité' ['ministerial rank is not title to impunity'].[79] However, Linguet considers disregard for laws natural under a triumvirate composed of Maurepas, who, recalled to office aged eighty, combines the 'frivolité de l'enfance avec la nullité de la décrêpitude' ['frivolity of childhood with the nullity of decrepitude']; Miromésnil, who was hand-picked by Maurepas on account of his feebleness; and Vergennes, who, after thirty years serving as a diplomat in Sweden and Turkey, is more a 'ministre étranger' ['foreign ambassador'] than a 'Ministre des Affaires Etrangères' ['minister of foreign affairs'].[80] Thus Linguet, like Fauques and d'Eon, identifies a clearly defined 'ministerial despotism' as his target, although he also depicts corruption as more endemic and intractable in French political culture than earlier *libelles* had implied.

With other challengers eliminated, the only credible remaining candidate among blackmail *libelles* for consideration as a 'proto-revolutionary text' is Darnton's classic *libelle*, Morande's *Gazetier cuirassé*, which he depicts as the prototype for the *libelle* genre, a nihilistic and systematic attack on an entire vice-ridden system.[81] At first glance this seems reasonable. Fictitious imprints attached to each of the three sections into which the text is organised flaunt the pamphlet's illegality, celebrate British power and freedom, and implicitly condemn the French by contrast.[82] The first section, *Le Gazetier cuirassé, ou anecdotes scandaleuses de la cour de France*, claims, like several later works attributed to Morande, to be 'Imprimé à cent lieües de la Bastille à l'enseigne de la liberté' ['printed one hundred leagues from the Bastille at the sign of liberty']; the second, *Mélanges confus sur des matières forts clairs* [*Confused Miscellanea about some Very Clear Matters*], was 'Imprimé sous le SOLEIL' ['printed under the Sun'], and the third, *Le Philosophe cynique*, was printed 'dans une isle qui fait trembler la Terre Ferme' ['in an island which makes terra firma tremble'].[83]

However, Darnton's view of Morande's work as a scathing indictment of the whole French regime fails to situate it adequately in the political framework of the Maupeou crisis, and over-states the nihilism and system of its approach.[84] For example, Morande's portrayal of the army lacks bite,

9 Frontispiece engraving from Charles Théveneau de Morande, *Le Gazetier cuirassé* (London, 1771) (this print is explained above, p. viii)

amounting to just three comments on military incompetence and three more on the sale of army offices.[85] It represents little more than a demand to abandon venality in assigning commands. Equally, although acerbic in its criticism of individuals, the *Gazetier cuirassé* operates within the traditional frameworks of Jansenist and *parlementaire* opposition, accusing the current ministry of 'ministerial despotism', rather than attacking the principles of monarchy and the social order. Moreover, the economy and religious policy of Choiseul's ministry are repeatedly praised.[86] Thus the *Gazetier* aims to link corruption to the current ministry and mistress and their allies. Suggestions that France has become despotic are aimed squarely at them. Morande is a reformer opposed to abuses rather than to monarchy or state *per se*. When he uses the word 'revolution', he refers to the overthrow of the ministry.[87] Nevertheless, like Fauques, he implies that universal opposition to the ministry legitimises rebellion, and he cites the historical precedent of the Fronde rebellions against Mazarin, whom he equates with Maupeou.[88]

Thus, the *Gazetier cuirassé* is primarily an ephemeral product of the Maupeou crisis. Its main targets are Madame du Barry and her ministerial allies, Maupeou, d'Aiguillon, and Terray. Indeed, Terray, Maupeou, and du Barry are represented metaphorically on the work's frontispiece, which depicts a man with cannons strapped to his armour repelling their thunder, lightning, and *lettres de cachet* with the blast of his weapons (see plate 9). Such priorities might indicate that Morande wrote on behalf of either the *parlementaire* opposition or Choiseul, who was supplanted in December 1770 in a ministerial coup orchestrated by Maupeou. However, the *Gazetier* is a deeply ambiguous document and does not lend itself to so clear a reading. Among the people it defames were a handful of influential *parlementaires* and Choiseulists, including Praslin, who, Morande asserted, was rumoured to have bitten himself and contracted rabies while gnawing his own nails.[89] Another member of the clan, the chevalier de Choiseul, is exposed as a bad debtor and womaniser,[90] and the prominent Choiseulist bishop of Orléans, Jarente, whose lechery was notorious, is denounced for improper relations with a dancer at the Opéra.[91] The princes of the blood, who, with the exception of the comte de La Marche, sided with the *parlements* in 1771, are also mistreated.[92] Nevertheless, the pamphlet's overall sympathy is evident.[93]

The *Gazetier cuirassé* begins with an extensive section of *nouvelles politiques* that frames Morande's opposition to Maupeou, repeatedly reiterating the tyrannical nature of his ministry,[94] which stands accused of despotism because it has abolished the *parlements* and banished those *parlementaires* who protested.[95] It is also, with considerable rhetorical licence, accused of widespread kidnappings and secret executions; use of *lettres de cachet* on an unprecedented scale; and preparing a machine capable of hanging 100 men simultaneously.[96] Nevertheless, the evil is associated specifically with the existing ministry and mistress: Choiseul's administration had proved that reform was possible. Morande therefore sees a strong tendency towards despotism within the French monarchy, but it is not inherently despotic. As his later journalism indicates, Morande believed that the monarchy could reform itself. His repeated but non-specific demands for liberty must be understood within these contexts. One passage portrays Britain as a country purged of *ancien régime* abuses, censorship, and arbitrary arrests, in which all citizens are equal and can criticise powerful individuals without fear of unjust retribution. The same passage equates French use of the Bastille with exile to the wastes of Siberia and strangulation in the Ottoman Empire.[97]

France is thus presented with a choice between English-style liberty and oriental despotism. Nevertheless, Morande's primary demand is for the restoration of the *parlements* as an intermediary body and safeguard against despotism. This position is, crudely speaking, that of Montesquieu in *L'Esprit des lois* [*The Spirit of the Laws*], and hence Morande examines England only in relation to France, and in order to provide a blueprint for reform.

As far as can be judged from the sample of texts examined here, there seems to have been an increasingly strident tendency by the 1770s to suggest that despotic practices were endemic problems, and not just the consequence of a single wicked minister or mistress. Morande's *Gazetier cuirassé* (1771) and Linguet's *Lettre à Vergennes* (1777), while continuing to hint at the possibility of improvement, imply that France's problems are much more systemic than Fauques's first edition of the *Histoire de Pompadour* (1758 and 1759) and d'Eon's *Lettres, mémoires et négociations* (1764) had suggested. It is tempting to link this development to the Maupeou crisis, but although it was consummated by the events of 1771–74, the shift appears to have begun several years earlier.

The nature and timing of the shift is best shown by examining the updated, two-volume English edition of Fauques's biography of Pompadour, published by Hooper in 1766, two years after Pompadour's death. This new edition was apparently aimed primarily at the British market, for it addresses several British preoccupations and flatters British national prejudice and martial pride, as well as ridiculing the 'Vatican's thunders' and 'Popish superstition'.[98] Nevertheless, it also seeks to undermine the Franco-Austrian alliance by attacking the British policy that drove the Habsburgs into the arms of the Bourbons, claiming that the controversial Peace of Paris harmed France more than Britain, and stating that the French had betrayed Austria by failing to crush Prussia in the Seven Years' War.[99] However, the most striking addition to Fauques's original text is a twenty-three page tirade against the French police, censorship, and use of spies. It denounces the Bourbon regime as systematically despotic, and accuses Pompadour of establishing an unprecedented tyranny.[100] It is no coincidence that Fauques reconceptualised her view of the French regime between 1758 and 1766. These years saw some important political developments, including French military defeat and the first rumblings of the Brittany affair, but above all the expulsion of the Jesuits from France, which began the uncoupling of political and religious discussion, and the d'Eon and Wilkes affairs, which catapulted discourses about liberty and despotism to centre-stage in the British press and public debate.[101] As the next chapter elaborates, Fauques's subtle but fundamental shift from attacking individual 'ministerial despots' to the denunciation of France's 'despotic system' is characteristic of the last twenty years before the prerevolutionary crisis.

Thus Darnton's depiction of the *libelles'* content and proto-revolutionary intent is erroneous. The London *libelles* were largely devoid of political pornography, spoke the language of loyalty, and contained little to desacralise the monarchy *per se*. Nevertheless, it seems probable that they had a subversive impact in the long term, by making important contributions to discourses which shaped French political culture in the late 1780s and early 1790s. The *libelles*' significance lies in the power of these discourses and the nuanced and sometimes paradoxical ways in which they were interpreted and transformed in the crucible of day-to-day politics. The analysis presented here suggests that, since most *libelles* attacked the corrupting effects of individual ministers and royal mistresses, their messages were ephemeral and probably, in the short run, deflected criticism away from the monarchy. However, Thomas Kaiser is probably correct to argue that on balance, in the longer term, it was almost certainly harmful for the monarchy to be depicted from this perspective once criticisms of royal diplomatic, religious, and fiscal policies gathered pace.[102] Ironically, the trope of royal weakness and female influence was more problematic for Louis XVI than for Louis XV, because he failed to take a mistress, and thus attacks focused on the person of Marie-Antoinette, who unlike a mistress was not easily removable and, to make matters worse, was a symbol of the despised Austrian alliance. However, such attacks took significant shape only from 1789, when the queen attempted to take a more direct role in politics and was first targeted by printed *libelles*. Likewise, the *libellistes*' repeated suggestion that their ministerial opponents were self-serving enemies of the public good, and stigmatisation of their allies as 'factions', became deeply problematic from 1789. Such modes of thinking were fundamental to revolutionary political culture and help to explain both the failure of the king, ministers, and revolutionary politicians to shape a functioning party system, and the wide incidence of allegations of faction and conspiracy.

On the eve of the revolution there also appears to have been an intensification of discourses linking female political influence to corruption and political decline. Under Louis XVI, the *libellistes* seem to have perceived that the malign effects of female influence were becoming more entrenched and generalised and that the number of women portrayed wielding nefarious power proliferated. Simultaneously, there is an increasing tendency to depict the royal court and courtiers as sources of corruption, unbridled greed, deception, and vice. Whereas the *libelles* from the reign of Louis XV imply that the removal of a few ministers and a particularly pernicious mistress would suffice to cut out the cancer of corruption and regenerate the French body politic, texts produced under Louis XVI – especially the *libelles* against Marie-Antoinette – suggest that the court itself is the source of corruption. While *libelles* aimed at Louis XV's mistresses display aristocratic disdain for their lowly origins and the crapulousness with which they infected the court, later *libelles* are impregnated with distaste for the imagined immorality and lifestyles of the entire court aristocracy. The court is also the locus of all conspiracies, both those to make and unmake mistresses and ministers, and more sinister plots to eliminate enemies by abusing *lettres de cachet* or administering fatal bowls of 'Versailles soup'.[103] From early 1789, *libelles* available to the public increasingly associate these conspiracies with the queen's party and begin to evoke the phantom Austrian committee that was to haunt the revolutionary psyche. However, among all the myths and discourses that were invented, perpetuated, reflected, or disseminated in the *libellistes'* works and contributed to the genesis of revolutionary political culture, the most important were those concerning despotism and freedom. As the next chapter reveals, the *libellistes* shaped these discourses more by their experiences than by their writings.

Notes

1 *Gulliver's Travels*, part I, ch. 4.
2 Marianne-Agnès Pillemont de Fauques, *L'Histoire de Madame la marquise de Pompadour* (London [Amsterdam?]: S. Hooper, 1759), pp. 103–4.
3 Ibid., p. 104.
4 Ibid., pp. 142–4.
5 Ibid., pp. 14–15, 144–5.
6 Ibid., pp. 50–1.
7 Ibid., pp. 56, 79–94.
8 Ibid., pp. 147–9.
9 See ibid., pp. 128–9.
10 See, for example, *Gazetier cuirassé*, part I, 31–2, 112–13. This work is complex to reference because it comprises three separate parts, each with separate title and pagination. The first section is titled *Le Gazetier cuirassé, ou anecdotes scandaleuses de la cour de France*, the second part is called *Mélanges confus sur des matières forts clairs*, and the third section *Le Philosophe cynique*. Sometimes these sections are found as stand-alone pamphlets in library collections, although it is not clear whether they were actually published as separate instalments. In notes, the sections are referenced as parts I, II, and III respectively. Page references are to the original 1771 edition.
11 *Gazetier cuirassé*, part I, 68–9; part II, 45–68.
12 Ibid., part I, 83, 84–5, 94–5, 116–17.
13 Ibid., part I, 30–1, 126; part II, 1, 27–8.
14 The definition of pornography is adapted from Hunt, 'Pornography and revolution', p. 305. See also Goulemot, *Forbidden Texts*, esp. p. 115.
15 *Gazetier cuirassé*, part III, 43–4. French use of 'chat', usually in the feminine 'chatte', to mean female genitalia is analogous to colloquial English use of 'pussy'. Although he uses it in the masculine here, Morande undoubtedly intended the pun.
16 Ibid., part I, 89–90.
17 Mairobert (attrib.), *Anecdotes*, p. 326. Mairobert (attrib.), *Lettres originales de Madame la comtesse Dubarry* (London: n. p., 1779), p. 178, informs readers that Morande's text described du Barry 'cuckolding' Louis XV with d'Aiguillon and her black servant Zamore. See also *CSP*, II, 314; Mairobert (attrib.), *Espion anglois*, II, 314–15. Dutens, *Mémoires*, II, 40, reports that Beaumarchais assured him that Mairobert's *Anecdotes* were very different from Morande's biography of du Barry.

18 Mairobert (attrib.), *Anecdotes*, p. 64.

19 On popular songs and street talk as reported by Mairobert see Darnton, *Forbidden Best-Sellers*, pp. 163–5. It is unclear how reliable or representative Mairobert is as a source for such material.

20 CPA 542 fos 37–42, Moustier [but probably ghost-written by Morande], 'Moyens simples . . . pour prévenir . . . attentats semblable à celui de Boissière', quote at fo. 38.

21 Anne-Gédeon de La Fite de Pelleport, *Les Petits Soupers et nuits de l'hôtel de Bouillon* (Bouillon [London: Boissière], 1783), p. 71.

22 Ibid., p. 87.

23 Ibid., pp. 76–7.

24 For his main characters see ibid., p. 8.

25 Ibid., p. 90.

26 Ibid., pp. 16, 19.

27 Ibid., p. 18. Tarquin was the legendary ravisher of Lucretia.

28 Ibid., p. 21.

29 Ibid., pp. 24–33.

30 Ibid., p. 47.

31 Ibid., pp. 50–1.

32 Ibid., pp. 52–68. Pelleport dates the coachman's death to 31 December 1778.

33 Ibid., p. 41.

34 Ibid., p. 84. The *bourrée* was a peasant folk-dance.

35 Morande, *Réplique à Brissot*, p. 20.

36 Morande, *Gazetier cuirassé*, part I, 51; part III, 1–2.

37 For Morande's allusions to du Barry's sexual past see ibid., part I, 57–8, 73, 80, 89–90.

38 Ibid., part I, 50.

39 Fauques, *Histoire de Pompadour*, 1759 edition, pp. 12, 24–5.

40 Ibid., pp. 136–7, 148.

41 Ibid., pp. 30–1, 73–5.

42 Ibid., p. 40.

43 Ibid., pp. 136–7.

44 Ibid., pp. 4–5, claims that Pompadour's nominal father, François Poisson, was a butcher who fled France after commiting a rape, and that Pompadour was conceived in his absence. In fact, Poisson was a solid bourgeois who worked for the Pâris brothers (one of whom, Pâris de Marmontel, as Fauques notes, may have been Pompadour's biological father) supplying arms to the French military. His flight in 1726, five years after Pompadour's birth, followed a financial scandal rather than a sexual crime. However, it is probable that Lenormand or Pâris de Marmontel was Pompadour's biological father. For more details see Christine Pevitt Algrant, *Madame de Pompadour: Mistress of France* (London: Harper Collins, 2002); Evelyne Lever, *Madame de Pompadour* (Paris: Perrin, 2000).

45 Fauques, *Histoire de Pompadour*, 1759 edition, p. 17.

46 Ibid., pp. 34, 36.

47 Ibid., p. 37.

48 Ibid., pp. 147, 152.

49 Ibid., p. 110. See also pp. 151–2.

50 Ibid., pp. 94–6.

51 Ibid., p. 52. This appears to be a distorted version of actual events: Maurepas was reputedly the author of an anonymous verse making the same point.
52 See, for example, ibid., pp. 58, 60, 64–9.
53 Ibid., pp. 23, 28–9, 39, 54–5.
54 Ibid., pp. 154–5.
55 Ibid., pp. 105–11, 148–9.
56 Ibid., pp. 153–4.
57 See esp. ibid., pp. 39–41.
58 See esp. CPA 474 fos 288–91, 'La Guerchiade, poème heroïcomique, extraits du 1er chant', lines 80–91, quote at lines 85–6.
59 Ibid., lines 153–9.
60 Linguet, *Lettre à Vergennes*, p. 23.
61 Fauques, *Histoire de Pompadour*, 1759 edition, pp. 34–5, 94.
62 Ibid., p. 41.
63 Ibid., pp. 150–1.
64 Ibid., p. 147.
65 Ibid., p. 101.
66 *Monthly Review*, June 1764, pp. 432–3.
67 D'Eon, *Lettres, mémoires et négociations*, pp. xxxi, 133.
68 Ibid., pp. xxiii, xl, xliii, 128–9.
69 Ibid., pp. xxxi, xxxv–xxxvii, 223–4. These allegations were expanded in a broadsheet entitled *The Extraordinary Intelligencer*, dated 23 June 1764, produced by d'Eon or his partisans, which also spoke of kidnap plans. For the text see *Public Ledger*, 26 June 1764; ULBC, file 58 between pp. 11 and 12. This file also contains cuttings concerning the smuggling allegation.
70 D'Eon, *Lettres, mémoires et négociations*, pp. xxvi, xxvii, xliii.
71 Ibid., pp. iii, xlv.
72 Ibid., pp. xxiv, 125–7, 148. See also below, chapter seven.
73 Ibid., pp. xxxix–xl.
74 Ibid., pp. xlix–l.
75 On this point see also Conlin, 'Wilkes, d'Eon and liberty'.
76 Linguet, *Lettre à Vergennes*, p. 42.
77 Originally a Persian term signifying the court, the ruler's council of state, or the chamber in which it met. Here Linguet apparently uses it to refer to royal ministers. To contemporaries the word smacked of oriental despotism and the decaying power of the Ottoman court.
78 Linguet, *Lettre à Vergennes*, p. 43.
79 Ibid., pp. 31–2, 44.
80 Ibid., pp. 45–6.
81 Darnton, 'High enlightenment'.
82 The three parts may originally have been published separately, but are usually found bound together.
83 In notes, these three sections, which are separately paginated, are referenced as parts I, II, and III respectively. See above, n. 10.
84 This analysis of the *Gazetier cuirassé* expands on Burrows, 'Literary low-life', pp. 78–80.
85 *Gazetier cuirassé*, part I, 37–8, 59–60, 66, 151–2; part II, 3–5.
86 Ibid., part I, 27–8, 30–1.
87 Ibid., part I, 22.

88 Ibid., part I, 14–15.

89 Ibid., part I, 45.

90 Ibid., part II, 23, 42.

91 Ibid., part I, 26–7.

92 Ibid., part I, 70–1, 95; part II, 32.

93 Agnani, 'Libelles et diplomatie', pp. 77, 120, supports a Choiseulist reading of the *Gazetier cuirassé*.

94 *Gazetier cuirassé*, part I, 13–72.

95 Ibid., part I, 14–23 and *passim*; part II, 2.

96 See for example, ibid., part I, 14, 17, 18–23, 48, 127; part II, 8, 37–8.

97 Ibid., part I, pp. v–vi.

98 Marianne-Agnès Pillemont de Fauques, *The Life of the Marchioness de Pompadour*, 4th edition, 2 vols (London: S. Hooper, 1766), II, 141, 200–1.

99 Fauques, *Life of Pompadour*, 1766 edition, I, 112–20; II, 128–9, 150–1.

100 Ibid., II, 1–23.

101 On Wilkes and d'Eon see chapter three above and esp. chapter seven below.

102 Kaiser, 'Pompadour and the theaters of power', p. 1042.

103 The image is from Jeanne de La Motte, *Memoirs*, p. 254, but allegations of poisonings are ubiquitous, occuring in the work of d'Eon, Fauques, the anonymous *Guerlichon femelle*, various texts associated with the comte and comtesse de La Motte, the *Essais historiques*, and elsewhere.

7

Discourses of despotism and freedom

The previous two chapters revealed that the *libellistes'* works bristled with suggestions that France had fallen victim to the despotism of ministers and mistresses, and that between 1760 and the prerevolutionary crisis they increasingly portrayed 'ministerial despotism' as an endemic problem within the Bourbon state. The current chapter examines two further types of work associated with this discourse – texts about French attempts to suppress *libelles* and other commentaries on Bourbon despotism – and demonstrates that accounts of the police pursuit of *libellistes* and other exiles supplied a significant empirical underpinning to denunciations of Gallic tyranny in both France and Britain. These texts ranged across a variety of genres and were far from marginal works. They included many of the best-selling *chroniques scandaleuses* of the French literary underground, books and pamphlets, underground newsletters, and British newspapers, and hence played a vital role in shaping political attitudes on both sides of the English Channel.

This exploration both rehabilitates and radically revises Robert Darnton's work on Grub Street and underground literature. According to Darnton, *libellistes* were responsible for perpetuating the 'myth' that France was a 'degenerate despotism'. However, on the whole, Darnton's work has emphasised the 'degeneracy' rather than 'despotism' of the Bourbon regime. It paints a captivating and titillating tableau of sexual corruption, inbreeding, and voluptuousness among the French elite. Previous chapters of this book have suggested that this view of the *libellistes* is problematic. It overlooks the likely roles of *libelles* in *ancien régime* political life, including their ability to buttress incoming governments; ignores the clear hiatus between scandalous pamphlets attacking Madame du Barry and those which attacked Marie-Antoinette; and has, together with early twentieth-century works by Fleischmann and d'Almeras, led other historians to infer, wrongly, that anti-Marie-Antoinette texts circulated widely before 1789.[1] Nevertheless, the current study argues that the *libellistes* played a major role in defining the Bourbon monarchy as a 'despotism' in the eyes of the French elite, both through their works, and, more importantly, in the way in which French attempts to suppress their activities were reported. These reports were sufficiently substantial to suggest that there was a concrete reality behind the 'myth' of French 'despotism', and they thus informed revolutionary mythology and paranoia. Tales of the *libellistes'* adventures and French secret police activities also had an impact in Britain. They helped to define Britons' views of France and the French government and, by means of contrast, their views of themselves. In this way they contributed to the emergence of a British national identity predicated, in large part, on the liberties supposedly enjoyed by Britons, but denied to the subjects of continental despotisms. The London *libellistes* are thus implicated in key cultural developments on both sides of the English Channel. In France, they promoted the conviction that the institutions, workings, and ideologies of government were despotic and required radical reform. In Britain, they buttressed nationalist discourses that celebrated the libertarian aspects of the British constitution.

Assessing the *libellistes'* significance therefore requires an understanding of how stories of their activities and adventures entered the public domain. While, in Britain, the *libellistes* and French police activities were freely discussed in newspapers and other publications, the French public could learn of such things prior to the revolution only via clandestine publications. To be sure, horror stories concerning the fate of dissidents pre-date campaigns against the London *libellistes*. One legendary victim, a journalist-blackmailer called Dubourg, was kidnapped by French police in Frankfurt in 1745 and carried to Mont Saint-Michel, where he was confined in the notorious iron cage, unable to sit or fully stand, until he died a year later.[2] However, the pursuit of the London *libellistes* in the decades before the revolution was better publicised than earlier incidents, and occurred at the very time when a strident critique of despotism was emerging in France's increasingly robust public sphere.

There appears to have been a clear developmental pattern to French denunciations of attempts at kidnap, attempted murder, and shady pay-offs, which stretch back at least as far as the comte de H***'s *Histoire de Mr. Bertin, marquis de Fratteaux* (1753). This work was primarily an *exposé* of the persecution of Fratteaux by his family, who wanted him arrested under a *lettre de cachet* and had nothing direct to say about the French government. It presented the kidnapping of Fratteaux on Good Friday 1752 as the work of the corrupt bailiff Blaisdell, a collaborator of Fratteaux named Vergnès, an unnamed Italian, and the defrocked French monk Dagès Desouchard. The conspirators were financed by Fratteaux's father, who, wishing to confer Fratteaux's birthright on a younger brother, tried to poison Fratteaux and falsely accused him of attempted parricide. Fratteaux's manuscript *libelle*, which he sent to 120 leading courtiers, was presented as a means of striking back at his father, by relating his purportedly habitual slanders against the royal family, ministers, and Pompadour. Fratteaux's kidnapping was thus presented as essentially a family affair, although his *libelle* compromised the monarchy. Although Dagès Desouchard was probably already a police agent and Fratteaux was eventually deposed 'par une enlevement injuste et contre le droit des gens dans une des plus affreux prisons de France' ['in one of the most terrible prisons in France by an unjust kidnapping and in contravention of the law of nations'], criticism of the French government and its laws remained implicit and muted.[3] The Fratteaux case's subsequent notoriety stemmed instead from the length of his detention: he died, still in the Bastille, on 9 March 1779.[4]

A decade after Fratteaux's kidnap, coverage of the d'Eon–Guerchy affair, perhaps the most publicised incident involving the *libellistes*, was much more problematic for the French government, exciting intense speculation in British newspapers and French underground publications. The British decision to allow d'Eon to be tried for libel poured oil on the fire, and ensured that the case was a *cause célèbre* even before Vergy's sensational confession to involvement in Guerchy's alleged plot to kill or kidnap d'Eon. D'Eon's allegations reached to the heart of the government, since he implicated both Pompadour and Praslin, and they acquired an aura of legitimacy when the bill of indictment against Guerchy was accepted by a jury. Moreover, d'Eon suggested that the French foreign ministry's ambitions extended as far as sinister plans to identify Frenchmen living in London, enquire into their business, and order home those whose reasons they considered unsatisfactory, on pain of confiscation of their property. D'Eon denounced this as 'une tentative que formoit l'esclavage pour placer sur les frontières de la France, les barrières que la sagesse de la Russie venoit d'arracher des siennes' ['an attempt dreamed up by slavery to establish at the frontiers of France, barriers that the wisdom of Russia has just seen fit to remove from theirs'].[5] This comparison was not made lightly: Russia was still considered a barbarian state, so the analogy was scathing.

These events made d'Eon a celebrity and hero of the British opposition, who drew obvious comparisons between his case and the position of Wilkes, who faced persecution for his writings in the *North Briton* no. 45 and had been arrested under a 'general warrant' – an order of dubious legality issued by the secretaries of state to authorise the arrest of unnamed persons. In 1764 Wilkes was in exile: the previous December he had fled to France to escape prosecution, having been released under a writ of *habeas corpus*. Hence, in the summer of 1764, when the London press was buzzing with reports that d'Eon was about to be snatched by French agents, a correspondent of the *St James Chronicle* stated, 'Ever since *Wilkes* and *Liberty* left this Kingdom, we have been alarmed for the Chevalier d'Eon – we are now told that this champion of liberty is to be carried to France.'[6] Other newspaper reports alleged that a skiff moored at London Bridge was waiting to spirit d'Eon away to an ocean-going ship at Gravesend. Several cited the precedent of Fratteaux or reported other supposed attempts to abduct or punish French refugees.[7] Others told of a gang of hired British rogues who, somewhat improbably, lay in wait in broad daylight for d'Eon and his companions by one of the main gates of the Spring Gardens pleasure resort.[8] It was even said that these thugs were employed by the British government, which, it was rumoured, wished to exchange d'Eon for Wilkes.[9] Such allegations should not be taken at face value: there is no hard evidence that French kidnappers were abroad in London. Nevertheless, d'Eon and his adherents had good reason to fear such an attempt, and the publicity helped the British opposition to recruit a bodyguard for him and mobilise protective mobs.[10] This mobilisation was accompanied by newspaper denunciations of alleged ministerial complicity in French plans; assertions that infringements of the liberty of one person violated the liberties of all citizens and sovereigns; and appeals to national pride. A weak, defeated, or enslaved power might acquiesce in French demands or turn a blind eye to their agents' violating the laws, but Britain had recently defeated France.[11]

Nor did the story quickly disappear. Over the next few years, the press used d'Eon's case for various purposes, including attacks on both British and French governments. In 1767, one newspaper argued that Wilkes and d'Eon would have made worthy citizens of ancient Rome. Their struggles had re-established public liberty in England by overthrowing the illegitimate powers of the secretaries of state, and establishing that general warrants – described as a 'type of *lettres de cachet*' – were tyrannical and illegal.[12] Hence the *London Evening Post* of 21–3 May 1765 [*sic*] carried the following acrimonious 'Interrogatories':

> Who made the peace? . . .
> Who issued general warrants?
> Who evaded the *Habeas Corpus*?
> Who declared Tryals by Jury to be a bad sort of Tryal?
> Who most strongly attacked the Liberty of the Press?
> Who thinks any legal course, in a just cause, ought to be stopped by a *noli prosequi*?[13]
> Did any man ever design to murder d'Eon?
> Does any man dare to sell No. XLV of the *North Briton*? . . .
> Who would not go to Tyburn, if some Great men were to be hanged?[14]

The story of Guerchy's indictment for poisoning resurfaced in the London press in 1767, following the ambassador's recall and death; in 1769, when d'Eon defended British ministers against allegations that they had taken bribes during the 1762 peace talks; in January 1774, following attempts to kidnap Morande; and the following October on the death of Vergy.[15] As late as 1777, when Beaumarchais finally purchased d'Eon's papers, the *Morning Chronicle* crowed, 'Notwithstanding the cabals of M. Le Duc de Praslin, who supported M. le compte [*sic*] de Guerchy, no-one is ignorant that the Chevalier has now carried his point with France.'[16] In addition, rumours that d'Eon had been kidnapped circulated whenever he slipped away from London.[17]

While Fratteaux's abduction could be dismissed as an *affaire de famille* and the conspiracy against d'Eon seen as the work of a powerful faction,[18] later attempts to silence the *libellistes* were presented in a way which directly implicated the French government and, sometimes, even the monarch. Tales of attempts to silence Morande rightly linked Bellanger's kidnap mission in January 1774 to ministry, king, and favourite, and continued to circulate for many years. The first printed account of the incident, apparently supplied by Morande, appeared in the *Morning Post* on 11 January 1774,[19] and was picked up by French underground publications within weeks.[20] Details of Morande's pay-off, negotiated the following April, emerged in August 1775.[21] The negotiation and kidnap plot also feature in Imbert's *Chronique scandaleuse* (1783)[22] and several anonymous best-sellers of the Mairobert corpus, including the *Anecdotes sur Madame la comtesse du Barry*, *L'Espion anglois*, and *Lettres originales de Madame la comtesse Dubarry*.[23] Morande's success in the negotiation is also flaunted in a letter appended to later editions of his *Gazetier cuirassé*, which relates how the miasma from the burning embers of his suppressed *libelle*, the *Mémoires secrets d'une femme publique*, wafted across the English Channel to Versailles, where Louis XV inhaled the fumes, provoking the illness which killed him in May 1774. The fanciful slaying of Louis XV by the *libelliste* Morande was a powerful metaphor: the fatal stench of corruption could not be extinguished.

Works recounting Morande's adventures enjoyed wide currency. If Robert Darnton's table of best-sellers is representative, the titles mentioned above accounted for over 6 per cent of France's massive trade in illegal books between 1769 and 1789.[24] Such literature, under the *ancien régime*, was required reading for even the most sober follower of politics.[25] Moreover, the story resurfaced in the *Diable dans un bénitier* and several revolutionary works, including Manuel's influential *Police dévoilée*, which claimed 'presque toute l'Europe sait que les officiers de la connétablie furent envoyés . . . pour l'enlever à Londres, et qu'ayant manqué leur coup, le gouvernement entra en négociation avec lui' ['almost all Europe knows that some officers of the constabulary were sent . . . to seize him [Morande] from London; and that having failed in their attempt, the government began negotiating with him'].[26] The story reappears as late as 1806 in Louis Dutens's *Mémoires d'un voyageur qui se repose*.[27]

In the same year as that in which the French secret police attempted to kidnap Morande, a remarkable anonymous work described and attacked a key aspect of French despotism. The *Rémarques historiques et anecdotes sur le château de la Bastille* was, as Hans-Jürgen Lüsebrink and Rolf Reichardt have noted, the first text on the Bastille to present the sufferings of prisoners there as something more than 'the extreme misfortunes of individual wretches' and 'made them seem typical and authentic by describing imprisonment at the Bastille in seemingly objective terms, systematically and with exact figures (including a ground plan), and presenting individual cases only in an appendix'.[28] Lüsebrink and Reichardt assert that the publication of this pamphlet marks a key turning-point in the literature on the Bastille, which thereafter became 'increasingly fundamental and radical on the subject of changing the system'.[29] This pamphlet is of interest here for three reasons. First, although it is sometimes attributed to Brossais du Perray, there is substantial evidence suggesting that Morande was the true author. His correspondence with d'Eon in 1773 reveals that he was researching a work on the Bastille, and from 1777 editions of his *Gazetier cuirassé* also contained the *Rémarques*.[30]

The *Rémarques historiques* were also significant because they prefigured more celebrated critiques of despotism, which used the penal system, judicial sovereignty of the king, and arbitrary arrest as means to indict the whole system of government. The most notable of these pamphlets were Mirabeau's *Des Lettres de cachet et des prisons d'état* (1782) and Linguet's *Mémoires sur la Bastille* (1783). A similar trend also seems to be evident in the trial briefs studied by Sarah Maza,[31] including those produced by Tort and Linguet's best-selling *Lettre à Vergennes*, which, as we have seen, sought to transform personal grievances concerning his expulsion from the bar and editorship of the *Journal de politique et de littérature* into a patriotic indictment of ministerial tyranny. Moreover, Linguet did not merely condemn the system: he also prophesied its overthrow, helping to generate self-fulfilling expectations of change. His *Lettre à Vergennes* predicts an imminent, cataclysmic struggle between the liberty espoused by the peoples of Northern Europe and forces opposed to it; his famous frontispiece to the *Mémoires sur la Bastille* prophetically associates Louis XVI with the ruins of the Bastille (see plate 10).[32] Linguet's pamphlet deployed the new language of sentimentalism to great effect, emphasising the tears, sighs, and melancholy of victims of absolutism to engage the sympathies of the reader. In the process, the *Mémoires sur la Bastille* confirmed the fortress's symbolic status as an emblem of despotism, without which its overthrow could never have acquired its potent symbolism.

Finally, the emergence of a more strident, systematic discourse on the Bastille and despotism in the *Rémarques historiques* coincides with the development of a more radical and systematic portrayal of despotism by *libellistes* other than Morande and Linguet. This is particularly evident in Pelleport's sensational *exposé* of Receveur's abortive mission, the *Diable dans un bénitier*, published in the summer of 1783, several months after Linguet's *Mémoires sur la Bastille*. Pelleport opens by stigmatising the French government system as a despotism with limitless ambition:

Le despotisme que le plus léger obstacle irrite et désespere, ne peut soutenir l'idée de l'existence de la liberté. . . Les droits sacrés de la nature, ceux des nations ne sont à ses yeux que des conventions ridicules: il emploie pour les détruire, la force, la ruse, l'argent et la calomnie; le poison et l'assassinat ne sont pas des ressources qu'il dédaigne, et s'il ne peut réussir dans ses desseins sinistres, au moins jouit-il de l'inquiétude qu'il cherche à semer dans le coeur des fugitifs. [Despotism, which is angered and driven to despair by the smallest obstacle, cannot abide the idea of the existence of liberty. . . in its eyes, the sacred rights of nature and of nations are only ridiculous conventions: in order to destroy them it employs force, trickery, money and calumny; it does not disdain poison and murder, and if it cannot succeed in its sinister designs, at least it enjoys sowing fear in the hearts of fugitives.][33]

10 Frontispiece engraving from Linguet's *Mémoires sur la Bastille* (London, 1783) (this print is explained above, p. viii)

The early pages of the *Diable*, which set the context for Receveur's mission, depict corruption as rife in the French administration and insinuate that the Bourbon government threatens the liberties of Frenchmen and foreigners alike. Pelleport observed that, in asserting that refugees' descendants remained French subjects down to the third generation, the Bourbons claimed authority over large sections of the Dutch and English populations.[34] He went on to connect the vice and despotism infecting the French political system. As in the *Petits Soupers*, Pelleport describes how Castries systematically embezzled naval funds, for which he was not even required to account,[35] and explained that his predecessor, Sartine, had betrayed a succession of French naval missions lest Castries reap the credit of his planning.[36] He also depicts the police of Paris as 'une pépiniere d'espions, de délateurs, et de bourreaux' ['a nursery for spies, informers, and executioners'] whose commanders happily resort to poison and strangulation, and systematically corrupt every generation to ensure a fresh supply of recruits and victims.[37] These recruits included the corrupt police spy d'Anouillh, who embezzled funds supplied for bribing British politicians;[38] the hapless Henri de La Motte, recruited for his fatal mission by the irresistible lure of riches;[39] and the loathsome Receveur, who boasted of sending thousands of men to rot in state prisons, or be broken on the wheel, branded, or flogged.[40] They also included Morande, who, he alleged, had brazenly sold out both sides in the American revolutionary war.[41]

Having offered extensive 'revelations' concerning French espionage and police networks, Pelleport offers a detailed, satirical account of Receveur's mission. It records how Receveur and the ambassador asked Morande to prepare a memorandum on *libellistes*, in which he advised ignoring them.[42] It also reveals that Morande won the support of several British MPs for a police plan for London. This allows Pelleport to imagine a scene in which Lenoir attacks the lunacy of existing English laws, which prevent a minister's ordering arbitrary arrests or interfering in sentencing, and provide no secrecy to veil the vengeance and passions of the great.[43] However, the most memorable scene in the *Diable dans un bénitier*, the inspiration for its title and a satirical print, parodies Morande's transformation from poacher to gamekeeper, and his readmission into the bosom of the monarchy. It imagines the ambassador symbolically baptising a Mephistophelian Morande to purge him of his past sins against the monarchy (see plate 8).[44] Such blasphemy is punished immediately, as Receveur's mission descends into farce. No trace of the *libelliste* is found; Boissière refuses to deal with Receveur, who is then exposed; and all the while Morande employs petty ruses to inculpate others through malice, revenge, or a desire to deflect suspicion from himself.[45] Deflated and defeated, Receveur sails for France hurling a final curse at England:

> j'ai souffert chez vous les tourments reunis dont j'ai accablé tant de misérables, mais n'importe, je suis assez vengé cruels Anglois, je vous laisse Morandes [*sic*].

[I have suffered among you the combined torments which I have myself inflicted on so many wretches, but it does not matter. I am sufficiently avenged, cruel Englishmen, [because] I leave you Morande.][46]

While parts of the *Diable* are comical, its central message was clear. The French ministry was composed of unaccountable, entrenched, petty despots, whose squabbles and feuds were as dangerous to state and subject as their greed and ruthlessness. They were served by brutal, corrupt, and amoral agents, who were as incompetent as they were cynical. Reviews of the *Diable* and details of Receveur's mission appear in several *chroniques scandaleuses* and underground *nouvelles à la main* including Imbert's *Chronique scandaleuse*, the *Correspondance secrète, politique et littéraire*, and the *Mémoires secrets*.[47] Reviewers did not miss Pelleport's main points, nor leave implicit the critique of France's system of government. For example, the *Mémoires secrets* explains how the afore-quoted opening passage of the *Diable*

> commence par établir le système de nôtre gouvernement, fâché de voir sur la terre quelque pays libre, parvenu à corrompre, à asservir tous les autres, sauf celui d'Angleterre. Ce n'est pas qu'il n'ait fait plusieurs fois de nouveaux essais pour cela . . . mais ils n'ont jamis réussi. [begins by establishing the means by which our government, annoyed to see any free country on the face of the earth, came to corrupt and enslave every other [country] except England. Not that it has not several times made new attempts against the latter . . . but they have never succeeded.][48]

This message is reinforced by similar contrasts of British freedom and French despotism in other pamphlets of the 1780s. For instance, Lanjuinais's *Supplément à l'Espion anglois*, whose criticisms of British policy make it impossible to dismiss as wartime anti-French propaganda, offers a condemnation of continental censorship, based on the language of the 'rights of man'. It questions the very legitimacy of the French government, arguing that:

> tout gouvernement, qui prive les particuliers de la liberté de communiquer leurs pensées, est un gouvernement ignorant, injuste, criminel, barbare, malintentionné, qui sent lui-même son illegitimité et sa tyrannie. Le premier droit de l'homme est celui *d'être*; le second c'est celui de *penser*. O! braves Anglois . . . vous êtes vraiment le seul peuple libre de l'Europe, puisque vous avez seul la liberté de la presse. [Any government which deprives individuals of the freedom to communicate their ideas, is an ignorant, unjust, criminal, barbarous, ill-intentioned government which senses its own illegitimacy and tyranny. The first right of man is to exist; the second is to think. Oh, brave Britons . . . you are truly the only free people in Europe, because you alone enjoy freedom of the press.][49]

In early 1789, this increasingly strident discourse was given fresh impetus by the publication of the comtesse de La Motte's memoirs, replete with their tales of courtly machinations to imprison the innocent, suppress her work, and kidnap or murder her husband.[50] The testimony of this tarnished and inconsistent witness was soon reinforced by discoveries in the Bastille, whose archives were ransacked by opportunist publishers. Compilations like Louis Charpentier's rapidly assembled *Bastille dévoilée*, which sold in cheap instalments in 1789 and early 1790, offered readers historical anecdotes of the prison, lists of prisoners, and dossiers on recent inmates.

Although, inevitably, the *Bastille dévoilée* had to recognise the criminality of many prisoners, it asserts that even the most guilty could complain of unjust imprisonment, because they were held 'sans l'aveu ou plutôt contre toutes les réclamations de la loi' ['without acknowledgement or rather in spite of all legal objections'].[51] Moreover, dossiers concerning several *libellistes* cast the authorities as the villains or allege that officials were complicit in the proliferation of *libelles*. For example, Charpentier claims maliciously that Lenoir always knew that Jacquet was behind the fabrication of the *libelles* he 'suppressed', but played along to impress Maurepas with his zeal. Besides, Jacquet made himself useful by tracing and seizing one of Lenoir's indiscreet former mistresses. He was therefore allowed to suppress his own *libelles* and conduct a roaring trade in illegal books, paying Lenoir a cut. However, when Jacquet was exposed, following a quarrel with an associate, Lenoir abandoned him in prison until 1789, for fear of being compromised.[52] Charpentier's dossier on Pelleport describes him as author of the *Diable dans un bénitier* but glosses over his *libelles* against the queen. Instead, it depicts the sufferings of Pelleport's family; Madame Pelleport's refusal to prostitute herself to save them; and Pelleport's noble attempts to save the deputy governor of the Bastille.[53] Brissot contributed his own dossier for the work,[54] which insists that Lenoir informed him that the real motive for his arrest was 'la haine du ministre [Vergennes] contre l'Angleterre, et la crainte qu'il a de voir répandre ici les principes de la liberté' ['the minister's hatred of England and his fear of seeing the principles of liberty spread here'].[55] In consequence, Brissot claimed to be a revolutionary *avant la lettre*, a martyr to the cause, gaoled for his zeal in propounding 'les principes qui triomphent aujourd'hui' ['the principles that triumph today'], and financially ruined by despotic orders that, on release, he remain in France.[56]

Charpentier's compilation condemned the cost of policing the *libellistes*, asserting that for Receveur's mission to Amsterdam in 1781 to suppress *libelles*, 'on a dépensé plus d'argent, soudoyé plus d'espions que si l'on eût voulu traiter de l'affaire d'état plus importante' ['more money was spent, more spies bribed, than when conducting the most important state affairs'].[57] This linkage of despotism with unbridled spending struck many contemporaries forcefully. Indeed, one usually moderate manuscript newsletter observed that the revelations in the *Bastille dévoilée*, when combined with the financial disclosures in the *Livre rouge*, were sufficient to justify the revolution.[58]

The most systematic *exposé* of French police despotism was Manuel's *Police dévoilée*, published in the summer of 1791, in the aftermath of the king's flight to Varennes. Manuel's revelations were even more explosive than Charpentier's, because they offered a more comprehensive overview of *ancien régime* police, backed with documentary evidence gleaned from police archives. In chapters devoted to the policing of *libelles* and the London exile community, Manuel revealed the precise sums lavished on suppressing pamphlets and employing and entertaining former *libellistes* and pamphleteers like Morande and Goudar in the 1780s. He also reproduced police dossiers on forty-one French exiles. Other chapters added to the scandal, by describing the policing of clerical morals, brothels, and gambling, adding flesh to Pelleport's assertions that the police actually encouraged these activities, to ensure a continuous flow of potential spies, victims, and protection payments. In this tale of corruption, villainy, incompetence, and waste on a massive scale, Receveur's mission served as a paradigmatic example of the Bourbon government's profligacy.[59]

Manuel proclaimed that a free people needed a free press and only a small police force. The greatest hero in the *Police dévoilée* was his political ally Brissot; the main villains, Lenoir, Vergennes, Morande, and lesser police spies. Manuel maintained that the worst crime committed by absolute monarchs was to deprive their subjects of liberty of expression. He therefore eulogised Brissot for being the first to clamour for freedom of publication.[60] Conversely, Manuel argued that absolutist censorship necessitated the underground book trade which had provided his livelihood before the revolution.[61] He was, however, careful to distinguish between public writers such as Brissot, who were persecuted for their virtues without the king's knowledge, and unworthy *libellistes* such as Pelleport, who loved only women and pleasure.[62] Nevertheless, even Pelleport had grounds to complain against Vergennes, Lenoir, and Morande.[63]

The demonisation of Morande in the *Police dévoilée* was no coincidence, for it appeared while he was campaigning against the Jacobin left in his *Argus patriote*. Manuel therefore wished to debunk Morande's claims to be a 'sentinel of the people'. He asserted instead that Morande was a thief even before he became a libertine, and that he had first visited a brothel to steal a gold ingot.[64] Having established Morande's moral character, Manuel repeated every tale of his depravity that he could muster, including allegations of his betrayal of Henri de La Motte and involvement with British pederasts, whom he later blackmailed. He also reminded his readers that Morande had been a deserter, gaolbird, sharpster, and pimp in Paris; allegedly fled to London to escape the noose; and served Lord North as well as Beaumarchais and Vergennes.[65]

Brissot and Manuel had good reason to fear Morande. In the summer of 1791, he unleashed a defamatory newspaper and pamphlet war against Brissot, hoping to prevent his election to the Legislative Assembly as one of twenty-four deputies for Paris. Morande accused Brissot of complicity in writing and producing *libelles*; swindling his partner Desforges; and being a British agent.[66] Brissot replied in kind, giving details of Morande's own career of defamation and crime, and republishing Morande's dossier from the *Police dévoilée*.⁶⁷ Brissot's allies believed that Morande's campaign took its toll. On 29 August 1791, the Girondin deputy François-Xavier Lanthénas wrote to a colleague that 'Morande répand en plus d'abondance encore ses poisons. Le corps électoral d'ici se montre mal.' ['Morande spreads his poisons in still greater abundance. The electoral assembly here shows itself ill-disposed.']⁶⁸ Lanthénas's concerns were well founded. The majority of the 964 member Paris electoral assembly were moderates, and only eight radical candidates were elected. Brissot, who enjoyed the highest public profile of any radical, was their chief hope, but lost in successive ballots for the first eleven deputies.⁶⁹ He finally scraped together the necessary majority in for-tuitous circumstances at the twelfth attempt, becoming the fourth radical to be elected.⁷⁰ The Jacobins of Chartres, Brissot's home town, wrote to the electoral assembly attributing his tribulations to calumny, which appears to have been justified. Indeed, Brissot's election provoked a bitter schism between moderate and radical members of the electoral assembly, who there-after discussed candidates in separate clubs.

Well-informed contemporaries were aware that Morande's assault on Brissot was the latest of a string of defamatory press campaigns, most of them conducted at the French court's behest.⁷¹ Morande conducted a vendetta against Mirabeau in the *Courier de l'Europe*, culminating in a cam-paign to discredit him during the elections of 1789;⁷² he repeatedly defamed Linguet and spat publicly in his face;⁷³ and in April 1789, Calonne bought the *Courier de l'Europe* partly to silence his attacks.⁷⁴ Morande had also, as already noted, betrayed Pelleport and Chamorand; had shadowed and exposed the La Mottes and Cagliostro; and probably wrote the defamatory *Vie privée du duc de Chartres*. By the 1780s, Morande was an object of curiosity for French travellers, including Madame Roland, whose account of him combines horrified awe with hints of sexual *frisson*.⁷⁵ In some revolu-tionary and prerevolutionary tracts, notably the *Police dévoilée* and the *Diable dans un bénitier*, he even stands alongside Lenoir, as a symbol of the worst excesses of despotism and the depravity of its agents.⁷⁶

To educated Frenchmen, Morande's victims must have seemed the tip of an iceberg, for underground publications had familiarised a generation of readers with their government's arbitrary acts. Ironically, during the latter part of Louis XV's reign and under Louis XVI, the French government was liberalising. However, when exposed to the scrutiny of an increasingly assertive public, its remaining despotic acts – whether ordered by the king's council or competing ministries – appeared intolerable. The rhetorical accu-sations of despotism that arose in the 1760s and reached a crescendo fol-lowing Maupeou's purging of the *parlements* was reinforced in succeeding years by growing public awareness of clandestine police actions that sug-gested that the problem was systemic and that an unfettered court was intrin-sically corrupt and tyrannical. These beliefs, in turn, were aggravated by denunciations of aspects of the despotic machine, including the celebrated works of Linguet and Mirabeau in the early 1780s. The Bastille, *lettres de cachet*, repeated attempts at kidnap, and, possibly, the murder of both political dissidents and criminal reprobates abroad, were part of a despotic system that was vilified in prerevolutionary pamphlets. These allegations seemed to be borne out by discoveries in the Bastille and police archives from July 1789. Against such entrenched despotism, Brissot's innocence proved no guarantee, and even blackmailer-*libellistes* like Pelleport had genuine grievances.

Could these observations help explain the siege mentality and fear of conspiracy which affected so many members of the revolutionary elite, anxieties which post-revisionist historians have seen as intrinsic to the dynamics of the revolution?[77] Recent historical work has depicted elite fears as consequences of short-term political events during the revolution, above all the crisis of July 1789.[78] However, this approach fails to explain why confidence in the king's benevolence was so quickly eroded. It thus seems reasonable to suggest that fear of court conspiracies was already deep-rooted in the revolutionary generation because of pamphleteers' tales of ministerial ruthlessness and police actions against dissidents, as well as the life-experience of some leading revolutionary politicians. The rational anxieties to which these gave rise interacted with Austrophobia and alienation from Marie-Antoinette's aristocratic coterie, to create a fear of an 'aristo-ministerial' conspiracy.

Certainly, paranoia is already evident in the works and behaviour of the *libellistes*. D'Eon and Morande both feared assassination; Pelleport panicked into exposing Receveur; the La Mottes' works are saturated with the phobias that literally propelled the comtesse to a premature death. Knowledge of police methods was also common currency: in his wife's *Mémoires*, the comte de La Motte alleges that Benevent dismissed a proposal to kidnap him with the assistance of a corrupt bailiff as a 'stale trick'.[79] Likewise, Morande and Pelleport both resorted to d'Eon's tried-and-tested tactic of public exposure to thwart supposed kidnap attempts. Their fears were shared by prominent figures such as Brissot or Linguet. The widely publicised personal experience of such men reinforced other causes for apprehension, including historical memories of royal attacks on Paris and, more recently, Bourbon repression of Genevan democrats. Hence the revolutionary elite were predisposed to believe that court factions would attempt anything to defeat political opponents, including conspiring to storm or starve Paris. Such fears helped precipitate the Parisian rising of July 1789. Equally, it was natural for the revolutionaries to consider the constitutional arrangements which had protected dissidents in Britain – freedom of publication and popular checks on government – as antidotes to the secret manoeuvres of the court, and to place them at the heart of the revolutionary programme of 1789. Subsequent experience in the revolution – which was punctuated and driven by real and imaginary conspiracies – reinforced the fears and prejudices of revolutionary leaders. It should therefore come as no surprise that in the autumn of 1791 it was Brissot, himself a celebrated victim of arbitrary government, who emerged as the leader of a war party whose members were convinced that foreigners and Frenchmen alike would rally behind this programme.

In Britain, media treatment of attempts to silence or extradite dissident writers gave rise to rather different discourses and effects. In particular, newspaper coverage reinforced images of France as Britain's continental antithesis and thereby shaped an emergent British national consciousness.[80] Where freeborn Britons enjoyed a free press and Parliament and lacked a continental-style police, France's absolute government had a police and censorship so despotic that it aspired to exercise influence over Frenchmen in England and even to suborn British liberties. Linda Colley has argued that the military threat posed by France across the entire long eighteenth century was, together with Protestant solidarity, instrumental in shaping a British national identity. However, British press discourse suggests that the peacetime ideological and practical threat represented by French police activities also played a role, by offering concrete examples of French despotism and hostility to fundamental British laws, values, and institutions.[81] Moreover, British press discourse on French police activity seems to support Colin Kidd's criticism of Colley's view of British exceptionalism. Kidd detects a 'universal francophobia' in the press, but nonetheless contends that the English (at least) viewed themselves as part of a brotherhood of originally free Germanic peoples and believed that continental absolutism derived from historical accident. Thus English critiques of Bourbon despotism were very specific and did not extend to a blanket condemnation of the French people.[82] By separating the French people from the acts of their government and demonising only the latter, press discourse left ample scope for British rejoicing when the French regained their liberty in 1789.

However, as in France, coverage in Britain of the *libellistes* was ambivalent, especially when they fell out among themselves. This is typified in reporting of Morande's pay-off, both in 1774 and at the time of his quarrel with d'Eon in 1776. Whilst satirical prints deride Morande as an ass or a French lawyer (see plates 11 and 12), elsewhere he was presented as a hero struggling against French despotism. A letter from 'François' in the *Public Ledger* of 2 September 1776 argues: 'Monsieur de Morande, is, I find, a gentleman of abilities, respectability and honour. He actually hath made the French ministry so much his enemies, that it would be dangerous for him to set his foot on French Ground. He is not playing a double game [the implied contrast is with d'Eon], nor acting in a sinister method, unbecoming of a man.'[83] Two days later, 'The Ghost of Guerchy' even justified Morande's sale of the *Mémoires secrets d'une femme publique* as his property, 'the fruit of much observation and the result of a thorough insight into the affairs of his country', whereas d'Eon 'sold papers which never belonged to her'.[84]

Although much of this coverage was undoubtedly planted by the *libellistes*, it contributed to a more general discourse contrasting French

11 'The wicked in triumph' (1774), caricature of Morande (this print is explained above, p. ix)

'despotism' with British liberties and laying special emphasis on British press freedom and the security of the person. Even if this discourse were entirely the creation of French exiles, hiding behind the mask of anonymity, it nevertheless reflected arguments that the most informed and media-savvy foreigners felt would appeal to British national sentiment and manipulate readers in their own interests. It must therefore be seen as reflective as well as formative of attitudes. The willingness of British mobs and gentlemen to protect Morande, d'Eon, and Pelleport confirms that it tapped into genuine sentiments concerning British virtues and identity.

THE FRENCH LAWYER *in London*.

THE BODY SOUL & MIND OF THE GAZETIER CUIRASSÉ

12 'The French lawyer' (1774), caricature of Morande (this print is explained above, p. ix)

One early exile contribution to this discourse, as we have noted, was the revised edition of Fauques's *Life of Pompadour*, which was published in 1766 and never translated into French, and alleged that Pompadour and successive lieutenants of police had established a systematic despotism based on spies, arbitrary arrests, and the policing of opinion. Fauques began her discussion by observing that:

> Among the most wretched, contemptible expedients of despotism, for the maintenance of that unnatural government, the employment of spies on its subjects has ever been, especially in France, since the loss of freedom, a point of state.

> But lately, that execrable practice has risen to an intolerable height, to the total destruction of public liberty and private happiness.[85]

Fauques attributed this sinister new development to two causes. First, Pompadour used scandalous anecdotes gathered for her by the lieutenant of police's spies and embellished by her imagination, to entertain and captivate Louis XV and damage the credit of her enemies. In this way, Fauques alleged that 'many useful and valuable subjects were, without their knowing it, and without the opportunity of clearing themselves, placed in so unfavourable a light, that they lost their fortune and the state service'.[86] Secondly, providing spy reports to Pompadour about 'such persons as took liberties with her name and character' was an ideal way for the lieutenants of police to curry favour with the favourite.[87]

As a result of this complaisance, Fauques asserts, a police service instituted for the 'prevention and detection of crimes, as well as the domestic order and oeconomy of . . . Paris' had been 'perverted' into a 'seminary of such wretches as spies and informers'.[88] She goes on to denounce the 'men of birth, of rank, of authority, who do not disdain to employ them [spies]' as 'the original tempters and authors of their baseness and guilt; a guilt which is, in fact, a crime of high-treason against human society'.[89] Moreover, she mocks official attempts to justify 'this horror' as 'one of the severest satires on the French government, in alleging the necessity of employing such rascals for the support of the royal authority; as if it could not exist without intruding on the private society of its subjects, like an enemy's camp, by keeping spies in it'.[90] The lieutenant of police, who orchestrated the espionage system, is literally demonised by Fauques, who depicts him receiving his spies 'with the air of the devil examining his imps on the mischief they have achieved'.[91] The result was a society where social intercourse was poisoned, every nobleman or gentleman feared that his most innocent words might be reported out of context, and 'ministerial servility', even more than Pompadour's resentment, 'crouded the prisons and dungeons with hapless victims'.[92]

This expensive police system was maintained after Pompadour's death. Despite 'a real nobleman' [Choiseul] stepping into the 'place of prime minister . . . there are detained in the prisons of Paris, persons, who have languished in their gloomy cells for years without any fault or crime but that of having offended the minister'.[93] Fauques also laments new restrictions on the press in France, which in 1757, 'under the plausible pretext of reducing . . . the licentiousness of writers', had forbidden 'on pain of death, the composing, printing, selling, or publishing of any thing against religion, . . . royal authority, or that might tend to disturb the public order or tranquillity'.[94] The real motive, according to Fauques, was 'to stifle the eruptions of the general indignation against La Pompadour'. Thus, 'the national interest in the commerce of books was sacrificed' to the private interests of the favourite.[95]

Although Fauques accuses the ministers of overall responsibility for this system of despotism, she also castigates the complicity of the French people: 'Should I even add, that the people who can endure such a government deserve such oppression. But when they boast of it, they provoke such a pity as the poor cacique of Cuba, who was betrayed into chains, by his taking them for ornaments.'[96] Elsewhere, Fauques rams her point home by dismissing plans to build flat-bottomed boats for the invasion of Britain as an attempt to deceive the credulous. It was, she said, inconceivable that 'the French, who could do less than nothing, with a superior force by land, should do every thing with an inferior one at sea; and especially, that a gang of French slaves, all dragging their chains after them, should conquer a nation of free-born Britons'.[97] Fauques thus contributed to a discourse that saw the French as contemptible, weak slaves of their rulers, and celebrated the martial virtues of the free British people.

Explicit and implicit comparisons of this sort were common-place in the British press by the 1780s. The following five examples, drawn from a five-month period in 1786–87, illustrate this point. On 1 August 1786, the *Morning Post*, a scandal-sheet that employed exiles of several nationalities, commented:

> There is something about a generous and manly mind, to hear of the frequent imprisonments in the Bastille of noble and literary characters, upon the most trifling suspicions. Yet to France we are ever willing to fly, though every day carries with it a fresh conviction of the dangers of residing in that country. When will Englishmen learn to justly estimate their own happiness!

On 4 August 1786, after Margaret Nicholson attempted to assassinate George III, the same paper detected a practical example of differences between the two countries. It compared her treatment to that of the deluded, unfortunate Damiens, who had attacked Louis XV with a pocket-knife, and been condemned to be broken on the wheel. In contrast, George III attributed Nicholson's actions to insanity and insisted she be treated kindly. 'Had a similar outrage been committed on a GALLIC DESPOT,' the paper commented, 'the foreign prints would, ere this, have been replete with RACKS, WHEELS, MOLTEN LEAD and all the other ACCESSARIES [*sic*] of AGONY.'

This contrast between the countries was also reinforced satirically, using the metaphor of the body politic:

> The *Bastille* is the *Sovereign* remedy in France for all *complaints* affecting the *Constitution*, and the state quacks of that country have found it to be an infallible prescription for all disorders of a *secret* nature. It is also a preventative more efficacious than any hitherto discovered. It differs, however, from all other *nostrums* in this, that it requires *confinement*.[98]

The more respectable sections of the press also drew attention to the lack of liberty in France. Commenting on the Eden trade treaty between England and France, the *Morning Herald* of 3 November 1786 reported: 'We hear that the French noblemen and gentlemen in this metropolis, who have fled from the persecution of the French court, the Bastille and *lettres de cachet*, are all against Sieur Rayneval's commercial treaty.'[99] Likewise, the *Morning Chronicle* of 1 January 1787 reported from Paris, with some rhetorical exaggeration: 'A pamphlet is circulated here, attributed to the Count de L——, intituled [*sic*], "Reflections of an honest Man on the criminal Jurisprudence of France" which will assure to the author, if discovered, a certainty of being hanged.'

The persistence of this press discourse facilitated the *libellistes'* use of the British newspapers to denounce the police agents sent against them, and the Wilkesite opposition's attempts to mobilise mobs to protect d'Eon. Fearing that d'Eon would be kidnapped, the London press published numerous articles and letters celebrating Britain's liberties and the rule of law. Among them was a letter from 'Publicus' reading:

> Hear this ye who know not the value of known and salutary laws, and the miseries you thereby are protected from, therefore may all offenders against them meet with the justly incurred infamy and execration that most abandoned villain Blazdell [Blaisdell] has done, for being the vile instrument of such misery to a deserving but unhappy gentleman [i.e. Fratteaux].[100]

A letter from 'Britannicus' was more explicit about the contrast between Britain and France, and celebrated Britain's record as a refuge for the persecuted:

> They [the French] are the slaves of a despotic power; we a free people whose country is the asylum of the oppressed; to violate it is a breach of public liberty and a crime against our country: let us never, therefore, suffer a stranger who flies to us for shelter, to be a sacrifice to a misguided fury or the horrors of the Bastille.[101]

Such rhetoric was a powerful weapon in the hands of the British opposition, allowing it to portray perceived breaches of customary liberties by the British government as French-style despotic behaviour.[102]

However, British attitudes to refugees were not unproblematic. This was highlighted by media coverage surrounding the arrest, trial, and execution of Henri de La Motte and the hunt for his accomplices in 1781. A notice in the *Public Advertiser* of 20 July 1781 implies that British liberty was perhaps too extensive for the national interest:

> How very different is the police of France from that of England! When an English Nobleman or Gentleman goes over to Paris, he has half-a-Dozen Spies placed about him in a Moment, nor can he visit the Hotel of a Heinel, or an Impure [prostitute] of less Note, but it is immediately known to the Lieutenant of Police. In England, instead of placing Spies over the Actions of any Foreigners who come here, we invite and encourage them to be Spies on ourselves.

Nevertheless, while the author of this passage is alarmist about the degree of freedom given to foreign visitors to Britain, he also clearly believes the

French espionage apparatus to be absurd, suffocating, and intolerable.[103] The *Morning Chronicle* of 27 July 1781, which warns against 'vipers' nourished in Britain's breast, also raised suspicions against those foreigners who lived better and enjoyed greater liberties and privileges than in their homelands. Yet the paper's solution was not to curtail these liberties, but to wish 'that those who are entrusted with our secrets would be more cautious of whom they admit into their company'. It advised that 'reason, justice and common sense' could help thwart treasonous designs.

Five years later, an article in the *Morning Post* entitled 'Compte Cagliostro. Gentle Strictures' by 'An English Spy' also sought to place parameters on the behaviour of refugees in Britain. It opened by asserting that the welcome that the British gave to foreign exiles was non-negotiable: 'This country has ever been considered as an asylum for the persecuted . . . to which every man may fly and be protected from tyranny.' However, those foreigners who wished to earn public esteem needed to behave as citizens 'casting aside' or 'at least . . . suppressing' personal resentments. Cagliostro's behaviour in 'censuring the justice of the French monarch, or that of his ministers', and expressing his dislike of 'French Spies, Bastiles, Lettres de Cachet', constitutes, according to the 'English Spy', an 'abuse of indulgence' accorded him by the British, and 'acting in a very offensive manner'. Cagliostro was exiled because of his 'obnoxious conduct', and his complaints concerned issues that were 'not grievances created by the present sovereign . . . He found these evils, on acceding to the throne, as the Stuart race found a species of absolutism annexed to the regal authority in England'. Attacks on Louis XVI on these grounds were therefore illegitimate. Despite his great personal virtue, he could 'no more be expected to alter the constitution of his empire, than our beloved sovereign can be expected to dispense with certain forms, indifferent, perhaps, in themselves, but deriving from ancient usage'. The 'English Spy' then proceeded to argue that Englishmen would 'abhor the meanness of traducing the magistracy, jurisprudence, local customs or forms of government of any nation under heaven, much less of France', a nation which had produced so many great men of science and literature. Vulgar prejudice against the French was almost extinguished in Britain, and it was mischievous to publish anything which suggested otherwise.[104]

This extraordinary article is highly suggestive and brings together several strands of the discourses investigated in this chapter. Although antagonistic to Cagliostro and defensive of Louis XVI, Bourbon monarchy, and French institutions (as well as highly conservative in a British context), it takes it as axiomatic that Britain should serve as a haven for foreign exiles and that the French 'constitution' contained fundamentally despotic elements. This juxtaposition helps to explain both the welcome given by the British to the revolution in 1789 and the warm reception afforded to the revolutionary émigrés in the early 1790s, despite their French nationality and the large numbers of Catholic priests in their midst.[105] Both phenomena suggest that the xenophobia of British nationalism and the British populace in the 1780s, especially among the elite, can be over-stated, and that other strands of nationalist discourse need further attention. Britain was more than a free country: it was also a place of asylum and a beacon of liberty for other nations. These virtues of the British character and constitution were celebrated in a further letter to the *Morning Post*, which, despite attacking Cagliostro, remarked: 'It requires little consideration to determine on a visit to this country. It is a land of liberty; we are a generous people; the Bastille is our detestation'.[106]

Thus, between about 1758 and 1791, the *libellistes* had contributed to the shaping of important discourses on both sides of the English Channel. In France they helped to reinforce the growing conviction that, in spite of its reforming zeal, the *ancien régime* monarchy was inherently despotic and, by inference, could be regenerated only by root-and-branch reform. By peddling tales of authetic and contrived police and factional machinations, they provided concrete instances of tyrannical disregard for the law in repressing dissent and free expression, and thereby helped to create anxieties and tensions that bore fruit in revolutionary conspiracy phobia. At the same time, by testing and extending the limits of British freedom, the *libellistes* contributed to the evolution of powerful political discourses on British liberty and national identity. These developments were shaped by political events, particularly the *de jure* abolition of general warrants, which made it easier to draw cut-and-dried distinctions between England and the continent, especially France. With the demise of the English *lettres de cachet*,[107] there appeared to be a practical and conceptual difference between the two states that was exemplified by Britain's burgeoning (and increasingly secure) freedom of the press. With the triumph of Wilkes, and his return from exile, Britain's claim to be home to all victims of persecution became more clear-cut. Only in the emergency of the 1790s, when ministerial persecution of radicals created new waves of exiles and political martyrs, were Britons reminded that *habeas corpus* remained insecure and the government still had an impressive range of repressive measures at its disposal. In the interim, the contrast between Britain and France, however over-drawn by *libellistes* and other commentators, had contributed to contradictory trends in both countries. It promoted the radicalisation of anti-regime discourses in France, whereas in Britain, while at times empowering legitimate, constitutional opposition, it ultimately helped to shape the strong, confident, libertarian nationalist discourse that would prove so powerful for mobilising Britons against the revolutionary threat in the 1790s.

Notes

1 D'Almeras, *Marie-Antoinette et les pamphlets*; Fleischmann, *Marie-Antoinette libertine*; Fleischmann, *Pamphlets libertins*.

2 On Dubourg see Eugène Hatin, *Les Gazettes de Hollande et la presse clandestine aux XVIIe et XVIIIe siècles* (Paris: René Pincebourde, 1865), pp. 68–75.

3 Comte d'H***, *Histoire de Fratteaux*, quote at p. 3. The comte describes the *libelle*'s content at pp. 103–8.

4 Funck-Brentano, *Lettres de cachet*, p. 324.

5 D'Eon, *Lettres, mémoires et négociations*, p. 148.

6 ULBC, file 58 p. 43, *St James Chronicle*, 11–13 September 1764 (cutting).

7 On attempts on refugees other than d'Eon and Fratteaux, see ULBC, file 58 pp. 33, 46, cuttings from *Public Advertiser*, 24 August 1764; *Lloyd's Evening Post*, 26–8 September 1764.

8 See ULBC, file 58 pp. 11–12, 23–4, 30, 37, 38, cuttings from *Gazetteer*, 25 June 1764; *Extraordinary Intelligencer*, 23 June 1764; *Public Advertiser*, 26 June and 4 July 1764; *St James Chronicle*, 9–11 August 1764; *Lloyds Evening Post*, 31 August – 3 September and 5–7 September 1764. For doubts about the story see ULBC, file 58 p. 41, *St James Chronicle*, 6–8 September 1764 (cutting). The alleged ambush was conveniently close to the Thames.

9 ULBC, file 58 p. 38, *Lloyd's Evening Post*, 5–7 September 1764 (cutting).

10 See Kates, *Monsieur d'Eon*, p. 126, and above, chapter three.

11 ULBC, file 58 pp. 11–12, 14, cuttings from *Gazetteer*, 25 June 1764; *Extraordinary Intelligencer*, 23 June 1764; *Public Ledger*, 26 June 1764; *Public Advertiser*, 29 June 1764.

12 ULBC, file 58 p. 67, 'note extrait de la *Gazette*, 1767' (handwritten). Unusually, d'Eon fails to attribute this snippet precisely. Usually 'la Gazette' signified the official *Gazette de France*, but the denunciation of *lettres de cachet* makes this unlikely. Chief Justice Pratt declared general warrants 'unconstitutional, illegal, and absolutely void' in December 1765.

13 This alludes to government pressure to stop criminal proceedings against Guerchy.

14 Cutting in ULBC, file 58 p. 57.

15 ULBC, file 58 pp. 60–1, 62–3, 65, 66, 70, 71, 75, 76, 79, 83, 89, cuttings from *Political Register*, September 1767, pp. 292–3, October 1767, pp. 369–80; *Public Advertiser*, 4 December 1767, 27–30 October 1769; *Gazetteer*, 18 December 1767; *North Briton*, 19 August 1769; *Morning Post*, 22 January 1774; *London Evening Post*, 27–30 August 1774, 1–4 October 1774, 20–22 October 1774; *London Packet*, 17–19 October 1774.

16 *Morning Chronicle*, 6 August 1777. The paragraph was purportedly lifted from the *Nouveau Journal françois, italien et anglois*.

17 See for example ULBC, file 60 pp. 332, 336, 338, cuttings from *Gazetteer*, 13 May 1771, *London Evening Post*, 9–11 May 1771, 14–16 May 1771, *St James Chronicle*, 18–21 May 1771, *Gazette d'Utrecht* (column dated London, 21 May).

18 Even Morande, *Gazetier cuirassé*, part II, p. 16, describes Fratteaux and d'Eon's kidnappers merely as 'scélérats' ['rogues'].

19 I have not located a copy of this edition. The *Morning Chronicle*, 5 January 1774, refused the story; the *Public Advertiser*, 6 January 1774, demanded authentication before it would accept it for printing.

20 *MSB*, 5 February 1774; see also 19 February 1774. Gotteville, *Voyage d'une françoise*, also appeared in 1774.

21 *MSB*, 25 August 1775.

22 Imbert (attrib.), *Chronique scandaleuse*, I, 33.

23 See Mairobert (attrib.), *Anecdotes*, pp. 314–17, 325–8, *Espion anglois*, II, 16–17, and *Lettres originales*, pp. 178–82.

24 Figures from Darnton, *Corpus* reveal that the five most popular of these titles accounted for 1,831 out of 28,212 clandestine book sales by the STN.

25 For example, the austere political commentator Mallet du Pan ordered a copy of Mairobert's *Anecdotes* from the STN on 15 June 1776. See BPUN, MS 1178 fo. 53.

26 Manuel, *Police*, II, 251.

27 Dutens, *Mémoires*, II, 39–40.

28 Hans-Jürgen Lüsebrink and Rolf Reichardt, *The Bastille: A History of a Symbol of Despotism and Freedom* (Durham, NC: Duke University Press, 1997), pp. 16, 18.

29 Ibid., p. 19.

30 CPA 503 fos 308–10, Morande to d'Eon, undated letter, received 21 December 1773 (copy), footnote annotation of d'Eon at fo. 308. Morande's authorship of a work on the Bastille is also mentioned in the preamble to a poem he placed in the *Morning Chronicle*, 23 June 1773.

31 Maza, *Private Lives*, esp. pp. 315–16.

32 Linguet, *Lettre à Vergennes*, p. 38.

33 Pelleport, *Diable*, pp. 3–4.

34 Ibid., p. 5.

35 Ibid., pp. 10–11.

36 Ibid., p. 15.

37 Ibid., p. 13.

38 Ibid., pp. 16–19.

39 Ibid., p. 14.

40 Ibid., pp. 22–3, 83.

41 Ibid., p. 32–4.

42 Ibid., 61–72, 95, and *passim*. Morande's memoir on *libellistes* is probably CPA 542 fos 37–42, Moustier, 'Moyens simples . . . pour prévenir . . . attentats semblable à celui de Boissière', which appears to have been ghost-written by Morande.

43 Pelleport, *Diable*, pp. 109–10. CPA 541 fos 196–9, Moustier to Vergennes, 16 March 1783, confirming the existence of this police plan, is reproduced in Manuel, *Police*, I, 242–9.

44 Pelleport, *Diable*, pp. 66–7. On this print see also Agnani, 'Libelles et diplomatie', p. 66.

45 Pelleport, *Diable*, esp. pp. 95–119.

46 Ibid., p. 120.

47 Imbert (attrib.), *Chronique scandaleuse*, I, 33–5; CSP, XVI, 94–7; *MSB*, 11 and 17 October 1784.

48 *MSB*, 11 October 1784.

49 Lanjuinais (attrib.), *Supplément à l'Espion anglois*, pp. 199–200.

50 The comte made allegations concerning the kidnap attempts as early as December 1786. See *Morning Chronicle*, 29 December 1786.

51 Charpentier, *Bastille dévoilée*, 'avertissement', pp. 1–2.

52 Ibid., 3rd livraison, pp. 36–9. Charpentier's allegations appear devoid of foundation, and his explanation for Lenoir's decision to abandon Jacquet does not tally with other sources. See chapter four above.

53 Pelleport's dossier, including an account of his attempt to save the deputy governor, is at Charpentier, *Bastille dévoilée*, 3ʳᵈ livraison, pp. 66–75; the description of the *Diable* is at p. 51.

54 Ibid., 3ʳᵈ livraison, pp. 75–9.

55 Ibid., pp. 77–8.

56 Ibid., p. 78.

57 Ibid., p. 56n. This passage erroneously identifies the *libelles* in question as the *Passe-tems*, *Amours du visir Vergennes*, and *Petits Soupers*.

58 *CSCV*, II, 439.

59 For Receveur's expense claim see Manuel, *Police*, I, 250–5. For Pelleport's allegations see Pelleport, *Diable*, p. 13. On Goudar's espionage: Hauc, *Ange Goudar*, pp. 164, 172–3.

60 Manuel, *Police*, I, 23, 63.

61 Ibid., I, 23.

62 Ibid., II, 28.

63 Ibid., II, 29.

64 Ibid., I, 265.

65 Ibid., I, 265–7; II, 250–3.

66 Morande's three main pamphlets were *Réplique à Brissot*; *Réponse au dernier mot de J. -P. Brissot et à tous les petits mots de ses camarades* (Paris: Froullé, 1791); and *Lettre aux électeurs du département de Paris sur Jacques-Pierre Brissot* (Paris: Froullé, 1791). All three appeared as supplements to his *Argus patriote*.

67 Jacques-Pierre Brissot, *Réponse à tous les libellistes qui ont attaqué et attaquent sa vie passée* (Paris: de l'imprimerie du *Patriote françois*, 1791); Brissot, *Réplique à Morande*; *Patriote françois* 740 (19 August 1791).

68 Lanthénas to Bancal, Paris, 29 August 1791, in Jeanne-Marie Phlipon Roland, *Lettres de Madame Roland*, edited by Claude Perroud, 2 vols (Paris: Imprimerie nationale, 1900–02), II, 361–2.

69 On the Parisian elections see Etienne Charavay, *Assemblée electorale de Paris*, 3 vols (Paris: Quantin, 1890–1905), II, pp. I–xlii, 512–38.

70 Brissot's victory occurred just after he drafted a protest against the violation of the electoral assembly by an officer intent on arresting one of its members: ibid., II, xxix, suggests that the two events were connected.

71 Besides widespread French comment, see, for example, *The Times*, 15 February and 17 October 1788; *Morning Post*, 14 October 1788.

72 See, for example, *Courier de l'Europe*, 18 March 1789; *BCE*, documents 454, 530, 533, letters of Morande to Beaumarchais dated 12 December 1785, 10 and 20 March 1789. Hostilities between Morande and Mirabeau stemmed from Beaumarchais and Mirabeau backing rival syndicates bidding for the contract to supply water to Paris. Desgenettes, *Souvenirs*, I, 133, tells of brokering an earlier truce between Mirabeau and Morande.

73 *BCE*, document 403, Morande to Beaumarchais, 3 October 1784; *MSB*, 3 and 23 April and 30 May 1785.

74 Burrows, *French Exile Journalism*, pp. 19, 88.

75 Roland, *Works*, p. 218.

76 See for example Pelleport, *Diable*; Manuel, *Police*, I, 242–50, 265–7; II, 250–3 and *passim*; Andrea de Nerciat (attrib.), *Julie philosophe*, II, 6–11.

77 For early expositions of the post-revisionist view, see François Furet, *Interpreting the French Revolution*, transl. Elborg Foster (Cambridge: Cambridge University

Press, 1981), pp. 53–6, and Lynn Hunt, *Politics, Culture and Class in the French Revolution* (Berkeley and Los Angeles: University of California Press, 1984), pp. 38–44.

78 See, for example, Timothy Tackett, 'Conspiracy obsession in a time of revolution: French elites and the origins of the Terror, 1789–1792', *American Historical Review* 105:3 (2000). Tackett surveys correspondence and diaries of National Assembly deputies and argues that conspiratorial modes of explanation can be correlated with revolutionary events and were primarily the result of the July crisis.

79 Jeanne de La Motte, *Memoirs*, p. 179.

80 On newspapers' importance in creating 'imagined' national communities, see Benedict Anderson, *Imagined Communities: Reflections on the Origins and Spread of Nationalism*, 2nd edition (London: Verso, 1991).

81 Colley, *Britons*.

82 Colin Kidd, *British Identities before Nationalism: Ethnicity and Nationhood in the Atlantic World, 1600–1800* (Cambridge: Cambridge University Press, 1999), esp. pp. 211–16, 234–5.

83 A cutting is preserved in Add. MS 11,340 fo. 16.

84 *Public Ledger*, 4 September 1776. Cutting in Add. MS 11,340 fo. 19.

85 Fauques, *Life of Pompadour*, 1766 edition, II, 1.

86 Ibid., II, 6. Similar comments concerning espionage date back at least to Saint-Simon.

87 Ibid., II, 7.

88 Ibid., II, 12–13.

89 Ibid., II, 15.

90 Ibid., II, 13.

91 Ibid., II, 15–16.

92 Ibid., II, 16–18, quote at p. 18.

93 Ibid., II, 20–1.

94 Ibid., II, 21–2.

95 Ibid., II, 22.

96 Ibid., II, 23.

97 Ibid., II, 140–1, quote at p. 141.

98 *Morning Post*, 23 September 1786.

99 Joseph-Mathias Gérard de Rayneval was the French commissioner at the negotiations.

100 *Public Advertiser*, 4 July 1764 (cutting in ULBC, file 58 pp. 23–4).

101 Ibid., 29 June 1764 (cutting in ULBC, file 58 p. 14).

102 See Kates, *Monsieur d'Eon*, pp. 124–7; Clark, 'D'Eon and Wilkes'; Conlin, 'Wilkes, d'Eon and liberty'.

103 For other examples of this paper's concern with spies, see *Public Advertiser*, 23 and 24 July 1781. These report that twenty-nine post-chaises and thirteen coaches of foreigners fled to Dover after La Motte was sentenced, and suggest that Britain was over-reliant on self-seeking American refugee spies.

104 *Morning Post*, 29 August 1786.

105 On the reception of the émigrés, see Kirsty Carpenter, *Refugees of the French Revolution: Emigres in London, 1789–1802* (Basingstoke: Macmillan, 1999); Weiner, *French Exiles*; Dominic Aidan Bellenger, *The French Exiled Clergy in the British Isles after 1789* (Downside Abbey: Downside Press, 1986);

E. M. Wilkinson, 'French émigrés in England, 1789–1802: their reception and impact on English life' (unpublished B. Litt. thesis, University of Oxford, 1952).

106 *Morning Post*, 2 September 1786, letter signed 'An Enemy to Deception'.

107 As Jonathan Conlin has noted, the comparison was made by contemporaries: see, for example, James Burgh, *Political Disquisitions: or, an Enquiry into Public Errors, Defects and Abuses*, 3 vols (London, 1774–75), III, 252. See Conlin, 'Wilkes and d'Eon', p. 1266 n. 67.

Conclusion

The London blackmailer-*libellistes* are a seriously misunderstood and misrepresented cultural phenomenon. They bore little relation to the classic description of alienated Grub Street hacks provided by Robert Darnton's early work, and close study of their output and influence conclusively refutes any 'pornographic interpretation' of the French revolution of 1789 predicated on scurrilous attacks on the monarchy. In consequence, this study offers a very different appraisal of the role and significance of *libelles* and *libellistes* in French and British political culture from that prevailing in existing works. This chapter draws together the main outline of this interpretation and highlights some of its implications.

A *libelle* industry developed and thrived in late eighteenth-century London primarily because London had a well-developed French publishing trade, *libellistes* had little fear of legal punishment, and successive French administrations were willing to pay suppression fees. Although some policy makers questioned the wisdom of such payments, the French government often felt that ignoring the *libellistes* was not an option, both because they might traduce the monarchy and because, on several occasions, their defamations permanently ruined the credit and reputation of key state servants, particularly diplomatic staff. More rarely, courtiers and politicians tried to turn the *libellistes*' activities to their own advantage in factional intrigues.

The *libellistes* had well-developed social networks and focal points in the London exile community to provide them with contacts, support, advice, and conviviality. They were also aided and abetted, advertently and inadvertently, by their contacts in the Paris police. Indeed, many of the agents employed to deal with *libellistes* in London and elsewhere were complicit in the *libelle* industry themselves, including Goupil, Jacquet, and, in all probability, Beaumarchais and Göezman. The *libellistes* therefore enjoyed a symbiotic relationship with the police and French foreign office, and several served as spies on their fellow exiles or the British. Their status as renegades and writers provided excellent and natural cover for such activities. The *libellistes*' links to political patrons remain rather more opaque, but it seems probable that most of them were encouraged to write by powerful political factions. Several certainly had contacts or sources at court, and thus the

Darntonian assumption that the *libellistes* were independent of patronage ties appears to be misplaced.

The typical *libelliste* was not an alienated hack driven to a career in gutter pamphleteering by literary failure, as Darnton's Grub Street model would suggest. Instead, they had in many cases already embraced criminality and tried their hands at a variety of other illegal activities before resorting to blackmail. Those who do not fit this profile, such as d'Eon and Linguet, tended to have a strong sense of personal grievance against the French government. Not infrequently – as in the cases of the comtesse de La Motte, Vergy, and Linsing – they had both a history of criminality and a grudge.

The *libellistes* mostly came from the lower levels of the social elite, rather than outside it. The majority had at least a tenuous claim to nobility. Substantial minorities were either women or lapsed members of the Catholic priesthood or religious orders. As a former nun, Fauques belonged to both groups. Most had been forced to fall back on their own resources – usually because of their own profligacy or crimes – and may have been motivated by an exaggerated sense of personal importance and entitlement, a sentiment probably not lessened by the priority that the government placed on silencing them. Their politics, as far as they can be traced, seem to have been generally reformist: they opposed ministerial despotism, the abuse of absolutist power, and the undue influence of 'the court', but they were first and foremost constitutional monarchists rather than republicans or nihilists. Perhaps because they lived in symbiosis with the monarchy, those *libellistes* whose political trajectory can be traced after 1789 tended towards counter-revolution or, in Linguet's case especially, were accused of doing so.

When the French government set its mind to the task, it was remarkably successful at silencing *libellistes*. Between 1759 and 1783, if no other method was feasible, it chose to do so by means of suppression payments or other forms of concession, practices which hit their peak early in the reign of Louis XVI, during the ministry of Maurepas. This runs contrary to the accepted chronology which suggests that material and payments more or less dried up following the death of Louis XV.[1] However, following the failure of Receveur's mission in 1783, the court abandoned the practice of paying off *libellistes* who threatened to attack the royal family, a decision which resulted in the temporary disappearance of the *libelliste* threat. No new pamphlets were threatened until late December 1786, when the comte de La Motte issued his first demands. Even then, no significant publication appeared until his wife published her *Mémoires* in February 1789. Moreover, unlike many *libellistes*, the comtesse had a highly marketable story and published in highly receptive political circumstances. Her resort to blackmail was thus probably just a means of keeping her options open. This chronology adds to a growing impression given by recent work on the press, that in the two decades preceding the revolution the French monarchy was remarkably successful at controlling its own image, at least in terms of suppressing hostile printed comment.[2]

The accepted chronology for the appearance of *libelles* and emergence of key themes within them also stands in need of significant amendment. In particular, this study endorses Gruder's contention that pamphlet *libelles* against Marie-Antoinette – particularly those containing sexual slanders – did not circulate in significant numbers before 1789.[3] Indeed, it goes further, and contends that notwithstanding the diamond necklace affair, printed pamphlets aimed specifically against the queen – as opposed to a handful of obscure works containing passing allusions – may well not have circulated at all. Many of the prerevolutionary pamphlets cited by students of anti-Marie-Antoinette literature were safely locked up in the Bastille: the rest seem never to have been published. The situation is not quite so clear-cut when it comes to popular songs and poems, caricatures, and broadsheets, but Gruder's work makes clear that these, too, were very few in number before the prerevolutionary crisis of 1787–89. In consequence, overt written criticism of the queen inside France, salacious, malicious, or otherwise, seems to have been confined to the rarefied world of the court and usually to manuscript libels. It was at the court, the centre of power, that her enemies wished to undermine the queen's credit during the *ancien régime*. It was there, where individuals' effective power depended primarily on perceptions of their standing with the king, that malicious gossip undermining confidence in the strength of her marriage, her influence over her husband, or the security of her children's claims to the throne could have a genuine impact on the queen's authority and perhaps undermine the Austrian alliance. Before the revolution, then, scandalous gossip about Marie-Antoinette was primarily related to the power plays and manoeuvres of courtiers and factions, and largely confined to the courtly arena. Those involved had little interest in taking such battles to a wider public, where their mudslinging and reprisals might seriously harm the image of the monarchy, and undermine the moral standing of the political elite. Moreover, before the revolution, there seems to have been little market for works attacking the queen, presumably owing to deeply ingrained habits of respect and fear. If this were not the case, entrepreneurial writers and publishers, especially those whose blackmail demands were ignored in 1783, would surely have speculated on the genre.

However, once revolutionary crisis transformed the *peuple* from passive observers into active participants in politics, hostile political actors had an interest in traducing the queen's reputation in the eyes of the public. The weapons with which to do so came readily to hand with the publication of Madame de La Motte's *Mémoires* and the texts liberated from the dungeons of the Bastille. Thus the legend of the Austrian Messalina, created by the London *libellistes* with the unwitting complicity of the French court, sprang fully formed into the revolutionary consciousness in 1789. The power of these foundational texts of revolutionary mythology and political pornography lay in their novelty and shock value, because nothing like them – not even genuinely political pornographic *libelles* – had previously circulated in

France. However, from 1789, pornographic attacks must be seen primarily as weapons with which to beat the queen, rather than root causes of disenchantment with her, especially as many post-1789 pamphlets are so unbelievable that readers must have viewed some of them, at least, as grotesque satires or political parables.

It must also be recognised that political pornography – designed primarily to stimulate hatred rather than libidos – was used by publicists of all political persuasions to attack their adversaries during the revolution.[4] Nevertheless, the London *libellistes* had provided the queen's revolutionary enemies with a made-to-measure mythology, and the provenance of their pamphlets, combined with the unique intensity and duration of revolutionary pornographic attacks upon her, gave readers a *prima facie* reason to believe that they might contain truths the monarchy had wished to bury for ever.[5] Thus if a pornographic interpretation of the origins of the revolution of 1789 must be rejected, the same does not necessarily hold true for the republican revolution and royal trials of 1792–93, in which *libelles* against the queen and her allies probably played a genuine, if subsidiary, part.

There are strong parallels between the timing of the publication of sexual libels against Marie-Antoinette and earlier sexual-political *libelles* against Louis XV and mesdames du Barry and Pompadour. Just as *libelles* against Marie-Antoinette began to circulate only when her power was on the wane, so the main *libelles* against *la Pompadour* and *la du Barry* also post-date their death and fall from grace respectively. Just as *libelles* against Marie-Antoinette were suppressed, so, with the notable exception of Fauques's biography of Pompadour, were those against royal mistresses while they remained in favour.[6] The best-selling scandalous biographies of the old *roué* Louis XV were also published after his death. It therefore seems that the purpose of the *ancien régime*'s notorious scandalous political literature was more ambiguous than hitherto supposed. Far from serving as weapons against a sitting government, most such pamphlets actually offered histories of administrations from the recent past. Their main political roles seem to have been to denounce abuses by superseded administrations, provide an ethical standard for the new government, defame the surviving personnel of an outgoing ministry, and provide moral underpinning for the incoming regime by offering an implicit contrast with the old. *Ancien régime libelles* appear to have been part of a political game practised by insiders to the elite, not mudslingers from beyond it. They are not as radical as they first appear. If this analogy also holds good for wider forms of pre-revolutionary erotica and scandalous texts, it would appear that any antithesis between radicalised French erotica and British pornography, which recent commentators have found to be often socially and culturally conservative, is false, or at least misleading. However, such a conclusion lies beyond the scope of this study, and must be a matter for further research.[7]

Nevertheless, the texts of the *libelles* prepared by the London *libellistes* are highly revealing, and even those that were not suppressed proved subversive.

As the revolution approached they reflected as well as influenced changing perceptions of the Bourbon regime. Over time, the works of the *libellistes* increasingly portray the French 'court' as a category apart from the rest of society and present it in a hostile light. From the 1750s to the early 1770s, the *libelles* consulted for this study, which are often couched in a language of loyalty, depict the court as a centre of power that can be infected by the corruption of evil ministers or mistresses. Implicitly, the body politic might be healed by cutting out a few cancerous cells, replacing a mistress or a few ministers. However, by the late 1770s the *libellistes* present the court itself as inherently corrupt and a source of contamination. Such a diagnosis implied a need for more radical surgery, although it should be stressed that the *libellistes* still saw the court, rather than the monarchy itself, as the root problem. This appears to be a stark reflection of the growing cultural and political divide between Versailles and the rest of French society, but it also reflects an increasing public for political literature, including scandalous texts, that extended beyond traditional elites.

One constant source of corruption in the *libelles* is politically active women, who are invariably portrayed as totally ill-suited to govern. Moreover, the court arena in which they operated is increasingly feminised and denigrated. This masculinist tendency is broadly consistent with feminist scholarship explaining how and why the revolutionaries excluded women from the French public sphere and, more controversially, that the revolution was made not only without, but against, women.[8] It is nevertheless worthy of note that the portrayal of political women is remarkably consistent in *libelles* across the period and pre-dates the emergence of Rousseau's publications concerning politics and gender, as well the rise of more masculinist cultural and political institutions which Dena Goodman has detected in the late 1770s and 1780s.[9] The *libelles* thus seem to have been drawing more on traditional misogyny than on enlightenment discourses. The revolutionary exclusion of women from public life had multiple and deep cultural roots.

The *libellistes* also had a symbolic significance, conveyed in representations of their activities and adventures, which transcends the importance of what they actually wrote. Stories about attempts to silence them and control other French exiles and dissidents invariably seeped into the public domain and were widely reported, usually with the connivance of the *libellistes* themselves. In the process they damaged the image of the Bourbon regime and could on occasion be used to accuse British ministers of complicity, collusion, and illiberality. Attempts to silence *libellistes* by assassination or kidnap appeared to prove the ruthlessness of the French court, and its lack of respect for law and process. Attempts to use the British legal apparatus also had the potential to backfire, while French campaigns to change British laws were denounced as despotic interference in the internal affairs of another sovereign state. Attempts to buy off *libellistes* were used as examples of the court's profligacy and corruption, and could accredit the *libellistes*' allegations. Finally, attempts to employ sullied individuals like Morande seemed both to illustrate the court's depravity and to prove that it prefered to reward vice, rather than virtue.

Tales of the draconian methods used to prevent *libelles* entered political folklore on both sides of the English Channel. A regime that orchestrated the persecution of d'Eon, the celebrated mission to kidnap Morande, the assassination attempts against the comte de La Motte, the ruthless imprisonment of Linguet and life-long incarceration of Fratteaux, the mysterious arrests of Goupil and Jacquet, the unjust gaoling of Brissot, and Morande's state-funded persecution of numerous exiles was self-evidently despotic and out of control. These tales and others, whether true or false, helped to underpin many of the celebrated pamphlet *exposés* of 'despotic' aspects of the regime that appeared in the 1770s and 1780s. Indeed, the most notable of them, including Linguet's *Mémoires sur la Bastille*, Mirabeau's *Des Lettres de cachet et des prisons d'état*, and Morande's *Rémarques historiques sur la Bastille* promoted elite distrust of the monarchic regime, despite its attempts at reform under Louis XVI. They thus contributed to the conspiracy phobia that affected the revolutionary leadership and drove the revolution.

These sensational stories also fed into public discourses on the nature of despotism and freedom that compared Britain and France. After the resolution of the Wilkes case and the apparent abolition of English general warrants in the mid-1760s and Maupeou's tyrannical suppression of the *parlements* in 1771, it became increasingly easy to draw contrasts between Britain as a land of liberty and France as a land of despotism. The persistent attempts of French governments to repress refugee scribblers and suborn British press liberties fitted naturally into this schema, and played a major part therein. In Britain, such comparisons fuelled a strand of nationalist discourse that celebrated Britain as a torch-bearer for liberty, haven for the persecuted, and home to a generous people, and was certainly less xenophobic, before the French revolution, than Linda Colley has argued.[10]

In France the comparison fed into a discourse, promoted not least by Linguet, Mirabeau, and Brissot, which condemned French institutions for despotism and a politics based on court intrigue and called for press freedom, popular sovereignty, political transparency, and the freedom of the individual. These demands formed the nucleus of the revolutionary programme in 1789. Clearly, for the men of 1789, despotism was rather more than a rhetorical device: it was a real and lived experience. It represented a clear and present danger to them and their aspirations. The antidote to this threat was called *liberté*.

Notes

1 See, for example, the potted history of the industry in Wagner, *Eros Revived*, p. 93.

2 For an overview see Burrows, 'Cosmopolitan press'. However, Goulemot, *Forbidden Texts*, p. 15 suggests that the authorities targeted erotic literature because they could not control philosophic literature.

3 Gruder, 'Question of Marie-Antoinette'.

4 Hunt, 'Pornography and revolution', pp. 315–17.

5 On the unique intensity of attacks on Marie-Antoinette see ibid., p. 324.

6 However, defamatory songs and poems disseminated by the favourites' enemies at court probably circulated more widely than similar prerevolutionary materials against Marie-Antoinette: see Kaiser, 'Pompadour and the theaters of power'.

7 On the conservatism of eighteenth-century British erotica see Peakman, *Mighty Lewd Books*, which also surveys other recent work tending to similar conclusions. It is tempting to view the historical paradigm shift away from viewing pornography as radical or socially subversive as a rejection of the values of the 'sexual liberation' campaigns of the 1960s' generation. Such a theory remains untested and may well prove too simplistic.

8 See esp. Landes, *Women and the Public Sphere*. On the feminisation of the image of the court see Maza, *Private Lives*, esp. p. 314.

9 See esp. Goodman, *Republic of Letters*.

10 Colley, *Britons*.

Appendix: the secret *dépôt* in the Bastille

According to Manuel's *Police dévoilée*, I, 37–9, the following fifteen items (probably comprising only fourteen works) were held in the secret *dépôt* in the Bastille under Lenoir's seal until shortly before his resignation in 1785, when he ordered most copies to be destroyed. However, Lenoir's instructions called for a dozen or so copies of each to be reserved for 'customary distributions' among key individuals, and twenty more to be preserved in the Bastille, where they were apparently discovered in July 1789 when the fortress was stormed.

400 copies of *Lettre de Dangui*, described as a *libelle* against the duc de Chartres.

73 copies of *Réponse de M. de Bourboulon au Compte rendu de M. Necker.*

A complete edition of *Les Amours de Charlot et de Toinette*, a *libelle* against Marie-Antoinette. (This is the illustrated London edition of 1779 bought from Boissière.)

A whole edition bought in London contained in a trunk bearing Lord North's seal. (This contained the *Guerlichon femelle*, a *libelle* against Marie-Antoinette and the princesse de Lamballe.)

The whole edition of Linguet's *Aiguillonade* (or rather *Aiguilloniana*.)

The whole edition of the *Préface de l'histoire de Louis XVI.*

385 copies of *Ministère du comte de Maurepas.**

A complete edition of *Le Portefeuille d'un talon rouge*, a *libelle* against the court containing extensive material against Marie-Antoinette.*

The following works, all of which were printed by Jacquet, are also listed:

200 copies of *Réflexions sur les pirateries du Sr. Gombault.*

300 copies of *Administration provinciale*. (Presumably the work by Le Trosne mentioned again below.)

* *Police dévoilée*, I, 257, also appears to link both *Ministère du comte de Maurepas* and *Le Portefeuille d'un talon rouge* to Jacquet and his collaborators. Shortly after Receveur smashed Jacquet's network, the *Mémoires secrets*, 7 February 1782, records that the police officer Henry retrieved five of his editions from Brussels, and reports rumours of a work on the life or administration of Maurepas.

79 copies of *Conversations de Mme Necker*.

534 copies of *Essai [historique] sur la vie d'Antoinette*, a *libelle* against the queen.

34 copies of *Les Joueurs et Dussault*, a *libelle* against Arnel and others.

500 copies of *Erreurs et désavantages de l'état* by Pélissery, a *libelle* against Necker.

700 copies of *De L'Administration provinciale* by M. Le Trone [Le Trosne].

Sources

Manuscript sources

France

Archives du Ministère des affaires étrangères, Paris
Correspondance politique, Angleterre (CPA), vols 441–2, 445, 450–1, 474, 496–577
CPA supplément, vols 13–14, 16–18, 20, 28, 30
Mémoires et documents (MD), Angleterre, vols 59, 73
MD, France, vols 150, 1351, 1398–1400

Archives nationales, Paris
Series AP: Archives privées:
  277AP/1 – D'Eon papers, dossier Morande
  297AP/1–2 – Calonne papers
  446AP/1–4, 7, 13 – Brissot papers
Series B^7: Marine:
  B^7 456 – correspondance arrivée, Angleterre, 1693–1788
  B^7 473–5 – Angleterre
Series F^7: Police générale:
  F^7 4224/46 – La Fite de Pelleport
  F^7 4336^1 – émigration
  F^7 4445^2 – affaire du collier
  F^7 4774^{51} dossier 3 – arrestation de Morande
Series K:
  K 157–9
  K 161–4
Series T: Séquestre:
  T 489/2 – papiers d'Alexis Guinet
Series W:
  W 251 dossier 27 – procès verbal de la perquisition faite chez le Sr Morande
  W 292 dossier 204 – affaire des Girondins
  W 295 dossier 246 – affaire Manuel

Series X – papers of the *Parlement* de Paris
X^{2B} 1417 – affaire du Collier

Bibliothèque de l'Arsenal, Paris
Bastille papers:
MS 6,798 – chevalier de Launay
MS 10,028 – Goupil
MS 12,247 – Théveneau de Morande
MS 12,345 – Théveneau de Morande
MS 12,433 – baron de Linsingen
MS 12,451 – Samuel Swinton
MS 12,453 – Jacquet, Duvernet, Marcenay
MS 12,454 – Pelleport, Chamorand
MS 12,517 – letters to the lieutenants of police, 1781–89

Bibliothèque historique de la ville de Paris
MS 268 – F. Jarry, dossiers biographiques, fos 18–22: Mme Latouche de Godeville [*sic*]
MS 691 – Papiers Target, affaire du collier
MS 713 fos 143–51

Bibliothèque nationale, Paris
nouvelles acquisitions françaises MSS 9533–4 – Papiers Roland

Archives départementales de la Côte d'Or
C7836 – Contrôle des Actes, Arnay-le-Duc, 1772–73
C7904 – Table de testaments d'Arnay-le-Duc
2E26/4–24 – Etat civil, Arnay-le-Duc, 1737–1858
3Q1 – Table des successions directes et indirectes, 1 vendémiaire X–1 janvier 1807

Archives communales, Arnay-le Duc
Table des mariages, 1668–1792
Table des baptêmes, 1701–30, 1731–60
Table des sepultures, 1701–92

Bibliothèque municipale, Tonnerre
D'Eon manuscripts, B27; H117–19; J62–3; J153–67; K9–12; K124–5; L11–22; L26–8; L41; L54; L102; O3; R1–2; R7–10; R18; R20–2; R24; Y3

Mediathèque d'Orléans
MSS 1421–3 – mémoires of Jean-Charles-Pierre Lenoir, 1732–1807

Private archives
Beaumarchais papers: Morande–Beaumarchais correspondence
'Notice sur M. de Morande' par César Lavirotte, présentée par Claude Guyot

Germany

Bayerisches Hauptstaatsarchiv, Munich
  Politische Korrespondenz des Herzogs von Pfalz-Zweibrücken, Kasten
  blau 405/34

Switzerland

Bibliothèque publique et universitaire de Neuchâtel
Archives de la Société typographique de Neuchâtel:
  MS 1000 – correspondants, répertoire géographique
  MS 1003 – rencontre (inventaire), January 1781
  MS 1004 – rencontre, May 1782
  MS 1005 – rencontre, December 1782
  MS 1006 – rencontre, 15 March 1784
  MS 1007 – rencontre, June 1785–87
  MS 1009 – inventaire, 1 June 1786, 1 June 1787
  MS 1028 – 'Journal C'
  MS 1113 – correspondence of Agassiz et Rougemont
  MS 1114 – of Jean-Baptiste Arnal
  MS 1128 – of Jacques-Pierre Brissot
  MS 1129 – of Bruzard de Mauvelain
  MS 1137 – of Etienne Clavière
  MS 1159 – of Pierre Gosse; Goëzman
  MS 1168 – of Huguenin de Mitand
  MS 1169 – of François d'Ivernois
  MS 1176 – of E. Lyde
  MS 1178 – of Jacques Mallet Du Pan
  MS 1179 – of [Bruzard de] Mauvelain
  MS 1181 – of William Owen
  MS 1190 – of [La Fite de] Pelleport
  MS 1192 – of François-Louis Perregaux
  MS 1212 – of Samuel Roulet
  MS 1228 – of J. G. Virechaux
  MS 1230 – of James de Winter
  MS 1240/4 – of Hans Moritz, comte de Bruhl

Great Britain

British Library, London
  Add. MSS 11,339–41 – d'Eon papers
  Add. MS 35,365 – Hardwicke papers

City of Westminster Archives, London SW1
  Printed marriage registers, parish of St George, Hanover Square, vol. 16,
  1768–71

Public Record Office (National Archives), Kew
C12 series: Chancery Court papers:
  C12/1389/27 – Latour versus de Callonne [*sic*], 1788
  C12/2002/26 – Linguet versus Boissiere, 1783
FO95: Foreign Office papers, miscellaneous:
  FO95/630–2 – Calonne papers
KB series – Court of King's Bench:
  KB33/5/13 – certificates relating to Lord George Gordon
PC series: Privy Council papers:
  PC1/124–31 – Calonne papers
SP78 series: State papers, France:
  SP78/259, 261–2, 264–5, 267, 273–4, 285, 300
TS series: Treasury solicitor's papers:
  TS11/46 – trials of Peter Stuart and J. S. Barr for libels on queen of France,
    1785
  TS11/388 – trial of Lord George Gordon, 1787
  TS11/506 – trial of John Bew for a libel on the Russian ambassador,
    1781
  TS11/793/2 – trial of François-Henri de La Motte, 1781
  TS11/1116 – trial of François-Henri de La Motte, 1781

London Metropolitan Archives, London EC1
Parish records of St John the Evangelist, Great Stanmore:
  A1/5 – baptisms and burials 1765–96
  F1/1 – overseers of the poor, accounts
  G1/1 – surveyors' accounts, surveyors of highways, 1772–1826
  MR/PLT 1418–68 – land tax records, 1780–1832

Brotherton Library, Leeds University
Brotherton Collection, d'Eon papers (NB Certain file locations in these
    papers appear to have changed as they do not match references given
    by Gary Kates. Documents are thus referenced by current file number,
    plus identifiable page or folio numbers.)
Ernest Alfred Vizetelly, *The True Story of the Chevalier d'Eon* (London:
    Tylston and Edwards and A. P. Marsden, 1895), 'extra illustrated'
    edition compiled by A. M. Broadley, bound in 7 folio vols

Harrow Public Library
Percy Davenport Collection, hand copies of original documents:
  Court rolls of the manor of Great Stanmore, 1764–99
  Land tax assessments, manor of Great Stanmore
  Surveyor of Highways accounts, 1772–1826, Great Stanmore
  Great Stanmore parish registers

Printed sources

Primary sources

Andrea de Nerciat, André-Robert (attrib.), *Julie philosophe, ou le bon patriote*, 2 vols (Paris: Le Coffret des Bibliophiles, 1910 [original edition, 1791])

Anon., *Les Amours de Charlot et Toinette* (Paris: 'à la Bastille', 1789 [original edition, 1779])

——, *Authentic Adventures of the Celebrated Countess de La Motte* (London: E. Johnson, 1787)

——, *Biographical Anecdotes of the Founders of the French Republic and other Eminent Characters who have Distinguished themselves in the Progress of the Revolution* (London: R. Philips, 1797)

——, *Essais historiques sur la vie de Marie-Antoinette d'Autriche, reine de France, pour servir à l'histoire de cette princesse* (London: n. p., 1789)

——, 'M. Demorande' in *Biographical Anecdotes of the Founders of the French Republic*, 131–2

——, *Le Portefeuille d'un talon rouge* (Neuchâtel: Société des Bibliophiles cosmopolites, 1872 [original edition Paris (London): 'de l'imprimerie du comte de Paradis, 178*'])

——, *La Reine dévoilée, ou supplément au Mémoire de Mde la comtesse de La Motte* (London: n. p., 1789)

——, *Sémonce à la reine* (n. pl., n. d.)

——, *The Trial at Large of the Hon. George Gordon* (London: R. Randall, 1787)

——, *The Whole Proceedings on the Trials of Two Informations Exhibited Ex-Officio against George Gordon* (London: M. Gurney, 1787)

Archives parlementaires de 1787–1860. Série 1, 1787–1799, edited by J. Mavidal E. Laurent, et al., 100 vols (Paris: Dupont et al., 1867–2000)

Bachaumont, Louis Petit de (attrib.), *Mémoires secrets pour servir à l'histoire de la république de lettres en France, depuis 1762 jusqu'à nos jours*, 36 vols (London: John Adamson, 1777–87)

Beaumarchais, Pierre-Augustin Caron de, *Correspondance*, edited by Brian Morton and D. Spinelli, 4 vols (Paris: Nizet, 1969–78)

——, *Lettres à Madame de Godeville, 1777–1779*, edited by Maxime Formont (Paris: Lemerre, 1928)

——, *Les Lettres galantes de Beaumarchais à Madame de Godeville*, edited by Maurice Lever (Paris: Fayard, 2004)

——, *Mémoires de Beaumarchais dans l'affaire Goëzman*, nouvelle édition précédée d'une appréciation tirée des *Causeries de Lundi* par M de Saint-Beuve (Paris: Garnier, n. d.)

Bertrand de Molleville, Antoine-François, *Private Memoirs Relative to the Last Year of the Reign of Lewis the Sixteenth, Late King of France*, 3 vols (London: A. Strahan, 1797)

Brissot de Warville, Jacques-Pierre, *Correspondance et papiers*, edited by C. Perroud (Paris: Picard, 1912)

——, *Mémoires de Brissot sur ses contemporains et la révolution française*, edited by F. de Montrol, 4 vols (Paris: Lavocat, 1830–32)

——, *Réplique de J. P. Brissot à Charles Théveneau Morande* (Paris: de l'imprimerie du *Patriote françois*, 1791)

——, *Réponse à tous les libellistes qui ont attaqué et attaquent sa vie passée* (Paris: de l'imprimerie du *Patriote françois*, 1791)

Broglie, Charles-François, comte de, *Correspondance secrète du comte de Broglie avec Louis XV*, edited by Didier Ozanam and Michel Antoine, 2 vols (Paris: Klincksieck, 1956–61)

Burke, Edmund, *Reflections on the Revolution in France* (Harmondsworth: Penguin, 1969)

Campan, J. L. H., *Mémoires (inédits) de Madame Campan*, 3 vols (Paris: J. Tastu, 1822)

Charpentier, Louis, et al., *La Bastille dévoilée*, 9 'livraisons' (Paris: Desenne, 1789–90)

Correspondance secrète entre Marie-Thérèse et le comte de Mercy-Argenteau, edited by A. von Arneth and M. Geoffroy, 2nd edition, 3 vols (Paris: Firmin-Didot: 1874–75)

Correspondance secrète inédite sur Louis XVI, Marie-Antoinette, la cour et la ville de 1777–1792, edited by M. de Lescure, 2 vols (Paris: Plon, 1866)

Correspondance secrète, politique et littéraire, ou mémoires pour servir à l'histoire des cours, des sociétés et de la littérature en France, depuis la mort de Louis XV, 18 vols (London: John Adamson, 1787–90)

Deffand, Marie, marquise du, *Lettres de la marquise du Deffand à Horace Walpole (1766–1780)*, edited by Mrs Paget Toynbee, 3 vols (London: Methuen, 1912)

Desgenettes, René Nicolas Dufriche, *Souvenirs de la fin du XVIIIe siècle et du commencement du XIXe siècle, ou mémoires de R. D. G.*, 2 vols (Paris: Firmin-Didot, 1835)

Dutens, Louis, *Mémoires d'un voyageur qui se repose*, 3 vols (London: Dulau, 1806)

Encyclopédie, ou dictionnaire raisonné des sciences, des arts et des métiers, 3rd edition, 17 vols (Livourne: Imprimerie des éditeurs, 1770–75)

Eon de Beaumont, Charles-Geneviève-Louise-Auguste-André-Timothée d', *Dernière Lettre du chevalier d'Eon de Beaumont à Monsieur le comte de Guerchy* (London: n. p., 1767)

——, *Letter Sent to His Excellency, Claude-Louis-François Regnier, Comte de Guerchy* (London: Dixwell, 1763)

——, *Lettres, mémoires et négociations particulières du chevalier d'Eon, ministre plénipotentiaire de France auprès du roi de la Grande-Bretagne* (London: Dixwell, 1764)

——, *The Maiden of Tonnerre: The Vicissitudes of the Chevalier and the Chevalière d'Eon*, transl. and edited by Roland A. Champagne, Nina

Ekstein, and Gary Kates (Baltimore and London: John Hopkins University Press, 2001)

——, *Pièces rélatives aux Lettres, mémoires et négociations particulières du chevalier d'Eon* (London: Dixwell, 1764)

——, *Suite des pièces relatives aux Lettres, mémoires et négociations du chevalier d'Eon* (London: Dixwell, 1764)

Fauques, Marianne-Agnès Pillemont de, *Die Geschichte der Marquisin von Pompadour oder das Galante Frankreich* (London [Amsterdam?]: S. Hooper, 1759)

——, *L'Histoire de Madame la marquise de Pompadour* (London [Amsterdam?]: S. Hooper, 1759)

——, *L'Histoire de Madame la marquise de Pompadour, réimprimée après l'édition de 1759 avec une notice sur le livre et son auteur* (Paris: Le Moniteur du bibliophile, 1879)

——, *The History of the Marchioness de Pompadour* (London: S. Hooper, 1758)

——, *The Life of the Marchioness de Pompadour, the fourth edition, revised and enlarged by the author of the first volume with a continuation from 1757 to her death*, 2 vols (London: S. Hooper, 1766)

Georgel, Jean-François, *Mémoires pour servir à l'histoire des evenemens de la fin du dix-huitième siècle depuis 1760 jusqu'en 1806–1810*, 6 vols (Paris: Alexis Eymery, 1817–18)

Gordon, George, *The Prisoner's Complaint to the Right Honourable George Gordon, to Preserve their Lives and Liberties, and Prevent their Banishment to Botany Bay* (London: n. p., 1787)

Gotteville, Anne Latouche de, *Voyage d'une françoise à Londres ou la calomnie détruite par la vérité des faits* (London: Mesplet, 1774)

Goudar, Ange, *L'Espion françois à Londres, ou observations critiques sur l'Angleterre et les anglois*, 2 vols (London: aux depens de l'auteur, 1780 [original edition, 1779])

——, *Examen des Lettres, mémoires et négociations particulières du chevalier d'Eon . . . dans une lettre à Mr. N********* (London: Becket and de Hondt, 1764)

—— (attrib.), *Mémoires pour servir a l'histoire de la marquise de Pompadour* (London: Samuel Hooper, 1763)

—— (attrib.), *Le Procès des trois rois, Louis XVI, de France-Bourbon, Charles III d'Espagne-Bourbon et George III d'Hanovre, fabricant de boutons, plaidé au tribunal des puissances européennes* (London: George Connaught, 1780)

The Grenville Papers, being the Correspondence of Richard Grenville, Earl Temple, K. G., and the Right Hon. George Grenville, their Friends and Contemporaries, edited by William James Smith, 4 vols (London: John Murray, 1852–53)

Gudin de La Brenellerie, Paul-Philippe, *Histoire de Beaumarchais*, edited by Maurice Tourneux (Paris: Plon, 1888)

H***, comte d', *Histoire de Mr. Bertin, marquis de Fratteaux* (Paris: aux depens de l'auteur, 1753)

Imbert, Guillaume (attrib.), *Chronique scandaleuse ou mémoires pour servir à l'histoire de la génération présente*, 3rd edition, 4 vols (Paris: n. p., 1788)

Joly de Saint-Valier, *Exposé ou examen des operations des ministres en Angleterre, depuis le commencement de la guerre contre les Americains jusqu'ici* (London: Boissière, 1781)

——, *Mémoire du Sieur Joly de Saint-Valier, lieut. colonel d'infanterie, ou exposé de sa conduite avant et depuis qu'il a quitté la France* (London: Boissière, 1780)

La Motte, Jeanne de Saint-Rémy de, *An Address to the Public Explaining the Motives which have Hitherto Delayed the Publication of the Memoirs of the Countess de La Motte* (London: Ridgway, 1789)

——, *Detection, or a Scourge for Calonne* (London: n. p., 1789)

—— (attrib.), *Lettre de la comtesse Valois de la Mothe à la reine de France* (Oxford: n. p., 1789)

——, *The Life of Jane de St Remy de Valois, heretofore Countess de La Motte*, 2 vols (Dublin: P. Wogan, P. Bryce, J. Moore, and J. Rice, 1792 [original edition London, 1791])

——, *Mémoire pour dame Jeanne de Saint-Rémy de Valois, épouse du comte de La Motte* (Paris: Cellot, 1785)

——, *Mémoires justificatifs de la comtesse de La Motte-Valois* (London: n. p., 1789)

——, *Memoirs of the Countess de Valois de La Motte* (Dublin: John Archer and William Jones, 1790)

—— (attrib.), *Second Mémoire justificatif de la comtesse de La Motte, écrit par elle-même* (London: n. p., 1789)

——, *Vie de Jeanne de Saint-Rémy de Valois* (London: John Bew, 1791)

La Motte, Marc-Antoine-Nicolas de, *Mémoires inédits du comte de Lamotte-Valois sur sa vie et son époque (1754–1830)*, edited by Louis Lacour (Paris: Poulet-Malassis et de Broise, 1858)

Lanjuinais, Joseph (attrib.), *Supplément à l'Espion anglois, ou lettres intéressantes sur la retraite de M. Necker; sur le sort de la France et de l'Angleterre; et sur la détention de M. Linguet à la Bastille* (London: John Adamson, 1781)

La Tour, Alphonse-Joseph de Serres de, *Appel au bon sens dans lequel M. de La Tour soumet à ce juge infaillible les détails de sa conduite relativement à une affaire qui fait quelque bruit dans le monde* (London: Kearsley, 1788)

Le Bac (pseud.), *Lettre curieuse de Mlle Le Bac, autrement Mlle St Amand, alias Mad^e Lescallier, Londres, 17 Octobre 1763* (London: n. p., 1763)

——, *Lettre de Mademoiselle Le Bac de Saint-Amant à Monsieur de la M*** écuyer, de la société roiale d'agriculture* (London: n. p., 1763)

Linguet, Simon-Nicolas-Henri, *Aiguilloniana, ou anecdotes utiles pour l'histoire de France au dix-huitième siècle, depuis l'année 1770* (London: n. p., 1777)

——, *Lettre de M. Linguet à M. le comte de Vergennes, ministre des affaires étrangères en France* (London: n. p., 1777)

——, *Mémoires sur la Bastille, et de la détention de l'auteur dans ce château royal, depuis le 27 septembre 1780 jusqu'au 19 mai 1782* (London: Spilsbury, 1783)

Louis XV, *Correspondance secrète inédite de Louis XV*, edited by M. E. Boutaric, 2 vols (Paris: Plon, 1866)

Louis XVI and the comte de Vergennes: Correspondence, edited by John Hardman and Munro Price, *SVEC* 364 (Oxford: Voltaire Foundation, 1998)

Mairobert, Mathieu-François Pidansat de (attrib.), *Anecdotes sur Madame la comtesse du Barry* (London: n. p., 1775)

—— (attrib.), *L'Espion anglois, ou correspondance secrète entre Milord All'Eye et Milord All'Ear*, nouvelle édition revue, corrigée et considéralement augmentée, 10 vols (London: John Adamson, 1785)

—— (attrib.), *Lettres originales de Madame la comtesse Dubarry* (London: n. p., 1779)

Manuel, Pierre-Louis, *La Police de Paris dévoilée*, 2 vols (Paris: Garnery, l'an II de la liberté, [1791])

Mercier, Louis Sébastien, *Parallèle de Paris et de Londres*, edited by Claude Bruneteau and B. Cottret (Paris: Didier érudition, 1982)

Mirabeau, Honoré-Gabriel de Riquetti, comte de, *Des Lettres de cachet et des prisons d'état*, 2 vols (Hamburg: n. p., 1782)

—— et al. (attrib.), *The Life and Death of Marie-Antoinette, Late Queen of France, from the French of Mirabeau and Others*, transl. W. S. Delome (London: W. S. Delome, n. d. [December 1793])

Morande, Charles-Claude Théveneau de, *Le Gazetier cuirassé, ou anecdotes scandaleuses de la cour de France*, 1st edition ([London]: n. p., 1771)

——, *Le Gazetier cuirassé, ou anecdotes scandaleuses de la cour de France*, 1777 edition (n. p.)

—— (attrib.), *La Gazette noire, par un homme qui n'est pas blanc* ([London]: n. p., 1784)

——, *Lettre aux électeurs du département de Paris sur Jacques-Pierre Brissot* (Paris: Froullé, 1791)

—— (attrib.), *Le Portefeuille de Madame Gourdan* ([London]: n. p., 1783)

—— (attrib.), *Rémarques historiques et anecdotes sur le château de la Bastille et l'inquisition de France* (London: n. p., 1774)

——, *Réplique de Charles Théveneau Morande à Jacques-Pierre Brissot: sur les erreurs, les infidélités et les calomnies de sa Réponse* (Paris: Froullé, 1791)

——, *Réponse au dernier mot de J. -P. Brissot et à tous les petits mots de ses camarades* (Paris: Froullé, 1791)

Morande, Charles-Claude Théveneau de (attrib.), *La Vie privée ou apologie du tres-sérénissime prince Monseigneur le duc de Chartres* (London: n. p., 1784)

Pelleport, Anne-Gédeon de La Fite de, *Le Diable dans un bénitier et le Gazetier cuirassé transformé en mouche, ou tentative du sieur Receveur et de la cour de France pour établir à Londres une police à l'instar de celle de Paris* (London: n. p., 1783)

——, *Les Petits Soupers et nuits de l'hôtel de Bouillon. Lettre de Milord Comte de * * * * * * à Milord * * * * * * * * au sujet des récréations de M. de C-stri-s ou de la danse de l'ours, anecdote singulière d'un cocher qui s'est pendu à l'hôtel de Bouill-n, le 31 décembre 1778 à l'occasion de la danse de l'ours* (Bouillon [London]: Boissière, 1783)

Ravaisson, François (ed.), *Archives de la Bastille*, 19 vols (Paris: Durand et Pedone-Lauriel, 1866–1904)

Roland, Jeanne-Marie Phlipon, *Lettres de Madame Roland*, edited by Claude Perroud, 2 vols (Paris: Imprimerie nationale, 1900–02)

——, *The Works of Jeanne-Marie Phlipon Roland*, edited by L. A. Champagneux (London: J. Johnson, 1800)

Ruault, Nicolas, *Gazette d'un parisien sous la révolution: lettres à son frère: 1783–1796*, edited by Christiane Rimbaud and Anne Vassal (Paris: Perrin, 1976)

Vergy, Pierre-Henri Treyssac de, 'Seconde lettre à Monsigneur le duc de Choiseul' in Charles-Geneviève-Louise-Augusten-André-Timothée d'Eon de Beaumont, *Suite des pièces relatives aux Lettres, mémoires et négociations particulières du Chevalier d'Eon* (London: Dixwell, 1764), 19–62

Voltaire, *Correspondence*, edited by Theodore Besterman, 107 vols (Geneva: Institut et musée Voltaire, 1953–65)

——, *Questions sur l'Encyclopédie par des amateurs*, nouvelle édition soigneusement revue, corrigée et augmentée, 9 vols (n. pl., 1771–72)

Walpole, Horace, *Correspondence*, edited by W. S. Lewis, 48 vols (New Haven, CT: Yale University Press, 1937–83)

Newspaper and periodical sources
  Annales politiques, civiles et littéraires du dix-huitième siècle
  Annual Register
  Argus patriote
  Bell's Weekly Messenger
  Courier de l'Europe
  Courier de Londres
  Daily Universal Register
  Extraordinary Intelligencer
  Gazetteer
  Gazette universelle
  Gazette d'Utrecht
  Gentleman's Magazine

Intermédiaire des chercheurs et des curieux
Lloyd's Evening Post
London Chronicle
London Evening Post
London Packet or New Lloyds Evening Post
Monthly Review
Morning Advertiser
Morning Chronicle
Morning Herald
Morning Post
North Briton
Patriote françois
Political Register
Public Advertiser
Public Ledger
St James Chronicle
The Times
Westminster Gazette

Electronic primary sources

Brissot de Warville, Jacques-Pierre, *Correspondance de Brissot de Warville* [with the Société typographique de Neuchâtel], edited by Robert Darnton, on the Voltaire Foundation website at http://163.1.91.50/x_vfetc/textual/corres/brissot/bris_intro/bris_intro_003.html   (consulted on 8 May 2001)

Selective secondary source bibliography

NB Only works mentioned more than once in the footnotes are listed below.

Aclocque, Geneviève, *Un Épisode de la presse clandestine au temps de Madame de Pompadour* (privately printed: Impressions du Carré, 1963)

Almeras, Henri d', *Marie-Antoinette et les pamphlets royalistes et révolutionnaires* (Paris: Librarie mondiale, 1907)

Arneth, Alfred von, *Beaumarchais und Sonnenfels* (Vienna: Wilhelm Braumüller, 1868)

Baecque, Antoine de, 'Pamphlets: libel and political mythology' in Robert Darnton and Daniel Roche (eds), *Revolution in Print: The Press in France, 1775–1800* (Berkeley and Los Angeles: University of California Press, 1989), 165–76

Baker, Keith Michael (ed.), *The French Revolution and the Creation of Modern Political Culture*, vol. 1, *The Political Culture of the Old Regime* (Oxford: Pergamon, 1987)

Barker, Hannah, and Simon Burrows (eds), *Press, Politics and the Public Sphere in Europe and North America 1760–1820* (Cambridge: Cambridge University Press, 2002)

Blanc, Olivier, *Les Espions de la révolution et de l'Empire* (Paris: Perrin, 1995)

Burrows, Simon, 'The cosmopolitan press' in Hannah Barker and Simon Burrows (eds), *Press, Politics and the Public Sphere*, 23–47

——, 'Despotism without bounds: the French secret police and the silencing of dissent in London', *History* 89:4 (2004), 525–48

——, *French Exile Journalism and European Politics* (Woodbridge: Royal Historical Society, 2000)

——, 'The innocence of Jacques-Pierre Brissot', *Historical Journal* 46:4 (2003), 843–71

——, 'A literary low-life reassessed: Charles Théveneau de Morande in London, 1769–1791', *Eighteenth-Century Life* 22:1 (1998), 76–94

——, 'Police and political pamphleteering in pre-revolutionary France: the testimony of J. -P. Lenoir, lieutenant-géneral of police of Paris' in David J. Adams and Adrian Armstrong (eds), *Print and Power in France and England, 1500–1800* (Aldershot: Ashgate, 2006), 99–112.

Chisick, Harvey (ed.), *The Press in the French Revolution*, SVEC 287 (Oxford: Voltaire Foundation, 1991)

Clark, Anna, 'The chevalier d'Eon and Wilkes: masculinity and politics in the eighteenth century', *Eighteenth-Century Studies* 32:1 (1998), 19–48

Colley, Linda, *Britons: Forging the Nation* (New Haven, CT: Yale University Press, 1993)

Colwill, Elizabeth, 'Pass as a woman, act like a man: Marie-Antoinette as tribade in the pornography of the French revolution' in Goodman (ed.), *Marie-Antoinette*, 139–69

Conlin, Jonathan, 'Wilkes, the chevalier d'Eon and "the dregs of liberty": an Anglo-French perspective on ministerial despotism, 1762–1771', *English Historical Review* 120:5 (2005), 1251–88

Cronin, Vincent, *Louis and Antoinette* (London: Collins, 1974)

Cruppi, Jean, *Un Avocat-journaliste au XVIIIe siècle: Linguet* (Paris: Hachette, 1895)

Darnton, Robert, *The Corpus of Clandestine Literature in France 1769–1789* (New York: Norton, 1995)

——, *Forbidden Best-Sellers of Pre-Revolutionary France* (London: Harper Collins, 1996)

——, *George Washington's False Teeth: An Unconventional Guide to the Eighteenth Century* (New York: Norton, 2003)

——, 'The Grub Street style of revolution: J.-P. Brissot, police spy', *Journal of Modern History* 40:4 (1968), 301–27

——, 'The high enlightenment and the low-life of literature in prerevolutionary France', *Past and Present* no. 51 (1971), 81–115

——, 'Ideology on the Bourse' in Michel Vovelle (ed.), *L'Image de la révolution française*, 4 vols (Paris and New York: Pergamon, 1990), I, 124–39

——, 'J. -P. Brissot and the Société typographique de Neuchâtel (1779–1787)', *SVEC* 2001:10 (Oxford: Voltaire Foundation, 2001), 1–47

——, 'A police inspector sorts his files: the anatomy of the Republic of Letters' in Robert Darnton, *The Great Cat Massacre and Other Episodes in French Cultural History*, first Vintage Books edition (New York: Vintage, 1985 [first edition, 1984]), 145–89

——, 'Trade in the taboo: the life of a clandestine book dealer in prerevolutionary France' in Paul Korshin (ed.), *The Widening Circle: Essays on the Circulation of Literature in Eighteenth-Century Europe* (n. pl.: University of Pennsylvania Press, 1976), 13–83

——, 'Two paths through the social history of ideas' in Mason (ed.), *Darnton Debate*, 251–94

De Luna, Frederick A., 'The Dean Street style of revolution: J. -P. Brissot, *jeune philosophe*', *French Historical Studies* 17:1 (1991), 158–90

Dictionnaire de biographie française (Paris: Letourzey et Ané, 1933–present)

Donvez, Jacques, *La Politique de Beaumarchais* (Leiden: IDC, 1980)

Eisenstein, Elizabeth L., 'Bypassing the enlightenment: taking an underground route to revolution' in Mason (ed.), *Darnton Debate*, 157–77

——, *Grub Street Abroad: Aspects of the French Cosmopolitan Press from the Age of Louis XIV to the Enlightenment* (Oxford: Clarendon Press, 1992)

Fleischmann, Hector, *Marie-Antoinette libertine. Bibliographie critique et analytique des pamphlets politiques, galants et obscènes contre la reine. Précédée de la réimpression intégrale de quatre libelles rarissimes et d'une histoire des pamphlétaires du règne de Louis XVI* (Paris: Bibliothèque des curieux, 1908)

——, *Les Pamphlets libertins contre Marie-Antoinette d'après des documents nouveaux et les pamphlets tirés de l'enfer de la Bibliothèque nationale* (Paris, 1908; republished Geneva: Slatkine reprints, 1976)

Funck-Brentano, Frantz, *L'Affaire du collier*, 12th edition (Paris: Hachette, 1926)

——, *Cagliostro and Company*, transl. George Maidment (London: Greening, 1910)

——, *Lettres de cachet à Paris: étude suivie d'une liste des prisonniers de la Bastille (1659–1789)* (Paris: Imprimerie nationale, 1903)

Gaillardet, Frédéric, *Mémoires du chevalier d'Eon*, réédités à Paris (Paris: Bernard Grasset, 1935 [original edition, Paris, 1836])

Girault de Coursac, Pierrette, *Marie-Antoinette et le scandale de Guines* (Paris: Gallimard, 1962)

Goodman, Dena, *The Republic of Letters: A Cultural History of the French Enlightenment* (Ithaca, NY: Cornell University Press, 1994)

—— (ed.), *Marie-Antoinette: Writings on the Body of a Queen* (New York and London: Routledge, 2003)

Gordon, Daniel, 'The great enlightenment massacre' in Mason (ed.), *Darnton Debate*, 129–56

Goulemot, Jean-Marie, *Forbidden Texts: Erotic Literature and its Readers in Eighteenth-Century France*, transl. James Simpson (Cambridge: Polity, 1994 [original French edition, 1991])

Granderoute, Robert, 'Serres de La Tour' in Jean Sgard (ed.), *Dictionnaire de journalistes, 1600–1789*, 2nd edition, 2 vols (Oxford: Voltaire Foundation, 1999), II, 917–20

Gruder, Vivian R., 'The question of Marie-Antoinette: the queen and public opinion before the revolution', *French History* 16:3 (2002), 269–98

Hauc, Jean-Claude, *Ange Goudar: un aventurier des lumières* (Paris: Honoré Champion, 2005)

Hunt, Lynn, 'The many bodies of Marie-Antoinette: political pornography and the problem of the feminine in the French revolution' in Hunt (ed.), *Eroticism*, 108–30

——, 'Pornography and the French revolution' in Hunt (ed.), *Invention of Pornography*, 301–39

—— (ed.), *Eroticism and the Body Politic* (Baltimore, MD, and London: Johns Hopkins University Press, 1991)

—— (ed.), *The Invention of Pornography: Obscenity and the Invention of Modernity* (New York: Zone Books, 1993)

Huot, Paul, *Beaumarchais en Allemagne: révélations tirées des archives de l'Autriche* (Paris: Librairie internationale, 1869)

Jones, Colin, *The Great Nation: France from Louis XV to Napoleon* (London: Allen Lane, 2002)

Kaiser, Thomas E., 'Ambiguous identities: Marie-Antoinette and the House of Lorraine from the affair of the minuet to Lambesc's charge' in Goodman (ed.), *Marie-Antoinette*, 171–98

——, 'Enlightenment, public opinion and politics in the work of Robert Darnton' in Mason (ed.), *Darnton Debate*, 189–206

——, 'Madame de Pompadour and the theaters of power', *French Historical Studies* 19:4 (1996), 1025–44

Kates, Gary, *Monsieur d'Eon is a Woman: A Tale of Political Intrigue and Sexual Masquerade* (New York: Basic Books, 1995)

Landes, Joan, *Women and the Public Sphere in the Age of the French Revolution* (Ithaca, NY: Cornell University Press, 1988)

Laugier, Lucien, *Le Duc d'Aiguillon* (Paris: Editions Albatros, n. d.)

Lever, Evelyne, *L'Affaire du collier* (Paris: Fayard, 2004)

Lever, Maurice, *Pierre-Augustin Caron de Beaumarchais*, 3 vols (Paris: Fayard, 1999–2004)

Levy, Darline Gay, *The Ideas and Careers of Simon-Nicolas-Henri Linguet: A Study in Eighteenth-Century French Politics* (Urbana, IL: University of Illinois Press, 1980)

Lintilhac, Eugène, *Beaumarchais et ses oeuvres* (Paris: Hachette, 1887)

Loménie, Louis de, *Beaumarchais et son temps*, 2 vols (Paris: Michel Levy frères, 1856)

Lough, John, 'The French literary underground reconsidered', *SVEC* 329 (Oxford: Voltaire Foundation, 1995), 471–82

Mason, Haydn T. (ed.), *The Darnton Debate: Books and Revolution in the Eighteenth Century* (Oxford: Voltaire Foundation, 1998).

McCalman, Iain, 'Mad Lord George and Madame de La Motte: riot and sexuality in the genesis of Burke's *Reflections on the Revolution in France*', *Journal of British Studies* 35:3 (1996), 343–67

——, 'Queen of the gutter: the lives and fictions of Jeanne de La Motte' in John Docker and Gerhard Fischer (eds) *Adventures in Identity: European Multicultural Perspectives* (Tübingen: Stauffenburg-Verlag, 2001), 111–27

McLaren, Angus, *Sexual Blackmail: A Modern History*, (Cambridge, MA: Harvard University Press, 2002)

Maza, Sarah, 'The diamond necklace affair revisited (1785–1786): the case of the missing queen' in Hunt (ed.), *Eroticism*, 63–89

——, *Private Lives and Public Affairs: The Causes Célèbres of Prerevolutionary France* (Berkeley, CA: University of California Press, 1993)

Mossiker, Frances, *The Queen's Necklace* (London: Victor Gollancz, 1961)

Peakman, Julie, *Mighty Lewd Books: The Development of Pornography in Eighteenth-Century Britain* (London: Palgrave Macmillan, 2003)

Pollitzer, Marcel, *Beaumarchais: Le Père de Figaro* (Paris: La Colombe, 1957)

Pomeau, Réné, *Beaumarchais ou la bizarre destinée* (Paris: PUF, 1987)

Popkin, Jeremy D., 'The business of political enlightenment in France, 1770–1800' in John Brewer and Roy Porter (eds), *Consumption and the World of Goods* (London: Routledge, 1993), 412–36

——, 'Pamphlet journalism at the end of the old regime', *Eighteenth-Century Studies* 22:3 (1989), 351–67

——, 'The prerevolutionary origins of political journalism' in Keith Michael Baker (ed.), *The Political Culture of the Old Regime*, 203–23

—— and Bernadette Fort (eds), *The Mémoires secrets and the Culture of Publicity in Pre-Revolutionary France* (Oxford: Voltaire Foundation, 1998)

Price, Munro, *The Fall of the French Monarchy: Louis XVI, Marie-Antoinette and the Baron de Breteuil* (London: Macmillan, 2002)

——, *Preserving the Monarchy: The Comte de Vergennes, 1774–1787* (Cambridge: Cambridge University Press, 1995)

Proschwitz, Gunnar and Mavis von, *Beaumarchais et le Courier de l'Europe: documents inédits ou peu connus*, 2 vols, *SVEC* 273–4 (Oxford: Voltaire Foundation, 1990)

Robiquet, Paul, *Théveneau de Morande: étude sur le XVIIIe siècle* (Paris: Quantin, 1882)

Schama, Simon, *Citizens: A Chronicle of the French Revolution* (London: Viking, 1989)

Shaw, David J., 'French émigrés in the London book trade to 1850' in Robin Myers, Michael Harris, and Giles Mandelbrote (eds), *The London Book Trade: Topographies of Print in the Metropolis from the Sixteenth Century* (London: British Library, 2003), 127–43

Sutherland, D. M. G., *The French Revolution and Empire: The Quest for a Civic Order* (Oxford: Blackwell, 2003)

Taylor, George V., 'Noncapitalist wealth and the origins of the French revolution', *American Historical Review* 72:2 (1967), 469–96

Thomas, Chantal, *The Wicked Queen: The Origins of the Myth of Marie-Antoinette*, transl. Julie Rose (New York: Zone Books, 1999)

Vizetelly, Ernest Alfred, *The True Story of the Chevalier d'Eon* (London: Tylston and Edwards and A. P. Marsden, 1895)

Vizetelly, Henry, *The Story of the Diamond Necklace*, 2 vols (London: Tinsley, 1887)

Wagner, Peter, *Eros Revived: Erotica of the Enlightenment in England and America* (London: Paladin, 1988)

Ward, Marion, *Forth* (London: Phillimore, 1982)

Weiner, Margery, *The French Exiles, 1789–1815* (London: John Murray, 1960)

Major database sources

British Book Trade Index at www.bbti.bham.ac.uk

Catalogue collectif de France at http://www.ccfr.bnf.fr

Copac at http://copac.ac.uk/copac

English Short Title Catalogue at http://eureka.rlg.ac.uk/Eureka/zgate2.prod

Gallica at http://gallica.bnf.fr

Unpublished secondary sources

Agnani, Paul, 'Libelles et diplomatie à la fin du dix-huitième siècle d'après la Correspondance Politique, Angleterre conservée aux Archives du Ministère des affaires étrangères, 1771–1783' (unpublished *mémoire de maîtrise*, University of Besançon, 2004)

Darnton, Robert, 'Trends in radical propaganda on the eve of the French revolution (1782–1788)' (unpublished D.Phil. thesis, University of Oxford, 1964)

Dehaudt, Christophe, 'Le Duc de Guines: un courtisan entre service du roi et affaires au temps des lumières' (unpublished doctoral thesis, University of Paris IV, 1998)

Kaiser, Thomas E., 'Nobles into aristocrats, or how an order became a conspiracy', unpublished chapter

Singham, Shanti Marie, ' "A conspiracy of twenty million Frenchmen": public opinion, patriotism, and the assault on absolutism during the

Maupeou years, 1770–1775' (unpublished Ph.D. thesis, Princeton University, 1991)

Wilkinson, E. M., 'French émigrés in England, 1789–1802: their reception and impact on English life' (unpublished B.Litt. thesis, University of Oxford, 1952)

Index

Notes: 1) Writings by, or attributed to, the comte and comtesse de La Motte appear under their names. 2) All other works [published or unpublished] are listed by title, except unpublished memoirs which appear under the author's name. 3) 'n.' after a page reference indicates the number of an end-note on that page. Illustrations are indicated by *italics*.

EU authorised representative for GPSR:
Easy Access System Europe, Mustamäe tee 50,
10621 Tallinn, Estonia
gpsr.requests@easproject.com

www.ingramcontent.com/pod-product-compliance
Ingram Content Group UK Ltd.
Pitfield, Milton Keynes, MK11 3LW, UK
UKHW021104160425
1799IPUK00011B/10